SEEING IS BELIEVING

SEEING IS BELIEVING

HOW HOLLYWOOD TAUGHT US TO STOP WORRYING AND LOVE THE FIFTIES

Peter Biskind

BLOOMSBURY

This book is dedicated to my parents,
Elliott and Sylvia, and to Betsy, with love.

First published in New York by Henry Holt and Company, LLC
115 West 18th Street, New York, New York 10011
First published in Great Britain 2001

Portions of this book first appeared, in different form,
in *Film Quarterly*, Autumn 1974 ('*Rebel Without A Cause*:
Nicholas Ray in the Fifties'); *Film Quarterly*, Autumn 1975
('The Politics of Power on the Waterfront'); and *Socialist Review*,
March–June 1980 ('Machismo and Hollywood's Working Class',
with Barbara Ehrenreich).

Bloomsbury Publishing, 38 Soho Square, London W1D 3HB

A CIP catalogue record for this title
is available from the British Library

ISBN 0 7475 5690 3

10 9 8 7 6 5 4 3 2

Printed in Great Britain by Clays Ltd, St Ives plc

Contents

Acknowledgments vii

Foreword · *Happy Days* ix

Introduction · *It's Only a Movie* 1

I · CONSENSUS AND ITS DISCONTENTS

Chapter 1. *Who's in Charge Here?* 9

We the Jury: 12 Angry Men 10

Docs and Robbers: Panic in the Streets 21

The Local Hero: My Darling Clementine 34

The Outsider: High Noon 44

Chapter 2. *The Organization Man Goes to War* 51

Must We Conform? 52

Babies and Bombers: Strategic Air Command 64

The Men in the Gray Flannel Uniforms: Twelve O'Clock High

and Flying Leathernecks 70

A Different Bugler: From Here to Eternity 79

At War with the Army: The Court Martial of Billy Mitchell 86

Prisoners of War: Attack! 92

II · US AND THEM

Chapter 3. *Pods and Blobs* 101

The Other Americans 102

The Russians Are Coming, Aren't They? Them! and The Thing   123

The Mind Managers: Invasion of the Body Snatchers   137

Friends in High Places: The Day the Earth Stood Still and
   It Came from Outer Space   145

Chapter 4.   *The Enemy Within*   161

Friendly Persuasion   162

Public Enemies: On the Waterfront, Underworld USA,
   The Big Heat, and Force of Evil   168

Wild in the Streets: Rebel Without a Cause, Blackboard Jungle,
   I Was a Teenage Werewolf, and The Space Children   197

Cochise, Si! Geronimo, No! Broken Arrow, The Searchers, and
   Apache   228

III · MALE AND FEMALE

Chapter 5.   *All in the Family*   249

Coming Home   250

Bringing Up Father: Red River   278

Mother Knows Best: Giant   285

The Taming of the Shrew: Mildred Pierce   296

I Remember Poppa: Executive Suite   305

The Right Man for the Job: The Fountainhead   316

The Man in the Red Flannel Shirt: All That Heaven Allows   323

Conclusion · *Coming Apart*   335

Notes   349

Photo Credits   355

Index   357

Acknowledgments

The roots of this book lie, of course, in the fifties, and I would like to thank, first off, my childhood neighbors Tom and Lillian Brandon, who laid the foundation for my affection for movies by exposing an impressionable boy to Charlie Chaplin films at a time when showing or watching them was considered almost a subversive act. Since then, I have benefitted over the years from the stimulating conversation with my friends Leo Braudy, Al LaValley, Jerry Peary, Bill Rothman, Kaja and Michael Silverman, and Paul Warshow, as well as my colleagues at *Cineaste*, *Jump Cut*, *Seven Days*, and *American Film*. I am indebted as well to Ray Durgnat, Barbara Ehrenreich, Al LaValley, Bill Rothman, and Michael Wood for scrutinizing the manuscript. Chick Callenbach encouraged me when I first began writing about film by publishing two essays in *Film Quarterly* that became the kernel of this book. I would also like to thank André Schiffrin, Tom Engelhardt, and Helena Franklin at Pantheon Books, as well as Barbara Humphrys and Emily Sieger at the Motion Picture Division of the Library of Congress; Eric Breitbart, and Martha Vaughan at *American Film*, for research help; Mary Corliss, who presides over the still collection, and Charles Silver, who presides over the script collection, at the Museum of Modern Art; the folks at the library of the Academy of Motion Picture Arts and Sciences; Carlos Clarens and Howard Mandlebaum for picture research; George Stevens, Jr., for permission to use stills from *Giant*; and Universal Pictures, Columbia, MGM/UA, RKO, Paramount, Warner Brothers, Twentieth Century-Fox, and American International (Orion) for so generously providing other stills.

I owe an incalculable debt of gratitude to my editor at Pantheon, Sara Bershtel. Sara's sure sense of organization helped shape a book difficult to structure; her unerring eye for contradictions saved me from embarrassment on occasions too numerous to mention; and her infectious enthusiasm kept it going when it was trapped in conceptual and emotional dead ends. Her refusal to settle for second best, in either word or thought, is at least as responsible as I am for whatever of merit this book contains.

And finally, I would like to thank Elizabeth Hess, for whom my constant refrain, "Gotta work, gotta work," became the only music for too many years.

Foreword: Happy Days

"Our fat fifties cars," John Updike wrote in "Museums and Women," "how we loved them, revved them: no thought of pollution." The cars were the least of it. The American fifties were the age of "guiltlessness," Updike said, they represented the "romance of consumption at its height." There was nuclear disaster to worry about, and the Cold War, but these were distant shadows, and in the short run nothing could take the brightness out of President Eisenhower's grin or the sheen off the long suburban lawn.

This was (and to some extent still is) the official story of the fifties, the way they have been packaged for us. Those who wish to darken the picture will murmur something about Senator Joseph McCarthy and the witch-hunts; otherwise it just seems, as Peter Biskind says, "a simpler, happier time." It's easy enough to refute this story, except that one scarcely knows where to begin. What's not so easy is to see quite what the story means. The deep argument of Biskind's mercilessly intelligent and funny book is that all this blandness is not just an error or loss of memory, a superficial interpretation of history or culture, or a product of simplifying nostalgia. It is the time's own attempt to invent itself, a contemporary cover-up. "The fifties" is what the fifties were trying to be, and this book documents in great detail the role movies played in that attempt. When Biskind says the movies "speak our language, and we learn to speak theirs," he means this language sounds natural but is actually a complicated cultural achievement.

The dominant fiction of the fifties was consensus, and Biskind shows us how the fiction works in films. The whole realm of what he calls "conflict and contradiction" has to be cast as a battle of unreasonable extremes against an eminently reasonable middle, often represented by technocrats, people who know how the world works. Science fiction films are full of aliens but more worried about the destruction of community than about the destruction of the earth. "Social control," the conservative's nightmare, is the centrists' dream. Even in war movies, Biskind suggests, "the real enemy is extremism" rather than Germany, Japan, or North Korea. When Arthur Schlesinger Jr., reaching for what Biskind calls a "dog-eared volume of Yeats," says "the center cannot hold," he may be saying that the shared moderate society of the fifties is giving way to the divided and radicalized society of the sixties. But what he ought to be saying, the films suggest, is that the old fiction won't work anymore, that the contradictions magically held at bay for a decade or more have come out into the open. The center never did hold; but it managed for a while to look as if it did. The movies didn't make this happen, but they helped to make a particular set of values seem universal, and to make a partial account seem like the whole story.

Of course the consensus, even within the movies, had its dissidents, critics on the left and the right who didn't believe in the system at all; but more often than not the system found room for them, or they turned out to be in some kind of dialogue with the system after all. The key films here, brilliantly discussed, are 12 *Angry Men*, *On the Waterfront*, and *Blackboard Jungle*, although Biskind has a prodigious knowledge of other movies of the time, and does a spectacular trawl through the genres.

The subject of 12 *Angry Men*, Biskind says, is consensus itself. The long-awaited jury verdict "feels like an anti-climax. What is important in this film is not that the jury acquitted the defendant but that the decision was unanimous. 12 *Angry Men* is more interested in consensus than in justice." This is a little harsh—maybe the movie is keenly interested in both—but it certainly maps out the implied argument. Henry Fonda, initially the only juror with doubts, has not only done the right thing, he has brought everyone else around, including the rabid, sweating bigots played by Lee J. Cobb and Ed Begley. "Their differences are all in the family," Biskind says.

What's surprising in *On the Waterfront* is not that Marlon Brando should inform on his companions, but that informing should so persuasively be made to seem "the only reasonable course of action for a just man." And not just reasonable, mature, the expression of self-knowledge. "I was ratting on myself all them years," Brando says, meaning he was betraying his own best self until he learned that betraying others was a good thing. This movie brings out all of Biskind's considerable sarcastic verve: "The lesson the film teaches is that it is smart to climb out of your class. There's nothing at the bottom except long hours and low pay." In a little riff of fantasy, Biskind imagines the later life of the Brando character. He will marry Eva Marie Saint, they will move to the suburbs, and she will "tidy up [his] diction so that he can become a professional commentator on working-class and urban problems."

In *Blackboard Jungle* Glenn Ford shows his unruly pupils a cartoon version of "Jack and the Beanstalk"—an early excursion into cultural studies. The students don't accept the traditional interpretation. They think Jack is a dope for trading in the cow and wonder whether he was right to kill the giant. Ford, seeing an opportunity for the right kind of lesson, argues that the giant doesn't have to be hated just because he is different, and Sidney Poitier, as the tough student about to cross onto the teacher's side, gets everyone to agree that the giant should at least have had a fair trial. This turns the class around, or most of it. Ford is no longer isolated from the kids, the really bad kids are isolated from everyone else. The center has long arms.

In his introduction Biskind says his book "returns to precisely those films we all saw but never really looked at." "We all saw," even in 1983, was a bit of a hyperbole, and most of his new readers will not have seen many of these movies, except as antiques or accidents of television programming. But we can think about movies before seeing them as well as after, and this book is full of excellent reasons for seeing as many of these films as we can, for the first or the twentieth time. And it does what the best cultural criticism always does: shows us society at the task of imagining itself, and then falling in love with the soft-focus image in the mirror.

—MICHAEL WOOD

IT'S ONLY
A MOVIE

For months after *The Day the Earth Stood Still* came out in 1951, grade-school kids drove their teachers crazy chanting "Klaatu barada nikto!" the words Patricia Neal uses to call off the tinfoil robot Gort, who's hell-bent on atomizing Washington. A few years later, in *The Wild One*, Marlon Brando did for motorcycles what Ike did for golf. While teen-age boys affected black leather jackets and ducktail haircuts modeled after Brando and James Dean, girls padded their bras so they could look like Marilyn Monroe, and mothers named their babies Jayne, after Mansfield, and spelled it with a *y*.

It has never been much of a secret, in other words, that movies influence manners, attitudes, and behavior. In the fifties, they told us how to dress for a rumble or a board meeting, how far to go on the first date, what to think about Martians or, closer to home, Jews, blacks, and homosexuals. They taught girls whether they should have husbands or careers, boys whether to pursue work or pleasure. They told us what was right and what was wrong, what was good and what was bad; they defined our problems and suggested solutions. And they still do. With their bigger-than-life impact on rapt, passive spectators spellbound in the dark, movies are peculiarly well suited to translate social values into felt needs that seem as authentic as the memories of childhood. Although we may not always agree with them, or even recognize that they are courting our consent, we tend to accept the frames of reference they supply. They speak our language, and we learn to speak theirs.

If we add up all that movies say and show about how we are supposed to be, we find that they present a "world-view," an "ideology," that conveys an attitude toward everything from the trivial to the profound, from what we eat for breakfast to whether we should go to war. Even the most apparently innocent aspects of script and casting, costumes and camera angle, are charged with meaning. Stories are perhaps the most obvious carriers of value. Happy endings, for example, are not only a recompense for the life well lived but also a pat on the back for the society that makes it possible to live life well. "America, as a social and political organization, is committed to a cheerful view of life," wrote critic Robert Warshow in 1948. "If an American or Russian is unhappy, it implies a certain reprobation of his society."[1] To understand the ideology of films, it is essential to ask who lives happily ever after and who dies, who falls ill and who recovers, who strikes it rich and who loses everything, who benefits and who pays—and why.

There were plenty of films in the fifties whose ideology was overt, anticommunist films like *Iron Curtain* and *My Son John*. But they pleased neither the public nor the critics, and did badly at the box office. On the other hand, the most popular movies, those with the biggest budgets, the brightest stars, the greatest impact, movies like *Giant*, *The Man in the Gray Flannel Suit*, and *Rebel Without a Cause*, seemed transparent, no more than windows on the world showing reality as it was. The attitudes they conveyed about growing up, work, leisure, and love appeared to be natural, commonsensical, or just plain American. And yet, when we come to these films from another time, another place, their ideology suddenly becomes dramatically clear; it materializes as if out of nowhere. We wonder how we could have missed it.

Seeing Is Believing returns to precisely those films we all saw but never really looked at, to excavate the hidden and not-so-hidden messages buried in Hollywood movies of the cold-war years, roughly from Harry Truman's victory in 1948 to the beginning of the Kennedy presidency in 1960. It is in these "everyday" films, westerns like *Red River* or sci-fi like *The Thing*, which seem to shoulder no ideological burden whatsoever, that the decade is best disclosed. It is these films that show us how people looked, what they cried and laughed about, while at the same time fashioning these mundane details of daily life into larger systems of ideas and values that are, finally, political.

Even a cursory glance at the films of the period reveals that they speak with fifties voices, draw upon a pool of common and characteristic themes, subjects, plots, dialogue, decor, and even sets that crop up over and over again. Whatever their genre, they share a preoccupation with the pressing issues of the day—conformity, dissent, minorities, delinquency, and sex

roles. All reflect the particular constraints of the fifties cultural and political climate. For example, every movie that was produced, no matter how
trivial or apparently escapist, was made in the shadow of the anticommunist witch-hunt, subject to the strictures of the House Committee on Un-
American Activities (HUAC) that dictated who worked and who didn't,
which subjects were appropriate and which weren't, how plots could be
resolved and how they couldn't. It comes, then, as no great surprise that
fifties films generally reflected the anticommunism of an anticommunist
decade, that sci-fi was a covert meditation on the Bomb, and that aliens,
consciously or unconsciously, were equated with Reds. Similarly, most
movies stressed the virtues of conformity and domesticity. The conventional view of the fifties focuses on just these themes, on the fifties as an
era of political and cultural uniformity, regarded either as a nightmare of
repression or a paradise lost, depending on the point of view. The left,
which has produced the most influential historical and cultural studies of
the fifties, has never been able to turn its gaze away from the witch-hunt,
so that the fifties, in its view, was a dismal decade, contemplated with the
distaste usually reserved for other bugaboos of American history, the ante-
bellum South or the Vietnam War. On the other hand, for the majority
of Americans, influenced by movies like *Grease* and *American Graffiti*
(sixties going on fifties) or television shows like *Happy Days*, the decade is
suffused with nostalgic yearning for a simpler, happier time when cars had
fins, gas was almost free, women were home and men were on the range.

But there is another picture of the fifties that remains to be revealed, a
picture of an era of conflict and contradiction, an era in which a complex
set of ideologies contended for public allegiance. Indeed, perhaps the most
striking thing about the films of the fifties is that they reflected not one
but several warring ideologies, so that it is possible to speak of radical (left-
and right-wing) as well as mainstream films. Moreover, they waged this
combat—slugged it out frame by frame across a battlefield of sounds and
images that stretched from one end of the country to the other, from
Times Square to Hollywood and Vine—without explicit political allusions. Films of the fifties, in short, pitted different ways of being and
acting against each other. While, say, sensitive men like Montgomery
Clift, Tony Perkins, and James Dean were quivering and quaking their
way through films like *A Place in the Sun*, *Fear Strikes Out*, and *East of
Eden*, John Wayne was still gunning down bad guys in films like *Rio*

Bravo. If there were teen angels, there were also teen wei
while sexpot Monroe was embodying one standard of fema
films like *Gentlemen Prefer Blondes*, tomboy Audrey Hepburn
larizing another in films like *Roman Holiday*.

I should say at the outset that my concern is not so much with the
intentions of the filmmakers as with the outcome of the filmmaking process.
Particular directors are often able to put their stamp on their work, intentionally insert messages into their movies. The films of Robert Aldrich
can usually be counted on to be somewhere on the left, just as the films
of Elia Kazan are frequently in the middle, while those of John Ford are
to the right of his and those of Alfred Hitchcock to the right of his. But
these are exceptions, and it often happens that the films of an individual
director, even one with a strong directorial personality, convey different
ideologies. A conservative director may work with a liberal writer, or vice
versa, and both, even if they are trying to impose their politics on their
films (which often they're not), may be overruled by the producer who is
only trying to make a buck and thus expresses ideology in a different way,
not as personal political preference or artistic vision, but as mediated by
mainstream institutions like banks and studios, which transmit ideology
in the guise of market decisions: this idea will sell, that one won't. The
very question "Will it play in Peoria?" masks a multitude of ideological
sins. Then there is the question of execution. Films often start out trying
to do one thing and end up doing another, because the delicate balance
between contending ideas is thrown off by a strong performance by this
actor or that actress. And, finally, there is the question of audience. Hollywood is a business, and movies avoid antagonizing significant blocs of
viewers; they have no incentive to be politically clear.

But in the end, whatever the intentions of the filmmakers or the exigen-
cies of the filmmaking process, the fact is that in one film Gary Cooper
throws down his badge while in another Henry Fonda picks his up, which
means that each film says something different. It is these conflicting
cultural messages that this book attempts to decode. Moreover, it examines some of the ways these messages are encoded. Fifties films engaged
in a cultural combat that was a reflection of the rhetorical campaigns
fought on the terrain of society, but they did so in terms that were peculiarly their own.

Toward the end of *Blackboard Jungle*, Glenn Ford shows a "Jack and the Beanstalk" cartoon to his high school class full of juvenile delinquents. All year he has been trying to "reach" them, and finally he succeeds. They love it. But now that he has reached them, what is he going to do with them? "All your lives," he tells them, "you're gonna hear stories— what some guy tells you, what you see in books and magazines, or the television and radio, what you read in the newspapers—but you gotta examine these stories, look for the real meaning, and most of all, fellas, you gotta think for yourselves." When Glenn Ford urges his students to think for themselves, what he means is that stories are opinions, often the "other guy's" opinions, systems of value, ideologies. One of his students gets so excited he says, "Hey teach, maybe I'll turn out to be a critic of the movies." Film criticism can be, although it rarely is, a way of getting at the "real meaning" of movies. I take film criticism to be a species of cultural criticism; I am interested in what film tells us about society and what society tells us about film. This book describes what we see when ideology becomes visible, which is another way of saying that it is a book about politics and film.

PART ONE

CONSENSUS AND ITS DISCONTENTS

WHO'S IN CHARGE
HERE?

We the Jury

12 Angry Men and the Anatomy of Consensus

We are presented with a shot of the massive façade of the Supreme Court Building in New York's Foley Square. The camera slowly crawls up the stone columns to the pediment above. Carved across it in bold letters are the words: "The administration of justice is the firmest pillar of good government." Ninety minutes later we will have seen justice served, and know that in the United States, government is indeed good. The Supreme Court Building is a monument, like the Lincoln and Jefferson memorials that are "quoted" in so many films, and as we look up with the camera at the majestic inscription over our heads, we realize that this will be a film that legitimates an American institution: the criminal justice system.

When the camera takes us inside a small, dingy room, we see a man staring moodily out the window at the steep sides of the skyscrapers beyond. The man is Henry Fonda, the film is Sidney Lumet's *12 Angry Men* (1957), and we are about to sit in on the deliberations of a jury. As the film unreels, we notice that the characters don't have names. And when one wryly says to another, after a particularly acrimonious exchange, "Nice bunch'a guys," and the latter replies, "I guess they're the same as any," we realize that these figures are symbols, standing for everyone, and that the film, more than legitimating this or that institution, is after bigger game. It will legitimate a process. For society to work, it was not only necessary that Americans hold certain beliefs in common, but that they agree on the mechanics of reaching agreement. The jury, with its frequent straw votes, its tug-of-war between opposing perspectives, its give-and-take, its stress on conciliation, on integrating clashing points of view, and its imperative of unanimity, was particularly well suited to dramatizing this process.

The defendant in 12 *Angry Men* is an eighteen-year-old, apparently Hispanic youth who is charged with stabbing his father to death. (I say "apparently," because although the film suggests that the defendant is a member of a minority group, it is a bit coy about saying just which one. Like the jurors, he is a "symbol"; he stands for all of them.) There is strong circumstantial evidence against him. The downstairs neighbor heard him threatening his father, heard the thud of the body against the floor, and saw the boy run downstairs immediately after the murder. The son admitted to owning a knife identical to the murder weapon, a switchblade with an unusual, intricately carved handle found sticking out of his father's chest. He implausibly claimed he had lost the knife before the murder, and further told police he was at the movies at the time of the killing, but when pressed by the prosecution, he couldn't remember the names of the movies or anything about them. The circumstantial case is apparently clinched by an eyewitness: a woman living directly across from the apartment of the murdered man on the other side of the elevated subway tracks. She claims she saw the boy kill his father through the window. Finally, to add insult to injury, the defendant has a long record of muggings, car thefts, and so on. But we know there must be something wrong, because in one extended close-up of the boy in the courtroom, before the jury retires, we see that he doesn't look like a murderer; on the contrary, he looks sensitive, soulful, and unhappy.

In view of the strong case against the defendant, it is not too surprising that the jury's first straw vote comes out 11 to 1 for conviction. The sole dissenting vote is cast by the hero, Henry Fonda. It's not that he's certain the boy is innocent; he's just not certain he's guilty. "It's not so easy to raise my hand and send a boy off to die without talking about it first," he says.

Fonda's dissent doesn't sit so well with the other jurors, for whom it's an open-and-shut case. Three of them take a hard line against the accused. We know they're bad guys even before they open their mouths. One, a salesman (Jack Warden), noisily chews gum, flicks the wrapper out the window, and sits on, not at, the conference table. He has tickets to the ball game that night and is anxious to have the deliberations over and done with so that he can get there in time for the first pitch. "The kid's dangerous; you could see it," he says. Another, a self-made businessman, Ed Begley, has a bad cold and keeps blowing his nose with a flourish of soiled handkerchief. "Human life doesn't mean as much to them as it does to us," he says between snuffles. We know yet another self-made businessman is bad news, because he's played by Lee J. Cobb, who always is, and because he too sits on the table, talks too loud, and is among the first to take off his coat in the sweltering heat. Cobb doesn't even think the boy should have been given a trial. "That's the system," he snarls, in his gravelly voice, "but I'm telling you, sometimes I think we'd be better off if we took these tough kids and slapped'em down hard *before* they make trouble." All three have already made up their minds, and they have nothing but contempt for the jury process. A fourth juror, E. G. Marshall, is a neatly dressed stockbroker who wears the kind of wire-rimmed granny glasses later made fashionable by Robert McNamara. We know he's a cut above the others because he doesn't sit on the table, but primly in his seat, and despite the heat, he keeps his jacket on. Nevertheless, he shares their dim view of the defendant. "Children from slum backgrounds are potential menaces to society," he says. The remaining seven jurors are fence-sitters, leaning first one way and then the other.

Despite the apparent strength of the evidence, there are some puzzling inconsistencies. Why did the boy return to the scene of the crime later that night if he indeed murdered his father? Could the woman across the way really have seen what she said she saw, when there was a train passing between the victim's apartment and her own exactly at the moment of the murder? As Fonda tugs at the loose ends, the prosecution's case begins to unravel, and it becomes obvious that the jurors will not be able to reach a quick decision. Under the press of the summer heat, tempers flare and the debate turns rancorous. The purpose of the deliberations, which is a straightforward, purely practical one—the determination of the guilt or innocence of the defendant—is forgotten, and the differences between Fonda and the others escalate into a battle to the death between irreconcilable principles, making it much more difficult to reach an agreement. In other words, the question at issue is obscured by a cloud of ideology; it has become politicized. "What is it, Love Your Underprivileged Brother Week, or something?" Cobb bellows at Fonda, smacking his lips like a beached flounder. "You come in here with your heart bleeding all over the floor about slum kids and injustice. Everyone knows the kid is guilty. He's got to burn." As Cobb, Begley, and Warden shout and carry on, they sweat like pigs, and even as we watch, dark, ugly rings appear under their

Cool Henry Fonda (left) faces down hothead Lee J. Cobb (right), who is throwing a roadblock in the way of consensus.

armpits. They are erratic, excitable, and irrational, leaping about, frantic with anger, always on the verge of losing control. "I'll kill you, I'll kill you!" thunders Cobb, threatening Fonda with a knife. He has no desire to debate or compromise with those who disagree with him. He just wants to destroy them.

As Fonda and Cobb go at it, the dialogue, plot, physical presentation of characters, and placement of the camera all make us sympathize with Fonda, make us see the issues his way, through his eyes. In contrast to Cobb et al., Fonda is cool as a cucumber; throughout Cobb's tirades, he sits calm and collected in his pale cord suit, like Marshall, declining to remove his jacket until well into the last reel. Moreover, he is mild and reasonable. Despite the fact that he initially defies the others, he is not out to polarize the group; rather, he tries to bring them together, convince them he's right. He is not content to splinter the original, false majority against him; he wants to fashion a new, true majority. Luckily, he has the "facts" on his side. As he analyzes the prosecutor's case, it turns out that both witnesses, the downstairs neighbor and the woman across the way, lied on the stand. Then he demonstrates that the boy's alibi is not so implausible as it sounded at first blush. These facts are enough to convert those who are poorer, weaker, and possibly to the left of himself: a refugee, presumably Jewish, from the Holocaust; a garage mechanic, presumably working-class; and a house painter. With these jurors in tow, Fonda proceeds to forge an alliance with the Wall Street stockbroker, E. G. Marshall. Marshall has been embarrassed by the antics of Cobb and his friends, but since he in essence agrees with their point of view, he has not been able to disavow them. According to Reginald Rose's script, however, "The stockbroker is a man of logic, a man without emotional attachment to the case," and therefore Fonda is able to convince him that the defendant is innocent.

The relative ease with which Fonda brings Marshall over to his point of view indicates that the two men play by the same rules, speak the same language. But this in itself is somewhat of a surprise. Why should they, in fact, share the same assumptions? After all, Fonda, the "bleeding heart," is a liberal, afflicted by the liberal's characteristic compassion for the victim, while Marshall, with his decidedly illiberal attitudes toward the defendant, is considerably to the right of him. In the thirties, during the New Deal, when an alliance of leftists and liberals, Communists and Democrats, faced an alliance of rightists and conservatives, reactionaries and Republicans, across the abyss of the Depression, Fonda and Marshall would have been enemies. But times had changed. This was the fifties, the decade in which it seemed that the United States had solved most of the basic problems of modern industrial society. The miracle of the economy, the seemingly endless flow of consumer goods, the constant technological innovation, ironically promised to realize Marx's dream of a harmonious, classless society, not in the Soviet Union, but right in the heart of capitalist America. The thirties, in other words, were obsolete, and the political alignments that characterized them had shifted dramatically. Liberals and conservatives made common cause against leftists and rightists; the center turned on the extremes. As David Riesman and Nathan

Glazer put it, "What happened is that the old issues died, and on the new issues former friends or allies have become enemies, and former enemies have become friends. Thus: liberal intellectuals have had to switch their attitudes towards Wall Street—symbolizing both the great financiers and the giant corporations they organize—and towards 'small business.' " "Liberal intellectuals" and "Wall Street" had become "natural allies."[1]

For its part, Wall Street was quick to respond to love calls from the left with cooing noises of its own. It realized that the New Deal reforms of "that man" (FDR) had saved capitalism, not buried it, that unions were here to stay, and that labor, with an assist from the witch-hunt, had traded in its vision of a socialist future for a car, a television, and a house in Levittown. In other words, if labor accepted the capitalist framework, capital reciprocated by agreeing to play by the rules of the game that had been laid down by the New Deal. Thus, when Eisenhower took over from Truman in 1953, far from rolling back New Deal reforms like social security and unemployment insurance, as some conservatives and most reactionaries had hoped, his administration accepted and consolidated them, gave them the imprimatur of the business community.

The components of this new alliance were the moderate wing of the Democratic Party, the so-called "cold-war liberals"—an assortment of disillusioned ex-Communists, old New Dealers, and social democrats who wholeheartedly embraced the cold war—bankers and lawyers like Averell Harriman and Dean Acheson, along with intellectuals like Daniel Bell, Arthur Schlesinger, Jr., Sidney Hook, and David Riesman. Their counterparts to the right were the "corporate capitalists," the left wing of the Republican Party, made up of the liberal business and financial leaders of the big East Coast, northern, and midwestern-based banks and corporations. The Truman (and later Stevenson) Democrats and Eisenhower Republicans played at the game of electoral politics, but it was this "corporate-liberal" alliance of the center, this "bipartisan" coalition of moderates from both parties, who made up the rules of the game.

12 *Angry Men* follows this script quite closely. It is, in some sense, a film written by ideology. Although its nameless cast of characters are meant to be just plain folks, fifties Everymen, they actually correspond to clearly defined political types. Fonda, an architect by profession, constructs the alliance of moderates. We know he is a liberal, but we can be much more precise than that. We don't find out anything about his views on

Communism or the witch-hunt, but we can also determine that he is a "cold-war liberal" precisely because he is engaged in building a bridge to those to the right of himself and bringing those to the left along with him. Stockbroker Marshall is, of course, the enlightened corporate capitalist, the symbol of Riesman and Glazer's "Wall Street." The understanding between Fonda and Marshall forms the backbone of the corporate-liberal alliance of the center.

The common language Fonda and Marshall speak was called pluralism. Pluralists believed that America was composed of a diversity of interest groups which competed on a more or less equal basis for a piece of the pie. Like the various blocs of jurors in 12 *Angry Men*, they could adjust their differences by reasoning together, if they would only avoid ideologizing their conflicts. With the example of Nazi Germany and Communist Russia fresh in their minds, fifties corporate liberals blamed ideology for polarizing societies, pitting one class or ethnic group against another, thereby rendering democracy unworkable. It was the glory of America that in the fifties, ideology was dead. As Schlesinger summed it up: "The thrust of the democratic faith is away from fanaticism; it is towards compromise, persuasion, and consent in politics, towards tolerance and diversity in society."[2] But the corporate liberals' obituary for ideology was premature. It was alive and well, dwelling where we had looked for it least, in the end-of-ideology ideology of the corporate liberals. It was pluralism itself.

Unlike Marshall, Cobb and his friends are old-fashioned ideologues. They don't care about the language of fact. Or, to put it another way, as Fonda continues to argue with them, we gradually see the ground shift from a dispute over the facts of the case to a dispute over the importance of facts per se. At the beginning of the film, as we have seen, Cobb et al. claim the facts for themselves. "I just want to talk about the facts," says Cobb. "You can't refute the facts." At this point, the facts seem to indict the defendant. Two witnesses, a motive, an alibi like Swiss cheese, apparent possession of the murder weapon, and a long criminal record, all say he's guilty. The facts seem to speak for themselves. "What's there to talk about? Nobody had to think twice except you," Warden complains to Fonda. Cobb derisively calls Fonda "preacher" and berates him for pandering to the passions of the jurors with emotional appeals. By the end of the film, the facts are on the other foot. The bleeding hearts have the facts on their side. "I don't think the kind of boy he is has anything to do with it," says one juror. "The facts are supposed to determine the case." In contrast, Cobb et al. are convicted of emotionalism. When Cobb assures the other jurors, "I have no personal feelings about this," it's just not true. His passionate outbursts, and his refusal to throw in his lot with the developing majority, are signs of psychological imbalance. His problem is his relationship with his son. In the final scene, this emerges as the true reason for his hatred of the defendant, and Cobb nearly has a nervous breakdown. And by this time, Fonda has succeeded in persuading his opponents to accept this framework. They dismiss the facts, ceding them to Fonda and friends. "I'm sick of the facts," admits Begley. "You can twist'em any way you like." Bereft of facts, Cobb et al. are content to fall back on intuition, on feeling, on subjectivity. They just *know* the boy is guilty.

In the same way that Fonda seizes the ground of fact from Cobb, so pluralists fought to secure the rights to reality from their enemies. In the forties, Lionel Trilling wrote that the future historian of the fifties, undertaking to describe the assumptions of his culture, "will surely discover that the word *reality* is of central importance in his understanding of us." Trilling knew what he was talking about, because he and others like him played a key role in prescribing just what could legitimately be considered "real" in the fifties. Pluralists were quite clear about what reality was not, but they were rather vague about what it was. They would say no more than that reality was complex, ambiguous, and mysterious. Trilling, for example, praised Hemingway and Faulkner for their "willingness to remain in uncertainties, mysteries, and doubts," their talent for seeing "the full force and complexity of their subject matter."[3] And it wasn't only poems and novels that required detailed exegesis. "The problems of national security," wrote Daniel Bell in a characteristic statement, "like those of the national economy, have become so staggeringly complex, that they can no longer be settled by common sense or past experience."[4] If reality was as complex as pluralists said it was, straightforward explanations of events were useless; phenomena had to be interpreted. In *12 Angry Men*, facts don't speak for themselves, and Cobb and friends are blinded by common sense, which assumes that they do. Those jurors who believe that reality is amenable to simple, lay, or amateur interpretation are not only wrong, they're dangerous.

What is at issue in *12 Angry Men* is not only what really happened, but how we find out what really happened, and whom we listen to. The answer, of course, is the corporate liberals themselves. Getting at the truth is a strenuous operation, requiring the intervention of a dispassionate, rational consciousness, which is why the jurors have to be tutored in the language of reality by Fonda. Fonda is an expert who qualifies for his role by virtue of his superior education. The cult of complexity implied that experts—intellectuals, scientists, and technocrats—were the only ones who could understand and therefore run society. Both capitalists and workers, wrote Schlesinger, are trapped in a state of "mutual bewilderment," leaving "the way open for . . . the politician-manager-intellectual types"[5] to step in. Like Fonda, they are well suited to deal with reality because they have the correct ideology, that is, no ideology.

If Marshall and Fonda represent the center, Cobb and his friends are archetypical versions of what centrists liked to call "extremists." From the vantage point of pluralists, extremists were trolls and goblins who dwelled in darkness outside the center; in short they were totalitarians of the right and left, Fascists and Communists who rejected pluralism, that is, had nothing but contempt for the democratic process. Extremists displayed a "tendency to convert politics into 'moral' issues," wrote Bell, whereupon "political debate moves from specific interest clashes, in which issues can be identified and possibly compromised, to ideologically-tinged conflicts which polarize groups and divide society."[6] Like Barry Goldwater, whose 1964 presidential campaign slogan was "In Your Heart You Know He's Right," they dismissed reason in favor of feeling. They were neurotic "indignants," as Riesman and colleagues called them in *The Lonely Crowd*, troublemakers who got "themselves worked up about political abuses; they have a positive tropism to evidence of race discrimination, police brutality, corporate skullduggery."[7] Extremists, in other words, were radicals, most often of the left, but also of the right, as in 12 *Angry Men*. Left or right, extremists, according to pluralists, were the way they were because they were anxious about their "status." They were insecure because they had risen or fallen too quickly through the ranks of class. In 12 *Angry Men*, the status-anxious extremists are either rags-to-riches self-made men like Cobb and Begley or petit-bourgeois losers like Warden.

Although Fonda manages to defeat his extremist opponents in debate, the rules of the jury process, like the rules of pluralism, require that he has to include them in the emerging majority for acquittal. As a good corporate liberal, he believes that a stable society is based on inclusion, not exclusion. So long as groups with competing ideologies subscribed to the ground rules of the center, submitted, as Bell put it, "to the discipline of compromise," to the rules of the game, the center was happy to have them on the team. Therefore, Fonda must conciliate the losers. In one scene, when most of the jurors have risen from the table to turn their backs on Begley, who has made a racist remark, it is Fonda who beckons them back, countering their indignation with a kind word for Begley: "It's always difficult to keep personal prejudice out of a thing like this," he says sympathetically. (A little indignation is a good thing, but too much would threaten to turn the jurors into extremist "indignants" themselves, and interfere with the good-natured give-and-take of pluralist politics.) Fonda finds it easy to forgive Begley, because Begley is essentially sick, not bad. Similarly, near the end, when Cobb sits shattered by the realization that he has failed his son, Fonda welcomes him into the fold by putting a comforting hand on his shoulder. At each other's throats throughout the film, they are now friends. Both have compromised. If Fonda has accepted Cobb into the group, Cobb has swallowed his pride and relinquished his hatred of Fonda. With Cobb on board, finally convinced that he too has a stake in society, the process is completed. When the jurors enter the courtroom at last, Cobb, Begley, and Warden take their places alongside everybody else, join Fonda and Marshall in closing ranks before the world. Their differences are all in the family.

When Fonda persuades Cobb et al. to join the others, he succeeds in domesticating the extremists, making bad reactionaries into good conservatives. Conservatives were the final ingredient in the fifties political pie. Somewhat to the right of the corporate liberals, they were nevertheless their junior partners. The economic base of conservatism lay in small and medium-sized farms and businesses, along with the new wealth of the Southwest, the area that would later be called the Sunbelt. Their party was the right wing of the Republican Party, the midwestern Old Guard gathered around senators like Dirksen and Knowland, often joined by the right wing of the Democratic Party, the so-called Dixiecrats. Their favorite son and perennial candidate for president was Robert Taft. Conservatives differed from corporate liberals on the details of how things should be run, but in times of crisis, like Cobb and friends, they closed ranks with their corporate-liberal allies, remaining well within the center.

The fruit of Fonda's labors has been the unanimous verdict for acquittal. But the verdict itself feels like an anticlimax. What is important in this film is not that the jury acquitted the defendant but that the decision was unanimous. *12 Angry Men* is more interested in consensus than in justice. Consensus, the shared agreement between corporate liberals and conservatives (however reluctant) on fundamental premises of pluralism, was—outside, perhaps, of the H-bomb—the fifties' most important product. Since *12 Angry Men* endorses consensus, it is a centrist film. And because the consensus is dominated by the corporate liberals and their ideology of pluralism, it is moreover a corporate-liberal or pluralist film.

In many films, however, the imposition of consensus, the assertion of the authority of centrists over extremists, is secondary, and the stage is given over to the quarrel inside the center between corporate liberals and conservatives for authority over consensus, the right to dictate its contents and set its limits. While Elia Kazan's *Panic in the Streets* (1950) also imposes the authority of centrists over extremists, it is the quarrel within the center that is crucial.

Docs and Robbers

Panic in the Streets and the Triumph of the Therapeutic

Near the end of *Panic in the Streets*, Clint Reed and police captain Tom Warren, at the head of a small army of cops, have trapped two fugitives on a pier in the New Orleans waterfront district. The fleeing men are gangsters, but that's not why the cops are after them. The reason is that they may be carriers of a deadly germ that threatens New Orleans with a plague epidemic. One man fires randomly at his pursuers as he dodges in and around sacks of grain being readied for loading onto the freighters that line the docks. As the bullets whine overhead, a cop reaches for his gun and prepares to shoot back, but Reed interferes. "Who is this guy, anyway?" the cop angrily asks Captain Warren, echoing a question that has been raised repeatedly by different people throughout the course of the film. But Warren tells him to shut up, put his gun away, and obey Reed. We concur. We know who Reed is, and when he stands up and shouts at the fugitives, "Stop! I'm a doctor. I can cure you," the cops know too. Although they may have the guns, Dr. Reed calls the shots. Had *Panic* been made earlier, it would have been straight cops and robbers. But in 1950, when it was released, it could not have been other than it was: a docs and robbers therapeutic thriller. *Panic* substitutes illness for crime, and cure for punishment. It prefers the needle to the gun, Bufferin to bullets. It was one of the first films of the "therapeutic society."

The therapeutic undertow of *12 Angry Men* was so strong that a film about the criminal justice system often threatened to give way to a film about the medical system, Perry Mason to Dr. Kildare. If American society was based on consensual values like persuasion and compromise, then the coercive, punitive component of the law ultimately disqualified it from speaking for pluralism. Fonda was an expert, but the kinds of experts corporate liberals liked best were doctors, because their preference for the values of health care over those of justice made doctors more suitable flag-bearers for consensus. In *Panic in the Streets*, Dr. Kildare comes into his own.

Faith in the efficacy of the therapeutic rode a wave of postwar optimism that suggested that evil was no more than a disease. Anthropologist Eliot Chapple, for example, wrote that "good and bad, right and wrong, are comparable to the concept of health and medicine."[8] In the late forties, the physician became a key figure in pluralist films. Bing Crosby and Barry Fitzgerald played priests in their big hit *Going My Way*, in 1944, but when they followed it up with *Welcome Stranger* three years later, they played doctors. In *Johnny Belinda* (1948), a young deaf-mute woman blossoms under the care of a handsome doctor, while in *The Sign of the Ram* (1948), a crippled lady who writes dreamy poetry on the Cornish coast holds her loving husband in thrall until a clever doctor sees through her act and exposes her wickedness.

Psychotherapy, in particular, which had enjoyed only a mixed reception in the United States during the twenties and thirties, finally came into its own. Called upon to minister to battle-weary, shell-shocked returning GIs, many of whom were obviously suffering from psychological disorders, psychiatry carried everything before it. The influx of psychiatric refugees from Europe, along with home-grown therapists, and their allies in academic sociology, psychology, and anthropology, were emboldened by the unprecedented prestige enjoyed by the medical profession and began to flex their muscles. In 1945, Harry Stack Sullivan called for a "world-wide mobilization of psychiatry" against social problems, while Harvard psychologist Henry A. Murray called on social scientists to become "physicians to society."[9] As Thomas Szasz put it sometime later, "whereas in the Age of Faith the ideology was Christian, the technology clerical, and the expert priestly; in the Age of Madness the ideology is medical, the technology clinical, and the expert psychiatric."[10]

In films, too, the image of the psychiatrist underwent a drastic transformation. During the twenties, thirties, and early forties, psychiatrists were secondary characters, most often either foolish or villainous, as in *The Flame Within* (1935), *Carefree* (1938), or *Bringing Up Baby* (1938). Often they were foreigners with gray beards and heavy Viennese accents, like the one in *Mr. Deeds Goes to Town* (1936), or greedy and unscrupulous, like the one in *The Cat People* (1942). The negative image of psychiatrists

persisted into the late forties, and fifties of course, but it was complemented, not to say overwhelmed, by a positive one. When Hitchcock
made *Spellbound* in 1945, change was already in the wind. In this film,
the villain is a psychiatrist, but so is the heroine, Ingrid Bergman. So
dramatically had the stock of psychiatry risen by 1946 that when Vincent
Price played a homicidal shrink in *Shock*, the film created an uproar. Dr.
Price murdered his wife and had the sole witness to the crime committed
to his own sanitarium, where he first convinced her she was crazy and
then tried to finish her off with a shot of insulin. *Variety* observed that
" 'Shock' should have the psychiatrists screaming," and wondered why the
witness's husband didn't get "further consultation with another doctor"
before packing her off to Price's hospital.[11] Bosley Crowther, writing in
the *New York Times*, called the film "bad medicine" and deplored its
negative image of the psychiatric profession: "The disturbing thing is that
this picture strives for emotional effect by presenting the villainous psychiatrist in the most fearsome light. He is made darkly diabolic behind his
quiet professional façade and all of his apparently standard treatments are
exposed as deliberately evil practices. . . . The basic design of the picture
is to create a phobia of psychiatry."[12]

It seems that Hollywood listened when psychiatrists screamed, because
post-*Shock* films turned its formula inside out. In *The Locket* (1946),
psychiatrist Brian Aherne is a hero, while his wife, Laraine Day, is a
kleptomaniac and murderer. She has *him* committed to an institution,
not he her, as in *Shock*. Eventually, she has a nervous breakdown, showing
us what we knew all the time, that she was the crazy one. At the end,
she's safely in the hands of another doctor. When psychiatrists appeared
to play villains, it turned out that they weren't really psychiatrists at all.
In Sirk's *Sleep My Love* (1948), shrink helps husband drive wife crazy, but
he's a phony, not a real one. We are led to believe a psychiatrist is the
villain of *Hollow Triumph* (1948), until we learn that he's being imperson-
ated by medical-student-turned-gangster Paul Henreid, who looks just like
him. In films like *Possessed* (1947), *The Snake Pit* (1948), *Home of the
Brave* (1949), *Shadow on the Wall* (1949), *So Young, So Bad* (1950), and
later *Fear Strikes Out* (1957) and *The Three Faces of Eve* (1957), the
competence and virtue of psychiatrists were unquestioned.

Not only did psychiatrists in particular and doctors in general come out
smelling like roses, they started crowding the cops out of their patrol cars.
In the thirties, movie doctors took out tonsils and were content to leave

Rico to the G-men. After the war, they threw away their tongue depressors
and began to usurp police functions. When cops did put in an appearance, they played a distinctly secondary role. First there was *The Crime
Doctor* (1943), which gave rise to a series of films in which the doctor-
sleuth was played by Warner Baxter. In *Spellbound*, all the evidence seems
to suggest that Gregory Peck is a murderer, and consequently he finds
himself hunted by police. But shrink Bergman knows that he's only sick,
and instead of going to jail, he goes into therapy. Bergman, meanwhile,
solves the crime of which Peck is suspected. In *High Wall* (1947), Robert
Taylor, like Peck, is an amnesiac who thinks he murdered someone. The
cops are not only unable to say who did, but they suspect him too. Enter
psychiatrist Audrey Totter, who first restores Taylor's memory with Pento-
thal and then induces the real murderer to tell all by shooting him full of
the same drug. In Otto Preminger's *Whirlpool* (1950), kleptomaniac Gene
Tierney is being gaslighted by Jose Ferrer, a sleazy hypnotist who's managed
to convince her that she's a killer. Luckily for Tierney, she's married to a
prominent psychiatrist (Richard Conte), who realizes that Ferrer is the
killer, not his wife. Where are the cops? Out giving traffic tickets.

Deceptive appearances have the police in a muddle once again in *The
Dark Mirror* (1946), where they are unable to tell which of twin sisters,
Terry or Ruth, is a murderer. (It's no wonder; they're both played by Olivia
de Havilland.) Only the psychiatrist, Lew Ayres, knows for sure. With the
aid of a battery of Rorschach tests, he quickly determines that Ruth is
sane and Terry is a psycho. When bad Terry tries to frame good Ruth,
she's thwarted by Dr. Ayres, and in the end, it is he, not the cop, who gets
the girl, in this case grateful Ruth. In *The Dark Past* (1948), gangster
William Holden takes over Dr. Lee J. Cobb's home. But Holden is tormented
by recurring nightmares. Cobb realizes that he's come down with a bad
case of the Oedipus complex and puts Holden into intensive therapy. Says
Cobb, "I believe in curing people, not killing them."

It was bad enough when docs put cops on unemployment, but in a
number of films, the tough cops who were the heroes of films of the late
thirties and early and mid-forties were themselves portrayed as sadists and
psychopaths. In William Wyler's *Detective Story* (1951), Kirk Douglas
plays a cop (McCloud) who would just as soon beat a suspect to death as
bring him before a judge. How do we know he's crazy? Everyone says so,
and at the end he confesses to a pathological hatred of his father. Had
McCloud been able to get his mind off dad long enough to attend a

meeting of the Patrolmen's Benevolent Association, he would have found himself in the company of men very much like himself, such as brutal Dana Andrews from Otto Preminger's *Where the Sidewalk Ends* (1950) and crazy Robert Ryan from Nicholas Ray's *On Dangerous Ground* (1951). There were no docs in these films, but the therapeutic cast a long shadow on the cops who were their "heroes."*

The rise of therapeutic imperialism allowed corporate liberals to translate political issues, encumbered by all those messy questions about values and social goals they found so irksome, into the spic-and-span, ostensibly value-free practices of science. It neutralized Marxism by arguing that discontent was a psychological, individual issue, not a social or class issue. If you were unhappy, it was because you were neurotic or psychotic, not because society was unjust. The therapeutic strategy enabled corporate liberals to portray themselves as "realistic" and "mature," at the expense of their enemies on the left, who were "infantile" or "childish."

On the other hand, it also allowed corporate liberals to turn around and mobilize these same "infantile" leftists against the conservatives, whose law-'n-order preference for the nightstick over the stethoscope came to seem positively medieval. In the fifties, when pluralists succeeded in further liberalizing the insanity plea, it appeared to conservatives that they were undermining the criminal justice system with psychiatric values, but in fact, the beauty of the therapeutic was that it achieved the same results as more traditional modes of authority, without the onus of coercion. What was the difference, after all, between a murderer in solitary confinement frittering away a lifetime in Sing Sing and a psycho in a padded cell doing the same in Dannemora? By mending bones, not breaking them, the therapeutic enabled docs to do for corporate liberals what cops had traditionally done for conservatives. One way was called treatment, the other punishment, and the apparent difference between them gave corporate liberals a decisive ideological advantage.

In *Panic in the Streets*, Dr. Clint Reed (Richard Widmark) is a Navy

---

*Of course, it wasn't only cops films that were bitten by the therapeutic bug. Every genre was infected. Take westerns. In *Pursued* (1947), Robert Mitchum is a neurotic cowboy addled by being an adopted child, while in *The Man from Colorado* (1949), Glenn Ford plays a crazy judge. In *The Fastest Gun Alive* (1956), Glenn Ford is again a nut, this time a quick draw paralyzed by guilt who goes up against outlaw Broderick Crawford also mad as a hatter. In *The Left-Handed Gun* (1958), Billy the Kid, played by Paul Newman, is depicted as a psycho.

doctor attached to the U.S. Public Health Service. As the film opens, he's out on the front lawn helping his cute, tousle-haired son, Tommy, paint a chest of drawers, when he gets a call from the coroner's office. There's something funny about the body that's just come in, and they need his help. After examining the dead man's blood, Reed quickly solves the puzzle that has stumped the coroner. The man was shot to death—but he was also infected with the plague.

Reed has his work cut out for him. He has only forty-eight hours to track down the killers, who by now are also carriers of plague germs. At a meeting of the city's top officials he gets no more than grudging coopera-tion. The politicians—the mayor and his aides—drag their feet. The situation is not so critical as he thinks, they say, treating Reed like an alarmist. The police commissioner says it's impossible to track down the plague carriers in so short a time, while Captain Warren (Paul Douglas) resents Reed as an arrogant outsider from back East. It quickly becomes clear that *Panic* is less about plague than about turf. Dr. Reed is the new authority figure on the block, and the film dramatizes the triumph of his values over competing notions of authority.

As we have seen, *12 Angry Men* concerned itself with the construction of the consensus of the center. *Panic in the Streets*, on the other hand, assumes consensus. It is a national emergency film, a subgenre popular in the fifties, and as such it takes consensus for granted. National emer-gencies were particularly well suited to dramatizing the necessity of consensus, because they implied that unless Americans agreed among themselves on fundamental issues, they would be an easy prey to internal or external enemies. Emergencies made consensus appear to be the only sensible way of dealing with trouble. The question in *Panic* is not whether consensus is or is not desirable, but rather who dominates the consensus, docs or cops, corporate liberals or conservatives, and according to what principles, therapy or punishment.

After some initial grumbling, politicians and police alike are convinced that New Orleans is indeed threatened by an epidemic, but the problems aren't over. Who is going to direct the investigation, Reed or Captain Warren?

Warren, of course, is the conservative. As Kazan himself put it, "the Doc was the New Dealer and the policeman Republican."[13] Warren doesn't like doctors. He blames his wife's death on a misdiagnosis: "The doc said she had neuralgia. It was a tumor." Reed's job is to make sure Warren takes his medicine and likes it. Both will have to work together in the coalition of the center to make consensus work. What makes it difficult for them to cooperate is not only their political differences but the desire of each to dominate the coalition. "Let's not get the idea that I'm a sailor in your navy," Warren tells Reed angrily. "I'll call you when I need you." But Warren is in for a nasty surprise. By choosing to focus on plague, not crime, Kazan, like Harry Stack Sullivan, Henry Murray, and Elliot Chapple, is telling us that those who threaten society are sick, and therefore doctors like Reed are better equipped to deal with the dislocations they cause than cops like Warren.

In *Panic*, the advantages of docs over cops are obvious. Cops elicit a response of defensive solidarity. When Reed enters a waterfront hiring hall looking for information, the suspicious seamen refuse to cooperate. "I'm

The hypodermic needle was the weapon of choice for gangbusting doctors like Richard Widmark who preferred Bufferin to bullets, therapy to force.

not from the police," he reassures them. "You won't get into any trouble." With his intense, authoritative manner, he gets results where Warren's official bluster only gets stares. "He's a doctor; he ought to know what he's doing," says one woman, urging her husband to come clean in another scene. But the difference between Reed and Warren, therapy and punishment, is one of means, not ends, and when push comes to shove, it becomes clear that the therapeutic is just a less obviously coercive form of authority. At one point, Reed forces a plague-ridden man to tell him what he wants to know by threatening to withhold the vaccine that will save his life.

The dispute between needles and guns is related to another issue: the conflict between experts and professionals. Reed is a college-educated whiz kid, and Warren reacts to his know-it-all manner with what corporate liberals regarded as the inclination of middle Americans to resent their intellectual betters. "You're a smart fella, a college man," says Warren. "You could make somethin' outa nuthin' just to be important." Warren, on the other hand, belongs to an older tradition, the tough professional who earned his stripes by pounding the beat, not reading a book. When Reed ridicules police methods ("They may not want to talk to the police"), Warren says, "You wanna send for a few experts from Washington to help me out?" "You could use 'em," retorts Reed, and in this film, he's right. Reality is once again too complex for normal folk to understand. What seemed like a simple homicide has turned into a medical mystery.

The emerging alliance between Reed and Warren, Democrat and Republican, corporate liberal and conservative, expert and professional, is the coalition of the center, and it is based on mutual admiration. Warren comes to respect Reed's brains, while Reed comes to respect Warren's experience. But the film makes clear that Reed, not Warren, dominates the coalition. In one scene, a cop asks him why the "boys" have to be inoculated. "Because the commissioner said so," snaps Warren, whereupon Reed, who has been eavesdropping, tells him that he too needs a shot, "because the commissioner said so, and I told the commissioner."

When Warren makes his crack about importing experts from Washington, he introduces another sensitive subject. Not only is Reed an expert, he is an employee of the U.S. Public Health Service, and as such is an agent of the federal government. Reed looks upon Washington as a source of help; nurtured on New Deal Big Government, corporate liberals defended the right of the feds to intervene at the state or municipal level to right local wrongs. "We must," urged sociologist Talcott Parsons, "have a stronger government than we have been traditionally accustomed to, and we must come to trust it more fully."[14] Warren, on the other hand, regards Washington with undisguised suspicion, a reflection of conservatives' preference for states' rights over federal power. As conservative educator Bernard Iddings Bell complained in 1951, "The central government has today almost unlimited and anonymous power. It overrides individual rights and local loyalties and peculiarities."[15]

In *Panic*, the clash between local and national takes the form of a conflict between the needs of the smaller community (New Orleans), represented by the mayor, and the needs of the larger community (the nation), represented by Reed. The mayor argues that the interests of the citizens of New Orleans are best served by breaking the story to the press, on the grounds that once the people realize what is at stake, they will help the police track down the plague carriers, while the carrier himself will in all likelihood turn himself in to be treated. Reed's argument, on the other hand, which is given a certain plausibility by the fact that the carrier is also a killer, is that if the story gets out, the people will panic in the streets and the carrier will flee, "endangering the entire country." "But we've got trouble in our own community, right here," protests the mayor. "What community? We're all in the same community," retorts Reed. "Do you think we're living in the Middle Ages? Within ten hours, you can be in any city in the world." In this debate, the mayor, partisan of local, concrete interests, is made to seem narrow, parochial, and old-fashioned, whereas Reed, partisan of national, abstract interests, is made to seem broad-minded, visionary, and up-to-date. Reed sees more, has the Big Picture, and is therefore right, while the mayor sees less, only the Little Picture, and is therefore wrong.

In *Panic*, local is bad, national is better, and international is best. This scale of values was characteristic of UN-loving corporate liberals and often found expression in the therapeutic globalism of men like Erich Fromm and Erik Erikson. Reacting to the nationalist passions stirred up by World War II, they saw the "local loyalties and peculiarities" cherished by conservatives like Bernard Iddings Bell as a threat to world peace. According to World Health Organization official C. B. Chisholm, "the critical intelligence" had been "crippled by local certainty, by gods of local moralities, of local loyalty, and personal salvation, and prejudice and hate and intolerance."[16]

The reason the mayor can see no more than the Little Picture is that he is a hostage of his constituents, the "people." Unlike experts and even professionals, Reed and Warren, who were insulated from the direct influence of the body politic, politicians danced when the people whistled, and thus could rarely be depended on to do the right thing.

In *Panic* the people are the problem, not the solution. They are parochial, unable to see beyond the ends of their own noses. If the doc is an expert and the cop is a professional, the people are unreliable, hysterical amateurs, know-nothings with neither the education nor the experience to do anything right. To tell them what's really going on could well lead to disaster. The mayor's worst mistake is to take the side of the reporter against the experts who know what's best. In films of the thirties, reporters were often attacked from below as cynical city slickers who betrayed the interests of the masses. By the fifties, the situation had changed dramatically, and journalists were often attacked from above for pandering to the vices of the mob. In this decade, a film's attitude toward the press is usually a good index of its attitude toward the people.

In *Panic*, the reporter indeed claims to act in the interest of the public. "I represent the people's right to know," he tells Reed, demanding the story. But in this film, the people don't have the right to know anything; information only flows one way, from the bottom to the top. Reed is a firm believer in the principle that decisions affecting the public must be made behind closed doors, and he has been hostile to the press from the very start, when he tells a photographer hanging around the coroner's office to get lost.*

In the same way that Reed and Warren compete for control of the center, so, too, the film asks, Who really represents the interests of the people, Reed or the reporter? The answer is, of course, Reed. The reporter is portrayed as a thoroughly dislikable loudmouth who dogs Reed's foot-

---

*In a later period, Reed's stonewalling would have been called a cover-up, as it was in post-Watergate films like *Jaws* (1975) and *All the President's Men* (1976), where officials who suppress the truth are villains, not heroes, selfish, not idealistic. In these films, the men of principle are the ones who break the story, and what is regarded as irresponsible behavior in *Panic* is positively civic in *Jaws* and *All the President's Men*.

steps and pokes his nose into places where it's not wanted. He's almost as bad as the certified heavies, played by Jack Palance and Zero Mostel. "Since when do you make the rules?" the reporter demands of Reed, threatening to break the story without "permission." Reed's "ally," Captain Warren, simply claps him in jail. The mayor is furious. "On whose authority?" he demands. "On my authority," replies Reed. And once again, Reed wins. "Take any emergency action you deem necessary," says the mayor wearily, caving in to Reed's Big Picture-ism.

Everybody in the film who is not a part of the investigation obstructs it and must be forced, against his will, by those who know better to act in his own self-interest. Not only do the people not have the right to know the truth; for their own sake they *must* not know the truth, because they are in essence irresponsible children.

Worse, the smelly morass of working-class ethnics—Greeks, Italians, Armenians, and Eastern Europeans that make up the waterfront community—incubate, nurture, and spread the plague; in fact, they *are* the plague, which becomes, finally, a metaphor for the threat the lower orders pose to the higher ones, that foreigners pose to the native-born. In the thirties, or even the mid-forties, these ethnics might have been heroes, as they were in Kazan's own treatment of Irish immigrant life in his first film, *A Tree Grows in Brooklyn* (1945), or in George Stevens's warm portrait of Norwegian ethnic life in *I Remember Mama* (1948). But by 1950, in the chill of the cold war, corporate-liberal directors like Kazan, reacting against the thirties, Popular Front deification of the people, had become xenophobic and virulently anti–working class; they turned away from the "little man" at the bottom to the big men at the top.

Pluralists made no bones about their contempt for the poor. "Slowness in altering opinion [is] characteristic of the lower classes," wrote David Riesman and Nathan Glazer. "The less educated are always the more suspicious; they have in the course of life gained a peasant-like guile." They called upon the "uneducated masses" to "practice deference and restraint which [are] understood and appreciated only among the well-to-do and highly educated strata," and went on to speak of the "poisonous tastes in politics and culture" of the "lower classes."[17]

The "people" had better leave the big decisions to the experts, because they were too dumb and depraved, and reality too complex, for them to decide for themselves. Moreover, people were a bad lot, floundering about in a quicksand of violence, hatred, and psychosis. Although many pluralists still clung to the traditional liberal notion of human perfectibility, influential intellectuals like Schlesinger traded it in for a darker view of human fallibility, long associated with conservatism. As Schlesinger put it, "The Soviet experience, on top of the rise of fascism, reminded my generation [of] a new dimension of experience—the dimension of anxiety, guilt, and corruption." Pluralists rationalized their disdain for people with fashionable psychoanalytic pessimism, on the one hand, and equally fashionable theological despair, on the other. "The psychology of Freud," wrote Schlesinger, "has renewed the intellectuals' belief in the dark, slumbering forces of the will. The theology of Barth and Niebuhr has given new power to the old and chastening truths of Christianity."[18] Beset by sex and sin, Freud and Niebuhr, without the saving correctives of education and the restraints of civilization, people were a bad lot, given to wreaking grievous harm on one another at the drop of a hat.

In their preference for experts over people, pluralists disclosed a fundamental elitism. In their view, the shape of society resembled a pyramid; the few at the top were better than the many at the bottom. The structure of authority in *Panic* is top-down and hierarchical, but it is a hierarchy based on science and expertise, one that gives a doctor the power over a cop and mayor. As we descend the ladder of authority from the leaders to the led, we leave the realm of competence to enter one of ineptitude. Reed, as we have seen, has to be called in to diagnose the plague, because the coroner, the local official with the provincial education, the Charles Bovary of New Orleans, is too dumb to do it himself. When Palance and Mostel are fleeing from the police, it is the lower-ranking cops who are itching to shoot to kill, and they have to be restrained by those above them. And finally, at the bottom, are the people, the panickers in the street for whom the film is named. *Panic* justifies this paternalistic arrangement by showing that the experts and professionals do, in fact, have the interests of the people at heart. They are benevolent, self-sacrificing, and hardworking. At the end, they do track down the plague carriers, and save the city.

Not all films swallowed the corporate-liberal line. Conservative films shared the same goals as films like 12 *Angry Men* and *Panic in the Streets*, but they preferred to realize them with different means, and argued that conservatives, not pluralists, should have the authority to administer consensus.

The Local Hero

My Darling Clementine and the Doctor's Dilemma

Somewhere about one-third of the way through John Ford's *My Darling Clementine*, Wyatt Earp (Henry Fonda), Tombstone's new marshal, faces off against Doc Holliday (Victor Mature) at the bar of the local saloon. "This is Doc Holliday's town," Earp has been told, and indeed Holliday acts like he runs the show in Tombstone. He controls the gambling and even tries to enforce the law, breaking up a poker game by ejecting a cheater. "Runnin' that tinhorn outa town—that's none of your business," drawls Earp. "Tombstone has the biggest graveyard west of the Mississippi," returns Holliday. "Marshals and I usually get along better when we understand that right away. I see we're in opposite camps."

Like *Panic in the Streets*, *My Darling Clementine* fights a two-front war, one on behalf of the center against extremists and one for control of the center. The ostensible enemy in *Clementine* are the Clantons, a gang of degenerate rustlers and killers who live in a shack outside Tombstone, but the real enemy is Doc Holliday, who lives right in town. The fight against the former frames the story—it gives it a beginning and an end—but the fight against the latter takes up by far the greater amount of screen time, and only when it is successfully concluded can Earp move against the Clantons.

Earp is the ex-marshal of Dodge City, but when the film begins, he's retired, just a cowpoke passing through town on his way to California. The Clantons steal Earp's herd and kill his younger brother, James. In order to avenge James's death and to make Tombstone a place where "kids will be able to grow up safe," Earp agrees to pick up the badge again and become the town marshal. From this point on, however, the fight against the Clantons takes a backseat to the tug-of-war with Doc Holliday. Like

A tense confrontation between Marshal Wyatt Earp (Henry Fonda) and Doc Holliday (Victor Mature) over who has the right to run Tombstone, the cop or the doc.

Panic, Clementine pits cop against doc, but this time, the cop comes out on top.

Clementine was released in 1946, right after the end of World War II. While the relation of films to their immediate historical context is often oblique, here it is not. Earp is the *ex*-marshal of Dodge City. Like returning GIs, he has put down the gun in favor of pacific pursuits. He finds, however, that he has been premature, that before Tombstone (read, the home front) and the West (read, the Western world) can be made safe for kids (read, democracy), he has to pick up the gun once again, in much the same way that both corporate liberals and conservatives alike basically agreed on the necessity of remilitarizing America for the cold war. But here they parted company. They disagreed on how to conduct affairs at home. Conservatives, as we saw in *Panic*, put their faith in the law, and therefore conservative films dramatized the breakdown of order. When Earp first rides into town, before his brother's death, he finds that, in effect, there is no law. A "drunken Indian" is shooting up the local hotel, and the marshal is too much of a coward to go in after him. Earp, a private citizen, has to do it himself.

But the real reason Tombstone is a mess is because it has been run by Doc Holliday. Holliday represents the same constellation of values embodied by Reed in *Panic*. Both Holliday and Reed are experts, M.D.'s educated in the East. Holliday is a cultivated man whose room is full of books. When the occasion arises, he can even recite soliloquies from *Hamlet*. He dresses like a fop, corrects his girl friend's grammar, prefers champagne to whiskey, and was formerly engaged to Clementine, a schoolteacher who, like him, comes from upper-crust Boston. (Boston plays the same role in this film that Washington played in *Panic*.) But Eastern values are not heroized in *Clementine*. On the contrary, they are decadent. Conservatives, as we have seen, preferred the West and South to the East, and local interests to the priorities of the federal government. When Holliday does manage to perform an operation, the patient dies. He is not only an alcoholic, he's in the grip of an advanced case of tuberculosis and is obviously unable to prescribe the kind of medicine Tombstone needs. In *My Darling Clementine*, the doctor is himself sick.

In contrast to Doc Holliday, Earp, who comes from no farther away than Dodge City, is the local hero. And when the film begins and ends, he's heading west to California, about as far from Boston as he can get. He is a professional, not an expert; his authority is based on experience, not books. And he's not only a professional, he's average, a little faster on the draw than most folks, but not in essence much different. He doesn't like champagne, doesn't know Shakespeare, and has never, so far as we know, been to school.

Clementine, like many conservative films, stressed the importance of being average and normal. Way back in Hitchcock's *Shadow of a Doubt* (1943), for example, Teresa Wright, the daughter of a nice American family from a nice American town in California, complains, "I don't like being an average girl from an average family." She welcomes a visit by uncle Joseph Cotten from Philadelphia because "his opinions aren't normal," but she finds out that his behavior isn't either. He's the Merry Widow Murderer, and after he tries to murder her too, her normal boyfriend, cop Macdonald Carey, drives the point home: "What's wrong with average?"

Seven years later, in Nicholas Ray's *In a Lonely Place* (1950), it was Humphrey Bogart's turn to be abnormal. He's a violence-prone script-writer, and Gloria Grahame, his girl friend, complains, "He doesn't act like a normal person. Why can't he be like other people?" "Other people" in this case are Bogart's old war buddy, Frank Lovejoy, a cop, and his wife. Wife says to Frank, "I'm glad you're not a genius. [Bogart] is a sick man." "No, he isn't," counters Frank. "There's nothing the matter with his mind except that he's superior." But in conservative films of the fifties, to be superior was to be sick, and the little lady has the last word: "I still like you the way you are—attractive and average." And at the end of the film, when Bogart tries to strangle Gloria Grahame, it turns out that she's right.

Conservatives liked to deride "geniuses." As a Monsanto Chemical recruiting film put it, "No geniuses here; just a bunch of average Americans working together."[19] But when they did so, they were not attacking achievement and old-fashioned Protestant striving, to which they were generally sympathetic, so much as experts and intellectuals. These films liked the heart as much as the head, emotion as much as fact. Earp is motivated by a deep, abiding attachment to his dead brother, and the film applauds his personal loyalty.

The emphasis on the average and on the validity of the heart accounts in part for the rejection of the top-down structure that characterized *Panic* and the comparatively generous treatment of the people. Many conservative westerns, particularly those of Ford and Hawks, displayed a populist streak that distinguished them dramatically from "bad town" westerns, in which the townies were either cowardly, finking out on the hero in the clutch, as in *High Noon* (1952), a left-wing film, or were likely to degenerate into a lynch mob, as in *Broken Arrow* (1950), a corporate-liberal film. When towns were bad in conservative films, it wasn't because the people were bad, but because the towns were lawless, which is to say they were being run by inept corporate liberals. Mostly, however, in films like *Clementine*, towns were good; the people backed the hero to the hilt. Here, two men volunteer, unasked, to stand by the Earps against the Clantons, and during the gunfight, they are dimly visible through the dust and flying lead, doing their part.

In one scene, the audience gathered for the performance of an itinerant thespian begins hooting and hollering when he doesn't show up. The film treats this display of popular choler indulgently; the townies are not a mob, but merely do-it-yourself critics legitimately expressing their displeasure with eggs and tomatoes. In fact, when they suggest riding the actor out of town on a rail, Earp backs them up. "That seems reasonable enough to me," he says.

American conservatism had traditionally been characterized by a patrician contempt for the people. In the thirties and early forties, the "masses" had been almost the sole property of the left, and in Ayn Rand's *Screen Guide for Americans*, Hollywood is warned not to "deify the common man." This made sense in terms of conservatism's pessimistic view of human nature, the same one that corporate liberals like Schlesinger were now discovering for themselves. But the authoritarian and repressive strain in conservatism had always collided not only with its equally traditional emphasis on individualism but also with the longing for the simpler life and an antagonism to Big Business that led to intermittent outbursts of populism. These themes were most movingly expressed in the prewar films of Frank Capra. In fact, Robert Warshow first called attention to the populist element in *Clementine*, when he characterized Earp as "a more dangerous Mr. Deeds," referring to Capra's man of the people.

After the war, influenced by ex-Communists like Whittaker Chambers and James Burnham, conservatives' affection for the common man became more pronounced. In a letter to William Buckley, Chambers wrote that "the rock-core of the Conservative Position can be held realistically only if Conservatism will accommodate itself to the needs and hopes of the masses."[20] According to historian of conservatism George Nash, "Chambers noted that the common people, humble people, 'the plain men and women of the nation,' had stood by him in his need. If the passions of the cold war drove some pluralist liberals to criticize 'populism' and mass society, these pressures also generated among some conservatives a hitherto forbidden identification with the people. On the Communist issue some conservatives sensed that *they* were on the popular side."[21]

It is significant, however, that in *Clementine*, Earp's support for the crowd against the actors only goes so far. When the Clantons—extremists—begin to bait an actor declaiming Shakespeare, Earp takes his side, punching out the offending Clanton. The populism of conservatives had its limits and did not extend to riffraff outside the law who truly rejected civilized values.

Moreover, regardless of the populist undertow of these films, people were, ultimately, awash in sin and depravity and behaved well only because they were forced to do so. Tombstone *does* need a marshal. And Earp can't persuade Holliday to shape up; he has to use coercion to put him in his place. In one scene he knocks him down, and in another he beats him to the draw, wounding him in the hand. But despite his resort to force, and despite his apparent repudiation of East Coast values, Earp, like the Fonda character in 12 *Angry Men*, plays a conciliatory role as well. His job is not only to enforce conservative over pluralist values but to construct a consensus that includes corporate liberals as junior partners. Although Holliday had at first insisted that he and Earp were in "opposite camps," it's not true. At one point, Earp momentarily suspects Holliday of murdering of his brother, James. It turns out, of course, that Holliday is innocent. The dispute between Earp and Holliday, after all, like that between Reed and Warren, is merely about means, and indeed, the rivalry between the two is muted by mutual admiration, respect, and even a marked resemblance. Earp is not without Eastern social graces. He dances—awkwardly, it's true—at a church social, and most important, he is on his way to winning teacher Clementine, whose heart still belongs to Holliday. The West, in other words, is heir to all that is best about the East. The question is merely who is in a better position to fight for those principles, the cop or the doc. The trouble with Holliday is not only the values he represents but the fact that he doesn't himself recognize what's valuable in them; he rejects Clementine, refuses to practice medicine, and even becomes a borderline outlaw himself. Nevertheless, Earp can't administer the coalition of the center without him, and when Holliday tries to leave town on the stagecoach, Earp brings him back. He has to incorporate Holliday within the consensus of the center, not drive him outside it or allow him to escape it.

For his part, Holliday, too, recognizes the imperatives of consensus and throws in with Earp, volunteering to aid him against the Clantons. As in 12 *Angry Men* and *Panic in the Streets*, the center—cops and docs, conservatives and corporate liberals—closes ranks in the face of extremists. And once his own house is in order, Earp, now the spokesman for consensus, can announce to the Clantons, "I'll give you a chance to submit to proper authority." They won't, of course, but with the hard job of consensus-building over, the Clantons can be easily dispatched in the climactic shoot-out at the O.K. Corral. Holliday dies too. "Death analysis" (who

dies and why) tells us that he must die so that on his way out of town at
the end, Earp can half hold out the promise that he will return for
Clementine, and cement the union of West and East by marriage.

The question who survives to speak for the center at the end of a film is
an important one, because it is often a confirmation of who has won the
struggle for authority. Moreover, the final speaker articulates the film's
ideology. Ford's *Fort Apache* (1948), released two years after *Clementine*,
presents a similar conflict, although here the embodiment of Eastern
values is not a dissolute doctor but a martinet colonel, again played by
Henry Fonda. Fonda's Colonel Thursday is the military version of the
expert. Educated at West Point (read, Harvard), he marches off to war
with visions of textbook battles dancing in his head. "The paper that
Captain Robert E. Lee wrote when he was at the Point impressed me,"
he says pompously, "particularly the maneuver Genghis Khan employed
in the Battle of Khin Sha in 1221." But the Apache wars of the late
nineteenth century have little to do with Genghis Khan, and Thursday,
pressed from the Custer mold, only succeeds in leading his men to
slaughter.*

The foil for Fonda is John Wayne, who plays a cavalry captain named
York. When Thursday blithely rides into an ambush, it is York who realizes there is something wrong. York reads the Apaches' smoke signals and
follows their trail. As in *12 Angry Men*, reality is opaque, and mediation
is necessary, but what is required is the conservative professional who
applies experience and common sense, not an expert who is blinded by
his education, here derogated as mere book learning.

Moreover, Thursday's cavalry, led by Ward Bond and Victor McLaglen,
are a rowdy bunch characterized by a spectrum of ethnic and regional
accents and by their generally boisterous and colorful behavior. The film
indulges them much as *Clementine* does its egg-throwing, foot-stomping
theater audience. The cavalry is an egalitarian melting pot composed of
working-class Irish immigrants, Confederate veterans, and assorted odd-

*Thursday has often been regarded as a conservative figure, because he is rigid and
authoritarian. But popular notions of what conservatives are like derive largely from the
dominant ideology—pluralism. Conservatives' own self-image was entirely different. They
did not regard themselves as rigid and authoritarian but, on the contrary, ascribed these
characteristics to their rivals.

balls, who fly in the face of the military and class hierarchy insisted upon by Thursday. When a soldier ends up in the stockade, it's a sign of his irrepressible high spirits and an occasion for humor, not an indication of his lack of discipline. Nevertheless, like those in *Clementine, Fort Apache's* populist inclinations have limits. The soldiers do need leadership and guidance. York respects Thursday for his integrity.

But York draws the line; he refuses to follow Thursday's orders and lead his men into suicidal combat, and in endorsing his point of view, *Fort Apache*, like *Clementine*, modifies the top-down structure that character- ized *Panic in the Streets*. Unlike corporate-liberal films, in which leaders are calm and followers are hotheads, in conservative films it is often the other way around. In *The High and the Mighty* (1954), for example, pilot Robert Stack chokes in the clutch, while co-pilot John Wayne (again) advises him to "throw away the book," and brings the plane in himself. And in *Fort Apache*, it is Thursday who is the nut, whereas York is cool and collected. Conservatives recognized that they had been playing second fiddle for decades, and sentimentalized themselves as men who knew best, or at least better than their overeducated superiors, the men who knew too much.

York's defiance, however, is confined within narrow limits. When Thursday threatens him with court-martial for refusing to fight and orders him to sit out the battle with the supply train, York does not appeal to the troops over Thursday's head and try to incite a mutiny, as well he might have. As Russell Campbell put it, York "is a fervid opponent of the official line. Yet he does not once disobey a command. . . . York is the obedient rebel. . . . The captain continues to place his trust in the ultimate virtue of the system to which he belongs. He questions, but he does not defy."[22] In other words, for all their unhappiness with the corporate liberals, conservatives remained the loyal opposition, firmly situated within the center.

But in *Fort Apache*, of course, the loyal opposition is the place to be; it is the moral center of the film. Thursday, after all, is killed, and York survives to deliver the coda at the end. In the final scene, he is talking with a reporter in front of a large oil portrait of Colonel Thursday. Thurs- day's Last Stand has become a legend. He is "the idol of every schoolboy in America," says the awestruck journalist. "He must have been a great man, a great soldier." "No man died more gallantly, nor won more honor for his regiment," replies York. Thursday's secret is safe with him, but how shall we take this posthumous praise for Thursday, whom we have just seen willfully lead his men to their deaths? Some critics have taken York's words ironically. Although the contradiction between what York says and what we know creates the potential for irony, it is precisely this film's job to raise the ironic option only to dismiss it, as York makes clear in his final tribute to Thursday: "They haven't died," he says, gazing out of the window into the middle distance at the cavalry of the mind, his fallen comrades. "They're still living and they will live as long as the regiment lives. They're better now than they used to be. Thursday did that." Once again, as in 12 *Angry Men* and *Panic in the Streets*, the center closes ranks before the world. It doesn't wash its dirty linen in public. Nevertheless, it is York, the conservative, who has the last word. It is York who eulogizes Thursday, York who is the teller of the tale, the guardian of the legend, the author of history, the producer of ideology. The reporter, it is important to note, is an ally in this process, not an enemy. As we might expect, conservative films, being more sympathetic to the people, were also more sympathetic to their surrogates.

In *The Man Who Shot Liberty Valance* (1962), fourteen years later, Ford replays this ending, but gives it a bitter, more conservative twist. The irony implicit in the conclusion of *Fort Apache* is stressed, not muted. Once again, a man is discussing a legend of the West with a reporter. The subject of the legend is Ransom Stoddard (James Stewart), known to all as "the man who shot Liberty Valance," a notorious outlaw. And the keeper of the flame is Stoddard himself, now a senator, a (corporate-liberal) politician from Washington. Stoddard has finally decided to tell the truth, that it was not he who shot Liberty Valance, but a gunslinger named Tom Doniphon (John Wayne), his rival in love and ideology. The reporter, however, doesn't want to hear the truth, and he tears up his notes. "When the legend becomes fact, print the legend," he says.

In both films, corporate liberals get the credit that conservatives deserved. Ford seems to be saying that this was all right and that legends are fine so long as it is the conservatives who live to tell the tale, as York does in *Fort Apache*. But in *Liberty Valance*, not only is Doniphon deprived of the glory that is rightfully his, but it is Stoddard who survives to embroider the legend, and *The Man Who Shot Liberty Valance* is bitter about it.

Conservatives did not, after all, inherit the America of the fifties, the way Ford suggests they would in *Clementine* and *Fort Apache*; on the contrary, the corporate liberals did. Stoddard rides in the saddle while Doniphon rests in his coffin, a forgotten man, not a hero but a victim of history—history made by the corporate liberals. A lot of water had flowed under the bridge by 1962, when *Liberty Valance* was released. Conservatives who had high hopes for Eisenhower, the first Republican president in two decades, saw him become captive of the corporate-liberal establishment, and they didn't like it. There is real anger in *Liberty Valance*, a sense of betrayal that looks forward to the conservative revival of the late seventies. Nevertheless, for all their anger at the pluralist inflection of consensus, conservatives remained loyal to the process by which it was reached. *Liberty Valance* shows grass-roots democracy at work. In one scene, the citizens debate statehood in a town meeting. As one after another stands up to have his and her say, the issues that divide them are articulated and compromised.

As we have seen, *Clementine*, *Fort Apache*, and even *Liberty Valance* quarreled with pluralist values, but they didn't question consensus itself. Some films did. Once we move out of the center into what centrists considered the never-never land of extremism, consensus and the struggle for authority over consensus look altogether different.

The Outsider

High Noon and the Conspiracy of the Center

Fred Zinnemann's *High Noon*, the critical and popular hit that won an Oscar for Gary Cooper in 1952, opens ominously with three deadbeat gunslingers riding into town while Tex Ritter mournfully warbles *High Noon*'s top-ten theme song: "If I'm a man, I must be brave/ I must meet that deadly killer/ Or lie a coward in my grave." Two of the three men are the Miller brothers, and they mean no good, but not quite yet. It's Sunday, the church bells are ringing, and Marshal Will Kane (Cooper) is in the midst of marrying blond, winsome Amy (Grace Kelly), yet another school-teacher (Quaker, this time) from back East. Kane is planning to retire and settle down with Amy on a ranch of his own. With its celebration of the rituals of community, this could be a Ford western of the cheerful *Clementine* period, but, as we shall see, it isn't.

While Will and Amy are tying the knot, the Millers are on their way to the depot to wait for brother Frank, who's arriving on the noon train. Just released from prison, Frank has sworn to get even with the man who sent him up, and he's heading to Hadleyville to do it. That man, of course, is Will Kane. When it becomes clear that before the day is out, at high noon, to be exact, there will be gunplay between Kane and the Millers, the goodwill that existed between the marshal and the community evaporates like a mirage.

At first, Kane doesn't turn a hair. "This is my town," he reassures Amy. "I have friends here. I'll swear in a bunch of deputies. Maybe there won't even be trouble." But Kane is in for a nasty surprise. The justice of the peace who married them folds up the American flag hanging on the wall of his office and prepares to leave town. He advises Kane to do the same. "This is a dirty little town in the middle of nowhere. Nothing that happens here matters. Get out." The hotel clerk sides with the Millers. "This place used to be busy when Frank Miller was around. Plenty of people around here think the marshal has a comeuppance coming to him." One man who does volunteer changes his mind when he realizes he's alone: "I got no stake in this. I got a wife and kids." Even Harv (Lloyd Bridges), Kane's deputy, won't lift a finger. He's miffed because he was passed over when Kane's job came up. As if this weren't bad enough, Amy opposes killing on principle. "I don't care who's right and who's wrong," she says. "There's got to be some better way for people to live." She's not fooling, either. She threatens to leave Kane unless he leaves town, ahead of the Millers.

As the clock ticks away, Kane goes into a bar, where the drunken patrons are giving one of the Millers a hero's welcome. Any volunteers? No! Next he walks over to the church, where he expects a better reception from the better element in town. But it's still no go. One parishioner maintains it's a personal thing between Kane and the Millers: "It's not our job." Another disagrees: "It ain't his trouble, it's ours, 'cause it's our town." It looks for a moment like his stirring speech will turn the tide in Kane's favor, when another man stands up. People up North are thinking of sending money down Hadleyville way, he says, to build factories and stores: shooting and killing are bad for business. "I think you better go while there's still time. It's better for you; it's better for us." The appeal to the pocketbook is decisive. Defeated, Kane walks out into the hot sun. Some boys are playing in the dirt. "Bang, bang, you're dead," says one, pointing a toy pistol at him. Even the kids are against him.

When high noon comes, the streets are deserted. Except for Amy, who has an eleventh-hour conversion, Kane doesn't have a friend in the world, and he has to go it alone. Luckily for him, he doesn't need anyone. He shoots the Millers down like the dirty dogs they are. When the gunfight is over and the people pour into the streets to congratulate him, he throws down his badge in the dust, turns his back, and rides out of town.

High Noon is a dark, pessimistic, bitter film. Both Earp in *Clementine* and Kane here find that retirement is premature, that they are forced, once again, to pick up the gun. But Earp does it in the name of consensus, the center, the community, whereas Kane does it in spite of the community. If citizens and ex-lawmen in centrist films pinned on the badge, in radical (extremist) films they threw down the badge. *

---

*Because "extremist" is a term with negative connotations fully intended by the centrists who coined it, I shall use "radical" to designate those films that attacked the center.

The debate in the church is analogous to the jury process in *12 Angry Men* and the town meeting in *The Man Who Shot Liberty Valance*, but the difference is striking. Those films identify with the emerging consensus, whereas *High Noon* denounces it. Consensus is bankrupt, the refuge of fools, knaves, and cowards, and values exist only outside it. Whereas pluralists applauded themselves for their "idealistic" pragmatism and ridiculed extremists for their preoccupation with fundamental questions of right and wrong, which they considered irrelevant and even obstacles to the smooth operation of democracy, *High Noon* does the opposite. The center is ridiculed for its obsession with mean, trivial, business-as-usual affairs, whereas Kane is applauded for his life-and-death confrontation with the Millers. Moreover, Kane can't transform consensus, redeem society, as Fonda did in *12 Angry Men*. Rather, he just gives up and walks

Whom are these people staring at? Why, Marshal Kane (Gary Cooper), of course, who finds that consensus seems different when you're on the outside looking in.

away from it. And of course, once consensus is repudiated, the question who holds authority within the center is irrelevant. Both corporate liberals and conservatives are bad.

High Noon, therefore, attacks both centrist models of the community: the federally focused, top-down model favored by the corporate liberals and the more bottom-up, populist model favored by the conservatives. On the one hand, Hadleyville's solid citizens, the ones with the solid-gold watch fobs, fail Kane in his moment of need. Moreover, it is because of the federal government that Frank Miller is free in the first place. "I sent Miller up five years ago for murder," Kane complains to Amy. "Up North, they commuted it." As a retired lawman tells Kane, "It's a great life. You risk your skin catching killers, and then the government turns them loose to shoot at you again." Kane blames those "up North" for letting Miller go, for coddling criminals. The corporate liberals have stabbed him in the back. The repudiation of Eastern, so-called civilized values associated with corporate liberalism is much stronger in *High Noon* than it is in conservative films, either *Clementine* or *Liberty Valance*. All three films feature schoolteachers from back East. In *Clementine* and *Liberty Valance*, the male pairs—Earp and Holliday, Doniphon and Stoddard—compete for the schoolteacher's favors and fight to possess the values she represents. In *High Noon*, she turns out to be wrong. Her values give way to Kane's.

On the other hand, if the northerners and easterners at the top are flawed, so are the locals at the bottom, right there in Hadleyville, the very people Ford celebrates in *Clementine*, *Fort Apache*, and *Liberty Valance*. Robert Warshow took producer Stanley Kramer to task for what he called *High Noon*'s "vulgar anti-populism," but the film was made by leftists on the receiving end of the blacklist, who felt betrayed and embattled for the same reasons conservatives felt secure and comfortable. In the fifties, many leftists felt let down by the "people," whom they had courted throughout the thirties and forties. Hence, for all *High Noon*'s contempt for the bourgeoisie, the lowlife (formerly, the salt of the earth) in the bar were little better. Earp is offered help and turns it down. In Hawks's *Rio Bravo* (1959), intended by Hawks as a conservative riposte to *High Noon*, the same thing happens: the townies volunteer unasked to help sheriff Wayne fight off the Burdettes, but Wayne refuses. In *High Noon*, on the other hand, Kane asks for help but doesn't get it. He must depend on himself alone if he hopes to survive. Hadleyville is a bad town, not just corrupt at the bottom or the top, but through and through, from top to bottom.

We know *High Noon* is a left-wing film because it was made by left-ists like Kramer and scriptwriter Carl Foreman, who later said it was. Once the Millers were equated with HUAC or McCarthy, the craven townies became friendly witnesses, as those who cooperated with the witch-hunt were called. "What *High Noon* was about at that time," said Foreman afterward, "was Hollywood, and no other place but Hollywood." But aside from its disdain for business values, it would be diffi-cult to tell *High Noon* apart from a right-wing film. Once stripped of its historical context, it becomes indistinguishable from, say, *Dirty Harry* (1971), which also ends with a lawman throwing down his badge in disgust.

It was no accident that left- and right-wing films resembled each other like two peas in a pod. Radical films generally obscured the difference between right and left in order to create a broad-based coalition against the center. They portrayed themselves as above politics, neither right nor left, but just "moral," and they did so for commercial as well as ideological reasons. The fear of ideological clarity was especially true of left-wing films. By the fifties, they had no real constituency. Communism had never, in spite of HUAC's claims, enjoyed any real purchase on American screens, save for the World War II period, when the fortunes of the U.S. and the USSR temporarily coincided, and even then it was virtually indis-tinguishable from mainstream New Dealism. In the fifties, what had, a decade before, been thoroughly respectable liberalism was driven under-ground. The radical right, on the other hand, thrust into the doghouse during the war for its isolationist and neo-Nazi inclinations, made a modest comeback. Rugged individualism—the Big Bertha of its ideological artil-lery—was, after all, as American as apple pie, and since the right attacked the center too, left-wing films often took on the protective coloration of right-wing films, waging their struggle in the name of individualism, attacking the center for coddling criminals, for being corrupt and conformist, rather than for being a class enemy, the accusation they traditionally flung at their opponents.

Yet individualism was far from a universally shared value in the fifties. Like consensus, it was a bone of contention among competing ideological blocs. In the following chapter, we will look at the conflict between individualism and its antagonist, conformity, as it worked itself out across the political spectrum in a single genre: the war film.

CHAPTER TWO

THE ORGANIZATION MAN GOES TO WAR

Must We Conform?

Back in 12 *Angry Men*, we saw that Henry Fonda managed to sway the jury because he succeeded in demonstrating that he had the facts on his side. But by themselves, facts weren't enough. All the facts in the world wouldn't have led Cobb and that bunch of loonies, deadbeats, and fence-sitters to a just verdict. Something more was needed, and Fonda found it in peer pressure, or "group politics."

In 12 *Angry Men*, group pressure restrains the pathology of the jurors and works toward consensus. In one scene, after Begley comes out with his racial slur and the entire table of jurors dramatically rises as one and turns its back on him, he moves to a smaller table and sits alone like a small child, crushed by the withdrawal of group affection, until he's allowed to rejoin the group by changing his vote to not-guilty. And again, at the the end of the film, when Cobb is the last holdout, the film cuts in succession to the faces of the others, staring intently at the lone dissident, until he breaks down and capitulates to the group by changing his vote. If people as solitary individuals were neurotic or sinful (depending on your point of view), if people in mobs—aggregates of solitary individuals—were hysterical and dangerous, membership in groups could be counted on to save them from themselves, protect them from their own worst instincts. The Big Picture possessed by experts was a group shot.

Individualism, as a professed value, had been on the skids for some time, but it was in the fifties that it got its final shove downhill. In "the past thirty years," wrote Daniel Bell, "not the *individual* but *collectivities*—corporations, labor unions, farm organizations, pressure groups—have become the units of social action. . . . Individual rights in many instances derive from group rights."[1] As individuals, in other words, people were likely to vote for Henry Wallace, make "irresponsible" demands on their employers, or support Joe McCarthy. But as Elks, middle-level executives for General Electric, or members of an ILGWU local, they could be expected to vote Democrat/Republican, fight in Korea, and invest in backyard bomb shelters.

The notion that membership in groups moderates individual behavior meant that despite their newfound affection for sex and sin, pluralists did not have to embrace the punitive methods of conservatism. They displayed a "combination," as Schlesinger put it, "of a certain operational optimism with a certain historical and philosophical pessimism."[2] This meant that they could flourish Freud and Niebuhr to fend off conservatives and attack the left, but essentially, they were able to carry on as before, insisting on therapy instead of force.

The emphasis on group politics coincided with the rise of what William H. Whyte, Jr., called the Social Ethic, as opposed to the older, individualist Protestant Ethic. In his influential book, *The Organization Man* (1956), he defined the social ethic as the belief that "of himself, [man] is isolated, meaningless; only as he collaborates with others does he become worthwhile, for by sublimating himself in the group, he helps to produce a whole that is greater than the sum of its parts."[3]

Although, as a rule of thumb, groups were better than individuals, not all groups were equally desirable. Simply, those that were governed by pluralist principles were good; those that were not were bad. Defying the former was a crime; defying the latter was *de rigueur*. That is why, in the beginning of 12 *Angry Men*, Fonda is correct to oppose his own solitary intuition to the collective wisdom of the group. This is a bad group dominated by extremists. Moreover, large groups were usually better, more ecumenical and inclusive than small ones. The rise, during the Progressive Era, of federal agencies that regulated competition and prices, along with the New Deal and wartime stimulation of American business, combined to rationalize the vagaries of the market and laid the groundwork for the final consolidation of monopoly capital, with its huge, bureaucratic organizations. Bigness, in the form of Big Business, Big Labor, and Big Government, became not only a fact of American life but a value as well. Bigness was desirable, efficient, natural, reasonable. In short, big was beautiful.

The men who worked in these large organizations, assembling Chevvies on the line or making decisions in the executive suites, were less slaves or captains of industry than wheels in machines that put a premium on cooperation, not competition; conformity, not individualism. Popularity with peers replaced creativity or even productivity as a criterion of performance. In 1956 psychiatrist Robert Lindner asked, "Must you conform?" in a book of the same name. Although fifties social critics often deplored conformity, the obvious consequence of this kind of group pressure, they more often found a silver lining. America's youth, argued Norman Podhoretz in the *New Leader*, were discovering "that 'conformity' did not necessarily mean dullness and unthinking conventionality, that indeed, there was a great beauty, a profound significance in man's struggle to achieve freedom *through* submission to conditions."[4]

In films made during World War II, the man who stood out from the crowd was an out-and-out villain, the Nazi *Übermensch*, like the heavy in Hitchcock's *Saboteur* (1942). But by the fifties, even the American Superman had become a cause for anxiety. In *The Lonely Crowd*, David Riesman quotes from an interview with a twelve-year-old girl who says, "I like Superman better than the others because they can't do everything Superman can do. Batman can't fly and that is very important. Question. Would you like to be able to fly? Answer. I would like to be able to fly if everybody else did, but otherwise it would be kind of conspicuous."[5] This girl's fear of flying was well grounded. It was better to blend in than stand out, better to be the same and safe than special and sorry.

The stress on conformity conflicted with corporate liberals' top-down elitism, their emphasis on experts and intellectuals, and created a fundamental contradiction. But pluralism was in the business of resolving contradictions, accommodating opposing values within consensus. It valued experts, but experts who would join the team and play ball. Similarly, once it established the authority of the group over the individual, it turned around and reconciled the two. In *12 Angry Men*, justice is served, but it is the system that serves it, despite the incompetence of its constituent parts. The defendant, who is only on camera for one or two brief moments at the beginning of the film, does nothing to help himself, but merely sits tight while the mills of justice grind on. Had *12 Angry Men* been a different kind of film, one in which the plot helps those who help themselves, he might have escaped, tracked down the real killer, and presented him to the astonished police at the end of the film. But the group process in *12 Angry Men* did in fact guarantee the rights of the individual, and moreover were it not for Fonda, the One Good Man, the system might have failed. In both these ways, the film accommodates the group and the individual. Conflict between them, like other social conflicts within the center, is only apparent; it is caused by a breakdown of communication. Like other centrist films, *12 Angry Men* tries to have its cake and eat it too.

The social ethic permeated every genre, even those that had tradition-ally provided a playground for individualism. All the solitary men-with-guns were in trouble. Look at the fate that befell the private eyes—Raymond Chandler's Philip Marlowe and Dashiell Hammett's Sam Spade—both of whom loomed large in the Hollywood landscape of the forties. The private eye was tough, cynical, urban, but above all, he was "private," a rebel against the organization, often an ex-cop who had been fired for insubor-dination, a man who had gotten fed up with the red tape and had acted on his own. He operated outside the organization, in the crawl space between the bureaucracy and the underworld. He was an individualist, a man with a code, almost as antagonistic to the police as he was to the criminals he was paid to catch. His independence was precarious, "licensed" by the state, and his license was always in danger of being revoked by the authorities, who resented his autonomy. His home was the city, and like the last cowboy, always one step ahead of the frontier, he was a victim of the suburbs, where town and country meet.

The film that marked the end of the line for the private eye was *Kiss Me Deadly* (1955), Robert Aldrich's farewell to the genre, a brilliant tour de force of stylistic pyrotechnics, atmosphere, and dialogue with the flair of the best *noir* writers: Chandler and Cain, Cornell Woolrich and James Hadley Chase. But the content is very different. Mickey Spillane, on whose book the film was based, was a perversion of this tradition, and even before Aldrich got his hands on Spillane's Mike Hammer, Hammer was a degenerate copy of Marlowe and Spade. He had their toughness without their morality, violence unrestrained by a personal code, rotted out by a barely concealed undertow of sadism. Whereas Chandler's Marlowe walked "these mean streets without himself becoming mean," untouched by the sordid milieu in which he worked, Hammer had not been so fortunate. He was as mean as they come.

In *Kiss Me Deadly*, the individualism that was sentimentalized in Chandler and Hammett is now sleazy and selfish. Living on the edge of the law is no longer romantic; it's dangerous to society. When worlds collide—Hammer's individualism and the needs of society—it's clear which one has to give way. Hammer has stumbled on a plot to steal a nuclear device, and the film expects him to lie back and let the cops take care of things. "You think you're so bright," a cop tells him. "Penny-ante gumshoe. Who do you think you are? Too many people like you have contempt for anything to do with the law. But when you do that, you might as well live in a jungle." When the cop appeals to Hammer's better nature, asking him to "step side and let us do our job," it doesn't work, because he doesn't have any. "What's in it for me?" Hammer replies. Then the cop gives him a glimpse of the Big Picture: "Manhattan Project, Trinity, Los Alamos—do those words mean anything to you?" the cop sneers. They do indeed. The Big Picture coincides with the national interest, and Hammer is properly ashamed of himself. By 1955, the stakes had become too high for the down-and-out shamuses doing their own thing. *Kiss Me Deadly* is a cold-war cautionary tale, and the message is clear. There's no room for neutrals playing both sides of the street. Either join the team or step aside. Hammer is squeezed between big crime and big government. The age of the private eye had ended.

Although the detective classics of the late forties were remade countless times in subsequent decades, the genuine article succumbed to the pressures of the fifties when, hats in hand, the private eyes became insurance investigators or returned to the force, happy to pound the beat alongside the men who had never left. Most crime films of the fifties dramatized the collective behavior of organizations in action, not the solitary struggles of individuals. The personal voice, the first-person narration characteristic of the genre in the forties, gave way to the third-person institutional narration; the shabby office with the pebbled glass door and the bottle of booze in the bottom drawer gave way to the precinct house and the crime lab. *Dragnet* (1954) replaced *The Big Sleep* (1946), Sergeant Friday replaced Marlowe and Spade, Jack Webb replaced Humphrey Bogart. Moreover, fifties cops were no longer single; they had wives and kids, who tied them securely to society, like Joseph Cotten in Bud Boetticher's *A Killer Is Loose* (1956) or Glenn Ford in Fritz Lang's *The Big Heat* (1953).

Cops who had a hard time clocking in in the morning and out again at night were individualists, characteristically derogated in therapeutic terms. In *Detective Story,* it becomes apparent that the real reason cop McCloud is depicted as crazy is because he won't play ball with the organization.

When he should be sitting at his desk filling out forms in triplicate, he's off stalking the "butcher," an abortionist named Schneider (George Macready). "I know I'm different from the others," he tells his easygoing partner, Lou (William Bendix). "I'm here out of principle. Criminals are a different breed. This is war."

McCloud's feud with Schneider disrupts the smooth functioning of the police bureaucracy. When Schneider's lawyer takes his complaints upstairs and bursts into Lieutenant Monahan's office railing against McCloud, Monahan takes the lawyer's side, accusing McCloud of bringing heat down on the department. Monahan is an organization man. "Your moral indignation is giving me a pain in the neck," he snaps, echoing Riesman on "indignants." A film from a different perspective, more indulgent of individualism, more suspicious of organizations, would have sentimentalized McCloud, treated him like an endangered species, a Last Cowboy, while here he's just a psycho, better off dead. He's rigid when he should be flexible; he thinks in absolutes when he should be pragmatic. "Bend with the wind or break," Lou warns him, but he won't listen. He's out of step, listening to an inner voice when Americans were marching to Muzak, and at the end, he has to be killed.

War films were better suited than those of any other genre to dramatize the clash between the Social Ethic and the Protestant Ethic. As Robert Warshow pointed out, "Modern war is a cooperative enterprise . . . heroism belongs to the group more than to the individual."[6] When General Eisenhower won the presidency in 1952, it was less a sign of the militarization of American society than of the triumph of the organization man. As I. F. Stone put it, Eisenhower's "one great gift [was] a gift of getting along with people, of solving and smoothing over organizational problems."[7] To the man in the gray flannel suit, the army was home.

Moreover, war films could help to create a cultural climate hospitable to cold-war objectives. This wasn't an easy job. The imperatives of the cold war, the war that wasn't a war, were difficult to dramatize because they demanded the passions of war in a time of peace. When McCloud said that society was in a state of "war," he didn't realize the war was over, and mistakenly thought that behavior appropriate to the battlefield was appropriate to the home front as well. In a society based on consent, men like McCloud were wrong. But on the other hand the specter of the Soviet Union could not be ignored; people had to prepare for the coming confrontation. When World War II ended in 1945, the military had been demobilized and conscription abolished. Returning vets came home to pick up the pieces of their lives and resume interrupted careers or begin new ones. When the Truman adminstration appealed for rearmament and a peacetime draft in the late forties, many turned a deaf ear. They had done their part, and now they wanted to tend their own gardens, not pay higher taxes to support a bloated military establishment. If postwar America was really the affluent society everybody said it was, and as indeed it seemed to be, the idea of sacrifice could go out the window. In a society in which everybody had everything, why should anyone have to sacrifice anything or ever want to? In 1954, Mary McCarthy, in her aptly titled novel *The Group*, attributed this sentiment to the generation of the thirties, but it was even more true of the time in which she wrote it. "Women in my day," says Mrs. Renfrew to her daughter, Dottie, "were willing to make sacrifices for love, or for some ideal, like the vote or Lucy Stonerism." "That was your day, Mother," Dottie explains patiently, as if to a child. "Sacrifices aren't necessary any more. . . . Sacrifice is a dated idea."[8]

By dramatizing the overwhelming importance of the public interest, war films could rehabilitate the idea of sacrifice by making private concerns appear petty. Since the biggest, best, and most important group was the government, the conflict between the organization and the individual could be easily translated into a clash between the public interest and personal life.

In Gordon Douglas's *Bombers ʋ-52* (1957), a general, alluding to some contretemps around Col. Efrem Zimbalist, Jr.'s passion for Sgt. Karl Malden's daughter, tells him, "Doesn't make sense unless there's something personal involved," rolling *personal* off his tongue as if it had a bad taste. "I don't want to interfere with your affairs," he goes on, "but when they get in the way of the Wing, it's our affair. We can't let anything get in the way of the job we've got to do. It's too big," he concludes, looking off into the middle distance at the Big Picture. Schlesinger complained that for extremists, "politics becomes, not a means of getting things done, but an outlet for private grievances and frustrations."[9] And indeed, that's what's wrong with McCloud—his war is a personal vendetta, not a socially sanctioned battle. Like *Kiss Me Deadly*, these films stressed that the postwar world was no place for people with personal agendas.

By V-J Day, however, Americans had seen all the war films they wanted to see, and then some. War films had become box-office poison, and from 1945 to 1949 Hollywood virtually stopped making them. Then came Korea, the answer to a prayer. The fresh crop of fifties war films started hopefully, even nostalgically. "Hollywood had blossomed in the war years," wrote critic Julian Smith, and its new films "tried to rekindle the romance by making the cold war as warm and appealing as the war that had given us the best years of our lives."[10] But Korea was a mixed blessing. "The trouble is," Robert Mitchum confided to Mai Britt in *The Hunters* (1958), "Korea came along too soon after the real big one. It's hard to sell anyone on it." Besides, the North Koreans were real losers, and neither they nor the Chinese, somewhat more respectable adversaries, were adequate stand-ins for the Russians.

Many fifties war films were indeed set in World War II (a more compelling war than Korea). Still, they differed markedly from films of the early forties by virtue of the fact that they were not much interested in war. Some, like *From Here to Eternity* (1953), which ended when the Japanese attacked Pearl Harbor, or *Operation Pacific* (1951), in which John Wayne spent half his time pursuing his ex-wife, Patricia Neal, barely managed to get their GIs into combat. The films made during World War II, mainly written by progressives like John Howard Lawson, Albert Maltz, Dalton Trumbo, and Lillian Hellman, were often preoccupied with articulating war aims—democracy, freedom, brotherhood—and went out of their way to explain why we fought. By contrast, Korean War films didn't know why we fought, and what's more, they didn't care. "I don't know why I'm here, but let's get it over with and go home," was a sentiment expressed repeatedly.[11]

If the films weren't unduly troubled by the absence of an adequate theater of operations, heroic purpose, and a suitable enemy, it was because the real enemy was behind the lines, just as the real drama lay, not in the battle with the Nazis or Commies, but in the deadly combat between the individual and society, represented by the army. This obsession with the contrasting claims of individualism and social organization overshadowed all other concerns. In these films, the army even looked different. In the fifties, as Whyte put it, the whole was more important than the sum of its parts, and the stress on consensus resulted in an army that was much more homogeneous than the one pictured in films of World War II, where, as Barbara Deming pointed out in her book, *Running Away from Myself*,

Catholics fought side by side with Jews; Brooklyn cabbies with philosophy teachers; black men with white.[12] In fifties war films, on the other hand, Protestants fought shoulder to shoulder with Protestants, whites dug foxholes with whites, middle-class college kids shared their K-rations with middle-class college kids. When there were differences among the men, they were much more likely to be those of rank than those of class or ethnicity. Films made in World War II often focused on enlisted men, privates or corporals at the bottom of the heap. The heroes of fifties war films were officers. Robert Mitchum played a colonel in *One Minute to Zero* (1952), Richard Widmark a lieutenant in *Halls of Montezuma* (1950), Clark Gable a general in *Command Decision* (1949), Van Heflin a major, then a colonel in *Battle Cry* (1955), and so on.

Fifties war films had the same cast of characters as films of other genres. They had their war correspondents, their doctors, and also their experts in officers' clothing—college-educated generals, colonels, or lieutenants who ran their battalions by the book—as well as their professionals, usually lifers, who threw the book away. And the films fought among themselves over what attitudes to adopt toward them. In pluralist films, the experts were genial Eisenhowers—wise, easygoing organization men—and the lifers who defied them, and depended on experience, hunches, or instinct, were nuts. Docs never quite shoved soldiers aside the way they did cops in thrillers, but in pluralist war films they lurked in the background, ready to ambush martial with therapeutic values when the occasion arose. They came into their own treating traumatized or wounded vets in postwar films like *Home of the Brave* and *The Men* (1950), and they had little trouble seizing the hearts and minds of GI Joes from the chaplains, who had had them pretty much to themselves in the early forties. In some films, soldiers acted like doctors. For example, in Fred Zinnemann's *The Search* (1948), GI Montgomery Clift helped a disturbed DP kid regain his speech. Humphrey Bogart played an Army doc in *Battle Circus* (1953), but it was not until Robert Altman's *M*A*S*H* in 1970 that therapeutic values won a decisive victory on the battlefield.

In conservative films, the experts were derogated as military bureaucrats, paper-pushing desk-bound generals or callow lieutenants, and the rogue officers or sergeants who threw away the book, pitting experience against education, were usually right. If pluralist war films liked Ike, conservative war films liked Douglas MacArthur, the maverick Truman had to fire because he tried to take the Korean War into his own hands. In Lewis Milestone's *Halls of Montezuma*, the expert is a public-schooled British officer who speaks Japanese and figures out where the Jap rockets decimating the U.S. Marines are coming from, but clever as he is, he's a secondary character, subordinated to the professional soldiers. The war correspondent, Jack Webb, is treated much more indulgently than the reporter in *Panic*, and the doctor, Karl Malden, rather than undermining Lieutenant Widmark's authority, helps him kick the therapeutic habit. Widmark is afflicted with migraine headaches and depends on Malden's pills to keep him going. "It's something you got to beat down in yourself without medicine," Malden tells him, "otherwise you'll be nothing but a grown-up baby hanging onto your mother's apron strings." At the end, Widmark smashes a bottle of pills with the butt of his M-1, looks up at his men, and says, "We're moving out."

In other films, doctors did no more than endorse the morality of the hardcore heroes. In *One Minute to Zero*, the doc provides the rationale that allows Col. Robert Mitchum to bomb a refugee column that Mitchum believes is concealing Reds. "War is the most malignant condition of the human race," says the doc. "We sometimes have to cut out the good tissue with the bad." But *Halls of Montezuma* and *One Minute to Zero* were somewhat unusual, because most conservative films dispensed with the services of docs entirely, leaving the field to chaplains, like Rock Hudson of *Battle Hymn*, or the one in William Wellman's *Battleground* (1949), to whom was entrusted the job of articulating America's war aims.

Ultimately, the real bone of contention between corporate-liberal and conservative war films was the army itself. Corporate-liberal films generally gave the army good grades, first because they were interested in prosecuting the cold war, second because it was an easy way of illustrating the necessity of sacrifice, and third because it was an organization permeated by the Social Ethic. If it came to a question of leaving the wounded to save the mission, these films did so without batting an eye, because the group was more important than the individual. At the same time, however, the army made corporate liberals nervous because it fostered authoritarian and military values inimical to pluralism. For pluralists, the question was always, How could the army be demilitarized? How could war be made safe for peace?

Predictably, conservative films, with their preference for force over persuasion, were comfortable with the army as the embodiment of martial values, but they disliked it for being a bureaucracy, hostile to individualism. Because they respected individuals, soldiers in conservative films were much more likely to return for their wounded, even at the expense of the group. It was the enemy, the alien hordes, who sacrificed the wounded, not us. In *Retreat, Hell!* (1951), Col. Frank Lovejoy says, "These Chinese would rather give us a wounded man than a dead one. They know we take care of our own wounded, and it slows us up." Comments like these were covert responses to the corporate liberals, the real enemy. Fifties films were war films, all right, but the war was between Ike and MacArthur.

Radical war films turned the scale of values implicit in both centrist types of films upside down. The individual and the group were irreconcilably at odds. Either the individual carried out the mission in spite of the group, or the mission itself was suspect. Like conservative films, right-wing films accused the army of smothering individualism with bureaucratic red tape, but they didn't encourage their rebel heroes to return to the fold at the end. Here, too, bad generals were paper-pushing Eisenhowers, but the MacArthurs were little better, because they didn't go far enough. Good soldiers were "fighting generals," like Claire Chennault, or even better, those lower down the ladder, like Chennault's Flying Tigers in the film of the same name—"adventurers, soldiers of fortune," as someone calls them, or the ragtag band of mercenaries in Sam Fuller's *China Gate* (1957). Essentially, they are all individualists, and in these films, personal motives—money, adventure, loyalty—are more than okay. When by-the-book lieutenants lecture tough-as-nails sergeants for letting their personal concerns warp their judgment, they're always wrong. If conservative films liked the heart as much as the head, right-wing films liked the heart more, and in war films, the heart became "guts"—a quality of individual heroism.

Left-wing films also disliked the army, but they did not elevate individualism to a matter of principle. The army was bad because it crushed people, not because it smothered individualism per se. Moreover, the army was regarded as a caste system that enforced class distinctions. Generals were usually bad, drunk with power, cowardly, or terminally inept. In these films, the brass invariably ordered GIs into suicidal missions.

To see how these recurrent motifs, conventions, and characters are inflected from left to right, we must first ask, How is the army presented, as a good organization or a bad bureaucracy? Is there a doctor? If so, is he a help or a hindrance? Who has the authority, an Eisenhower, a MacArthur, or neither? Does he go by the book or throw the book away? Does he believe in going back for the wounded at the expense of the mission, or does he put the mission first and leave the wounded behind? Men in battle often die or break down emotionally or physically, and we have to ask, Who dies and who survives, who collapses and who pulls through, and what kinds of values do they represent? Are small groups—squads, platoons, battalions—pitted against the army as a whole? Mutiny is the form dissent takes in the army, and conversely, court-martial is the method used by the army to discipline mutineers. Consequently, we have to ask, Are mutineers heroes or villains? Is court-martial just or unjust, fair or foul?

Babies and Bombers

Strategic Air Command and the Domestication of War

It's spring training time at Al Lang Field in Saint Petersburg, Florida, the winter home of the Saint Louis Cards. On a hot, sunny day in April 1955, the stands are sparsely populated by kids, players' wives, and a couple of fans drinking beer and gazing absently at the men on the field. Nothing could be further from their minds than South Vietnam, which was just beginning to receive American aid for the first time, but as a B-36 flies overhead, we're reminded that without the constant vigilance of the Strategic Air Command, we'd be dodging bombs, not watching baseball. Meanwhile, on the ground, a figure in the uniform of a United States Air Force general, incongruous among the madras shorts and Cardinal caps, makes its way toward the playing field. The figure's name is Rusty Castle (James Millican), and he wants to talk to the third baseman, Dutch Holland (Jimmy Stewart). Dutch and Rusty are old war buddies, and when Sally, Dutch's wife (June Allyson), sees Rusty, she grimaces. "I know Dutch. The last thing he wants to do is hash over old times," she says. She thinks the war is over, but she's in for a nasty surprise when Rusty announces that Dutch, who is in the reserves, has been called up for active duty. "Where's the fire?" asks Dutch. "We're the only thing that keeps the peace," Rusty replies, gravely, but Dutch isn't buying. Another twenty-one months in the service will ruin his baseball career, and he's not pleased. "I've done my share," he says bitterly. And Sally is even more adamant. She's just finished decorating their new home, and the house-warming party is that very night.

But it looks like the pleasures of civilian life are going to have to be sacrificed to the rigors of military service, the small group to the big group, the Cards to SAC. In this film, the authority of the organization is unquestioned, and Dutch needs no more than a nudge to join up. And like Dutch, Sally is a real trooper. She agrees to follow him to Fort Worth, Texas, where he's stationed. "If you go, we both go on active duty. Anything you do is fine with me—just as long as you don't leave me behind," she says breathlessly.

Cut to Carswell Air Force Base. Dutch and Sally have plenty of time to read the billboard at the entrance to the base, which says, "The Nation and Your Security Are at Stake," because they're detained at the gate by

James Stewart is a team player. The only question is, which team? The Cards, the little team on the ground, or the Strategic Air Command, the big team in the sky?

the MPs. Dutch doesn't have proper identification, and even his driver's license has expired. He grows impatient with the red tape, but we know the security officers are just doing their job. It's not the army that is a clumsy bureaucracy, but the civilians who are a mess without the discipline of the organization.

Before long, Dutch and Sally get used to the routine of life at the base, which is little different from life at home. They move into a new house, just like the one in Saint Pete, and every evening Sally picks Dutch up at the airfield in the family car. Dutch even begins to like his job. His boss, General Hawkes (Frank Lovejoy), is firm but friendly; working conditions are strenuous but challenging, and there is plenty of opportunity for a good man to get ahead. The Air Force, of course, is hierarchically organized; those at the top are better than those at the bottom. Highest and best is General Hawkes; he sees the Big Picture, has the firmest grasp on the role and rationale of SAC. Beneath him is Rusty Castle, who recruited Dutch, and beneath him is Dutch himself, who quickly suppresses his reservations about leaving civilian life and learns to live with the organization. Below Dutch are a variety of lieutenants and sergeants, many of whom, as we shall see in a moment, don't see the Big Picture. They want out. Since the film looks with favor upon this top-down structure, promotion up the ladder is an unambiguous reward for a job well done, just as demotion down the ladder is punishment for one done badly. During the course of the film, Dutch is promoted to colonel.

The fact that the army was both an organization and a hierarchy made it a perfect vehicle for resolving the contradiction between pluralism's preference for the superior to the average, on the one hand, and its preference for conformity over individualism on the other. The army nurtured both sets of values; it was the natural habitat for the expert as well as the organization man, and the two often coexisted in the same person. General Hawkes both educates Dutch about the modern weaponry of the fifties and supervises the working of the group.

Despite the fact that Dutch is fast becoming a high-level executive, Sally isn't happy. She begins to chafe at the bit; she doesn't like the life of an army wife, and resists the organization. "I want a husband right here on the ground, not in Alaska, Timbuktoo, or Greenland," she complains. Sally's going to have a baby, and when Dutch is about to leave on a four-day mission, she protests, "Do you have to go on this trip?" "Do you realize that there are fifteen hundred babies born a month in SAC?" Dutch replies. "We can't schedule the flights according to the birth schedule." When Dutch decides to sign on for the duration, she blows her top, bursting into General Hawkes's office to accuse him of "manipulating" Dutch with praise and promotions. "Wasn't one war enough for you?" she cries. And Sally isn't the only one who favors family over flying. One sergeant is leaving SAC because "A fella likes to get home once in a while and see his wife and kids." And it isn't just family life that beckons. In one scene, the crew enviously refer to a former radar man who quit to go into business for himself. He gave up the security of the organization to take his chances as an old-fashioned entrepreneur, putting private life (and private enterprise) ahead of the public interest.

By the time *Strategic Air Command* is a third over, the lines of battle have been drawn: big groups over small, public interest over private life, martial against civil, General Hawkes against Sally. How does the film reconcile these contending values? No problem. We find that, contrary to appearances, they are really two sides of the same coin. The Air Force is repeatedly described as a team, as in this instance, when General Hawkes, speaking to Dutch, says, "The B-47 is on third base. It'll be up to you to bring it home." And, if SAC is a team just like the Cards, only bigger and better, it is also a family, like Dutch's, only bigger and happier. The Air Force and the family are repeatedly equated, both metaphorically and structurally. When Dutch asks an old flying buddy if he has any kids, the man replies, "Sure, one on the ramp, one in the hangar." Dutch brings his baby down for a crash landing at the same moment Sally gives birth to hers. While she's nursing, General Hawkes shows Dutch another baby in the hangar, a spanking new B-47, the first of the next generation of strategic bombers. "With the new *family* of nuclear weapons," Hawkes whispers reverentially, "a B-47 with a crew of three carries the destructive power of the entire B-29 forces used in World War II." As Dutch caresses the sleek metallic skin with his eyes, he becomes excited, evincing considerably more enthusiasm for it than he did just moments before when he got his first look at his flesh-and-blood baby (a girl). "She's the most beautiful thing I've ever seen in my life," he says, referring to the B-47, a catch in the Jimmy Stewart voice. Cut to Dutch's real baby, one of, we recall, fifteen hundred born to SAC every month. In other words, if right-wingers like McCloud in *Detective Story* applied martial metaphors to civilian life, corporate liberals would apply metaphors drawn from civilian life—team and family—to war. If teamwork was warfare for rightists, warfare was teamwork for corporate liberals. And in this way, they resolved another major contradiction.

Babies and bombers. With the cross-cutting emphasizing the equivalence between the two, the plot steps in and moves Dutch from Texas to MacDill AFB in Florida, so that Dutch and Sally can reclaim their old home. But Sally still isn't satisfied. She wants him to return to the Cards. Dutch refuses. "I'm staying in the Air Force permanently," he announces. "And you made the decision all by yourself?" she snaps. "If there was a war on, you wouldn't feel that way," Dutch replies. "But that's just it, there isn't. You're getting to sound more like General Hawkes every day. You don't have a responsibility to me? to the baby?" "There is a kind of war on—we've got to stay ready to fight without fighting—that's harder." Sally just can't understand the logic of the cold war, and while she's sobbing, the phone rings. Dutch has to leave on the big mission. Where to? Sally can't know. There's a security blackout. "Let's do it first and talk about it later," says one of the officers. Sally's like the people who mustn't know what's going on behind closed doors, else she might panic in the kitchen.

While Sally is left with the baby, Dutch is getting it on in the air, copulating with a tanker in midflight by way of a long, slender tube. As we contemplate the limpid blue Vista-Vision sky, criss-crossed by feathery white vapor trails, we finally realize what *Strategic Air Command* is all about. This was, after all, the film whose visual and verbal metaphors linking war and sex inspired Kubrick's *Dr. Strangelove* (1964). But Dutch is not yet out of the clouds. He may have run Sally into the ground, but in the air he has a hard time keeping it up. As he brings his bomber in to land, the control tower tells him, "Stand by for immediate jet penetration." Dutch, however, has a bum shoulder, and smack in the middle of jet penetration his arm goes limp. God may have been the co-pilot in some films, but here it's Freud. It's the revenge of the therapeutic; Dutch should have let the doctor take a look at his shoulder when Sally told him to, earlier in the film, and now it's too late. They land safely (the crew takes over—it's truly a team effort), but Dutch's flying days are over. General Hawkes isn't pleased that Dutch kept his bad shoulder to himself; he jeopardized the lives of the team, the success of the mission, the health of the organization. He has let his personal desire to continue flying override the prerogatives of the group, and beyond that, the national interest.

The equation of war with sexual and familial metaphors was by no means unique to *Strategic Air Command*, and sometimes the latter cannibalized the former. In *Bombers B-52*, Sergeant Malden's adolescent daughter, Natalie Wood, is "restless," which, in the vocabulary of the fifties, meant she had the hots for Colonel Zimbalist. Malden doesn't like him, and puts an Oedipal chill on their affair. Women and planes are linked by picture and sound; the military drama is reduced to symbolizing the family drama. In one scene, an airborne tanker extends its long phallic tube to refuel a B-52, but the plane's doors are jammed, and "she's unable to receive fuel," that is, she's frigid, and risks a crash landing. Later in the film, they try again. "Request jet penetration," says the bomber to its escort. This time, the coupling works so well that the B-52's control panel catches on fire; she's too hot for daddy Malden to handle, and he has to bail out. It's all a message for him (and us) about "restless" Wood. How much sex is enough? Somewhere between too little and too much—and when Malden, Wood, and Zimbalist learn this lesson, true love can take its course.

Back at *Strategic Air Command*, we find that Dutch and Sally both win. Sally apologizes for giving him a hard time: "I'm proud of you and ashamed of me." But she gets her way: Dutch is grounded. He wins in principle; she wins in fact. Public and private, army and family (and team), civil and martial (and marital) are reconciled. Consensus was big enough for all. Once again, corporate-liberal films had the best of all worlds. Either/or was not for them.

The Men in the Gray Flannel Uniforms
Twelve O'Clock High, Flying Leathernecks, and the Tyranny of the Organization

From the vantage point of the fifties, it was clear that World War II was the first job opening for the organization man, even before we knew there was such a creature. Solemn, bland, buttoned-down Gregory Peck submitted the most impressive résumé, and in Henry King's *Twelve O'Clock High* (1949), Peck had a dry run for his role as the man in the gray flannel suit he would play several years later. Here Peck's suit is a uniform, and the corporation is the United States Air Force.

When the film opens, it is 1949, and former Major Stovall (Dean Jagger) is standing on the weed-covered runway of an abandoned airfield somewhere in England, dreaming of the way they were. No sooner does he lift his eyes to the sky than it becomes black with B-17s, the air is filled with the deafening roar of bombers, and we're transported backward in time, to the thick of battle. Peck plays Frank Savage, a brigadier general sent in to take command of the 918th Bomber Wing, a "hard luck outfit." Their job is a difficult one, the controversial "daylight precision bombing" of German targets. But the 918th is a mess. Its casualty rate is high, its morale is low. Where is the problem? Col. Keith Davenport (Gary Merrill), the wing commander, thinks it is upstairs. He blames the Air Force, the inhuman bureaucracy, for pushing the men beyond endurance. "It's there, where a bunch of boys are nothing but a set of numbers. You're gonna drive'em till they crack," he accuses Savage. But in this film, organizations aren't rigid, unfeeling bureaucracies, and Davenport is wrong. The problem isn't with the organization, it is with the individual, with Davenport himself. He's too much of an individualist, too unwilling to share the burden of leadership, and moreover, as Savage tells his superior, General

Pritchard (Millard Mitchell), Davenport's problem is that he's "overidentified with his men." Pritchard wants to see for himself. And sure enough, when one of Davenport's "boys" makes a costly mistake, Davenport defends him: "That boy's got a persecution complex," he says. "He wants to fly every mission to live down the fact that his parents were mixed up with the German-American Bund." But General Pritchard has heard enough. He relieves Davenport of his command and sends in General Savage to take over.

Normally, talk about "persecution complexes" would be encouraged in a film like this. Davenport's diagnosis—his navigator is neurotic, not negligent—and the therapeutic framework it implies would be welcome, would rate a promotion, not a transfer. But what worked in peacetime didn't always work in wartime; what was good for Americans wasn't necessarily good for Russians (or, in this case, Germans). Compromise, flexibility, negotiation were fine at home, but disastrous abroad, where compromise was foolhardy, flexibility fatal. *Twelve O'Clock High* is a corporate-liberal film because it favored the organization at the expense of the individual; but in times of war, tougher, more traditional measures were necessary, and corporate-liberal war films often found themselves saddled with more or less conservative heroes like Savage who preferred force to therapy. (Easygoing Dutch Holland was something of an exception.) Marine Sgt. John Wayne in Alan Dwan's *Sands of Iwo Jima* (1949) was typical. He enforces corporate-liberal values with conservative means: "Any man who doesn't want to cooperate will wish he'd never been born." Therapy was a casualty of war, but even in *Twelve O'Clock High*, as we shall see, the therapeutic got in its licks.

Changes in command were a good way to dramatize the clash of corporate liberals and conservatives, and were frequently used for this purpose. Just about the time that General Savage was taking over from Colonel Davenport, Major Kirby (John Wayne) was taking over from Captain Griffin (Robert Ryan) on the other side of the Pacific in Nicholas Ray's *Flying Leathernecks* (1951). There the organization is the Marine Corps, but Kirby's job is the same as Savage's; he has to whip a raggedy-ass bunch of pilots into shape. Kirby is a disciplinarian, unpopular with his men, but he doesn't care. "I'm not in a popularity contest," he snaps, flying in the face of the popularity-plus ethic of the organization man. "We've got a job to do." Although he's tough, he's not a "lifer" like Sam Fuller's sergeants, Zack and Rock, in *Steel Helmet* (1951) and *Fixed Bayonets* (1951). The army is not his whole world, and he has a family back home with whom he spends his time off. Nevertheless, he's a lot tougher than "Griff," whom the flyguys love, but who the brass feels isn't yet ready for command, because, like Davenport, he's too soft, too reluctant to discipline his men.

Under Griff's brief tenure, individualism has begun to raise its ugly head. Major Kirby puts his foot down, threatening to court-martial anyone who doesn't toe the line, while Griff takes the fliers' side, accusing Kirby of being a bully. Griff hangs out with the men, drinking and listening to their problems, while Kirby is aloof, preferring his own company or that of his superior officers. We know who's right, because every time one of the fliers peels out of formation on his own, he's shot down, runs out of gas, or otherwise comes to grief. Only the squadron affords protection to the individual.

Like *Twelve O'Clock High*, this film locates authority in the group, and the worst offender against group solidarity is Griff's brother-in-law, "Cowboy," an individualist contemptuous of group discipline. The men call him "Cowboy" because he comes from Texas, wears cowboy boots instead of the regular issue, and because he's a hotshot, a show-off. For corporate liberals, "cowboy," with its connotations of unbridled individualism, was a dirty word.

For a disciplinarian like Kirby, standardizing dress is a top priority. Since the film takes the side of the army against the GIs, the officer's job is to enforce the rules. Kirby has to go by the book, and the first thing he does when he takes over is order Cowboy to leave his Tony Lamas in his locker. But Cowboy doesn't listen; instead, he makes jokes during briefings and clowns around on missions. The big mission that concludes the film is his last. Before the squadron reaches its target, his engine conks out. It's not his fault—this time. But he's been asking for it. Griff tells him to return to base. Cowboy starts back, but when he realizes he's got two Jap Zeros on his tail, he radios for help. Griff, learning fast, says no dice. As Savage told his men, "A damaged bomber is expendable." One of Griff's fliers volunteers to help, but Griff stands firm. He won't allow anyone to break formation. Kirby, monitoring this exchange over the radio, smiles warmly when he hears Griff enforcing group discipline over both individualism and personal ties. Cowboy is shot down and killed, but Griff has finally earned his wings.

Flying Leathernecks rewards conformists who toe the organizational line. Individualists who go off on their own get hung up in trees.

Like Kirby, General Savage stamps out all vestiges of individualism. Organization man Peck was not really cut out to be a disciplinarian (he can't help offering his driver a smoke), but those are the boss's orders, and he does his best. When he arrives at the base, he insists on being saluted; like Kirby, he becomes a stickler for dress, and busts a sergeant for wearing a T-shirt. He threatens to court-martial one officer for being a "traitor to the group," and reprimands a pilot for leaving formation to help a pal whose plane was under attack. "For the sake of your roommate you violated group integrity?" Savage bellows. "The group, the group—that has to be your first loyalty!"

The pilots know where they stand. "I'll take Colonel Davenport any day," says one, and they all apply to transfer out of the unit. "You got what amounts to a mutiny on your hands," Davenport points out to Savage. Mutinies were a serious business in films like this, because they challenged the legitimacy of the organization. Savage's job is to make sure it doesn't happen, and indeed, this one never comes off. Contrary to expectations, Savage, by taking a hard line, succeeds in instilling "pride in the group," and his men withdraw their transfer requests.

The context was the army, but the moral was clear. The organization required cogs, not cowboys. As a Socony-Vacuum Oil pamphlet put it, with a curtsy toward the Cult of Complexity, "Business is so complex . . . there is little room for virtuoso performances."[13] Or, as Lionel Trilling phrased it, "The nature of our society requires the young man to find his distinction through cooperation, subordination."[14] The only people who knew how it really worked were those on top.

Savage usually knows best because he's a general; as we saw in *Strategic Air Command*, the army wedded the expert and the organization man. General Pritchard knows even better, because he's the highest-ranking officer, a wise father figure, the Eisenhower of this film. As we descend the chain of command, we go from good to bad to worse. Colonel Davenport is relieved of his duty, Colonel Gately is arrested, and the garden-variety captains, lieutenants, and sergeants are guilty of infractions too numerous to name.

Like the Air Force in *Twelve O'Clock High*, the Marine Corps in *Flying Leathernecks* is also a top-down affair. The officers at the top are wise and understanding, and promotion from one rank to the next is an unambiguous reward for services rendered. Kirby begins the film as a major, and before the end he is promoted to colonel. Nevertheless, despite their similarities, *Twelve O'Clock High* and *Flying Leathernecks* are not identical; one index of their slightly different ideological coloring is the different way they portray the army. Another is their contrasting attitudes toward the therapeutic.

Twelve O'Clock High does not regard its Air Force as a rigid bureaucracy, but, on the contrary, as a flexible organization receptive to innovative ideas, in this case, the "daylight precision bombing" of German targets. In fact, the initiative for this procedure comes from the organization itself, from General Pritchard, not from the ranks. In *Flying Leathernecks*, the Marine Corps does not come off quite so well. It is a shade more rigid and bureaucratic. The novel tactic here is "close ground support" of the "mud Marines" on land. Planes come in at treetop level and spray the enemy with bullets, napalm, and whatnot. This is Kirby's idea, not the generals' (innovation springs neither from the top nor from the bottom, but from the middle); although some of the brass over his head think that close ground support is a dandy idea, others have their reservations, and Kirby has to demonstrate his theory to the skeptical bureaucrats. "After we prove our point," he says wryly, "the information will probably go through channels, and we'll use it in the next war."

The more conservative tinge of *Flying Leathernecks* is evident on the health front, too. In *Twelve O'Clock High*, General Savage is running into flak. He's done his job, whipping the fliers into shape, so that they can bomb the daylights out of the Jerries, but just when he's flying high, he's shot down. He comes to grief because in the process of enforcing group discipline, he's forgotten that he, too, is no more than a member of the group.

Although General Pritchard recalls a mission, gung-ho Savage disregards orders and continues on to target. "The 918th got there when no others did," he says proudly, but Pritchard is not amused. Savage has gone too far, setting the small group, the 918th Bomber Wing, against the organization as a whole. Like Cowboy, he's closed his eyes to the Big Picture, let down the team. He's not playing by the rules, and Pritchard tells him so: "You're swinging after the bell." Savage has become too individualistic. Making the same error that Davenport did, he's taken the whole burden of leadership on his own shoulders.

Savage's insubordination is the beginning of the end. Perhaps the strain of acting like a conservative has been too great, and Peck begins to break. His performances were notoriously wooden (although this was one of his best), and when he falls into a state of catatonia, it is hard to tell. If he didn't run his hands over his forehead several times, we'd never know the springs inside were coming loose. As Savage sits immobile, staring straight ahead, the doctor finally comes into his own. "He's in a state of total shock," he explains to the puzzled officers. But we know that like Dutch Holland, he's suffering from the revenge of the therapeutic. Even though the doctor, who would normally dominate the coalition of the center in this kind of film, plays a subordinate role, he is still the leader of the therapeutic opposition to Savage's big-stick tactics once Davenport is gone. "Ease up," Doc Kaiser (Paul Stewart) had advised. "Give 'em a chance to get used to you." "I can't enter a popularity contest with Keith Davenport," Savage replied, echoing Kirby's repudiation of popularity. But Savage

The revenge of the therapeutic: against doctor's orders, General Savage (Gregory Peck) has thrown himself over the edge, and falls into a catatonic stupor.

has pushed himself beyond his limits, and now he pays the consequences. Davenport has the last word. "They call it maximum effort," he says sorrowfully, staring at Savage. Davenport's been right all along; you can't push a man too far. But Savage is right too; he was "gonna make 'em grow up," and now they have. They're both right, the corporate liberals and the conservatives, both elements of the coalition of the center. As peace finally comes to Savage, we know his day is done. He lies down for a long-overdue rest; Davenport removes his shoes and covers him with a blanket. His words are an elegy; his motions a sort of burial. Savage is a martyr to the organization; he sacrifices himself for the good of the group. Corporate liberals acknowledged their debt to conservatives, but they knew the future was theirs. And the tale was theirs too. At the end, we dissolve back to the present, the deserted airfield, and former Major Stovall, now a lawyer again, listening to his memories.

Flying Leathernecks, on the other hand, explicitly repudiates the therapeutic. Kirby is not laid low by the strains and stress of leadership, as Savage is; he is not judged by therapeutic criteria. There is a doctor in *Flying Leathernecks* too, and at one point, he warns Kirby that Griff is at the breaking point. "I might be getting eighty bucks an hour for this and grow a little beard," quips the doc, but Kirby doesn't think its funny and doesn't want to hear about Griff's state of mind. With a brusque wave of the hand, he dismisses the doctor and his therapeutic baggage: "Knock it off, Dr. Freud." In *Flying Leathernecks*, in other words, it is not the therapeutic but the military that has the last word.

Despite the fact that *Flying Leathernecks* mildly chides the Marine Corps for bureaucratic rigidity and repudiates the therapeutic, the conflict between the individual and the group is unambiguously resolved in favor of the group. When Kirby is transferred at the end, Griff is able to take command because he has earned it. He has learned to speak the language of games and teamwork: "I'll try to call the plays right. I had a good coach."

In *The Organization Man*, William Whyte described a typical conservative predicament in which the collision between the Protestant Ethic and the new Social Ethic is sharp and emphatic. "If you wanted to put in fiction form the split between the Protestant Ethic and the Social Ethic of organization life," wrote Whyte, you might come up with a plot like this one: "A middle-management executive . . . finds that the small branch plant he's helping to run is very likely to blow up. . . . If he presses a certain button the explosion will be averted. Unfortunately, however, just as he's about to press a button, his boss heaves into view. The boss is a scoundrel and a fool, and at this moment he's so scared he is almost incoherent. Don't press the button, he says. . . . Thus, his dilemma: if he presses the button he will not be acting like a good organization man and the plant will be saved. If he doesn't press the button he will be a good organization man and they will all be blown to smithereens."[15]

As we move right, we encounter an increasing number of plots similar to the one Whyte describes. The heroes of conservative films are no longer agents of the organization but, to one extent or another, rebels against it.

A Different Bugler

From Here to Eternity and the Conservative Predicament

In Fred Zinnemann's *From Here to Eternity*, (1953) the organization is, of course, the army, and the individual is Robert E. Lee Prewitt, played by Montgomery Clift. The place is Schofield Barracks, in Hawaii, and the time is 1941, right before Pearl Harbor. Prewitt is a maverick, and he gets into trouble every time he opens his mouth. He's an all-around boy, an ace bugler and middleweight champ, but his skills are less a help than a liability.

As the film opens, Prewitt has just transferred into a company commanded by Capt. Dana Holmes. When Holmes asks him why, Prewitt replies, "A personal matter." "Personal" is a danger signal in organization life, and we know Prewitt is headed for trouble. In Holmes's company, he's out of the frying pan into the fire. "I have a fine, smooth-running outfit," says Holmes, the organization man. He's the boxing coach, and he's dead set on winning the regimental championship. He wants his team to win, and he wants Prewitt on his team. The only trouble is, Prewitt won't play. He's given up fighting. It seems he blinded a man named Dixie Wells, and since then he hasn't touched the gloves. "Looks to me like you're trying to acquire the reputation of a lone wolf, Prewitt," says Holmes. "You should know that in the army, it's not the individual who counts." But Prewitt doesn't; he knows something else instead. "I know where I stand. A man don't go his own way, he's nuthin'." "Maybe back in the days of the pioneers a man could go his own way," chimes in Sgt. Milt Warden (Burt Lancaster), but "today, you gotta play ball. I know your type. You're a hardhead."

Holmes won't take "no" for an answer. He's going to force Prewitt to box by giving him the works. "I can take anything you can dish out,"

Prewitt taunts him. "You wanna put the screws on, go ahead." Holmes does. He has him washing latrines and peeling potatoes. He puts him on forced marches with full pack. He trips him when he's running and kicks him when he's down, but Prewitt won't break or complain. In one scene, he's on his hands and knees scrubbing the floors in the gym. Holmes makes a heavyweight knock over a slop bucket where Prewitt is working. The man tells Prewitt to clean it up. "Clean it up yourself. I've never liked being spit on," Prewitt returns. Holmes orders him to apologize. Prewitt won't. "Prepare the court-martial papers," Holmes tells Warden angrily.

Like Major Kirby in *Flying Leathernecks*, Holmes threatens to discipline a subordinate. This time, however, court-martial is not a means of enforcing obedience to the reasonable expectations of the organization, but rather a way of securing conformity to the irrational demands of a

Champ Robert E. Lee Prewitt (Montgomery Clift) won't play ball—or in this case, box—so the army teaches him teamwork the hard way.

bureaucracy, and therefore Prewitt has to stand his ground. Both Major Kirby and Captain Holmes are organization men faced with insubordination; both Cowboy and Prewitt are individualists. But *From Here to Eternity* is considerably more sympathetic to individualism than *Flying Leathernecks*, so that whereas Kirby is a hero, Holmes is not; whereas Cowboy is a show-off, Prewitt is a man of principle. The individualists in *Flying Leathernecks* frivolously flout authority, selfishly endangering the other members of the team. But in *From Here to Eternity*, the members of the team are time-servers and yes-men, and therefore the team's authority is illegitimate.

Midway through the film, however, we begin to realize that individualism has its limits, whereas the army, on the other hand, suddenly reveals virtues we didn't know it had. Prewitt has a friend named Maggio (Frank Sinatra), who is even a worse case than he is. Prewitt is just stubborn and independent; Maggio is flaky and self-destructive, in the guardhouse one moment and out again the next. He humiliates Fatso (Ernest Borgnine), the stockade honcho and a notorious sadist, and Fatso vows revenge. "Guys like you end up in the stockade sooner or later," he warns Maggio, and he's right. Maggio's jailed for some infraction of the rules, and Fatso carefully beats him to death with a club. It's a repeat of Prewitt's torment at the hands of Holmes's boxers, only worse. Like Prewitt, Maggio won't complain; he spits in Fatso's face. But Maggio's defiance is a dead end. All it gets him is six feet under.

Now it's Prewitt's turn to vow revenge. By this time, Prewitt has gotten over his reluctance to fight; it has been nothing more than a momentary lapse, an eccentricity of peacetime. He corners Fatso in an alley. "The army's gonna get you sooner or later," Prewitt tells him, with unaccustomed optimism, "but before they do, I'm gonna get a piece of you myself." Fatso pulls a switchblade, but it ends up in him, not Prewitt. Grabbing his gut, he keels over, dead. Prewitt goes AWOL and holes up with his girl friend, Loreen (Donna Reed), while he recuperates from his tussle with Fatso.

The date is December 7, 1941, and while the Americans are fighting among themselves, the Japanese are preparing a surprise. (See what happens in the absence of consensus?) Prewitt turns on the radio and hears that the Japs have attacked Pearl Harbor. "They're picking on the best army in the world," he says angrily. Unshaven and still elaborately bandaged, he pulls on his pants. "What do you want to go back to the army for?" asks Loreen, appalled. "What has the army done for you besides treat you like dirt and give you one awful going over?" "What am I going back to the army for?" repeats Prewitt, incredulously, wondering how she could be so dumb. "I'm a soldier. A regular soldier of the regular army. A thirty-year man!" And he rushes out, leaving her weeping bitterly.

Prewitt may think he's a soldier, but the army doesn't know it. Back at Schofield Barracks, patrols are out looking for "saboteurs," while Prewitt is creeping around in the trees, trying to find his way back to base. "Halt!" shouts a GI. But as usual, Prewitt has his own ideas. Instead of stopping he runs for it. Shots ring out, and Prewitt is killed. No sooner does he breathe his last than Sergeant Warden emerges from the darkness in time to deliver the moral to the tale. "He must have been trying to reach our company position," says Warden. "Then why didn't he halt?" an officer interjects. "He was always a hardhead, sir," replies Warden. "But he was a good soldier. He loved the army more than any soldier I ever knew."

Prewitt had to die, of course, because his individualism had gotten out of control. It was okay to get drunk, but not to kill a sergeant and go AWOL. When he took the law into his own hands, he became little better than a vigilante. Conservative films sanctioned so much and no more. From the center's point of view, Prewitt had become a liability. He was a "saboteur" after all, threatening the army's monopoly on violence.

Still, although the army looks better as Prewitt looks worse, it's not the same army as the one we find in *Flying Leathernecks* and *Twelve O'Clock High*. In those films the hierarchical chain of command worked the way it was supposed to. The men at the top got there because they were the best; the men at the bottom were troublemakers. Hierarchy rewarded excellence and punished mediocrity. In *From Here to Eternity*, the reverse appears to be true. Integrity is found at the bottom, not the top. The higher you go, the worse it is. At the bottom, Prewitt and his pal Maggio are ornery and stubborn, but here that's a virtue. Warden, whom one GI calls "the best soldier I've ever seen," is only a sergeant. Warden carries the ball for his incompetent superior, Holmes, and what's more, he has no desire to become an officer himself. When Holmes's wife, Karen (Deborah Kerr), whom Warden has been snuggling on the beach, urges him to apply for a commission, he refuses: "I hate officers. I've always hated officers. I'm happy where I am." (Like Warden, Audie Murphy turned down his commission in another conservative film, *To Hell and Back*

(1955), because he didn't want to be separated from his buddies.) But the virtue of promotion itself is only apparently called into question. Holmes, too, has been bucking for a promotion, and doesn't get it because he's not worthy of it. Karen tells him, "If you spent less time chasing after generals and more time with your company, maybe you'd get that promotion." She's criticizing him for the same thing Griff attacked Kirby for in *Flying Leathernecks*: fraternizing with the brass, not the men. There, it's necessary for discipline; here, it's regarded as currying favor. There, Griff was wrong; here, Karen is right. *From Here to Eternity* does not ultimately question the goal of promotion itself. Rather, it questions the means.

On all these issues—promotion, individualism, cooperation—*From Here to Eternity* is ambivalent and waffles from left to right. "From now on, nobody's gonna earn his stripes by boxing," says the captain who replaces Holmes, explicitly repudiating the pluralist metaphor of game and team, and apparently vindicating Prewitt's view of himself as his own man instead of a team player. But when Prewitt is killed for being too much of an individualist, we understand that Warden was also right when he warned him, "You gotta play ball." It seems that there is some life left to the team-and-game metaphors after all. Similarly, the film can't make up its mind whether those at the top are good or not. Holmes is punished for cruelty to Prewitt by those above him, which seems to indicate that they are not all bad.* And both Prewitt and Maggio are foolhardy and die, which suggests that those at the bottom aren't all good.

From Here to Eternity tries to carve out a middle ground between

---

*Although all films are subject to conflicting ideological pressures, war films are particularly vulnerable, because they often depend on the armed forces for expensive props: planes, ships, tanks, and so on. The army's military aid to Hollywood had strings attached, and the Department of Defense's Motion Picture Production Branch existed to pull them. Donald Baruch, the department's chief, told Julian Smith, for example, that in the case of Clift's persecution in *From Here to Eternity* and again (for being Jewish) in *The Young Lions* (1958), "it was the Motion Pictures Production Branch's duty to see that audiences were reassured that this harassment would not go unnoticed and unpunished by higher authority (as it had in the novel by James Jones, for instance)." Department of Defense guidelines for Hollywood films mandated a "true interpretation of military life," and "compliance with accepted standards of dignity and propriety in the industry."[16] Support was forthcoming only for scripts that satisfied the army's interpretation of these requirements. Those that didn't, like Aldrich's *Attack!* (1956), were denied customary use of equipment and banned from U.S. bases around the world. The army rejected Sam Fuller's request for combat footage for *Steel Helmet* because the script called for the killing of an unarmed North Korean POW by a GI.

corporate-liberal films on its left and radical films on its right. After purging Prewitt and Holmes, one wormy apple and one rotten one, the center once again closes ranks, as it does in 12 *Angry Men*, *Panic in the Streets*, and *My Darling Clementine*. It is Warden, not Prewitt, who emerges as the hero of the film. He's an organization man like Holmes, and an individualist like Prewitt; he combines the best of both worlds. Warden is ready to cut through army red tape when he has to, but he's not about to go AWOL. In one scene, during the Japanese attack, Warden tries to get weapons for his men, but they are locked up. Although bombs are exploding all around them, the dumb cluck guarding the ammo won't let Warden at it "without authorization from an officer." Warden's common sense tells him the base is under attack, but the guard needs an expert to tell him what to do, and Warden has to brush him aside and break the door down, disobeying orders and risking court-martial. In *Twelve O'Clock High*, disobedience like Warden's was a symptom of an incipient nervous breakdown. Here, it's *de rigueur*. The organization is a bureaucracy, and therefore upon occasion it has to be defied, but it still commands our basic allegiance. By breaking rules, Warden, like York in *Fort Apache*, is not turning his back on the organization, but merely saving the army from itself. It's all right to take the law into your own hands, if you have the interest of the group at heart.

From Here to Eternity tries to avoid having to resolve the contradiction in Whyte's either/or scenario in a clear-cut way. Like corporate-liberal films, conservative films managed to have it both ways. Conservative heroes typically found themselves in a paradoxical role, at once martinets to those below them and mavericks to those above. They threatened individualists with court-martial and then turned around and risked it themselves by acting like individualists.

Maj. Van Heflin in Raoul Walsh's *Battle Cry* (1955) is a typical conservative martinet/maverick who amuses himself when he has nothing better to do by leading his men on sixty-mile forced marches, while the next moment he's defying his superior, paper-pushing General Massey, in his efforts to get his battalion assigned to a prominent position in the assault on Saipan. Massey is a by-the-book bureaucrat, not a fighting general. He is Eisenhower, the organization man viewed from the right. "You're getting the reputation as a troublemaker. You're ready to question the brains and labor that went into this plan?" he warns Heflin, pointing to a book a foot thick. "You can take that book and throw it into the ocean," retorts Heflin, angrily. "Insubordination!" thunders Massey. "You might as well court-martial me," shouts Heflin, and so it goes. In *Battle Cry*, it's worth risking court-martial to buck the organization, but in conservative films, it's not much of a risk, and Heflin never does get court-martialed. Warden defies the boss and saves the factory, but he's not fired and doesn't quit, because when it came right down to it—two outs in the last of the ninth—conservatives preferred to play ball till the end, rather than cry foul and withdraw.

Once we move out of the center, we finally find films that do pose clear-cut answers to the dilemma Whyte posed. In right-wing (as well as left-wing) films, Whyte's hero either pushes the button to save the plant, and tells the boss to go to hell, or allows the plant to blow up and the boss along with it.

At War with the Army

The Court Martial of Billy Mitchell and the
Critique of Bureaucracy

As we have seen, the ostensible enemy in war films of the fifties—the Germans, Japanese, and North Koreans—played a relatively unimportant role. In corporate-liberal films like *Flying Leathernecks* and *Twelve O'Clock High*, the real enemy is extremism, in the guise of the individualist who jeopardizes the survival of the group. Conservative films fought a two-front war, against individualists on the one hand and bureaucrats on the other, against extremism and corporate liberalism. But, as we have seen, conservative films were still well within the center; *From Here to Eternity* attacked Holmes the man, not the army as an institution. In Otto Preminger's *The Court Martial of Billy Mitchell* (1955), the enemy is not the man but the army, the organization, the system, the center itself. The reevaluation of the relationship between the individual and the group begun by conservative films like *From Here to Eternity* is completed in radical-right films. The group is wholly wrong; the individual is wholly right.

The Court Martial of Billy Mitchell is set in 1921, just after the end of World War I. Brig. Gen. Billy Mitchell (Gary Cooper) is an advocate of air power at a time when the other services thought the airplane was merely a toy. Mitchell tries to show a bunch of skeptical admirals and generals that his fliers can sink the "unsinkable" German battleship *Ostfriesland*, but at first they fail, because Gen. Jimmy Guthrie (Charles Bickford) won't let them fly low enough with large enough bombs. When Billy asks to use 2,000-pounders at 1,000 feet, Jimmy says no. The fact is, Jimmy and the other brass don't want Billy to succeed. "I think it would be most unfortunate if you sank that ship," Jimmy tells Billy. He thinks that if the government is convinced that the United States can be defended by air power alone, the army will be as unprepared for the next war (World War II) as it was for World War I. "No war will be won until the foot soldier puts his bayonet to the neck of the enemy," says Jimmy. Billy thinks differently. "One day, strategic bombing will leave half the world in ruins," he says prophetically. "I want this country to be in the other half." Moreover, Billy does something about his beliefs, deliberately disobeying orders by instructing his fliers to come in low with 2,000-pounders. The *Ostfriesland* sinks like a stone, but Billy's career goes down with it. He is demoted to colonel by his angry superiors and reassigned to Texas. "General Mitchell's course has been lawless, lacking in teamwork," sputters General Jimmy, an organization man. "There can be no progress if your officers are undisciplined."

Guthrie pits law, teamwork, and discipline against what he considers unbridled individualism. But this film upends the values of centrist films, both conservative and corporate liberal; what they regard as unbridled individualism it regards as common sense, just plain principle. Here the army and navy are the selfish ones, only concerned with protecting their own turfs, with exacting obedience from their officers regardless of the cost, while individualism is equated with generosity of spirit. Billy's not in it for himself. He does what he does because he sees the Big Picture. "There's more at stake than me," he tells Guthrie. "It's a new weapon. The biggest in the world." In *Twelve O'Clock High* and *Flying Leathernecks*, the army was a flexible organization that readily adopted innovative tactics, like daylight precision bombing and close ground support. Both these films stressed teamwork and punished those who wouldn't play. *From Here to Eternity* was more ambivalent about teamwork; it ridiculed Holmes's mania for boxing, but it ultimately accepted the "team" as a metaphor for society. But in *The Court Martial of Billy Mitchell*, the army is a rigid bureaucracy totally resistant to innovation, and loyalty to the team is selfish and short-sighted. Billy is the victim of bureaucratic infighting and the old ideas of his fossilized superiors. The film backs his defiance of the group, his betrayal of the team, his lawless disregard for order. It is the individual, not the group, that is the vessel of truth.

In *Battle Cry*, it was only General Massey at the top who insisted on going by the book, but in *The Court Martial of Billy Mitchell*, the entire army is infested with bookworms. "We have to go by the book," insists

Billy's pal, Zachary Landsdowne. "Suppose some other country throws away the book," retorts Billy, but Landsdowne is unmovable. He's a sensible centrist. "You can't do the impossible," he says, reasonably. "I can try," replies Billy. But Landsdowne remains loyal to the team, though here loyalty is not a virtue, it's cowardice. "Why should I stick my neck out?" he says, showing Billy the door.

Billy, of course, is right and Landsdowne is wrong, and this film drives home the dangers of playing by the rules. At one point, Billy urges Landsdowne to disobey orders, refuse to fly a blimp that Billy thinks is dangerous. But Landsdowne is too good an officer, too much a team player to take his advice. The blimp crashes in the next scene, and Landsdowne is killed, but since the organization is bad, his death is not a martyr's death. Rather, it is a "needless, futile sacrifice," as one man calls it. In direct contrast to *Twelve O'Clock High* and *Flying Leathernecks*, where you die if you don't obey the organization, here you die if you do.

Even after Landsdowne dies, Billy is reluctant to confront the army, go outside channels. When his pal, Congressman Reid (Ralph Bellamy), urges him to quit the army and run for Congress, he's reluctant. "I don't want to turn the service into a political football. We're both professionals. You play by your book, and I'll play by mine," he tells Reid. But when he tries to go through channels, he gets the brush-off, and he learns that he has to throw away the book, get out of the game. And when Reid then advises Billy to compromise with the brass, he refuses. Billy knows that what works for corporate liberals will not work for him. He'd rather break than bend.

Billy becomes a fanatic, a nut, the kind of man who writes letters in longhand to the president, badgers secretaries, lurks in doorways to buttonhole officials, petitioning them to correct some imaginary wrong. He literally invites court-martial by accusing the brass of "criminal negligence and the almost treasonable administration of our national defense."

The Court Martial of Billy Mitchell, however, takes Billy's wild charges seriously. It is a film in which the loonies are sane and the sane are loonies. Billy, the man who would be crazy in a centrist film, is here played by Gary Cooper; far from being a candidate for the nuthouse, he's a prophet, a dreamer, the Edgar Cayce of the army. During his trail, he predicts the use of paratroopers, Lindbergh's flight across the Atlantic, and the Japanese attack on Pearl Harbor (remember, this is supposed to be in the twenties). When the prosecutor, the army's ace legal brain Maj. Allen Gullion (nastily played by Rod Steiger), tries to suggest that he's unbalanced ("You are an expert in palmistry, in table-tipping, the reading of tea leaves?" he asks sarcastically), Billy angrily replies with Cooper's homespun authority: "You mean, am I crazy? The answer is no." The therapeutic is introduced, as in corporate-liberal films, to discredit and undermine dissent. But here it is irrelevant, itself discredited as manipulation.

Although, of course, it is true that Billy is neither normal nor average. In contrast to the careerists and bureaucrats of the center, whose vision is clouded by petty vanities, he is a visionary who would do the impossible. In right-wing films, the supermen who were banished from centrist films come into their own.* When Billy finally sees that he won't get a fair trial, he is forced to pit his own personal vision against his loyalty to the army. "Are you ready to give unquestioned obedience to your superior officers?" Gullion demands. "If being a good soldier is your kind of soldier, unable to think for himself and say what he thinks, you can have the uniform," says Billy at last, realizing that his principles have forced him to hang up his number. In Billy's army, the MacArthurs as well as the Eisenhowers are bad news. (Both types of officers sit on his court-martial panel, although predictably, "General MacArthur" is more willing to give him a fair shake.)

With the single exception of "MacArthur," those at the top in *Billy Mitchell* are wrong. The film overturns the hierarchical, top-down view of society that characterized corporate-liberal films and ultimately conservative films as well, despite their reservations. Right-wing films mistrusted the brass. In Fuller's bottom-up *Fixed Bayonets*, a series of officers are knocked off so that Cpl. Richard Baseheart, the lowest man on the totem pole, can take command. When Billy first began rising through the ranks, he believed that the system was rewarding him for a job well done, and he was rewarding the system with fresh ideas. But this view turns out to be naïve. "I thought that when I became a general, I could change every-

---

*Witness the group of films that reconciled us to our erstwhile enemy: *The Desert Fox* (1951), with its loving portrait of Afrika Korps Field Marshal Erwin Rommel (James Mason); *The Sea Chase* (1955), with its noble Prussian commander (John Wayne); and *The Enemy Below* (1957), with its dedicated U-boat captain (Curt Jurgens). Supermen were safer if they were German.

Downward mobility for Gary Cooper: in this man's army, there's no room at the top for mavericks, and promotion is only another word for selling out.

thing," he says. "But there's always some bigger general. General Yesterday." The further up Billy goes, the worse it is. Promotion from the bottom to the top is therefore not even the ambiguous virtue it is in *From Here to Eternity*, but rather a joke, a reward for a job badly done. Whereas in corporate-liberal films such as *12 Angry Men* one good man makes the system work, Billy learns that one good man makes no difference at all; one good man is crushed. When Gullion accuses Billy of calling individual officers traitors, Billy answers, "I was thinking of the system."

The attack on rank changes the attitude toward the press and the people as well. If the press was an enemy in *Panic*, and an uneasy ally in *Fort Apache*, here it is praised for being genuinely oppositional. When Billy first blows the whistle on the army, he does it in the press. Because in the final analysis, his last and only court of appeal is the public, which is here the solution, not the problem. At the bottom of the ladder are the people who, uncompromised by selfish special interests, are equated with the good of the nation. They are not presented as an irrational mass prone to panic and hysteria; they can make informed, rational judgments. When prosecutor Gullion makes a centrist attack on Billy's call for air-raid precautions, arguing that Billy's claim that the United States is vulnerable to air attack is alarmist, "could result in panic," Billy makes the classic extremist response: "I'd rather see them scared than dead." Whereas centrist films encourage people to leave action to the experts or professionals, *The Court Martial of Billy Mitchell* tries to alarm them, mobilize them. The film presents a right-wing alliance of superman Billy at the top, with the aroused people at the bottom.

The court-martial itself, good in corporate-liberal films, ambiguous in conservative films, is here plainly bad. The army is simply wrong, and Billy is simply right. Court-martial becomes a procedure for muzzling the few creative souls who lurk in the interstices of the bureaucracy. And Billy is convicted, not vindicated. He's not miraculously cleared; he doesn't convince the panel of military judges at the last moment that he is right. In centrist films, the legal system invariably works; here, it fails.

This is not a conciliatory, have-your-cake-and-eat-it-too film. The right often ridiculed the center's attempts to accommodate contradictions. William Buckley wrote disparagingly about the Eisenhower era as a "middle of the road" period, an "age of modulation" that shrank from "principle: because principles have edges, principles cut; and blood is drawn, and people get hurt." He criticized Ike's inclination to "reconcile opposites" and called for a break with "modulation's trance" that acknowledged irreconcilable facts like "Original Sin," and so on.[17] In *Billy Mitchell*, conflict is not suppressed, nor is it attributable to poor communication. It is a product of fundamental differences.

Prisoners of War

Attack! and the Critique of Authority

Traditionally, right-wing war films like *The Court Martial of Billy Mitchell* were antiarmy, not antiwar; left-wing films were both. There was a venerable line of Hollywood antiwar films going back at least as far as Lewis Milestone's *All Quiet on the Western Front* (1930), but the witch-hunt and the Korean War at the beginning of the decade created an inhospitable climate for the sentiments these films expressed. The so-called Eisenhower Thaw at mid-decade (the cease-fire in Korea, the fall of McCarthy in 1954, the "Spirit of Geneva" generated by the Summit Conference the following year) made it easier to cast a jaundiced eye on the chauvinism of the center. The new crop of war films, however, like *Time Limit* (1957), *The Bridge on The River Kwai* (1957), *The Naked and the Dead* (1958), and *The Young Lions* (1958), contented themselves with mildly questioning militarism or fell back on a comfortable war-is-hell humanism. But some, like Robert Aldrich's *Attack!* (1956) and Stanley Kubrick's *Paths of Glory* (1957), did a bit more, conducted a kind of veiled class warfare. In these films, the army is not a stuffy bureaucracy but a symbol of oppression.

Attack! is a savage, blistering film, more like Fuller's Korean War films on the right than the sleek, domesticated war films of the center, such as *Strategic Air Command*, which were more about the nuclear family than nuclear or any other kind of war. The film opens with a bang, somewhere in France during World War II. Lt. Joe Costa (Jack Palance) is on the walkie-talkie to Sgt. Ingersoll (Strother Martin) telling him he's got to take a murderous-looking cement pillbox high up on a hill, assuring him that Capt. Erskine Cooney (Eddie Albert) will back him with reserves. Ingersoll leads his men into withering German machine-gun fire, while Costa frantically appeals to Cooney for help. When the film cuts to Cooney, we see the walkie-talkie lying next to him on the seat of his jeep, ignored, Costa's voice an all but inaudible squeak. Ingersoll and his men are slaughtered, and it's clear that Costa has been stabbed in the back by Cooney, his own superior. As in *The Court Martial of Billy Mitchell*, the center is as dangerous as the enemy; the center is the enemy.

Cooney is a coward who finks out on his men in the clutch. But he's protected by Col. Clyde Bartlett (Lee Marvin), a crony of Cooney's dad, who's a judge in Riverview, deep in the heart of Dixie. Bartlett is another organization man, here depicted as a high-rolling, smooth-talking operator. He likes to play poker, and when he does, he usually wins, because he knows the rules of the game. Bartlett is playing World War II for high stakes. He wants to use his combat record to further his political ambitions back home in Riverview, when the war's over. He is counting on the judge to help him, so he covers Cooney's ass.

While Bartlett and Cooney are sampling fine French wine in a commandeered chateau, we find Costa in a blacksmith shop, sweating like a pig amid flames and flying sparks. What he's doing there is anybody's guess, but it sets him up as a muscular working man against the upper-crust courthouse gang from down South.* Costa is hip to the old-boy network that binds Bartlett and Cooney together, and when his buddy, Lieutenant Woodruff (William Smithers), says he's going to ask Bartlett straight out to transfer Cooney before he jeopardizes any more lives, Costa just laughs. "He's a lieutenant colonel and you're just a lieutenant," Costa says. Woodruff is a liberal who can't quite give up on the system, while Costa is a radical who has a corrosive, uncompromising, and, as it turns out, realistic assessment of power and rank. And he's no Billy Mitchell, no visionary prophet nor superman, just a regular guy at the bottom of the class heap.

Woodruff disregards Costa's advice, and complains to Colonel Bartlett about Cooney. Bartlett tells him not to worry about it. "I got it from the top. It's one hundred to one this company will never see combat again," drawls Bartlett, sipping his French wine. If he got it from the top, we

---

*In centrist films, by way of contrast, class divisions are denied or bridged. Sgt. Karl Malden's daughter, Natalie Wood, marries Col. Efrem Zimbalist, Jr. in *Bombers B-52*; and Sgt. Warden, in *From Here to Eternity*, could have married the boss's wife had he wanted to.

know that it's a hundred to one that it's wrong, but Woodruff doesn't. "Bartlett was straightforward and understanding," he reports back to Costa. Costa only scoffs: "Just little ole country boys up to the knees in blood," and before he can finish his sentence, a GI comes running over to tell him, sure 'nuf, they're about to go into battle again. Costa swears he'll kill Cooney if he loses another man on his account. "I'll shove this grenade down your throat and pull the pin," he growls. "That's court-martial talk," responds Cooney. Court-martial, as in right-wing films, is bad news, but not because it is a mechanism for crushing individual initiative; here, it represents the exercise of unjust authority.

The trouble with Costa is that he loves his men. Costa is Griff in *Flying Leathernecks* and Davenport in *Twelve O'Clock High*, but here this figure is heroized; no longer a bleeding heart, he is tough and hard-boiled. Despite his better judgment (it's hard to kick the system habit), Costa allows Cooney to talk him into one more foolish mission where once again he will have to rely on Cooney's assistance. And when the moment of truth comes, once again Cooney panics. "Maybe there's more Krauts than we can handle," he whimpers. "Pull back and call for artillery. You want me to risk the whole company for one lousy platoon?" That seems right; wasn't that the lesson Griff learned from Kirby in *Flying Leathernecks?* Wasn't that the reason he let his brother-in-law go to his death, rather than risk the mission to save him? But *Attack!* is a different kind of film. Here the same principle, the priority of the organization over the individual, of the large group over the small, is regarded as no better than a rationale for cowardice. There, the individual betrayed the group; here, the group betrays the individual.

Costa survives the Germans, but before he has a chance to make good his threat against Cooney, his bazooka jams, and he's crushed by a German tank. More dead than alive, he collapses at Cooney's feet, his gun clattering harmlessly across the stone floor of the farmhouse in which the Americans have taken refuge from the advancing Germans. The men have been brought to the point of open mutiny by Cooney's cowardice; he holds them at bay with his rifle as he prepares to surrender to the Germans. That's the last straw. Woodruff picks up his gun and shoots him to death. Aghast at what he has done, he wants to give himself up, but his men tell him not to. "I got faith in justice, but the army ain't got no sentiment," says one. "It'll make you out a bloodthirsty maniac." Each man in turn pumps a bullet into Cooney's body, in support of Woodruff; the murder becomes a ritual act of rebellion, not the immoral, irrational action of one man. The mutiny threatened in *Twelve O'Clock High* is carried out here. "If ever a man needed killing, it was that no-good piece of trash lying there," is the verdict of another GI, and apparently of the film as well.

Woodruff, like Warden in *From Here to Eternity*, mediates between authority and rebellion. In the beginning, he went by the book and couldn't quite bring himself to get behind Costa's homicidal designs on Cooney (Cooney is "the commander of this company, for better or for worse," he said). Later, he turns against the center. It's Woodruff who finally pulls the trigger, Woodruff who carries out Costa's desires. He realizes that the real enemy is behind the lines and that force is the only power illegitimate authority understands. The hierarchical chain of command, dear to the hearts of the corporate liberals, is here equated with the class structure and thoroughly savaged. The higher you go, the worse it is; the lower down, the better. Captains are worse than lieutenants; colonels worse than captains. In one scene, Costa and company capture two German soldiers. One is an officer, one a private. One is blond, arrogant, and intransigent; the other is cooperative. Which is the officer? Which the enlisted man? "The mean one's the captain," observes a GI. "It's the same in any army." In corporate-liberal films, followers undo leaders; in radical films, it's the other way around.

Attack! portrays Cooney as a coward and Bartlett as an opportunist, but many left-wing films depicted their officer-villains as maniacal authoritarians. In Raoul Walsh's *The Naked and the Dead* (1958), Raymond Massey is a mad general, the left's answer to the right's paper-pusher. Walsh's egalitarian hero, Lt. Cliff Robertson, is bothered by the inequalities of rank the army encourages. "How do you think the enlisted men feel when they see us eating meat?" he asks Massey. "They don't hate us; they fear us," Massey replies. "The morality of the future is a power morality. Power can only flow from the top down." Massey flicks a cigarette butt on the floor and orders Robertson to pick it up. Robertson refuses. Massey threatens him with court-martial and five years in the stockade. Robertson picks it up, but in this film, he's making a mistake. We want him to disobey orders and risk court-martial.

The Naked and the Dead and *Attack!* share some common ground with *The Court Martial of Billy Mitchell*, but there are important differences.

Defiant Lieutenant Costa (Jack Palance) doesn't like the blond gentleman in the center, not because he's a Nazi, but because he's an officer.

For one thing, the left-wing films are much more rebellious. It is one thing to vilify the brass for being bureaucrats who stifle innovation. It is quite another to attack the army for constituting a patrician class of vested interests that oppresses the proletarians in the ranks. And still another to advocate not only insubordination but mutiny (*The Naked and the Dead*) and murder (*Attack!*). Films like *The Court Martial of Billy Mitchell* are more comfortable with insubordination than mutiny, the lone rebellion of one man than the uprising of the many. When they did indulge in right-wing populism, they regarded their rebels as aggregates of individuals, as vigilantes, not masses. Left-wing films were of two minds about this. Some, as we saw in *High Noon*, were easily as antipopulist as their pluralist cousins. Others, particularly in the later part of the decade, when the witch-hunt had abated, reverted to the left's traditional fondness for the common man. *Attack!* is one of the latter sort. It likes its GIs, and when they fire into Cooney's body, there is a strong sense of solidarity, of the (small) group acting as one, a rarity in right-wing films.

Attack! goes pretty far for Hollywood. Did Aldrich manage to slip a *Potemkin* past the front office? Not likely. Woodruff is no incipient Lenin, and before we can pick up the phone to call the American Legion, he has changed his tune. Although he has almost been convinced by the sensible advice of his men not to throw himself on the mercies of the army, Colonel Bartlett's cynicism makes him change his mind.

Bartlett couldn't care less who killed Cooney; all he wants to do is make sure Woodruff doesn't tell all to his superior, General Parsons. He promises to promote Woodruff to captain and get a Distinguished Service Cross for Cooney, and even a posthumous one for Costa too, if that will make Woodruff happy. But Woodruff is outraged at Bartlett's business-as-usual cynicism. "No phony medals with my signature," he says angrily. "I may have pulled the trigger, but you aimed the gun. You set the whole thing up." Bidding a final farewell to Costa, Woodruff decides, "You know what I've got to do. You'd do the same thing." As the film ends, Woodruff has got General Parsons on the phone. If Captain Cooney was a coward and Colonel Bartlett an opportunist, surely General Parsons at the top will be okay. Woodruff's back in the fold. By deciding to confess, he has accepted the moral framework of the center, even if the turnabout back to the center is disguised as whistle-blowing. But of course, Costa wouldn't have done it. And that is why he has to die. He was too bitter to be the voice of the film, too relentlessly hostile to survive. That is Woodruff's role, because Woodruff still believes in General Parsons, in the army, in the system. And the film supports his views. We never see Parsons cleaning up the mess, but the film implies that he will.

Thoroughgoing, unrelenting radical films like *Billy Mitchell* are rare— right or left. One was Stanley Kubrick's *Paths of Glory* (1957), where the conflict between authority and conscience is uncompromising. It is World War I, and we are with the French army. Once again we have a court-martial situation, and this time it is Col. Kirk Douglas who defends his proletarian troops for refusing to precede their aristocratic officers into suicidal combat. "If those little sweethearts won't face German bullets, they'll face French ones," rants Gen. George Macready, a vainglorious martinet, and indeed, three men are chosen at random to face court-martial for cowardice. The mutineers rebel against the army, not in the name of bigger and better methods of war, as in *Billy Mitchell*—they are not fighting red tape—but in the name of resisting class oppression. The men are convicted and executed; there is no final court of appeal, no benevolent general to set things right. Colonel Douglas, the man of conscience, is helpless. Whereas *Attack!*, like *12 Angry Men*, tries to reconcile the individual and the group by holding out the hope that the one good man can make the system work, *Paths of Glory* closes all the exits. As in *The Court Martial of Billy Mitchell*, the one good man is powerless, and in *Paths of Glory*, even worse, he becomes an accomplice in the charade of military justice by playing a role in the trial. The contradiction between the individual and the group is insoluble.

We shall now turn to science fiction, which was a genre peculiar to the fifties, one that was born with the atom and died in the late fifties when, as Stanley Kubrick put it, we learned to love the bomb. Sci-fi, in addition to repeating the same systematic patterns we have observed in war films, complicated the picture with several new factors: science and technology, Us/Them, the treatment of the Other, the politics of utopias, and the ideological deployment of the concepts of nature and culture.

PART TWO

US
AND
THEM

CHAPTER THREE

PODS AND BLOBS

The Other Americans

Destination Moon and *Rocketship* XM, both released in 1950, began the cycle of fifties science fiction films that before the decade ended would produce a veritable invasion of little green men, flying saucers, born-again dinosaurs, predatory plants, diabolical juveniles, and enormous insects. But beneath the green slime and behind the horny scales were some familiar faces, some old themes in new guises.

Like war films, sci-fi often presented America in the grip of an emergency, and once again, these emergencies dramatized the necessity of consensus, of pulling together. But in sci-fi, the emergencies were much more serious than they were in war films. They jeopardized the future of the race; they were not national, nor even international, but planetary. The vast scale of destruction also differentiated sci-fi from the horror films of the thirties and forties that preceded them. In *Frankenstein* (1931) and *Dracula* (1931), the scale of misfortune was small, a few villagers mugged by a monster, a little blood let by a vampire. But films like *When Worlds Collide* (1951) or *War of the Worlds* (1953) were suffused with what Susan Sontag called the "imagination of disaster," fear of the cataclysmic destruction of civilization, mayhem of an unimaginably higher order than we had ever seen before, the beginning of the end of life-as-we-know-it.

Although the stakes were raised in fifties sci-fi, stylistically these films were much more restrained than their horrible predecessors. Whereas *Frankenstein* and *Dracula* were drenched in atmosphere—dramatic lighting, fairy-tale sets with their castles, crags, sinister dark woods, and rushing streams—and employed actors with strong screen presences, such as Boris Karloff and Bela Lugosi, sci-fi was (mostly) shot in flat, matter-of-fact black and white and employed a series of colorless, almost interchangeable actors: John Agar, Richard Carlson, Richard Denning, Hugh Marlowe, Jeff Morrow, and Rex Reason. Their affectless performances (before as well as after they were "taken over" by pods or blobs), in addition to the visual blandness of these films, were most appropriate to the prevailing mood of conformity, and provided an ironic counterpoint to their alarming premises. It was sci-fi, more than any other genre, that caught the hysteria behind the picture window.

In sci-fi, the federal government in Washington plays the role the army does in war films. Conflicting attitudes toward the state are articulated in the clash between East and West, national and local, city and country. The alien invasion often begins in the heartland, a small town somewhere in (the) middle (of) America, and moves toward the big cities. Help, on the contrary, flows from national to local, from D.C. to Podunk. Some films expressed confidence that the government, with its bombs and missiles, was equal to any emergency, along with the conviction that everything west of Washington and south of the Mason-Dixon Line was an emergency—the backwoods in rebellion. In *The Giant Claw* (1957), for example, it takes federal fighters to down "the bird as big as a battleship." In *Destination Moon* (co-written by Robert Heinlein), on the other hand, the government is a myopic bureaucracy, only this time it doesn't turn its back on Billy Mitchell's bombers, but instead refuses to finance a moon shot (read, human progress), and worse, after a visionary Mitchell-like industrialist has seen to it that the rocket is built, tries to abort the launch.

If sci-fi recast familiar fifties themes in terms that were peculiarly its own, it also introduced new ones. Science replaced therapy as the guiding light of corporate-liberal sci-fi, in which the coalition of the center was managed by scientists and soldiers, not cops and docs.

Scientists and soldiers were first thrown together in a big way during the war, in the Manhattan Project, and the romance that blossomed then reached its climax at Hiroshima. In the fifties, when their infant A-bomb grew like a beanstalk into a strong and sturdy H-bomb, scientists became alarmed, and fell to fighting not only with soldiers but among themselves over their child's future. Albert Einstein and J. Robert Oppenheimer began to wish they had strangled him in the cradle, while Edward Teller wanted to pack him off to military academy, instead of reform school. But the struggle was an unequal one, and the soldiers easily seized control of defense policy from the likes of Oppenheimer, who was ultimately humiliated as a security risk.

The corporate-liberal intellectuals were caught in the cross-fire. They didn't have much sympathy for doves like Einstein and Oppenheimer, and they agreed with the army that scientists who couldn't get behind the Bomb were better off at Princeton than the Pentagon. But they took a lively interest in defense matters and firmly believed that war was too important to be left to the generals. "The military establishment," wrote Bell, "is ill-equipped to grasp modern conceptions of politics, or to use the tools (computer simulation, linear programming, gaming theory) of strategic planning."[1] It wasn't until the Kennedy era, when McNamara's new generation of "military intellectuals" snatched the war toys from the professional soldiers, that Bell had his way. Pluralist sci-fi, in which scientists told soldiers what to do and brawn deferred to brains, anticipated the reign of RAND by a decade. And in the same way war films made us choose between Ike and MacArthur, sci-fi not only made us choose between scientists and soldiers but between Oppenheimer (or Einstein) and Teller as well.

Many of the monsters of fifties sci-fi were at least partially attributable to science; nevertheless, where science caused the problem, science often solved it too. In *It Came from Beneath the Sea* (1955), for example, the giant octopus in question is spawned by nuclear testing, but it is also destroyed in the end by an atomic torpedo. Thanks in part to the dramatic success of the A-bomb, the prestige of science was so high by the beginning of the fifties that the mad scientists of thirties and forties films, like Dr. Thorkel who not so long ago had shrunk his colleagues down to the size of chickens in *Dr. Cyclops* (1940), were frequently working for Bell Labs. They were no longer mad, but on the contrary, rather pleased with the way things had turned out. Of course, not all films relegated the mad scientist to the dustbin of history. The idea of science, like other elements of fifties ideologies, was inflected from left to right.

Conservative films, as we might predict, were more inclined to let soldiers have their way, as in *Lost Continent* (1951), where the expedition, which includes scientists, is led by Maj. Cesar Romero, or in *The Deadly Mantis* (1957), where the team of soldiers and scientists is led by Col. Craig Stevens. If there were two groups of scientists pitted against each other, these films preferred the Tellers to the Oppenheimers. Conservatives were considerably more suspicious of science than their allies to the left. In 1943, for example, Richard Weaver, author of *The Southern Tradition*, called science a "false messiah."[2] Scientists in conservative films were likely to be brothers beneath the beard of Baron Frankenstein, which is to say, the mad scientists who had disappeared from the labs of corporate-liberal films were alive and well in conservative films. In Roger Corman's *It Conquered the World* (1956), for example, scientist Lee Van Cleef helps some Venusians do just that. If scientists weren't mad in these films, they were obnoxious, and sometimes both. In Jack Arnold's *Tarantula* (1955), an irate sheriff says of Leo G. Carroll, the nutty professor who's been breeding guinea pigs as big as donkeys, "Some of these big brains never learn manners." There aren't any soldiers in this film, at least until the end; just two scientists, bad Professor Carroll, who worked at Oak Ridge and is thus tarred with the brush of federal Big Science, and the hero, a small-town M.D. ("I'm just a country doctor, but I know what I know"), who represents local interests.

Despite *Tarantula*'s attack on Big Science, it is suggestive that the hero is a doctor. Conservative films questioned science, but they by no means rejected it wholesale. Science was fine, so long as it was under control, subordinated to traditional values. Likewise, for all *Tarantula*'s localism, in the end the spider is destroyed by napalm in an Air Force strike led by Clint Eastwood.

The center's infatuation with science was part and parcel of its love affair with machines, with technology. If we examine the language of pluralism, we will discover that society itself was often imagined as a machine. Talcott Parsons wrote of the "institutional machinery" of society,[3] and Norman Vincent Peale even gave machines God's blessing. "A machine is an assembling of parts according to the law of God. When you love a machine and get to know it, you will be aware that it has a rhythm," he wrote. "It is in God's rhythm."[4]

Since centrists imagined society as a machine and looked fondly on science and technology, they rarely regarded computers and robots as dangerous. (We have only to recall the love affair between Dutch Holland and B-47s in *Strategic Air Command*. Characters in films like this were fond of applying mechanical metaphors to one another. In *Bombers B-52*, Karl Malden exclaims, "Women! And they say a B-52 is an involved hunk of machinery!") In *Unknown World* (1950), a trip to the center of the earth is facilitated by a giant mechanical mole. There were a number of films like *Tobor the Great* (1954) and *The Colossus of New York* (1958), in which robots and little boys were pals, while in *Forbidden Planet* (1956),

Robby the Robot was a servant and tool, not a master nor enemy. Robby was the Artoo Deetoo of the fifties. He was the latest thing in labor-saving devices, a Waring Blender, Mixmaster, and Electrolux vacuum cleaner all rolled up into one. Robby wouldn't think of hurting a hair on a human's head, because it was prevented from harming people by the "Laws of Robotics." When ordered to shoot Comdr. J. J. "Skipper" Adams with a blaster, it grinds to a halt amid a flurry of sparks, victim of a "subelectronic dilemma," a sort of robot gridlock.

Technology, however, was merely a special case of the artificial, the man-made. Pluralists like Trilling, Riesman, Schlesinger, and Bell identified the center with no less than civilization itself, with the highest achievements of humanity, with the totality of man-made objects, the aggregate of human production: in short, with culture. Riesman observed that in America, "society is no longer felt as a wilderness or jungle as it often was earlier,"[5] and pluralists invariably imagined it not only as a machine but as a business, a building, and a game.

That which is not-culture is, most generally, nature—not merely trees, animals, and bugs, but all that is not-human—so that the conflict between moderates and extremists, the center and the Other, Us and Them, was often presented as a conflict between culture and nature. To the center, culture was good, and nature was generally bad; it was all that threatened to disrupt or destroy culture. Bell, for example, spoke of the "*flash-fire* of McCarthyism,"[6] of the "turbulence" created by the right, and of "a *rogue elephant* like Huey Long or Joseph McCarthy . . . rampag[ing] against the operations of government."[7] Adlai Stevenson commended J. Edgar Hoover for "catching Communist agents like killing *poisonous snakes* or *tigers*" (italics mine).[8] When Billy Graham opened the 1952 session of the U.S. Senate with a prayer, he warned against the "barbarians beating at our gates from without and moral *termites* from within."[9] "Termites," "flash-fires," "poisonous snakes and tigers," "rampaging rogue elephants"—these images themselves conjure up disasters and emergencies. They were the coming attractions for the sci-fi films that did no more than literalize the metaphors of the center.

It is not surprising, then, that the Other in pluralist films was most often nature. Society may no longer have been experienced as a wilderness or a jungle, as Riesman said, but the "jungle" remained, a favorite fifties epithet for the world outside society, as well as for the pockets of primitivism that lingered on within society. There was Richard Brooks's *Blackboard Jungle*, William Witney's *Juvenile Jungle* (1958), John Huston's *Asphalt Jungle* (1950), Vincent Sherman's *Garment Jungle* (1957), the "chromium jungle" in *The Man in the Gray Flannel Suit* (1956), as well as the "jungle" that Mike Hammer inhabited in *Kiss Me Deadly*. And, not surprisingly, the jungle was the natural habitat of extremism, of survival-of-the-fittest Social Darwinism, which is to say, Whyte's old-fashioned Protestant Ethic. Recalling the lessons he had learned in his youth at the Vicks VapoRub School of Applied Merchandising, Whyte wrote that in those days, "combat was the ideal. . . . It was a gladiator's school we were in."[10] But by 1950, when the country was fast becoming the city, or at least the suburbs, more asphalt than jungle, the Protestant Ethic was paved over too, and Demetrius, surveying the gladiators' school in *Demetrius and the Gladiators* (1954), could say in disgust, "This is a place where men are trained to kill each other like animals."

Sci-fi has always been fascinated with the Other, and critics of popular culture have been quick to point out that the Other is always other than itself, which is to say, the pods and blobs are "symbols" standing for something else. Ever since Susan Sontag pointed to the fact that the Other in fifties sci-fi was often linked to radiation, it has been customary to equate the Other with the Bomb. John and Jane Doe may think they're being attacked by elephantine aphids run riot in their garden, but we know better. The hypothetical film informs us that a tactical nuclear weapon has been set off at the desert test site just ten miles away from the Doe residence; one step ahead, we realize that it is radiation that has caused the ravenous aphids to double in size every ten minutes, and jumping to conclusions, we decide that *The Attack of the Giant Aphids* is really about the arms race, and that John and Jane are down with a severe case of nuclear anxiety. But centrist films like this are not primarily worried about the Bomb; they loved the Bomb, or at least the technology that made it possible. The Does may not be as dumb as we thought, and to understand what these films did worry about, all we have to do is look at what's before our very eyes: it's aphids after all, nature run amok.

In films of the center, then, pluralist and conservative, the enemy is the natural world, as in big-bug films like *The Beginning of the End* (1957) (grasshoppers), *The Black Scorpion* (1957), *The Deadly Mantis*, and *Tarantula*. In the same category fall films set in the jungle or remote, wild places, like *The Creature from the Black Lagoon* (1954); *From Hell It Came* (1957), where the Other is a deranged tree stump; *The Attack of the Crab Monsters*, where the Other is an army of king-sized crabs on a Pacific atoll; or *The Monster That Challenged the World* (1957), where the Other is a school of jumbo-sized marauding snails. Then there are the films that assert a correspondence between the villains and the natural world, like *The Leech Woman* (1960), part of which takes place in the jungle; *The Wasp Woman* (1959); and *The Cult of the Cobra* (1955). In these films, nature may attack from the past, or occasionally the future, but rarely from the present. The American, European, Asian, or African past is equated with "primitive," "barbarous" nature, and expresses itself, for example, in the antediluvian beast from 20,000 fathoms or the "prehistoric" monsters of *King Dinosaur* (1955) or the Transylvanian curses that hovered over the heroine of *The Cat People* and the hero of *I Was a Teenage Werewolf*. Even relatively benign manifestations of nature like rivers, waterfalls, and open spaces are often dangerous in centrist sci-fi. The Other in *The Monolith Monsters* (1957) is nothing more exotic than giant crystals. Deserts, like the one in *Tarantula*, were notorious for spawning aliens of one sort or another.

Nature may also attack from within, as in *Forbidden Planet* (1956), a highly unusual, Freudianized sci-fi version of *The Tempest*, directed by Fred Wilcox, best known for his Lassie movies. When the film opens, the Skipper (Leslie Nielsen) has arrived in United Planets Cruiser C-57-D at Altair 4, to search for the remnants of the Bellerophon expedition of twenty years earlier. (It still took a long time to get things rolling, even in the twenty-third century.) All he finds is Morbius (Walter Pidgeon) and his daughter, Alta (also called Altaira), played by Anne Francis. They are the sole survivors of Expedition 1. Despite the death of their friends, they have been living happily ever after in a patriarchal paradise. Alta has never seen a man other than her father; she worships the ground he walks on.

The only fly in the Oedipal ointment is the mysterious "planetary force" that tore the members of the first expedition limb from limb. It is invisible to the naked eye, and the Skipper's crew finds that it is impervious to their most powerful weapons. Alta and the Skipper fall in love, but the more they pet, the more the planetary force wreaks havoc. Running for their lives, Morbius, the Skipper, and Alta take refuge in the bowels of the ancient Krel kingdom, far beneath Altair's surface. The Krel were an advanced civilization that mysteriously vanished overnight, thoughtfully leaving their technology intact for Morbius to play with. As the door of hardened Krel steel begins to buckle before the incredible power of the planetary force on the other side, the Skipper confronts Morbius with the awful truth: the monster is Morbius himself, his own unconscious, the so-called "monster from the id," stirred into a jealous rage by the Skipper's attentions to his daughter. The Krel, it turns out, in the extremity of scientific progress, had succeeded in "freeing themselves from any dependence on physical instrumentality." This seemed to be all very well for the Krel; they just pushed some buttons, sat back, and let their thoughts do the working. But at the same time that they managed to instrumentalize their waking thoughts, they inadvertently unleashed the power of their own "baser selves," the unconscious, and were destroyed. By fussing with Krel technology, Morbius unwittingly learned the Krel trick and exposed himself to the same fate. "Like you, the Krel forgot their own subconscious hate and lust for destruction," explains the Skipper. "The beast, the murderous primitive. Even the Krel must have evolved from that beginning," replies Morbius sadly.

Forbidden Planet is a conservative film in which the scientist has to make way for the soldier, in which technology, apparently, has gone too far. Despite Robby, and all the screen time lavished on a loving display of the Krel's futuristic hardware, a riot of dials and switches, machines were their downfall. Morbius, of course, is the neo-mad scientist, given to saying things like "The fool—as if his ape's brain could fathom the secrets of the Krel," and worse, for a film like this one, "I'm not in need of any military assistance." But just as conservatives were sympathetic to individualism, only to repudiate it in the end and fall in line with the corporate liberals behind groups, so they ultimately fell in line behind technology too. "A conservatism that cannot face the facts of the machine and mass production," as Buckley put it, "is predoomed to futility and petulance."[11] Despite the dire consequences of technological overdevelopment—the transformation of Morbius's own id into the dread planetary force—here there is nothing essentially wrong with machines. No, the trouble isn't with the microchips and semiconductors. In *Forbidden Planet*, people betray technology, nature betrays culture. Trouble comes from "human error." When machines make it possible for people like Morbius to harness their brain power, the result is disaster, because people are still imperfect, insufficiently machinelike. They harbor dark, irrational forces, primitive throwbacks to their natural origins. Neither Morbius nor the Krel, the race that knew too much, were up to their own technology.

Forbidden Planet's emphasis on the "monster from the id" allows us to refine our analysis of the therapeutic. Although conservatives repudiated it in principle, Freudianism was close enough to their own traditional Christian pessimism about human nature for them to find it serviceable. As we have seen, Freud and Niebuhr, sex and sin, were able to make common front. And similarly, although corporate-liberal films embraced the therapeutic, this did not necessarily mean Freud, but rather the so-called "neo-Freudians" like Karen Horney and Erich Fromm, who argued that neuroses were caused more by environment, "interpersonal relations," than by deep-seated disturbances in infantile sexuality. In fact, cold-war liberals like Trilling often deplored "the tendency of our educated liberal class to reject the tough, complex psychology of Freud for the easy rationalistic optimism of Horney and Fromm."[12]

Corporate liberals, in other words, may have absorbed some of Freud's pessimism—they believed in the monster from the id—but, as we have seen, this did not make it necessary for them to abandon their customary permissiveness. They still embraced the therapeutic. If people were sick, they could be cured. If humans were corrupt, society did not have to be a jail to contain them. But when conservative films like *Forbidden Planet* embraced Freudian premises, they did not draw therapeutic conclusions. If nature, the id, the "baser self," was as dangerous as it seemed to be, what was needed was repression, not permission. The Skipper puts it nicely: "We're all part monster in our unconscious," he explains patiently to Alta. "That's why we have laws and religion." The dramatic moment in which Morbius, with a shock of recognition, realizes that the planetary force is his own id would be a therapeutic breakthrough in a different kind of film, but here, it doesn't work. "Stop, I deny you. I give you up," he screams. The force, however, is implacable, and only disappears when Morbius dies. Therapy is useless. There's a doctor in this film, but he's no more than the Skipper's sidekick, and it is the Skipper who gives the orders and gets the girl. And like Morbius, the doc dies too; it is the Skipper who answers the riddle of the planetary force.

The emphasis on the monster from the id lets technology off the hook.

In the last scene, the Skipper, his crew, and Alta head home, taking Robby with them. But Robby isn't cleaning rugs in the control room. It's the "astrogator." While Skipper and Alta settle down for the ride, Robby pilots the ship. Technology is back in the driver's seat.

Nature, whether within or without, was merely the most general category of Otherness. The Other took different forms in different films, and we can specify it considerably more precisely than we have so far. It has long seemed evident, from the moment the first blob oozed its way across the screen, that the little green men from Mars stood in the popular imagination for the clever red men from Moscow. The media portrayed Communists in such a lurid fashion that the connection was inevitable, even if unintended by writers and directors. But like the Bomb, the Red Menace theory stands in the way of thinking through the idea of the Other. I. F. Stone, among others, pointed out at the time that the Soviet threat was as much a function of the squabbles between Democrats and Republicans as it was a reality: "The Republicans fought Russia in order to prevent a New Deal, while the Democrats fought Russia as a kind of rearguard action against the Republicans."[13] Indeed, the red nightmare was so handy that had it not existed, American politicians would have had to invent it. Movies did invent it, and it served somewhat the same purpose in Hollywood as it did in Washington. More often than not, the Communist connection was a red herring, allowing the center to attack extremists, extremists to attack the center, and both centrists and extremists to quarrel among themselves (corporate liberals against conservatives, right against left), all in the guise of respectable anticommunism. But this was no more than a smokescreen for a domestic power struggle. Fifties sci-fi was more concerned with Main Street than monsters.

The idea of the alien was profoundly influenced by the Manichean Us/ Them habit of thought that was an occupational hazard of the cold-war battle of ideas. The Other was everything the center was not, and we can get a good idea of what the center was not, at least in its own estimation, by again examining the language of pluralism. If the center was modern, the Other was ancient. Bell referred to "*archaic* Europe" and the "*backward* colonial system.*" If the center was civilized, the Other was primitive. Bell criticized the "barbarous" behavior of the radical right,[14] and Alan Westin warned liberals and conservatives against "the *spear thrusts* of the radicals."[15] If the center was scientific and technological, the Other was magical. Bell accused the right of entertaining the illusion of the "*magical* rollback of Communism in Europe" (italics mine).[16] If the center was middle-class, the Other was lower- or occasionally upper-class. If the center was normal, the Other was abnormal. If the center was sane, the Other was insane. If the center was the ego, the Other was the id or occasionally the superego. If the center was heterosexual, the Other was homosexual. If the center was white and Anglo-Saxon, the Other was alien cultures: Martians in sci-fi; Indians in westerns; traditional societies like the American South in period pieces; Italian, Irish, or Jewish ethnic enclaves in American cities, or European, Asian, or Latin societies in "realistic" dramas.

The equation between some familiar aspect of the world-as-we-know-it with the Other was in effect a polemical device that dehumanized, Other-ized people, ideas, and values the center disliked, transforming them into Them while at the same time guaranteeing that the ideas, people, and values it did like were cozily considered to be Us. Centrists were fond of ridiculing the left and right for dehumanizing their enemies, adopting a crude, vulgar, uncomplex division of life into black and white. The left and the right did indeed dehumanize their enemies, but so did the center. The only difference was, of course, in who was Us and who was Them.

Other-izing qualities, life-styles, or groups that threatened the center was not only a way of discrediting specific alternatives to the as-is but a way of discrediting the very idea of alternatives to the orthodox manner of living and being. If alternatives to mainstream institutions were dystopian, there was no place to go but home, that is, back to the center.

The whole genre of forties and fifties fallen-away, ex-Communist liter-ature, from *Darkness at Noon* to *The God That Failed*, was anti-utopian in character. Orwell's *Animal Farm*, made into a feature-length cartoon in 1954, and *1984*, adapted for the screen in 1956, along with Aldous Huxley's *Brave New World*, were virtually canonized in the fifties. The attack on utopias and utopians, dreams and dreamers, was a constant refrain in centrist literature. Utopians are our old friends, extremists, and utopianism was worked over so thoroughly that *utopian* and *millennial*, like *ideological*, became epithets of abuse. Thus Alan Westin derided "dangerously millennial proposals" of the left and right,[17] while Talcott Parsons ridiculed the "utopianism" of Republican isolationists.[18] It was Schlesinger who put the centrist case against utopianism most cogently.

"We must grow up now and forsake the millennial dream," he lectured those who persisted in cavorting in the sandbox of progressivism. Why? Utopians were not only foolish, they were dangerous. They had paved the way for Hitler and Stalin. "Men in a conviction of infallibility can sacrifice humanity without compunction on the altar of some abstract and special good," he wrote, going on to praise *The Blithedale Romance*, which was based on Nathaniel Hawthorne's brief flirtation and bitter disillusionment with the utopian community of Brook Farm: "Hawthorne extrapolated unerringly from the pretty charades of Brook ·Farm to the essence of totalitarian man."[19] For Schlesinger, it was only a hop, skip, and a jump from Brook Farm to the Third Reich.

In *Forbidden Planet*, Alta's Garden of Eden is a utopia in its natural form—an arcadia. She lives in perfect harmony with the beasts of the jungle: deer appear at the snap of a finger; tigers nibble bonbons out of her hand. But since nature can't be all good in a centrist film like this one, we know she's in for a disappointment. When Alta and the Skipper are in the middle of their first big kiss, a tiger springs toward them. As the Skipper draws his blaster, she restrains him. "Stop! It's my friend," she says, but sure enough, the tiger keeps on coming, and the Skipper has to zap it. Although Alta doesn't know it, she's just fallen in love and out of nature. Yet her transformation is not presented as a "fall," but as growth. She's better off with the Skipper than she is frolicking about with tigers and deer. As a utopian, Alta is dangerous. She is promiscuously given to kissing whomever she pleases, swimming in the nude, and wearing scanty, see-through clothing. Her naïve sexuality threatens to stir up the tiger in the members of the Skipper's sex-starved crew, who have been in space for eighteen months. "Go home and put something on," he tells her testily, and she does. Her innocent intercourse with the natural world is exposed as parochial and limited, and when it ends we don't mourn it, because now it feels artificial, even "unnatural," which is to say, nature has been redefined as culture.

Sci-fi was particularly well suited for conveying the anti-utopianism of the center, because visions of the future were a staple of the genre. Even if utopias began well, they ended badly and were apt to degenerate from the best of all worlds to the worst. Given the center's fondness for technology, we might expect that these films would present an upbeat vision of the future, but their repudiation of utopianism was so strong it overrode

Paradise-about-to-be-lost: Alta's arcadia looks great, but in this film it's forbidden, because utopianism is parochial, dangerous, and even "unnatural."

their technophilia. Fifties sci-fi was full of futuristic civilizations that had fallen on hard times. In *This Island Earth* (1955), for example, the advanced civilization is Metaluna, but its gleaming array of gizmos and gadgets by no means guarantee peace and prosperity: on the contrary, the Metalunans are locked in a battle to the death with Zahgon, their archenemy, and have to kidnap scientists from Earth to help them. To judge by films like *Flight to Mars* (1951), *The 27th Day* (1957), and *Not of This Earth* (1957), Earth must have been the choicest morsel of real estate in the galaxy, because it was repeatedly invaded by advanced civilizations that had fouled up in one way or another—exhausted their resources, polluted their atmosphere, overpopulated their cities, and so on. To be an advanced civilization was to look for trouble. *

And from another perspective, it is worth noting that when danger arose in centrist films, it most often did so during an expedition, as in *Forbidden Planet, The Thing, From Hell It Came, Creature from the Black Lagoon,* and *Attack of the Crab Monsters.* The trouble they saw was another warning not to go poking about for utopian alternatives. Home was safe; danger lurked Out There. But that was all right, because "home" was Earth, the real utopia. Even though utopia after utopia fell on hard times, we were not to worry, because we weren't missing anything. Earth, by which they meant the U.S.A., circa 1955, was utopian enough for anyone. It was there, after all, that the contradictions—nature versus culture, individual versus society—that bedeviled advanced civilizations (read, other ideologies) were reconciled.

Centrists believed, quite simply, that their country had the endorsement of the Almighty, the Divine Seal of Approval. A booming consumer economy offered ample proof that the God who had abandoned twentieth-century Europe to physical and spiritual destruction had come home to roost in America. "Why should *we* make a five-year plan," wondered historian Daniel Boorstin in *Partisan Review,* "when God seems to have had a thousand-year plan ready-made for us?"[20]

Boorstin wasn't alone in his faith. It was clear to almost everyone that God had jumped on the Free World bandwagon. After a decade of relative lack of interest in things theological, the fifties saw a major revival of organized religion. Between 1949 and 1953 the annual distribution of Bibles rose by 140 percent. Almost 10 million Bibles were sold in 1953 alone, and stories from the scriptures regularly appeared in Sunday comics

---

*Utopias and dystopias were by no means confined to sci-fi. Ancient civilizations played the same role in the biblical spectacles of the fifties as advanced civilizations played in sci-fi. Like them, they were on the skids; the only difference was that they happened to be situated in the past, not the future. In Rome's case, being advanced was linked to decadence, and in most films, Rome loses out to Christians, who were the apostles of the Social Ethic.

In westerns, we often find romanticized outlaw communities that are destroyed by their own contradictions, like Chuck-a-Luck (a sort of bandit MacDowell Colony) in Lang's *Rancho Notorious* (1952) or the thieves' haven behind the waterfall in Ray's *Johnny Guitar* (1953).

and popular magazines like *Readers Digest*. Helping to open the American Legion's "Back to God" crusade, President Eisenhower said, "Recognition of the Supreme Being is the first, the most basic, expression of Americanism. Without God, there could be no American form of government, nor an American way of life." And when Ike was inaugurated in 1953, "the parade of floats representing the 48 states was headed by a float to God."[21]

But, as the theology of therapy appealed more to corporate liberals, so the therapy of theology appealed more to conservatives, and their films worshipped at the altar of religion. Christian allusions occasionally popped up in corporate-liberal sci-fi, but in these films, religion ultimately had to yield to science. Whereas in a film like *The Conquest of Space* (1955), the soldier hero deteriorates into a religious fanatic who believes that God would have given us rockets if we were intended to fly, and tries to wreck his ship, in conservative films religion is used to chastise science. These are the films in which the Faustian mad scientist is warned by a woman, a minister, or a soldier not to mess with God's work. In Kurt Neumann's *The Fly* (1958), when the scientist exclaims, "I can transport matter!" his wife replies, aghast, "It's like playing God." Utopians were totalitarians to corporate liberals; to conservatives they were the Antichrist.

If America was itself utopian, this meant that spiritual values of any sort—whether Christian or humanistic—were immanent, not transcendent; they were immediate, palpable, accessible in the activities of everyday life, not remote, distant, unreachable. Utopia, whether specifically Christian or not, lay in humdrum routine; "authenticity," "significance," even salvation, were to be found in our own backyards.*

---

*Like the idea of utopianism, the problem of incarnating transcendental values in everyday life was not peculiar to science fiction. Barbara Deming has pointed out that in the returning-vet films of the late forties, the problem of readjustment to civilian life was often rendered as the clash between the hero's loyalty to a moment of transcendence that occurred during the war and the mundane routines of office, factory, or home.[22] He has to learn to recognize the one in the other, transcendence in the here-and-now. For Clark Gable in *Adventure* (1945), it was the sea that gave him that certain thrill. A Navy man, he resists the charms of Greer Garson, insisting that it was on the "black ocean" that he came closest to experiencing "it"—the Eternal, the Truth. "There's nothing on land," says Gable, "that doesn't leak itself to death." "It, it, it," says Garson, impatiently. What is this "it" he's looking for? "You, you, you," admits Gable, finally. He realizes that the ocean, the "it," the sense of authenticity he longed for, was right in front of his eyes all the time, in Garson's eyes, in fact. "I never found it in any eyes before," he says happily.

In George Pal's *War of the Worlds*, a conservative film, salvation comes from an unexpected quarter: the common germ. An A-bomb, "the latest thing in nuclear fission," is ineffectual against the attacking Martians. Science has to throw in the towel, and near the end, the defeated scientist hero is reduced to wandering from church to church in search of his girl friend. In one, the hymns of the terrified flock momentarily drown out the sounds of battle, as the priest says, "O Lord, we pray thee—grant us the miracle of Thy divine intervention." No sooner said than done. A few frames later, an alien comes crashing through the roof of another church—dead. "We were all praying for a miracle," says the hero as church bells toll. But the film doesn't end there; the narrator goes on to give the miracle a rationalist explanation. It seems that the Martians were not immune to our bacteria, and once infected, they curled up and died. In other words, God's miracles, while potent, are not handed down from on high. Rather, God works through His creation, not behind its back or over its head. "After all that men could do had failed," says the narrator, "the Martians were defeated by the littlest thing that God in His wisdom had put upon this earth."

Radical films were the mirror image of centrist sci-fi. There, Us was the "extremists" and Them was the center. When the center became the enemy, both scientists *and* soldiers were vilified. The state, the federal government, was either bad or ineffectual. Often, the government was not called upon to help at all, or if called upon, could not be reached because the aliens controlled the phones. Sometimes the government tried to destroy the aliens and failed, its weapons useless against their armor, whereupon they were destroyed by the resourceful citizens of Smallville without the benefit of federal aid. The aliens were defeated, not by bombs and missiles, but by water in *The Night the World Exploded* (1957), a dog in *I Married a Monster from Outer Space* (1958), and fire extinguishers in *The Blob* (1958). In some films, the government's weapons, far from being ineffectual, were all too powerful, more dangerous than the alien itself.

Since in radical films, the enemy was the center, it was not too surprising that the form in which this enemy, this Other, was imagined was not nature but culture, specifically technology. If people betrayed technology in centrist films, like *Forbidden Planet*, where disaster was caused by "human error," in right-wing films technology betrayed people. Disaster was caused by "mechanical error." The editors of the *National Review*, for example, writing about John Glenn's space flight, preferred men to machines: "This and that went wrong with the mechanism, and man took over and brought Friendship 7 to its strange harbor," they wrote. To them, the flight "reminds us that there is no such thing, and never will be, as a 'thinking' machine. Only man thinks, wills, decides, dares. No machine, on land, in sea, air or space, can do man's job for him: can choose, for good or ill."[23] For the right, "robot" and "mechanical" were epithets of scorn, and the center, perceived from the right as dehumanized and technocratic, was represented in sci-fi by a whole army of robots, androids, and mechanical pod people that trudged across the screens of the fifties with their characteristic jerky motions. Whereas in centrist films robots like Robby were friendly, they were dangerous in right-wing films, such as *Target Earth* (1954), *Gog* (1954), and *Kronos* (1957). In *Invisible Boy* (1957), Robby the Robot, making its first (and last) appearance since *Forbidden Planet* one year earlier, is itself taken over by an evil computer that removes its Asimovian prohibitions against killing people. At the end, Robby destroys the computer, but it's not a centrist technology-saves-us-from-technology finale, because cuddly Robby by this time feels like one of Us, a human. It's a triumph for humanity over technology.

Right-wing films often used nature to flog culture. They did so, not from any particular passion for roots and berries, but partly because the center had been largely successful in arrogating culture to itself, and ennobling nature was an easy way to strike back. Alta's arcadia would indeed have been an Eden for the right. Similarly, they used the past to flog the present, the primitive to attack the modern. (*Billy Mitchell* is an obvious exception.) Therefore, the past was not a barbarous time, as it was in centrist films, but rather a simpler, purer one, while the primitive was often looked upon with nostalgia. It was the locus of utopian values.

Susan Sontag first called attention to the fear of robots, which she contrasted with the older fear of the animal. "The dark secret behind human nature used to be the upsurge of the animal—as in *King Kong*. The threat to man, his availability to dehumanization, lay in his own animality," wrote Sontag. "Now the danger is understood as residing in man's ability to be turned into a machine."[24] But Sontag was only partly right. While it is true that in the fifties the imagination of disaster took a mechanical turn, this new metaphor for dehumanization did not supersede the older one of animality. Rather, it coexisted alongside it. As we have seen, there were plenty of films in which dehumanization was imagined either as the eruption of the primitive, the return of the repressed unconscious—the monster from the id—or an attack by the natural world deranged by radiation. (In fact, *King Kong* itself was rereleased in 1952, and was a surprise hit, grossing more in its second outing than it did when it was first issued in 1933.) The alien as primitive, animal, natural was a centrist fantasy, while the alien as mechanical or technological was a nightmare of the right.

Occasionally, it was a left-wing fantasy as well. Unlike the right that disliked them, and the center that worshipped them, the left was of two minds about science and technology. Much of the left, anticipating the sixties rejection of postindustrial society, resembled the right in their antipathy for machines and fondness for nature. In Oboler's *The Twonky* (1953), the robot is a Big Brother–like television set that tries to control its human owner. *

But many elements on the left did not share the right's nostalgia for the preindustrial world, and conversely retained the confidence in technology (properly used) they imbibed in the intellectual climate of the twenties and thirties, made up in part of futurism, the Bauhaus, and Marxist utopianism. Many left-wing films smiled on technology. Like the films of the center, they favored culture over nature, head over heart, and prescribed larger doses of technology for the illness technology caused. In *When Worlds Collide* (1951), technology builds the spaceship that saves a handful of beleaguered humans from a head-on collision with the comet Bellus.

Radical films were more tolerant of utopianism than films of the center. Utopian aspirations did not find themselves realized in daily life; they were transcendent, not immanent. Right-winger Eric Voegelin, in *The New Science of Politics* (1952), decried the liberal tendency to "immanentize" Christianity, to reduce its otherworldly perspective to an "intramundane range of action" while at the same time striving for the "re-divinization of society."[25]

---

*Left-wing war films often portrayed Nazi supermen and right-wing American officers as robots or automatons, cool, efficient, and unfeeling, in contrast to the warm, undisciplined, chaotic world of the enlisted men. In *The Naked and the Dead*, Lieutenant Robertson tells General Massey, "I don't think warfare is like chess. You're dealing with human beings. You're like my father. He thinks workers are machines."

The right may have been negative about society, but it was hopeful that utopian values could thrive outside it. In *Red Planet Mars* (1952), the planet in question is the seat of a thriving advanced civilization, a utopia ruled by Christian precepts. The Martians pass the word along to Earth, where it effects a miraculous transformation of life-as-we-know-it, particularly in the Soviet Union, where peasants help the Orthodox Patriarch dust off his icons, overthrow the Reds, and establish a prerevolutionary theocracy. Divine intervention it is, but unlike the miracle in *War of the Worlds*, this one is not rationalized; it does not operate circuitously, by way of God's creatures, but directly. It is intervention from without.

To the left as to the right, utopian aspirations were transcendent, not immanent. They did not inhabit the center but, on the contrary, existed without, in future worlds, or within, beating in the breasts of disaffected, alienated heroes. In *When Worlds Collide*, the space voyagers are naturally afraid that Zyra, their destination, will prove to be inhospitable, either too cold or too hot, crawling with fierce beasts or covered with noxious gases. But luckily for them, it's not so. As the film ends, the hatch opens, and they peer out at the green hills of Zyra, as pretty a place as you're likely to see this side of Disneyland. They've found the paradise that Alta lost, but not on Earth, which is a graveyard for utopianism. Technology has carried them to a bucolic world that accommodates nature and culture.

If the right used the past to flog the present, the left used the future, either in the positive guise of prospering advanced civilizations—the same ones the center disparaged—or with the negative example of civilizations sadly destroyed by nuclear war a few years hence, as in *Rocketship XM* or Oboler's *Five* (1951). Whereas the center used the destruction of futuristic societies to knock utopianism, the left used it to knock the center.

But these films' stances toward technology, nature, and utopianism were not sufficiently distinct to allow us to discriminate between right and left. More crucial was their attitude toward aliens. The right's hospitality toward utopian aspirations did not extend to aliens. Right-wing films were doubly paranoid, afraid of the alien on the one hand and the center on the other. In other words, aliens did not offer an alternative to the status quo, because they symbolized the status quo. The aliens and the center were the same. Like right-wing war films such as *The Court Martial of Billy Mitchell*, they tried to alarm and mobilize people against the enemy.

Left-wing sci-fi was afraid of the center and the right, but the alien was neutral or benevolent, which is to say, these films tried to defuse the paranoia toward the Other. If right-wing films favored rollback, left-wing films favored appeasement of the alien. In the context of the Red scare, which saw Commies behind every bush, these were anti-witch-hunt films, which tried to reassure the people that there was no clear and present danger. When aliens in these films weren't neutral or benevolent, they were victims, like the mole people in the film of the same name (1956), or the famous Gill-Man in John Sherwood's *The Creature Walks Among Us* (1956), the concluding film in the Creature Trilogy. In the first film, made two years earlier by Jack Arnold, the Creature was mildly appealing, more sinned against than sinning, almost but not quite a noble savage tormented beyond endurance by the arrogant scientists who mucked about in his lagoon, and driven into a frenzy by the proximity of Julia Adams in a one-piece bathing suit. (The Creature's distinctive costume was reputedly derived from a sketch of the Oscar statuette.) In the second and third films the Creature gets increasingly put upon. In Sherwood's 1956 version, "he" has been taken out of his natural habitat entirely, removed in chains to a cage on land. Here, he's unambiguously sympathetic, protecting a flock of sheep that shares his pen from a mountain lion. But he's unable to protect himself from the mad scientists who perform all sorts of grim experiments upon his body while prattling about "reality and facts." They transplant this, amputate that, move a fin here, a gill there, until his own mother wouldn't recognize him. One of the scientists even tries to frame him for murder, and in the end, the Creature is killed. When, occasionally, aliens in these films were hostile, they were driven to it by villainous earthlings, like the scientist in Edgar G. Ulmer's *The Man from Planet X* (1951), who provokes the title character by turning off its air supply. Even then, its consequent rampage is defensive in character.

What will we be looking for in these films? First, we will ask some of the old questions: Who dominates the coalition of the center, scientists or soldiers, experts or professionals? Is society top-down or bottom-up? How are reporters and just plain everyday folks treated? Who saves the world? Individuals or groups? And if groups, are they small or large? Then some new questions: Are the scientists mad or sane? Are they Tellers or Oppenheimers? Where is the alien encountered? Does it come to us in Los Angeles, or do we come to it, say, on Mars? Is the alien friendly or hostile? If it is hostile, and comes to us, does the invasion proceed from the country to the city, from local to national, or is it the reverse? What is the alien—animal, vegetable, or mineral, that is, nature or culture? Does it come from a utopia or dystopia? Is it Us or Them, and if it is Us, which Us is it? What or who does it stand for? And finally, how is the alien killed, and by whom, the government in Washington or the people on the spot?

The Russians Are Coming, Aren't They?

Them!, The Thing, and the Extremists from Beyond the Center

When Ben Peterson (James Whitmore), a New Mexico state trooper, comes across a little girl wandering around in the desert, clutching a doll to her chest in Gordon Douglas's Them! (1954), he knows there's something amiss. "Look, she's in shock," he says, and sure enough, she is. Her dad has just been killed and their trailer squashed like a beer can. The sides are caved in, the interior is a mess, and curiouser and curiouser, there are sugar cubes strewn about the ground, not to mention strange tracks in the sand. Pretty soon the scene of the crime is crawling with fingerprinters and police photographers, but no one can make head or tail of the sugar cubes, tracks, and above all, the peculiar high-pitched ringing sound that fills the air with a maddening throb. No money has been taken, and the whole thing "doesn't make sense," as one cop says to another. Indeed, the police procedure seems completely inappropriate. As in 12 Angry Men and Panic in the Streets, reality defies common sense; this is clearly a job for experts, not professionals; docs, not cops.

Later, we find out that the culprits were oversized ants who have a correspondingly lusty appetite for sweets, and that the destruction of the trailer was incidental; it happened while they were rummaging around for sugar, which they love more than life itself. But what may not have been so incidental is the identity of the little girl's dad, the ants' first victim: he was an FBI agent on vacation. The ants, in other words, spawned in the desert of the Southwest, have struck at J. Edgar Hoover's G-men, agents of the federal authority from the East.

Them! goes on to build this whisper of regional rivalry into a structural contrast by cutting between shots of desert locales, with the ants wreaking havoc and spilling sugar every which way, and shots of Washington, D.C. When the dry, dusty landscape of the Southwest fades away and the U.S. Capitol Building, lit up like a Christmas tree on a dark Washington night, fades in, we breathe a sigh of relief. We know that once the authorities in Washington are alerted to the danger, everything will be under control. In other words, if the threat arises in New Mexico, strikes at Washington through the death of the FBI agent, and then against Los Angeles, a major urban center, the solution moves from the national to local. When the time comes to declare martial law, and the words we have been waiting for boom out over the loudspeakers—"Your personal safety and the safety of the entire city depend on your full cooperation with the military authorities"—we know it's true. People in the street after the curfew are subject to arrest by the MPs, but we don't care. After all, it's a national emergency. *Them!* has effectively established the legitimacy of state power. *

The federal government in Washington responds to the crisis by dispatching Dr. and Pat Medford (Edmund Gwenn and Joan Weldon), a father/daughter team of "myrmecologists" from the U.S. Department of Agriculture (remember the U.S. Department of Health in *Panic?*), a general, and an FBI agent named Robert Graham (James Arness) bringing up the rear. Although the national elite, the coalition of the center, runs the show, it does not sweep aside local authority, but works through it, forming an alliance with Ben Peterson, the state trooper. He becomes the agent of the federal government within the local community. Federal interests are administered, mediated by local officials.

It is the scientists who have pride of place. Dr. Medford is a benign, avuncular fellow, a far cry from the demented Thorkels of yesteryear. Although he wonders what God hath wrought ("We may be witnessing a

---

*In centrist films, the most memorable images were not aliens, but reassuring scenic views of Washington, D.C., which is one reason the conclusion of *Earth vs. the Flying Saucers* (1956) is so startling. After playing a symphony of fascinating variations on the themes of national and local, therapy and force, friendly and unfriendly aliens, good and bad robots, the film ends on a magnificently ambiguous note, designed (by Ray Harryhausen) to warm the hearts of centrists and radicals alike. The government wins, but Washington is obliterated in the attack of the saucers. Lincoln and Jefferson, who had to endure the maunderings of so many actors in so many movies, are put out of their misery; the Washington Monument is snapped in two like a toothpick, and the sequence concludes in a storm of pillars and pediments, great chunks of concrete and flying glass hurtling every which way, when a saucer crashes through the dome of the U.S. Capitol Building, smashing it like an overripe melon.

biblical prophecy come true . . . The beasts will reign over the earth"), he also knows that the test tube is mightier than the cross, and that once again, if it was science (in this case nuclear testing) that had caused the problem, science would solve it too.

Them! reflects the new prestige of science by placing scientists at the center of world-shaking events. Dr. Medford meets with the president, lectures top public officials, and is able to command the full resources of the state. In the same way that the mayor in *Panic* had to take orders from Dr. Reed, so here the general has to take orders from Dr. Medford. In fact, he flies Medford around in his Air Force plane like a chauffeur, and Pat Medford observes, "It's like a scientist's dream." Poor agent Graham complains that the scientists are keeping him in the dark and won't tell him their theory. "We're on this case, too," he says plaintively. The cachet of science is so great that it even seems to upset the traditional hierarchy of sex roles. When the men get ready to climb down into the ants' nest,

Big-bug films like *Them!* put scientists in the center of the picture. Here, Dr. Edmund Gwenn explains the habits of ants to a room full of bureaucrats and brass.

Pat Medford wants to go along. "It's no place for you or any other woman," says agent Graham manfully, but she puts up a fight. "Somebody with scientific knowledge, a trained observer, has to go," she says, and not only does she have her way, she takes over, ordering the men to torch the queen's chamber. Far from resisting her power, agent Graham falls in love with her, raising the prospect that the alliance between science and the military, or, in this case, the law, will be ratified by marriage.

Often, in films like *Them!*, the military was not able to use its big guns because it was fighting on its own turf. Even the army, eager to bomb the ants in the desert, hesitated to nuke Los Angeles, so that the search for the appropriate weapon, more discriminating and selective than the H-bomb, became a major theme in corporate-liberal sci-fi, a distant echo of the fight within the defense establishment over big bombs or tactical nuclear weapons. The search for a flexible, limited response to the alien threat reflected corporate liberals' uneasiness with the all-or-nothing strategy of massive retaliation championed by conservatives like Dulles. In *Them!*, the appropriate weapon is gas, not guns; in *The Beginning of the End*, it is sound, not bombs, a sonar imitation of the grasshoppers' mating call, that lures them to a watery death in Lake Michigan.

While the scientists and soldiers were quarreling among themselves over the appropriate weapon, another group of scientists and soldiers was having its own troubles up north, in Howard Hawks's *The Thing* (1951). This film was based on a 1938 novella called *Who Goes There?* by John W. Campbell. Like *Them!*, *The Thing* is not only preoccupied with hierarchies of authority, the authority of groups, and groups in conflict, but also with the struggle between science and the military, and the nature of aliens. *The Thing*, however, is a conservative film, and so the outcome of these conflicts is somewhat different.

When Air Force Capt. Pat Hendry (Kenneth Tobey) arrives in a remote Arctic outpost of scientists to help them investigate a strange item buried in the ice, he finds an enormous object apparently shaped like a frying pan. His men fan out around it and quickly find that they have made a circle. "We found a flying saucer," someone shouts, and indeed they have. "This isn't any metal I know," says another, examining a fin protruding from the ice.

But Hendry's problems are just beginning, because it seems that the passenger aboard the saucer has survived; it is the Thing-from-Another-World, as the ads put it, and it lives on blood. As if this weren't bad enough, Hendry discovers that the head scientist at the base, Nobel Prize-winner Dr. Carrington (Robert Cornthwaite), is almost as dangerous as the Thing, much as Wyatt Earp in *Clementine* discovers that he has to deal with Doc Holliday before he can face the Clantons. We're tipped off right away by his goatee (facial hair in the fifties was about as popular as bad breath) and his Russian-style fur hat. When he's not wearing that, he's attired in a dressing gown and ascot, a thinking man's David Niven, out of place among the rough-and-tumble soldiers.

Carrington is no Medford. He's a borderline mad scientist, and in *The Thing* the tension between science and the military that was latent in *Them!* not only becomes much more pronounced, it is resolved in favor of the military. FBI agent Bob Graham complained in *Them!* that he couldn't understand the Medfords because they used too many big words ("Why don't we all talk English?" he says testily), but Graham was something of a clod anyway, and if he couldn't make out their technical lingo, it was probably his own fault. But when Captain Hendry asks a question and gets only mumbo jumbo in return, it's another matter. "You lost me," he says, and this time it's the scientists' fault, a symptom of technocratic arrogance. In *Them!*, Medford's admiration for the "wonderful and intricate engineering" of the ants' nest is reasonable, not unseemly or unpatriotic. But in *The Thing*, Dr. Carrington's scientific curiosity is given a sinister twist. He develops an altogether unhealthy interst in the Thing. "It's wiser than we are," he says. "If only we could communicate with it, we could learn secrets hidden from mankind." Whereas Medford merely restrains the military because he wants to find out if the queen is dead, Carrington betrays it, defecting to the Other side. He helps the Thing reproduce itself, finds a nice warm spot in the greenhouse for it to lay its spores, and even sabotages Hendry's attempts to kill it.

Carrington's scientific disinterest, which reflects the value-free pragmatism of the corporate liberals, is regarded as appeasement. "There are no enemies in science, only phenomena to be studied," he says, but he's wrong. There are no neutrals. When he rushes up to the Thing, alien groupie that he is, crying, "I'm your friend," it swats him aside like a fly. The enemy is remorseless and cruel; negotiations with it are useless, and those who try are self-deceiving at best. Carrington is an unreliable element—private, moody, reclusive. He's soft on aliens, a Thing-symp, the J. Robert Oppenheimer of the Arctic base. The genial scientist and expert of *Them!* is transformed into an extremist "egghead," a head-over-heart zealot, a

In *The Thing*, soldier Kenneth Tobey *(left)* calls the shots, not Thing-symp scientist Robert Cornthwaite (with goatee), who nurtures the alien's spores.

man who can't be trusted because "he doesn't think like we do," a man who has contempt for the average and is therefore dangerous. Unlike Dr. Medford, Carrington is derided as a genius or superman. "These geniuses," says Hendry with contempt. "They're just like nine-year-olds playing with a new fire engine."* Carrington's behavior justifies the soldiers' mistrust of science, even turns them against the Bomb itself. "Knowledge is more important than life. We split the atom," Carrington shouts in a transport

---

*Notice that conservatives caricatured corporate liberals in two ways. In *Fort Apache* and *From Here to Eternity*, the corporate liberal is portrayed as an ambitious organization man, while in *The Thing*, he is depicted as a subversive genius. These contrary characterizations corresponded to the contradiction in pluralism alluded to earlier that pitted elitism against the group.

of enthusiasm. "That sure made everybody happy," comes the sour reply from one of Hendry's men.

But even here, science is by no means rejected wholesale. There are good scientists as well as bad, Tellers as well as Oppenheimers, and the difference between them is that the good scientists side with and defer to Hendry, instead of Carrington. Carrington's real crime, that is to say, worse than consorting with the enemy, is setting his own authority against that of the military. As in *Panic*, it is a question of turf. Hendry's appearance at the base signals a change in command like the ones in *Twelve O'Clock High* and *Flying Leathernecks*, and the figurative one in *Clementine*. When he first arrives, he is warned that he is treading on alien territory. "Dr. Carrington is in charge here," says one of the scientists. Hendry's job is to seize control of the base and assert the authority of the soldiers over the scientists. Eventually confined to his quarters, Carrington shouts, echoing the mayor and reporter in *Panic*, "You have no authority here," but when one of Hendry's men pokes a revolver in his face, Carrington learns that power grows out of the barrel of a gun.

And what about the people, the average Joes and plain Janes who are neither scientists nor soldiers? In *Them!*, it seems that they are almost as much of a problem as the ants themselves. They spend most of their time in films like this fleeing for their lives, obstructing the best efforts of the government to save them from themselves. Occasionally they pause long enough to riot, destroying valuable scientific equipment or medical supplies. Since the people are helpless to help themselves, the war against the ants has to be carried on by experts behind closed doors. In one scene, pilot Fess Parker, who has seen a queen in flight winging her way west to Los Angeles, has been thrown into a loony bin. The doctors and the local authorities, who have been kept in the dark by the scientists and soldiers, think he's crazy. When agent Graham questions him, it becomes clear that he isn't nuts—the pilot did see the flying queen—but nevertheless, he is not vindicated, as he would be in a radical film. On the contrary, Graham tells the doctors to keep him locked up in the hospital, his therapeutic prison: "Your government would appreciate it if you kept him here." Reporters, as in *Panic*, threaten official secrecy. Like their readers, they have to be kept in the dark. "Do you think all this hush-hush is necessary?" someone asks Dr. Medford. "I certainly do," he replies. "I don't think there's a police force in the world that could handle the panic of the people if they found out what the situation is." When it's no longer possible to cover up the facts, and the ants are strolling down Sunset Boulevard, the mayor of Los Angeles finally calls a press conference, but "there is no time for questions."

There is bad blood between the authorities and the press in *The Thing* too, but this conflict is resolved differently than it is in *Them!* A nosy reporter named Scotty (Douglas Spencer) realizes there's a big story afoot, and he wants to tag along. "This is Air Force information," says Hendry, refusing to let Scotty near the saucer. "The whole world wants to know," replies Scotty, sketching in the Big Picture for Hendry. But here, Big Picture-ism fails. "I work for the Air Force, not the world," snaps Hendry, voicing the conservative preference for the concrete and local over the abstract and general. But instead of the reporter being thrown in jail, an amiable arrangement is reached. Scotty is allowed to accompany Hendry to the Arctic base in exchange for agreeing to withhold the story until he gets permission from the authorities to release it. And at the end of the film, when he does tell part of the story in a broadcast to the world, he is allowed to speak for everyone, Hendry and Carrington, the soldiers and the scientists. As the voice of the center, he goes out of his way to pay special tribute to Carrington (who by this time has learned his lesson), papering over the differences that factionalized the group, as Fonda does in 12 *Angry Men* and York does in *Fort Apache*. Once again, the center closes ranks before the world.

Scotty can be accommodated more easily than the reporters in *Panic* and *Them!*, because *The Thing* is more populist. Within the community of soldiers and scientists at the base, relationships are more egalitarian than they are in similar communities in corporate-liberal films. When Tex, one of Hendry's men, enters a room and sees the group mobilizing against the Thing, he quips, "What's up? It looks like a lynching party." In corporate-liberal films that regard people acting on their own as mobs or would-be vigilantes, it would be; here, it's not. Hendry may give the orders, but a number of ideas bearing on the disposal of the Thing originate with others, are adopted by Hendry, and ultimately work. Even the best lines of what for sci-fi is an unusually talky script (by Charles Lederer) are democratically distributed among the officers, noncoms, civilians, and (one) woman alike. There is a good deal of overlapping dialogue; people continually interrupt one another with wisecracks and good-natured insults.

There is a real sense of community, of people engaged in a common effort, which nevertheless doesn't prevent them from expressing their individuality.

If people in *Them!* obstruct authority, authority in *The Thing* frustrates people. The conflict between soldiers and scientists is complemented by another, this one between Hendry, his superior officer General Fogarty in Anchorage, and the brass back in Washington. Hendry begins his odyssey as the perfect Air Force organization man. He can't blow his nose without clearing it first with headquarters. Not only won't he allow Scotty to wire his paper without authorization from Fogarty, but Fogarty himself has to refer back to Washington. "That's what I like about the Air Force," quips Scotty, "smart all the way to the top."

The critique of bureaucracy, an obligatory preoccupation of conservative films, is given some new twists in science fiction. The absurdity of "going by the book," the limitations of "standard operating procedure," are never more apparent than when you're dealing with flying saucers and little green men. When Hendry goes by the book, it's a recipe for disaster. Using standard operating procedure to free the saucer from the ice, he accidentally blows it up with thermite. The film is filled with jokes about military bureaucracy. As the men stare at the frozen saucer, someone recalls that the Air Force dismissed UFOs as "a mild form of mass hysteria," but in *The Thing*, the masses aren't hysterical. On the contrary, the problem is the brass. Red tape, finally, immobilizes Hendry altogether. "Until I receive my instructions from my superior officers about what to do," he says, "we'll have to mark time."

When the orders finally do come, they are worthless. Although the Thing has been making Bloody Marys out of the boys at the base, Fogarty instructs Hendry to "avoid harming the alien at all costs." Like York in *Fort Apache* and Sergeant Warden in *From Here to Eternity*, Hendry is forced to disobey orders, even at the risk of court-martial. He can't go too far, like Carrington, but he has to do something, because the organization is out of touch with reality. And reality here is not national and abstract, but local and concrete. The problem has to be resolved on the spot. Like most conservative films, *The Thing* ultimately deals with the problem without calling in the federal government. The Thing is dispatched by means of a do-it-yourself electric chair, improvised out of the materials at hand. But what keeps this from being a right-wing execution is that although the men at the base do it themselves, they are still soldiers employed by the government, working ultimately in its interests. By this kind of sleight of hand, conservative films avoided having to make the either/or choice Whyte presented to his organization man. For all the ambivalence *The Thing* expresses toward the Air Force, Hendry's rebellion, like York's in *Fort Apache* and Warden's in *From Here to Eternity*, is confined to the parameters of the organization. He remains an Air Force man to the last.

What about the Thing itself, and the ants? What do they "represent"? First, on a level so obvious that it is usually ignored, the ants represent an attack by nature on culture. Nature, for all mankind's technological expertise, is still a threat, red in tooth and claw. But the anthropomorphic gravity of American films is so strong that they have difficulty dramatizing genuine otherness. Aliens, no matter how seemingly strange and exotic, end up resembling humans in one way or another. It would be hard to imagine anything more Other than, say, giant ants, until Dr. Medford explains that "ants are savage, ruthless, and courageous fighters. They are the only creatures on earth aside from man who make war. Ants campaign, they are chronic aggressors, they make slaves of those they can't kill." In other words, the humans of *Them!* find that their adversaries are very much like Us.

If the ants are like humans, which humans are they like? In 1954, when *Them!* was made, those humans that Americans regarded as antlike, which is to say, behaved like a mass, loved war, and made slaves, were, of course, Communists, both the Yellow Hordes that had just swamped GIs with their human waves in Korea, and the Soviets, with their notorious slave-labor camps. Sci-fi films that presented Communists directly, like *Invasion U.S.A.* and *Red Planet Mars*, were rare. The analogy was usually oblique, but so close to the surface (in *The Naked Jungle*, also released in 1954, the ants that climbed all over Charlton Heston were actually red, and attacked private property to boot) as to be just below the level of consciousness. Presenting Reds as ants or aliens served to establish their Otherness. As Gerhart Niemeyer of Notre Dame put it, the Red mind "shares neither truth nor logic nor morality with the rest of mankind."[26] They were *not* just like Us.

To corporate liberals, Russians in turn stood for the eruption of primitive aggressive behavior. Reds, in other words, were monsters from the id. If we press *Them!* a little further, it quickly becomes apparent that the ants are not only Reds, they're females. *Them!* has as much to do with the sex war as it does the cold war. The film's attack on extremism becomes an attack on women in a man's world.

Centrist films, as we have seen, feared the eruption of nature within culture and were therefore afraid of sex and mistrusted women, particularly sexual women. In *Forbidden Planet*, we recall that the Skipper made Alta exchange her skimpy tennis dress for a long gown and put an end to her promiscuous kissing. The monster from the id, nature within, was provoked by Alta's burgeoning sexuality. Like Natalie Wood in *Bombers B-52*, she had become "restless."

Them! balances somewhat contradictory attitudes toward sex and sex roles. On the one hand, as we have seen, it explicitly presents an independent woman scientist, whose strong will prevails over agent Graham's this-is-no-place-for-a-woman conservatism. On the other hand, it implicitly presents, in slightly disguised form, a paranoid fantasy of a world dominated by predatory females. The ant society is, after all, a matriarchy presided over by a despotic queen. The queen, it seems, strikes only at patriarchy. Not only does she kill the male drones, but all her human victims are male (one man's phallic shotgun is bent like a paper clip), including two fathers. When the ants are finally cornered, they take cover in Los Angeles's womblike storm drains that conceal the queen's "egg chamber." "Burn'em out," is the verdict of the male scientists and soldiers at the end of the film, as they perform a hysterectomy by flamethrower.

Them! examines on a fantasy level and on an apocalyptic scale what it leaves unexamined on the "realistic" level: the conflict between Pat Medford's independence and the chauvinism of the men. It conveys two complementary cautionary messages. To men the moral is: Better give an inch than lose a mile, better let Pat Medford assert herself, or face a far more serious challenge to male power in the future. To women: Don't be too assertive or you'll be punished for it. Centrist films often defined and negated the extremes, the limits of behavior, leaving it to the audience to negotiate an acceptable compromise within those limits.

Like *Them!*, *The Thing* in its most abstract aspect depicts nature's inhuman assault on civilization. The vast, bleak Arctic wastes play the same role here that the desert plays in *Them!* The film's final lines, the celebrated injunction to "watch the skies," ask us not only to fear that which comes from space, but space itself, absence, emptiness, the negation of culture. Like the expanse of ice, the sky is an image of Otherness, and that which is not-culture is dystopian. By contrast, enclosures, manu-factured spaces, mean safety. The tiny Arctic base does not feel claustro-phobic, nor is it experienced as a prison; rather it becomes a fortress of human warmth, albeit a fragile one, easily destroyed, like the trailer in *Them!*

Like the ants, the Thing bears multiple meanings. The Russians imme-diately come to mind. Hendry actually speculates early on that the puzzling occurrences in the Arctic "could be the Russians—they're all over the pole like flies." But Hendry finds out that the problem is *not* the Russians, but the Thing—or does he? What is the Thing? Despite the fact that it is apparently part of the natural world, more vegetable than mineral, the Thing is a robot. Some films rendered the distinction between nature and culture as one between animals and vegetables, where vegetables take on the characteristics usually associated with machines: they don't feel pain, have no emotions, and aren't retarded by moral scruples. In *Invasion of the Brain Eaters* (1958), for example, once the plantlike parasites have taken over, people become "like robots—machines taking orders." But the Thing, like the ants in *Them!*—like most film symbols—"depends on associations, not a consistent code,"[27] as critic Raymond Durgnat puts it. It slips and slides from one meaning to another. Although the Thing is supposed to be an entirely alien form of life, it looks like nothing more unusual than a large man. Which man is it like? Carrington, of course, the Thing's pal, the cold, unfeeling genius who is as superior to his colleagues as the Thing is smarter than garden-variety humans, and whose development has not been, as someone says of the Thing, "handicapped by emotional or sexual factors." (In one version of the script, Carrington is actually killed by the Thing, and Scotty says, "Both monsters are dead.") Carrington, as we have seen, is a pluralist mad scientist, but with his beard and Soviet-style fur hat, he is also a Russian, so we have come full circle. This film attacks pluralists by equating them with Reds. And if a film like *Them!*, through its linkage of nature, ants, women, and Russians, imagines Reds as monsters from the id, conservatives imagined them as emotionless veggies or robots, repressive, not eruptive. They represented reason run amok; they were monsters from the superego.

Finally, however, conservative films fell in line behind their corporate-liberal allies in time for the final fade-out. In *The Thing*, this means that although the blood-sucking carrot from another world is a head-over-heart veggie robot Red monster from the superego one minute, it is an extremist heart-over-head monster from the id the next.

When Hendry arrives at the Arctic base, before introducing himself to Carrington or investigating the strange "disturbances," he makes straight for the only woman, Nikki Nicholson (Margaret Sheridan). * First things first. It seems that the two are romantically involved, although Nikki is piqued because, on their last date, Hendry got drunk and took liberties. "You had moments of making like an octopus," she tells him. "I've never seen so many hands in all my life." If the head can get out of hand, hands can lose their heads, and Hendry has to learn to keep his to himself. "You can tie my hands, if you want to," he suggests, and in a bizarre scene, she does just that. As he sits in a chair, his hands safely tied behind his back, she pours a drink down his throat and then kisses him on the lips. In other words, she has to emasculate and infantilize him before he can become a safe and acceptable suitor. But the joke is on her. His hands aren't tied after all; he's just pretending, and at the end of the scene, he flings off the ropes and grabs her. Cut directly to a large block of ice bound with rope, just like Hendry. Inside the ice is the Thing, just as inside Hendry is the id. The ice accidentally melts, and the Thing gets loose, in the same way that Hendry escapes Nikki's bonds. At the end of the film, when the Thing is destroyed, the monster from Hendry's id is symbolically subdued, clearing the way for the union of Hendry and Nikki. The extremes of head (Carrington) and heart (Hendry's id), culture and nature, both represented by the Thing, have given way, once again, to the golden mean. But the denouement is a characteristically conservative one. As in *Forbidden Planet*, force, not therapy, is the solution to the problems of the self.

This confusing plurality of meanings is at least in part an expression of the center's inclination to reconcile contradictions, to be all things to all people. Conservative films, as we have seen, were torn between extremists on their right and corporate liberals on their left. They fought against and

---

*Women in centrist sci-fi often had masculine names, like Nikki, here; Pat (*Them!*); Steve (*Tarantula*); and Terry. They were just one of the boys, part of the male group that restrained the monster from the id. Pat Medford, we recall, leads the expedition to torch the queen's egg chamber.

borrowed from both in an attempt to achieve their own distinctive equilibrium. Both *Them!* and *The Thing* want soldiers and scientists to work together. The differences between the two films are those of emphasis. Each, in a slightly different way, equated the cold war with the sex war, politics with personality, the Russians with the id or superego or both. Each implied that not only did the Soviets pose an external threat and, worse, an internal one through unreliable, wrong-thinking elements like Carrington, but worst of all, they penetrated our very selves. We were all potentially extremists inside. As Schlesinger put it, "There is a Hitler, a Stalin in every breast."[28]

The Mind Managers

Invasion of the Body Snatchers and the Paranoid Style in American Movies

"At first glance, everything looked the same," begins the narrator of Don Siegel's *Invasion of the Body Snatchers* (1956), Dr. Miles Bennell (Kevin McCarthy), a general practitioner in a small town in California. "It wasn't. Something had taken over the town." The town is Santa Mira, and when Bennell returns from a trip, he finds that his office is filled with people complaining that their friends and neighbors aren't what they seem to be; they're imposters. "There's something missing," says Wilma, referring to Uncle Ira. "Always when he talked to me there was a certain look in his eyes. Now it's gone. There's no emotion. The words are the same, but there's no feeling." Similarly, Miles's sweetheart, Becky (Dana Wynter), thinks there is something peculiar about her father.

At first, Bennell adopts the therapeutic approach. "The trouble's inside you," he tells Wilma, and advises her to see a psychiatrist. "It's a waste of time, there's nothing wrong with me," she replies defiantly, but it looks bad for Wilma. When Miles pays a call on Uncle Ira, he's mowing the lawn as usual.

Were there not other stories like Wilma's, Miles would be ready to ship her off to the funny farm. But if it's happening to others as well, how can it be "inside" her? Dan Kaufman, the psychiatrist, has an explanation: it's an "epidemic of mass hysteria." We've heard that one before, and Bennell is convinced otherwise when his friend Jack, a writer, shows him a body laid out on the pool table in his game room that is almost a perfect reproduction of Jack. "It's like the first impression stamped on a coin," exclaims Miles. When Jack cuts his hand a moment later, the body develops a similar cut on *its* hand in exactly the same place. As if this weren't bad enough, Miles finds another clone, this time a replica of Becky. He summons Kaufman to look at the two bodies, but when he arrives, they've disappeared. "You saw it only in your mind," the psychiatrist says. "Stop trying to rationalize everything. We have a mystery here," replies Jack-the-writer, relying on common sense. Before they can decide which it is, the cops burst in. "I have a good mind to throw you both in jail," says cop number one, referring to Miles and Jack. But Dr. Kaufman intervenes: "These people are patients, badly in need of psychiatric help." The cops and doc argue about whether Miles and Jack are felons or patients, requiring punishment or therapy, but we know they're all wrong. In this film, the docs are sick and the cops are criminals. *

By contrast, all those who complain about their relatives acting strangely are members of relatively powerless groups whose perceptions are often mistrusted: women and children. Little Jimmy complains about his mom, Wilma complains about Uncle Ira, and Becky complains about her dad. As we have seen in *Them!* and *Forbidden Planet*, women in centrist sci-fi are either one of the boys or like children; as the latter, they fit the description of extremists: they are irrational, hysterical, and subjective; they see the world in personal terms, not objective and factual terms the way men do. But this film will take their side against the center. In *Invasion of the Body Snatchers*, it is women and children first.

The following day Miles's patients suddenly announce that they're all okay. Everything has returned to "normal," but Miles is left wondering what "normal" is. "How could Jimmy and Wilma seem to be normal now?" he asks himself. "Certainly I had done nothing to cure them." We're a far cry from *Panic*, where the relation of sickness to health was clear and unambiguous, and the doctor was king. In Santa Mira, there is illness without cause and recovery without cure. When Miles discovers an oversize "pod" ("They're like huge seed pods!") in his own likeness, the plot thickens. This irrefutable evidence removes the matter from the realm of the psychic for good. Becky, too, learns that she must have faith in her own perceptions of the world and not let experts and professionals mediate between herself and reality. Intuition and common sense are

---

*Miles is a doc, too, of course, but he's only a GP, and he's not operating in the capacity of a doctor. Before Jack shows him the body, he asks, "Would you be able to forget you're a doctor for a while?" Miles agrees.

pitted against expertise, which is seen as fallacious. Contrary to what the psychiatrist told her, the problem isn't in her mind, it's out there, in the real world. "I knew something was wrong, but I thought it was me," she says. In a pluralist film it would have been; here it's not.

Dr. Kaufman is not only wrong, he's evil. He's one of Them. The vehemence of the film's villainization of Dr. Kaufman is an indication of the degree to which radical films insisted on the primacy of the individual over the community vision. In conservative films, on the other hand, the clash is not so sharp. The psychiatrist in *The Beast from 20,000 Fathoms*, who spends several minutes trying to convince the hero that he didn't see the "rhedosaurus" that we saw him see, is also wrong, but he's not evil; he's just foolish. And in corporate-liberal films, the conflict is again sharp, but the decision goes the other way. In *Them!* poor pilot Fess Parker is imprisoned in a hospital despite the fact that he isn't crazy, which is to say that although the individual vision may be truthful, it is irrelevant to the good of the community and can, nay, should be overridden in its interests. But right-wing sci-fi, like right-wing war films, was in the business of validating individual vision, and consequently the rift between the public and the private was exacerbated. If centrist films dramatized consensus, right-wing sci-fi dramatized conflict, polarization and the antagonism between self and society. There was no question that giant ants were crawling about Los Angeles in *Them!*, nor that a homicidal carrot threatened to overrun the North Pole in *The Thing*. Everyone who had eyes could see it. The focus of these films was not the strenuous efforts of those who knew to alert those who didn't to the fact that there is trouble afoot, a blob in the basement or green slime in the attic. Right-wing sci-fi, on the other hand, focused on the struggle of the outsider, the kook, the end-of-the-worlder, to force the community to acknowledge the validity of the self's private vision, even if it violated the norms of credibility that govern the expectations of experts and professionals. Far worse than invasion, what these films anxiously imagined was the loss of community, the estrangement of the one-who-knows from those who don't, Us from Them.

Once the bond between the individual and the group is ruptured, normality itself becomes sinister. "It's just like any other Saturday morning," says Becky, staring out at the town square full of pod-people going about their business. And when Becky and Miles further realize that the cops and docs are podded-out too, they understand that the enemy is not the alien but the familiar, their friends and neighbors. The center and the aliens are one, which is to say, the paranoia of radicals is directed at the center itself.

But it wouldn't do to attack the center directly; those who did were immediately labeled "extremists," and so *Invasion* necessarily speaks an Aesopian language. The conceit of "take-overs" by aliens who assume human form, making people act like machines, was admirably suited to a sortie against the center, because it allowed the local druggist, the PTA chairwoman, or the cop on the beat to become the enemy, at the same time that they really weren't, because they really weren't themselves. Possession by pods—mind stealing, brain eating, and body snatching— had the added advantage of being an overt metaphor for Communist brainwashing, which had just turned GIs into Reds in Korea, and a covert metaphor for pluralist therapeutic authority, which operated by entering the mind and directing behavior from within. As in *Them!* and *The Thing*, Communism was somewhat of a diversion. It allowed those films to attack extremism in the guise of attacking the Red menace, to suggest that like Communism, extremism was subversive. Here, it enables extremists to turn the tables. In *Invasion*, therapy is brainwashing, and centrism—the docs and the cops—is subversive.

Once Miles and Becky recognize who the real enemy is, the battle starts in earnest. They try to call the FBI, but the operator tells them there's no answer. They phone the governor in Sacramento, but the Sacramento circuits are dead. They try Los Angeles, but the lines are down. "They" control the telephones. "I needed somebody I could trust," Miles tells us; "I figured my nurse was my best bet," but when they get to her house, it's too late. A pod is being lowered into the baby's playpen. The cops put out an all-points bulletin on Miles and Becky. The enemy is everywhere. Miles and Becky take refuge in Miles's office, only to be cornered there by Dr. Kaufman and Jack, now one of "them." Miles reaches for a scalpel to attack the pod-people, but changes his mind and stabs them with a hypodermic needle instead. It's the wrong weapon for this film, but he's a doc too, and old habits die hard.

Before Kaufman and Jack fall into a therapeutic slumber, they make their pitch. "People are nothing but problems," sighs Dr. Kaufman, but for those with pods in their futures, "there's no pain. [They'll] be born

Miles Bennell (Kevin McCarthy) and Becky (Dana Wynter) run from the real enemy in *Invasion of the Body Snatchers*—the business-as-usual townies.

again into an untroubled world." The pod society is the familiar mechanistic utopia usually (and rightly) taken as a metaphor for Communism. This is a world in which "everyone is the same," a collectivist millennium to which all citizens contribute, as they do here, systematically distributing pods in a parody of political activism. But to the right, this rationalist world in which the head rules the heart and people act like robots is the dream of the "creeping socialist" center, with its statists and planners, as well as the left. In 1957, for example, *National Review* publisher William Rusher wrote that "the Liberal Establishment . . . shares Communism's materialist principles."[29] As in *The Thing*, Reds and corporate liberals were the same, but *Invasion* does not then turn around and attack extremism the way *The Thing* does.

If the center favors the head over the heart, the right unambiguously favors the heart over the head. By contrast with the mechanical pods, nature-within is no monster from the id, but "natural" human warmth, normal emotion. When Becky at one point tries to pass for a pod-person, tries to merge with the crowd, she gives herself away by expressing her feelings, screaming when a dog is run over. In Freudian terms, the enemy here is not the id, but once again the superego, embodied by the rationalist authorities, the cops and docs.*

In *Them!* and *The Thing*, no one expressed a yen for utopias, except perhaps Carrington, and he was a villain. Alternative forms of life were simply monsters, while alternative societies, such as the matriarchy of ants, were dystopias. But this didn't matter, since utopian aspirations were realizable within the institutions of society, the as-is. Agent Graham will marry Pat Medford, and Hendry will marry Nikki Nicholson. But Miles and Becky have each been married before—and divorced, which is to say, both have discovered that their aspirations *cannot* be realized within society. Their dreams did not and cannot come true, because society is inimical to dreams and dreamers. It transforms dreams into nightmares.

Dr. Kaufman writes off their dreams, their utopian aspirations, altogether. "There's no room left for love. You've been in love before. It doesn't last. Life is simpler without it." To the right, the centrist solution implies giving up dreams and accepting life without them. The center is a dystopia, a wasteland without love, without feeling. Against this vision, *Invasion* opposes back-to-basics values. "I don't want a world without love or faith or beauty," wails Becky. The film is suffused with a nostalgia for the past, for the old-fashioned pretechnological GP, rather than the newfangled psychiatrist with his glib talk of "mass hysteria." It presents us with a vision of the perversion of small-town life. The family is no longer what it seemed; traditional bonds have eroded. "He was always like a father to me," says Wilma of Uncle Ira. "Now there's no emotion." Science has

---

*Since the superego, not the id, is the enemy in right-wing films, their women are more sexual than the male-identified women with masculine names in centrist films. If they are scientists, their profession is no more than a cosmetic veneer. In Sam Fuller's *Hell and High Water* (1955), somebody says of lovely philologist Bella Darvi, "What makes a girl who looks like that get mixed up in science?" Darvi snaps back, "Perhaps in your estimation I am a female. But first I am a scientist—and a good one." But she obviously hasn't read the script, which says: "We reveal as much as we can of [Darvi] taking her shower. . . . She looks good enough to eat—and the men know it. There's nothing 'scientific' about her; she is all female."

upset the natural order of things. Wondering about the peculiar behavior of the townies, Miles says, "So many things have been discovered in the last few years, it could be anything."

Invasion of the Body Snatchers is an activist film that dramatizes the need for eternal vigilance. Falling asleep is dangerous. When people doze off, become unaware, pods snatch their bodies: "A moment's sleep, and the girl I loved was an inhuman enemy bent on my destruction," says Miles, after Becky has succumbed to the pods. The film strives not to reassure, but to alarm, not to tranquilize, but to mobilize, both the audience watching the film and the audience within the film, that is, the psychiatrist whom we see listening to Bennell's story. For it turns out that the entire film is a flashback. The psychiatrist is from a "state" hospital, and it is he (rather than the "town" shrink, Kaufman) whom Bennell convinces that the danger is real. In the final scene, the doctor grabs the phone: "Operator, get me the FBI."

The end of *Invasion of the Body Snatchers* could be the beginning of a national emergency film like *Them!* or *Panic*. Here are the institutions of the center, the docs and the FBI, gearing up for martial law, preparing to nuke the pods or at least douse them with Malathion. The danger originates on the local level—Santa Mira is a hotbed of podsnappery—and from there threatens the urban centers. Help, on the other hand, originates at the national level, and from Washington moves to the heartland. *Invasion of the Body Snatchers* is beginning to feel like one of those radical films that scampers back to the center at the last minute, and indeed, the conclusion was tacked on by the studio against Siegel's wishes. The producers apparently felt that the original ending, in which Miles, eyes popping, glares at the camera and screams, "You're next!" was too pessimistic, which meant, translated into ideological terms, too radical.

Centrist films were optimistic and antiparanoid. They employed paranoid structures only to diffuse them, as in Lang's *Woman in the Window* (1945), in which the hero wakes up in the end to find that the nightmare world he has inhabited is *only* a nightmare. He's been dreaming. These films contained and transcended right-wing films, in much the same way that *Them!* assumes *Invasion of the Body Snatchers*, takes up where it leaves off. But *Invasion*'s framing story, insisted upon by the studio, works as a right-wing ending, after a fashion. What Bennell experienced was not a nightmare. But even more important, the new resolve, the common purpose that now binds Miles and the center, is based on *his* vision rather than theirs. The breach between him and the community that was opened up by his access to special knowledge of the alien is healed on his terms. He does not relinquish his perceptions, he is not convinced by the authorities, like the "loony" in *Them!*, that he is deluded; rather, he convinces them that his view of the world is valid, and what's more, he mobilizes them for action.

Both *Invasion* and *Them!* imagine attacks from exotic aliens, but the issue at stake in the two films is who's right, the individual or the group, and who commands authority, amateurs or experts, the people or the state. *Invasion* challenges the government's monopoly on wisdom and violence— the reassuring cross-cutting to Washington that characterized *Them* is simply absent. Individuals must not only act for themselves, they must think for themselves as well. The fact that the hero succeeds in convincing his neighbors he's right is not only an expression of the radical right's populist optimism, but also a rehabilitation of common sense, discredited by the center. The kook knows the alien has landed because he's seen it, and he has faith that what is evident to him is true.

We never see the counterattack against the pods, because that is not what the film is about. It is about the loss and restoration of community or, rather, the creation of a new community defined by the alarmist perspective of the right—as opposed to the business-as-usual somnolence of the center—and based on the integrity of the self. *

Left-wing films shared the right's aversion to the center, but because they were more tolerant of Otherness, they presented a dramatically different picture.

The Court Martial of Billy Mitchell seems to be an exception to this rule of right-wing films. Billy fails to convince the authorities that he's right; he's not vindicated, and a new community fails to coalesce around him. But at the end, he appeals over their heads to us, the audience, and when we look up and see the sky filled with bombers, we are convinced he was right. We are the utopian community of true believers.

Friends in High Places

The Day the Earth Stood Still, It Came from Outer Space, and the Suppression of Paranoia

It's a fine spring weekend in Washington, D.C. The year is 1951, and American boys are still fighting in Korea, six thousand miles away. The Rosenbergs are in jail, waiting to be executed, and before the year is out, a bootblack in the Pentagon will be questioned seventy times by the FBI for once giving ten dollars to the Scottsboro Boys defense fund. But the balmy weather makes it easy to forget all that. Kids are playing baseball in the park, picnickers are scattered about with their lunch baskets, flicking ants off their peanut butter sandwiches and dozing in the warm sun. Suddenly a spot appears above the horizon, pale against the blue sky. Is it a bird, a baseball—or a Soviet "buzz bomb," as someone suggests? No, none of the above. It is a flying saucer, and this will be a day to remember: the day before the day the earth stood still.

As the silvery disc streaks silently over familiar landmarks—the U.S. Capitol Building, the Lincoln Memorial, the Smithsonian Institution—pandemonium breaks out. Elmer Davis, H. V. Kaltenborn, and Drew Pearson, all real-life news commentators, take to the air to further alarm a jittery public. Police cars flood the streets, and at a nearby army base, tanks gear up for action. It's looking like a national emergency, and let it never be said that Harry Truman was asleep at the helm. By the time the saucer glides to earth in the middle of the Washington Mall, the authorities are ready. It is quickly ringed with troops, tanks, and the latest in military hardware: howitzers, cannons, and so on. It's better than "Howdy Doody," and the American nation watches expectantly over national television for the payoff. Suddenly a ramp extends from the seamless skin of the ship, and Klaatu (Michael Rennie), a tall, slender emissary from outer space, walks forth. The turrets of a hundred tanks swivel as one, following his progress down the incline. "We have come to visit you in peace, and with goodwill," says Klaatu, in excellent English, but as he pulls a "gift to your president" out of his tunic, a nervous GI with an itchy trigger finger squeezes off a round from his M-1. Klaatu falls to the ground, apparently dead.

But Klaatu still has a few tricks up his sleeve. He didn't come all this way to be shot to death by some earthling. The sliding door in the side of the ship opens again, and out walks Gort, a nine-foot robot. (Inside Gort was Lock Martin, doorman at Grauman's Chinese Restaurant, the tallest man in Hollywood.) Gort is entirely featureless, except for a visor in the middle of what should have been its face. The howitzers fire away, but the shells bounce off Gort's metallic skin like pebbles. The panel on the robot's face rises, and a laserlike beam flashes forth, reducing everything in its path to a fine black ash. Just as it seems that Gort is about to barbecue Washington, Klaatu raises himself on one elbow, shouts a few words in his own language, which sounds a bit like Swedish, and Gort is immobilized. The visor closes, and the beam goes back to wherever it came from. So ends a close encounter of the third kind in 1951.

Klaatu is carted off to Walter Reed Army Hospital for treatment. But before we can say, "Klaatu barada nikto!" he's all better and asking the president's aide for a meeting with a delegation of world leaders! He's not one of those diffident aliens who land on a farm somewhere in Iowa and take years to make their way to Washington or Los Angeles. Klaatu means business, and goes right to the top. "I want to meet with representatives of all the nations on earth." "That's impractical," protests the aide. "Our world is full of tensions and suspicions, and in the present international situation, such a meeting is impossible. I'm sure you know about the evil forces on our planet which have caused trouble," he says, referring obliquely to the Russians. "I'm not concerned with your petty squabbles," replies Klaatu, testily. But the aide is right. After all, he's the expert, and Klaatu is only an amateur. The president issues invitations to the world's leaders. The Soviets accept, only they want the meeting in Moscow. The British accept, too, but they insist on London. A general meeting proves to be out of the question. Truman, however, offers to meet with Klaatu alone. Never a charismatic president, and having just fired General MacArthur, he needs all the help he can get. Maybe Klaatu can teach him some tricks, lend him Gort to chase the Chinese back across the Yalu River.

But Klaatu won't let himself be "politicized" for partisan ends. "I will not speak to the representative of one nation and increase your petty jealousies," he says severely.

If Klaatu can't meet with the leaders, at least he can meet with the followers. He wants to "go among the people" to conduct a Gallup poll of his own. He doesn't trust the experts. But the president's aide forbids it, and Klaatu realizes that he is a virtual prisoner, locked in his hospital room, like the unfortunate pilot in *Them!*, except that he has little difficulty escaping.

Klaatu wasn't the only alien having his troubles. Some Others were having a sticky time of it in Jack Arnold's *It Came from Outer Space* (1953), based on a short story by Ray Bradbury. When the film opens, John Putnam (Richard Carlson) and Ellen (Barbara Rush), seated together in John's ranch-style home somewhere in the Southwest, are speaking of marriage, as couples often did in the fifties. Suddenly, they see a fiery object shoot across the evening sky. It crashes to earth at the site of an abandoned mine nearby, and John goes to investigate. There, in the middle of a crater, partially obscured by rock and sand, is a spaceship. "It's some kind of spaceship," John says excitedly. "It's like nothing we've ever seen before. This may be the biggest thing that's ever happened." But alas, before anyone else can confirm his discovery, a landslide buries the ship with tons of dirt. Thus begin John's fruitless attempts to convince the solid citizens of Nowheresville, USA, that creatures from another world have landed near their town. No one will believe him. He first encounters the folks from the center. Dr. Snell, an astronomer from a nearby observatory, makes no bones about the fact that he thinks John is crazy. "Facts, John, facts," he says derisively, echoing Fonda in *12 Angry Men*. "Imagination—the willingness to believe that there are things we don't understand," counters John. "Be realistic," returns Snell, and they're off, fact and fancy racing neck and neck along the ideological track. Like Miles and Becky, John finds the center's rationalism sterile and reductive.

Then there's Matt (Charles Drake), the sheriff. He already has it in for John, because Ellen is his old girl friend, and he's jealous. Moreover, he's not alone. John is a writer and an amateur astronomer, something of a visionary, and Matt lets him know that people in those parts just don't like him. John is not a team player. "He's more than odd," says Snell. "He's individual and lonely. He's a man who thinks for himself." John even lives apart, outside of town in the desert. The distance people live from town is always an index of their relations to the community. In centrist films, to live outside town, beyond the suburbs, is to be beyond the safe perimeter of society, and therefore to look for trouble. Those who live in the sticks are either villains, like the Clantons in *Clementine* who live all the way out in nowhere, or about to become targets of outlaws, Indians, Martians, and so on. In radical films, on the other hand, those far-out subdivisions shunned by soberer souls are just fine. Here, John's desert hideaway affords him the opportunity to make contact with other worlds. But the sheriff doesn't see it that way. "This town doesn't understand geniuses, you poking around out here in the desert," says Matt. "Putnam, you frighten 'em, and what frightens 'em they don't like." There it is again, the tension between the individual and the community, the hostil-

"It's like nothing we've ever seen before," says John Putnam (Richard Carlson), carried away by his enthusiasm for the ship from outer space.

ity toward geniuses voiced by Hendry in *The Thing*. Ellen, the town schoolteacher, and thus the vessel of culture in this film, is the prize in the tug-of-war between the nonconformist writer and the conservative sheriff. Matt warns John to lay off Ellen. She has, he says, "a responsibility to the community."

While John, Matt, and Dr. Snell are hithering and dithering about facts and imagination, geniuses and normals, the aliens are busy taking over the locals. They assume the shapes of humans, rendering what seem to be the genuine article affectless shadows of their former selves. "There's something wrong," complains one woman, alarmed at her spaced-out husband. "He never touched his food."

So far, *It Came from Outer Space* could be a right-wing film like *Invasion of the Body Snatchers*. The center—the scientists and police, the guardians of the community—are dumb bunnies with, so to speak, their heads in the sand. We're firmly behind John-the-loner in his dispute with the authorities. They think he's crazy, but we know he's not, because we know that in a film like this one, people whom the authorities regard as crazy are liable to be sane. Besides, we've seen the spaceship land, and we've even witnessed a number of take-overs from Their point of view— through the compound eye of the aliens, no less. And that's the rub. *It Came from Outer Space* begins like a radical-right film, but it is gradually transformed into a left-wing film as it becomes clear that the aliens mean us no harm. These visitors from outer space have merely gotten lost and landed on earth to repair their ship. "Don't be afraid," they tell John in a disconcerting monotone. "We don't want to hurt you. We have souls and minds, and we are good." Not only are we relieved, we feel sorry for them, because this accident has screwed up their chances for exploring the universe. They had struggled thousands of years to reach the stars, only to end up in the middle of a godforsaken desert someplace on Earth harassed by a bunch of dumb yokels. Moreover, they are only borrowing, not snatching, our bodies for the very good reason that they are so hideously ugly, by human standards, that they are afraid the earthlings will attack them if their true selves are revealed. "Your people and ours must be kept apart or there will be very great destruction," they tell John. And as John later explains to an incredulous Matt, "They don't trust us because what we don't understand we destroy. That's why they've been hiding behind other men's faces."

What John says about the aliens sounds familiar; it is exactly what Matt had said about the townies and him, only moments before: they don't like him because he frightens them. This suggests that the kind of equivalence that existed between Dr. Carrington and the Thing exists here between John and the aliens. John underlines his resemblance to the aliens when he jokingly tells Matt, "Wouldn't it be a fine thing if I was something from another world here to give you a lot of false leads." Ha, ha! John *is* like them; they *are* like him: metaphors for difference, dissent, resistance to the community. Like Communists, the aliens hide behind false fronts because Americans destroy what they don't understand. But *It Came from Outer Space* uses the conceit of visitors from another world to imagine a much more mundane but nevertheless prickly problem: the "egghead," the person who is liable to be investigated because he thinks differently, because he is sympathetic to alien systems of thought.

Like right-wing sci-fi, left-wing sci-fi polarized the center into a conflict between the individual and the community. The heroes of these films who saw the spaceship land or shook hands with little green men were also estranged from society, but the difference was that right-wing heroes were just average Joes. At the beginning of *Invasion of the Body Snatchers*, Miles Bennell wasn't different. He didn't think unconventional thoughts, wasn't equated with aliens, and while the film attacks conformity, it doesn't defend nonconformity, the right to be alien. On the contrary, it uses the concept of "alien" to derogate those it dislikes. In *It Came from Outer Space*, on the other hand, John Putnam was estranged in the first place, long before the lost-in-spacelings made their way to Earth. He is an Einstein, an Oppenheimer. Neither an expert nor a professional, he is an amateur, the genius that centrist films distrusted. ("Genius" is here associated with imagination, a world beyond facts that the center could not accommodate.) The special knowledge of the alien he comes to possess does not destroy his ties with the community, because he never had any; it merely ratifies a preexisting alienation. John Putnam *is* subversive; he is not interested in re-creating the community in his own image. Like him, left-wing heroes just wanted to get the hell out. Unlike the right, the left, as we saw in *High Noon*, was pessimistic about the posssibility of transforming the community into a utopia—another reflection of its bitter, disillusioned antipopulism.

Unlike the weirdos with their polyfaceted compound eyes in *It Came from Outer Space*, who, for all their good intentions, are too ugly for words, Klaatu is eminently presentable. Soft-spoken, mild-mannered, cultured, Michael Rennie, more Milquetoast than Martian, is surely the best behaved, most polite alien who ever hopped across hyperspace, so we know there's nothing to worry about when he gets loose. But when the authorities discover that Klaatu has flown the coop, escaped from his therapeutic hospital prison, all hell breaks loose. There's panic in the streets. "Man from Mars Escapes" reads the big, bold headline, splashed across the front pages of the capital's press. As Klaatu, now nattily attired in a business suit, walks down Washington's quiet, tree-lined residential avenues, he hears the hysterical voices of radio and TV commentators booming through the open windows. "A monster is loose," says one, and as we glide inside a rooming house to join the boarders at dinner, we hear

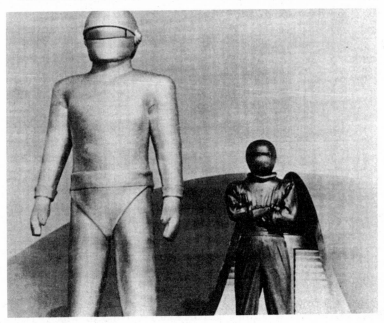

Alien chic: Klaatu (Michael Rennie), shown here with robot Gort, is neither a pod nor a blob but a deluxe model human, with some bad news for rowdy earthlings.

Gabriel Heatter, another real-life newscaster, his voice crackling with alarm, using metaphors drawn from nature to denounce poor Klaatu: "This creature must be tracked down like a wild animal. He must be destroyed." As Klaatu enters, unseen, the boarders are discussing the "monster." "What can the government do? After all, they're only people," says one. "They're not people, they're Democrats," says another. One woman accuses Klaatu of being a Red from Russia, but we know that isn't true because we saw him land, and besides, she's chubby and shrill. Another woman, Helen Benson, springs to his defense. Why do we assume he's an enemy? she asks. After all, it was he who was shot, not us. We know she's right, because she's slim and attractive. She's Patricia Neal. As the newscaster announces that "we may be up against a power—" the boarders turn, sensing an alien presence. Klaatu is standing quietly in the shadows. He says his name is Mr. Carpenter, and he wants to rent a room.

In case there was any doubt that Klaatu was on the side of the angels, the film equates him with Christ himself. After all, his adopted name is "Carpenter," he "goes among the people" with a message of peace, and he's crucified and resurrected not once but twice. When Gort revives him the second time, Helen asks, wide-eyed, "Do you have the power over life and death?" "That power is reserved for the Almighty Spirit," Klaatu replies solemnly, and explains that his resurrection is only temporary, subject to revocation by God at any time. (The scriptwriter, Edmund North, referring to the Christian motifs, later commented, "It was my private little joke. I never discussed this angle with [producer Julian] Blaustein or [director Robert] Wise because I didn't want it expressed. I hoped the Christ comparison would be subliminal."[30]) Bigotry against aliens by extension becomes the heathen denial of Christ.

Like *It Came from Outer Space*, *The Day the Earth Stood Still* pits the individual, with his or her unpopular, idiosyncratic views, against the center. The individual with the most idiosyncratic and least popular views is, of course, Klaatu, and he is joined by Helen and Bobby, a woman and a child, the Others who first blew the whistle on the pods in *Invasion of the Body Snatchers*. When Helen eventually finds out who Mr. Carpenter really is, she doesn't turn him over to the authorities like a patriotic citizen should; she helps him escape. She defects to the Other side.

Klaatu quickly makes friends with Bobby (dad died at Anzio), and together they make a pilgrimage to the Lincoln Memorial, which Klaatu had flown over earlier but had been too busy to notice. Now, gazing up at the immense statue of Lincoln, he's filled with admiration. Lincoln must have been a great man. "That's the kind of man I'd like to talk to," Klaatu tells Bobby (alas, poor Harry Truman), and then goes on to ask him who is the greatest man on earth. Bobby doesn't know what he means by "greatest." "I mean the best philosopher," Klaatu explains. "Oh, you mean the smartest man," replies Bobby, the light dawning in his eyes. "That's Professor Barnhardt—the greatest scientist." Barnhardt is a theoretical physicist who, as played by Sam Jaffe, bears a striking resemblance to Albert Einstein. Einstein was never a favorite of the authorities; he was even more troublesome than Oppenheimer. In 1945, Congressman John Rankin, an ornament of HUAC, attacked Einstein on the floor of the House of Representatives for being a "foreign-born agitator," and added that "It's about time the American people got wise to Einstein." In 1953, Einstein publicly urged witnesses before Congressional investigatory committees to refuse to testify. By making an Einstein figure a hero of sorts, *The Day the Earth Stood Still* was crawling far out on a very thin limb.

Klaatu breaks into the professor's study when he's not there, glances disdainfully at the blackboard covered with equations, and scribbles a few symbols of his own. When he finally meets the professor in person, he explains, "Soon one of your nations will apply atomic energy to spaceships—that will threaten the peace and security of other planets." He asks the professor to convene a meeting of the world's scientists. But the professor demurs, and Klaatu has to show a little muscle, demonstrate his power, "the only thing your people understand."

Klaatu is as good as his word. Precisely at noon, he sees to it that the earth stands still. Everything, everywhere, as we notice in a montage of scenes from around the world, comes to a halt. The professor is impressed; after all, he invented the atomic bomb, and he knows power when he sees it. He agrees to call the meeting. The subsequent congress of East/West scientists bears a passing resemblance to the Cultural and Scientific Conference for World Peace held at the Waldorf-Astoria Hotel in New York amid a storm of protest in 1949. While American progressives like Lillian Hellman on the inside tried to thaw out the cold war by talking to their opposite numbers, anticommunist pickets on the outside marched angrily in the streets. In *The Day the Earth Stood Still*, however, scientists who participate in East/West dialogues are not regarded as subversive. Klaatu has managed to turn the scientists against the soldiers by drawing Barnhardt out of the center. Barnhardt has become the Carrington, the scientist soft on aliens, but here that is good, not bad. In left-wing films, idealists like Barnhardt are not mad, evil, or foolish, but sensible. Utopians are realists, while "realists" are crackpots.

The Day the Earth Stood Still's respect for intellect makes heroes of professors and aliens (the Thing was smart, too, but in that film brains weren't enough) and creates a top-down hierarchy. The intellectual elite are the only people smart enough to hear Klaatu's message. Professor Barnhardt's secretary, on the other hand, is so dumb she tries to erase Klaatu's equations. Even though the military as an institution is discredited, rank still has its prerogatives, and the lower we go, the worse shape we're in. Like the cop who wants to shoot Jack Palance in *Panic*, here it is a lowly GI, not an officer, who acts irresponsibly and wounds Klaatu in the first scene. Down at the bottom with the secretary is Tom (Hugh Marlowe), Helen's boyfriend, the worst person in the film. Klaatu makes the mistake of using diamonds for money, and when Tom has them appraised, he's told that there are no stones like those anywhere on earth. Tom only sells insurance, but even he realizes that Helen's pal Carpenter, like his diamonds, comes from another world. Helen tells him to shut up about it, because it's more important than he knows. "Of course it's important," he replies, " and we can do something about it." If this were a right-wing film, he would do something about it, and this would be the beginning of the end for the pods and blobs. Tom would be the hero, the whistle blower of the right, like Miles Bennell, the Paul Revere who takes matters into his own hands and justifiably panics the populace. But the left, like the center, sought to avoid panic in the streets: the center because the panickers, although they were right, interfered with the government's prerogatives; the left because the alien was benign and panic therefore was just panic. In this film, the problem with the people is not that they are too rational, too reliant on head over heart, as a right-wing film like *Invasion of the Body Snatchers* would have it—but not rational enough. Brainy Klaatu, kin to the Krel, complains about the "unreasoning attitudes" of earthlings and says, "I'm fearful when I see people substituting fear for reason." As the Martians put it in *Angry Red Planet* (1960), "You are technological adults, but spiritual and emotional infants." Since there is no real threat in *The Day the Earth Stood Still*, Tom is just a jerk. He can't see beyond the tip of his nose. "I can write my own ticket," he says excitedly. "I can be the biggest man in the country. You'll feel different when you see my picture in the papers." When he goes off to inform on Klaatu, we're not with him, we're against him.

Tom's information is all the authorities need to nail Klaatu. Far from being sobered by Klaatu's show of force, they have become more agitated than ever. With Gort immobilized in a block of KL9T, a new plastic "stronger than steel," the army announces that Klaatu is wanted dead or alive. "Washington Quarantined," scream the headlines. Roadblocks are thrown up across Chevy Chase Circle, and Pennsylvania Avenue vibrates with the rumble of heavy military equipment pouring in from nearby bases. It's national emergency time again, but here martial law is the problem, not the solution. Like Miles and Becky, Klaatu and Helen find themselves fugitives, with all the resources of the center ranged against them. Finally cornered by the army, Klaatu is shot and again apparently killed. But no sooner is his body laid out on a slab in the morgue than Gort melts the plastic "stronger than steel" as easily as if it were an ice cube, seizes the body, and revives it in time for Klaatu to address the scientists who have assembled near the edge of his saucer. "The universe grows smaller every day," he says, making a lame start, but getting better as he warms to his subject. "Threats of aggression cannot be tolerated. There must be security for all." The scientists have to learn that the life-and-death struggle between war-mongering capitalism and Godless Communism is small potatoes compared with the global, even galactic question of nuclear conflict. Because if warfare among Them threatens Us in films like *This Island Earth*, in films like *The Day the Earth Stood Still*, warfare among Us threatens Them. At the end of *Angry Red Planet*, irritable Martians deliver a lecture to some visiting American astronauts virtually identical with the one Klaatu delivered a decade earlier. "Your civilization has not progressed beyond violence and destruction," they say. "Remember this warning—do not return to Mars." As the scientists ponder Klaatu's message, he delivers the punchline: "We have created a race of robots as policemen. They have absolute power over us. At the first sign of violence, your earth will be reduced to a burned-out cinder. Your choice—join us and live in peace or face obliteration. The decision rests with you." On that note, without so much as an "Are there any questions?"

Klaatu turns on his heel, summons Gort, and retires to his ship. The saucer begins to glow with an unearthly light, rises from the ground without a sound, and disappears into the heavens.

Klaatu has given the scientists a lot to think about, and while they're mulling over his words, we can look in on John Putnam, who, when we last saw him, had just realized that his neighbors didn't like him much better than they liked the aliens. Once John realizes who his real friends and enemies are, he stops trying to rouse the townies and begins trying to protect the spacies. John doesn't try to heal the breach between himself and the community; the community is too far gone. Besides, there is no need for the community to support the individual against the aliens, since in this film, too, the aliens are harmless.

The principal danger to the aliens, however, doesn't come from the sheriff. Although he's a little dense, Matt is an okay guy. But he's egged on by his deputy, who wants to take the aliens by storm. "I'd get rifles into the hands of some men and clean it up, whatever it is," he says fiercely. In a right-wing film, this fire-eater would be the hero, but like Tom-the-insurance-salesman, here he's just a nuisance. The panic gets worse as we descend the pyramid of authority. The deputy is more hysterical than the sheriff; the riffraff he rounds up for a posse are more dopey than the deputy.

Under these circumstances, John, now completely isolated from his own kind, has no choice but to throw in with the creatures. Like Carrington in *The Thing*, he tells them, "Whoever you are, I want to help you. I want to understand you," but unlike Carrington, he is not slapped down for his curiosity, for his idealism, for his utopianism; he is rewarded instead, both with their trust and with a glimpse of their "faces," which are indeed as hideous as they warned us they would be. A glimpse is all we get; by leaving the aliens up to our imaginations, by stressing that they are indeed unlike ourselves, but nevertheless benign, this film gives expression to a genuine sense of Otherness. Unlike the Thing or the ants in *Them!*, the Other is neither just like us nor bad. And like *The Day the Earth Stood Still*, this film suppresses hysteria and defuses paranoia.

In order to protect his friends, John is thrust into a direct collision with the center. He slugs the sheriff to prevent him from mobilizing a posse of vigilantes. He steals a police car and helps the pod-people escape. Like Helen Benson, by siding with the aliens against his own kind, he is going over to the enemy, defecting to the Other side. In the end, the aliens escape the clutches of the townies, and *It Came from Outer Space* finally comes out of the closet. There's no doubt that We are Them; the alien leader refers to the posse as a "mob," and the fact that he has taken John's shape confirms what we had suspected all along: John-the-oddball was an alien under the skin. But nobody in the audience is yelling, "If you don't like it here, go back to outer space," because by this time, we're all on Their side. When they do indeed go back to outer space, we feel sad. John, who gets his body back, waves good-bye, and we realize that we have just learned a lesson in peaceful coexistence.

In both *The Day the Earth Stood Still* and *It Comes from Outer Space*, Earth, not the alien culture, is dystopian. Their message is that Earth (including the U.S.A.), far from being the last word in civilization, as centrists thought it was, exists in a state of virtual barbarism. And we've seen this confirmed in the films themselves. Both imagine a utopian alternative to the center. Neither Klaatu nor the sympathetic aliens with the compound eyes are fleeing one of those advanced civilizations on the fritz, the ones that in centrist films invariably get themselves into hot water. Their people are not wracked by war, like the Metalunans in *This Island Earth*, nor are they victims of their own ids, like the Krel in *Forbidden Planet*. On the contrary, they are prospering. At the end of *The Day the Earth Stood Still*, Klaatu does not fall in love with Helen Benson, settle down in Chevy Chase, and become a consultant for Brookings, as he might in a centrist film, in which utopian values are immanent within society. He just picks up and heads back for the Milky Way, leaving the survival of "civilization" in doubt.

What kind of utopia does *The Day the Earth Stood Still* present? On the one hand, the film seems to project a technological utopia. We ooh and aah over Klaatu's bag of tricks, his high-tech spaceship, and his robot, Gort, with its rays and beams. As in *Forbidden Planet*, people—irrational and unreliable—let technology down. But technology by itself is not the answer either. There are two sides to Gort. He may be a Robby-the-Robot from Klaatu's point of view, but to mere mortals he's a veritable engine of destruction. When Klaatu is harmed, Gort runs amok, and his first move after his master is "killed" is to stalk pretty Helen Benson. Gort and Helen are, of course, a replay of King Kong and Fay Wray with one crucial difference, and here Sontag's observations on dehumanization are pertinent. King Kong, from darkest Africa, was the very avatar of a monster from the id if there ever was one, while smooth and shiny Gort, easily as dangerous, looks like it just dropped off the assembly line. Without the restraint of reason, technology is as dangerous as nature run wild. Like the right, the left knew that machines could kill; galactic cop Gort is a silverized pod-person threatening beauty and feeling in the person of Helen Benson. Once again, it's a monster from the superego. The left feared repression from above as much as the center feared eruptions from below.

Yet where Klaatu comes from, the robot cop is trusted. It is only on Earth (and here, Earth stands for society, as society stands for the center) that Gort is dangerous, only on Earth, the world of disharmony and intolerance, that Gort would menace Helen Benson, that technology and humanity, head and heart, are at odds. Where Klaatu comes from, Gort is either an obedient servant or a benevolent master—the film is not sure which—but in either case, the two work hand in hand, which is to say, although either/or radical films attacked the center's attempts to reconcile opposites, they often turned around and tried it themselves. In other words, both the covert utopianism of the center and the overt utopianism of the extremes tried to overcome the dualisms that bifurcated Hollywood films into clashes between nature and culture, the group and the individual, fact and fancy, and so on.

It is difficult to appreciate the impact of films like these three decades later, but in the fifties, as critiques of the witch-hunt and the cold war, they skated close to the edge of permissible dissent. The doctrine of peaceful coexistence emphasized in *It Came From Outer Space* was regarded by many in the fifties as no more than Soviet propaganda. But this film was fairly well camouflaged; with its topical allusions *The Day the Earth Stood Still* was on much thinner ice. Its worst crime was not taking sides, was lumping the United States together with the Soviet Union in its indictment of world politics. When Klaatu refused to meet alone with the American president, it was tantamount to treason. And when it recommended empowering the Gorts of the worlds, those who are above the fray, the neutrals who would shortly give Dulles ulcers, it was merely rubbing salt in the wound. Even apparently innocuous remarks had reverberations in the highly charged atmosphere of the cold war. When Bobby asks Klaatu what makes his spaceship go, Klaatu replies, "A highly developed form of nuclear power." "I thought that was only for bombs," replies Bobby. "It's used for a lot of other things, too," says Klaatu. By "other things," Klaatu was alluding to the peaceful uses of atomic power, but in 1951, Eisenhower's Atoms for Peace program was still some years off, and the only people talking about the peaceful uses of the atom were the Russians. Such sentiments were regarded in many quarters as more Soviet propaganda, an unpatriotic slur on America's nuclear arsenal. With all his talk about atoms for peace and collective security, Klaatu indeed sounded more like a Soviet agent than an emissary from outer space. Maybe the chubby lady was right after all.

Certainly, in these instances, the filmmakers were conscious of the ideological burdens of their films: "I wanted to have some meaning to it all," said Jack Arnold, who directed *It Came from Outer Space*. "I think science fiction films are a marvellous medium for telling a story, creating a mood and delivering whatever kind of a social message should be delivered. . . . If ten percent of the audience grasped it, then I was very successful."[31]

On the whole, science fiction, as a genre, afforded more freedom for uncompromising left-wing statements than, say, the war films, precisely because it was so thoroughly removed from reality, so well insulated by its own peculiar conventions. After all, it was "just entertainment," wasn't it?

CHAPTER FOUR

THE ENEMY WITHIN

Friendly Persuasion

Pods and blobs were by no means the only aliens with which American films had to contend. There were enemies within as well as without, and in many ways, those on the inside were considerably more dangerous. True, pods and blobs often seemed to stand in for domestic fifth columns of one sort or another: subversives, monsters from the id, or even predatory women. But these connotations were secondary, metaphorical, and it is important to remember that despite the fact that these films often blurred the distinction between inside and outside, they still presented themselves as confrontations with threats from without.

The external/internal distinction was an important one, because films reacted differently to each. For all the hostility *The Thing* directed at Dr. Carrington, he survived to be included within the consensus, whereas the Thing itself was killed. Centrist films preferred to portray aliens as outsiders and outsiders as aliens, because to admit that they were insiders was to admit that real conflict existed within society, when everybody knew that this wasn't true.

"Realistic" films gave up the charade and dealt directly with aliens inside society. These were the topical films that took their cues from the headlines of the day. Who were the troublemakers they focused on? Communists, of course, but also gangsters, juvenile delinquents, and minorities—blacks, Jews, Hispanics, and Indians. We will skip Communists, not only because the witch-hunt has been lengthily examined elsewhere, but also because the two hundred or so anticommunist films produced by Hollywood between 1948 and 1953, with a few exceptions like Leo McCarey's *My Son John* (1952), had little impact. The rest we will take up in turn, but before doing so, it will pay to look at what they had in common. Because the delinquents, say, in *Blackboard Jungle* or Nicholas Ray's *Rebel Without a Cause* (1955) recall the longshoremen in Elia Kazan's *On the Waterfront* (1954), who in turn feel very much like the Indians in Delmer Daves's *Broken Arrow* (1950). Despite their topical differences, there was an important way in which *Blackboard Jungle*, *Rebel Without a Cause*, *On the Waterfront*, and *Broken Arrow* were all the same film. Whether they were dealing with delinquents, dockers, or Indians, they all set out to solve the same problem: social control.

All films, both centrist and radical, influenced the values of their audience. Radical films tried to undermine or subvert mainstream values that the audience had absorbed from sources like school, work, family, media, church, and so on. Centrist films, on the contrary, reinforced these values. They encouraged viewers to conduct themselves in the manner society wished, and discouraged them from doing what society abhorred. In this sense, every centrist film was a social-control film. But in the films we shall discuss here, social control was not only a purpose, it was a theme as well. Sci-fi films like *Them!*, for example, let their audiences know that they favored scientists over soldiers, national over local, but they were rarely concerned with social-control issues per se. In *Panic*, the film's primary concern is the fight between corporate liberals and conservatives for domination of the center. Social-control issues—getting witnesses to cooperate with the authorities—are present, but decidedly secondary. Films like *Broken Arrow*, on the other hand, set out to manage unruly groups and individuals within society. They tried to stop bank robbers from knocking over banks, delinquents from stomping teachers, Indians from scalping settlers, Communists from sneering at the flag. We have had a glimpse of social control before—Henry Fonda marshaling facts and manipulating groups in *12 Angry Men*—but in the films that follow, social control is primary and explicit.

What was the best way to keep troublemakers in their place? In sci-fi, force was okay. No matter how long scientists restrained soldiers, there eventually came a time when the military had its way and the aliens were blown to smithereens. But what was good for pods and blobs wasn't necessarily good for delinquents—some of them nice, white, and middle-class, like James Dean in *Rebel Without a Cause*, or even blacks, some of them so light they passed for white, like Jeanne Crain in *Pinky*. Dean and Crain were almost like Us, and corporate liberals (and occasionally conservatives) realized it was shortsighted simply to write off dissidents—throw the gangsters in jail, send the delinquents to reform school, massacre the Indians, and ship the Reds back to Russia.

We have already seen that pluralists preferred therapy to coercion, talk to force. Force was a last resort because it contradicted the permissive, consensual model of society in which pluralists believed. Americans acted not because they had to, but because they wanted to. Force implied power, and power in America simply did not exist. Power was one of those pesky notions that neo-Marxists like C. Wright Mills were always nattering on about, with their "ruling classes" and "power elites." Look as they might, in every status nook and class cranny, power eluded the keen eyes of America's finest sociologists. "The multiplication of interests and the fractioning of groups make it difficult to locate the sources of power in the United States," complained Daniel Bell.[1]

In America, power was dispersed among the people, in which case everyone and no one had power. It was the bad guys, the Reds and Nazis, who exercised power, not us. Corporate-liberal films went out of their way to disguise, deny, or attack the idea of power, particularly naked, unconcealed power. Agents of power were either punished by death for using it, as in "power corrupts" films such as Rossen's *All the King's Men* (1949), Walsh's *A Lion Is in the Streets* (1953), or Kazan's *Viva Zapata!* (1952) and *A Face in the Crowd* (1957)—all covert anti-Stalinist films—or forced into exile, like Shane in George Stevens's 1953 film of the same name, who had to ride out of town at the end because he killed a man. Part of the fascination and exhilaration of sci-fi was that, unlike these films, it provided the occasion for the guilt-free exercise of power. Corporate liberals, who flinched when people were maimed, didn't bat an eye when pods and blobs were gassed, burned, nuked, or otherwise dispatched to sci-fi heaven.

The second and perhaps more important reason force was rejected as an instrument of social control was simply that it didn't work. It made things worse, drove dissidents into active rebellion, and over the long haul it destabilized society. Therefore, pluralists rejected the Big Stick and adopted a strategy of divide-and-conquer instead. Since they preferred to include rather than exclude, they tried to separate the good apples from the bad, salvaging the majority and expelling the intransigent minority of irreconcilables and *refusés*. Better that the have-nots pursued their interests inside the consensus than outside, making demands against it.

Dissidents were factionalized by judicious use of the carrot and the stick. First, it was necessary to locate and identify among the dissidents what pluralists, thinking of foreign policy, liked to call the Third Force, the moderate equivalent of the center at home, those who were neither too far left nor too far right. In practice, the Third Force usually turned out to be social democrats, nationalists, and "modernizers," Diem in Vietnam and the Shah in Iran. Pluralists employed the Third Force strategy at home as well as abroad, and domestically, the Third Force was often the ex-Communist informers who played a key role in the Congressional investigations of the fifties. If the informer was already a leader among the dissidents, so much the better, because pluralists were so infatuated with elites, they believed that once the leaders were "turned," as they say in the spy novels, the followers would fall into step behind them, and the job would be done. If none of the collaborators were leaders, and none of the leaders was willing to collaborate, leaders would have to be created from among those who were.

Pluralists were schizophrenic on the subject of leadership. Although they needed leaders for social-control purposes, they knew that if America were really the democracy they said it was, there could be no leaders. "Who *really* runs things?" asked Riesman rhetorically. And he answered, "What people fail to see is that, while it may take leadership to start things running or to stop them, very little leadership is needed once things get under way. . . . The fact they do get done is no proof that there is someone in charge."[2] Discussions of leadership took on the aspect of theological debates over the existence of God. Pluralist agnostics like Riesman would admit to a Prime Mover, a First Cause, but no more.

The creation of leaders was at once a strategy to snare the followers, a way of making sure that those who were turned would stay turned—as leaders they now had a stake in the system that made them leaders and were therefore more moderate than their followers—and a reward for coming in out of the cold.

The carrot was the key ingredient in the control recipe. Pluralists not only wanted to stop people from doing the Wrong Thing, they wanted them to do the Right Thing—go to the cops, inform on their fellows, bring an apple to the teacher, make peace with the white man—and they realized that rewards were considerably more effective than punishment. The carrot that made the stick unnecessary was simply the right to dream the American dream, with some assurance that at least part of that dream would be fulfilled. The hero who betrayed his friends, as Terry Malloy does in *On the Waterfront*, who turned her son over to the FBI, as Helen

Hayes does in *My Son John*, or delivered his people to the Indian Bureau as Cochise does in *Broken Arrow*, could sit down at the table with Ozzie and Harriet and be assured of a piece of the pie.

Since the use of force was out of the question, agents of control, those who persuaded the heroes of pluralist films to do the Right Thing, did not represent traditional forms of authority. They were not, for the most part, cops or soldiers, but our old friends the therapists, along with some new ones: social workers, teachers, clergymen, lawyers, and especially women, the hero's wife or girl friend. We recall that in sci-fi, women played a dual role: some were extremists, more intimate with nature than culture, but others, like scientist Pat in *Them!* or Nikki in *The Thing*, were the reverse. They helped to control the uncontrollable. Therapists and clergy were particularly well suited to this purpose, because each in their own way provided a model for informing. In both analysis and confession, the patient or penitent made public what had once been private, became transparent to the gaze of authority. Moreover, in both cases, the Right Thing is made to appear as if it came from within; it is experienced as uncoerced, a result of emotional or spiritual growth, "maturity" on the one hand or "salvation" on the other.

Pluralists made no bones about employing manipulative social-control techniques; they were doing us a favor. "We must ask anyone who opposes the manipulation of men in modern industry whether he prefers to return to their brutalization," wrote Riesman. "In my scheme of values, persuasion, even manipulative persuasion, is to be preferred to force."[3] Riesman had a point, of course, but it was William Whyte who put his finger on the problem: "No one wants to see the old authoritarian return, but at least it could be said of him that what he wanted primarily from you was your sweat. The new man wants your soul."[4]

Despite their aversion to force, when the carrot failed, these films had few qualms about using the stick. Those who couldn't or wouldn't join the team were simply Other—extremists: gangsters, crazies, Commies, or bad Indians. Their private, oppositional world was a dystopia, a jungle, forever excluded from the world of culture. They were beyond the pale, and if they wouldn't play with Us, there was no reason why we should play with Them. Pluralists made a show of using the courts to deal with dissidents, but in reality they didn't bother pussyfooting around their civil liberties, respecting their Constitutional rights. Extremists went directly to jail without passing "Go."

Controlling gangsters, delinquents, and Indians, getting them to do the Right Thing and preventing them from doing the Wrong Thing, was a small although pressing part of a larger problem: motivating people in general, getting John and Jane Doe to act as "mature" citizens of the center. We have already seen how centrist war films of the fifties tried to neutralize the demoralizing effects of peace, tried to mobilize Americans for the cold war in general and the Korean War in particular, tried to dramatize the national interest at a time when self-interest was paramount, when "sacrifice" was out of style, when public and private were out of step. In wartime, it was easy to assert the prerogatives of the national interest. General Savage in *Twelve O'Clock High* could tell his boys, "Stop thinking about going home. Consider yourselves already dead," and nobody said otherwise. National emergencies also required people to subordinate their personal inclinations to the needs of the state. In *Them!*, we recall, if a resident of Los Angeles wanted to take out his Olds 98 for a spin up the Coast Highway, he couldn't do it, because martial law had been declared. But peacetime was not wartime, and films couldn't pluck a national emergency out of the air every time they wanted their heroes to do the Right Thing. The demands of private life could not be just brushed aside. It was the Russians, after all, who subordinated private life to the needs of the state. It wasn't merely individualism that was at issue, because, as we have seen, pluralists didn't much care about that. It was the right to personal fulfillment, career and family, the "pursuit of happiness," that was, after all, the bread and butter of the American Dream. If private life and public interest were out of step, how could they be made to march together? How could people be motivated to do what society wanted them to do without using force, without becoming like the Soviet Union? How could society make Americans do anything at all? The way it dealt with dissidents—gangsters, delinquents, and minorities—gives us some answers.

Public Enemies: Gangsters

On March 12, 1950, the TV cameras started to grind, and Senator Estes Kefauver of Tennessee began summoning members of the underworld to testify before his Special Committee to Investigate Organized Crime in Interstate Commerce. By this time, Americans were used to Congressional investigations, the parade of friendly or unfriendly witnesses, talking or not talking, dramatizing their loyalty or taking the Fifth Amendment and then scurrying for a taxi, their faces shielded with a coat sleeve from the photographers who chased them into the streets. Usually, these witnesses were ex- or current Communists and fellow travelers, but gangsters like Frank Costello and Joe Adonis were little different; it was the same old song, although this time the lyrics were written by Damon Runyon, not Bertolt Brecht. When gambler Frank Erickson, for example, took the Fifth, he refused to answer a question on the grounds that "it might intend to criminate me." A Mrs. Virginia Hauser, suspected of being a gangland courier, wasn't quite so reticent. She yelled at photographers, "You bastards, I hope a goddam atom bomb falls on every goddam one of you."[5] The Kefauver investigation, in other words, was a good show, and before long, it blossomed into the *Roots* of its day, chalking up a good 30 million viewers, far and away the largest audience in the history of television. Crime was suddenly battling Communism for the headlines.

Hollywood tapped the crime craze with films such as *Hoodlum Empire* (1952), *Kansas City Confidential* (1952), *The Miami Story* (1954), *New Orleans Uncensored* (1955), *Chicago Syndicate* (1955), *The Phenix City Story* (1955), *Inside Detroit* (1955), *The Houston Story* (1956), *Portland Expose* (1957), and *The Case Against Brooklyn* (1958).

On the Waterfront

On the Waterfront was far and away the best of these films. (It won numerous Oscars in 1954, including Best Picture and Best Director for Kazan.) It harnessed the conventions of the social-problem films of the late thirties and forties—the drama of the common man rendered in stark, neo-documentary black-and-white photography on real locations with colloquial dialogue—to the purposes of the fifties: informing. The social problem it addresses is racketeering in a waterfront local. In the early fifties, waterfront racketeering was a fat target for government probers. The main culprit was the International Longshoremen's Association led by waterfront boss Joseph P. Ryan. Ryan's influence reached far up into the power structure of New York City. He held notorious annual dinners, attendance at which was obligatory for every politician in the city, the mayor and police commissioner included. But as we have seen, one gang was very much like another, and although Kazan himself did not draw an explicit analogy, *On the Waterfront*'s emphasis on informing, along with the political climate, made it inevitable that the film's subject would slide from waterfront racketeering to domestic Communism. It may have seemed like dirty pool equating the union thugs with the Communist Party, but the submerged analogy between the two made perfect sense. To pluralists, remember, both Communists and criminals fell outside the traditional Constitutional guarantees. As Sidney Hook put it, "Heresy, yes; conspiracy, no!"[6] Kazan himself went before HUAC twice, once on January 4, 1952, and again on April 10, 1952. He named names, told chairman John S. Wood, Richard Nixon, and other members of the committee that his former friends and colleagues in the Group Theater, people like Art Smith, Morris Carnovsky, and J. Edward Bromberg, were Communists. Kazan was one of the few major directors to throw himself enthusiastically into the witch-hunt; by publicly repudiating his left-wing past, by abasing himself before his accusers, and by naming his colleagues, he behaved not dissimilarly from the victims of the Moscow Trials whose capitulation cold-war liberals never tired of deploring. The punishment for defiance may have been greater in Moscow, but the fruits of compliance were sweeter in Hollywood.

The sweetest fruit of all, of course, was simply that Kazan was allowed to make films like *On the Waterfront*, rather than having to cool his heels in Mexico or Europe like so many of his former friends who refused to talk. *On the Waterfront* was a weapon of the witch-hunt, a blow struck in the ideological and artistic battle between those who talked and those who didn't. Many of its personnel, in addition to Kazan, like Budd Schulberg, who wrote the script, Lee J. Cobb, who played boss John Friendly, and Leif Erickson, who played one of the Waterfront Crime Commission investigators, had been friendly witnesses. One of Kazan's closest friends (whom he didn't name) was Arthur Miller, with whom he had worked on *All My Sons* and *Death of a Salesman*. In 1953, Miller's play *The Crucible*, a thinly veiled attack on the witch-hunt, was a smash hit on Broadway. In it, Miller had his central character, John Proctor, go to his death rather than inform against his friends. When Deputy Governor Danforth, his accuser, demands names, Proctor replies, "I speak my own sins; I cannot judge another. I have no tongue for it. . . . I have three children—how may I teach them to walk like men in the world, and I sold my friends?"[7]

On the Waterfront was Kazan's answer. It constructs a situation that makes informing the only reasonable course of action for the just man. This was not an easy task, because it wasn't only *The Crucible* that Kazan had to break. John Ford's *The Informer* (1935) had etched the features of miserable Gypo Nolan (Victor McLaglen) into the minds of a whole generation of American audiences. Gypo sells out an Irish revolutionary leader for thirty pieces of silver. "An informer is an informer," explains one character when Gypo is discovered. "He's got to be wiped out like the first sign of a plague as soon as he's spotted. He's a common enemy." As Victor Navasky reminds us in *Naming Names*, "Playing the informer runs against the American grain."[8]

On the Waterfront, and other films like it, tried to change all that, but not merely in the interests of moral reeducation. Informing in these films was the highroad to a greater good: social control. *On the Waterfront* presents nothing less than a pluralist paradigm for dealing with dissent. The first step is the construction of sympathy, the creation of good guys and bad guys. We're presented with two groups that are at odds with each other. How do we know which one we're supposed to root for? This is partly the job of the script and plot, partly the job of casting. The film heroizes one group and criminalizes the other. Father Barry, the waterfront priest, risks his life for no other reason than a passion for social justice. Edie Doyle, the heroine, is principled and courageous. The Crime Commission investigator is a benign, hardworking man whose feet hurt because he has to climb so many flights of stairs. He sounds more like an American Civil Liberties Union lawyer than he does the character assassins who played HUAC investigators in real life, and spends more time advising the hero of his rights than interrogating him: "You have every right not to talk if that's what you choose to do," the investigator tells him sweetly, and again, "You can have a lawyer if you wish, and you're privileged under the Constitution to refuse to answer questions that may implicate you in any crime." All these roles are performed by appealing actors and actresses: Marlon Brando, who plays Terry Malloy, with "the battered prizefighter's face, the slouching walk, the shoulder-shrugging gestures completing half-spoken sentences, and cock-sure, gum-chewing arrogance and the gentle, uncertain half-smile," as critic Penelope Houston describes him, is crucial to the sentimentalization of the common man, characterized by the poeticized speech and romantically blighted aspirations that Kazan learned from characters like Clifford Odets's Golden Boy.[9] Father Barry is played by mush-nosed Karl Malden, Edie by blond, angelic Eva Marie Saint, the investigators by upright Leif Erickson and Martin Balsam. It wouldn't do, say, to have Lee Marvin or Lee Van Cleef play the priest, nor a morally ambiguous woman like Barbara Stanwyck or Lizabeth Scott play Edie.

The other group is derogated as the "mob," and its members are clearly bad news. They open the film by pushing Joey Doyle, Edie's brother, off a roof, and continue their mayhem until the last frame. This characterization is also aided by the casting: snarling Lee J. Cobb as John Friendly, and hissing Rod Steiger as Friendly's right-hand man, Terry's brother, Charlie-the-Gent.

The second step is to define the extent of the problem. Corporate liberals did not take crime very seriously. It was indeed a "problem" to be "solved," and the solution, often the result of a little social engineering, technological tinkering, showed that reform was possible and therefore revolution unnecessary. To Daniel Bell, for example, waterfront racketeering was no more than a side effect of dockside congestion, which in turn gave rise to the occupation of "loading" (goods had to be physically picked up off the docks and loaded onto trucks), which came to be a major source of graft. The remedy? Wider streets! They, reasoned Bell, would allow trucks to drive right up to the ships, thus eliminating loading and the graft that went with it.

In real life, one of the many virtues of corruption was that it was a mechanism for defusing labor conflict. Management purchased "protection" from crooked unions, freedom from strikes and disruptions over pay and workplace grievances. Even Daniel Bell knew this. "Industrial racketeering," he wrote, "performs the function . . . of stabilizing a chaotic market and establishing an order and structure in the industry."[10] But it wouldn't do to suggest that racketeering might be endemic, not incidental, that it was a form of mutually beneficial and politically expedient collusion between unions, management, and the Tammany Hall machine, that graft was merely a way of lubricating and stabilizing the system. The connections between the particular and the general that might suggest structural contradictions in society had to be supressed. Kazan too is careful to circumscribe the tumor of corruption so that it can be neatly excised from the body politic without undue injury or embarrassment. Despite one rhetorical gesture toward generality (there is a "Mr. Upstairs," and a single shot shows him watching the Crime Commission hearings on TV), Kazan emphasizes the limited and exceptional nature of his subject. Lest this be misunderstood, he has one of his dockers exclaim, "The waterfront . . . ain't part of America." And not only ain't the waterfront part of America, but boss John Friendly's union ain't like other unions. "No other union in the country would stand for stuff like that," says Father Barry, the crusading waterfront priest.

The HUAC investigators who had just patted Kazan on the head might well have been expected to watch this film by their new recruit; in case they were deaf, as well as dumb, as many suspected, *On the Waterfront* is prefaced with a title:

It has always been in the American tradition not to hide our shortcomings, but, on the contrary, to spotlight them and to correct them. The incidents portrayed in this picture were true of a particular area of the waterfront. They exemplify the way self-appointed tyrants can be fought and defeated by right-thinking men in a vital democracy.

In other words, as children of the "social problem" films, corporate-liberal crime films acknowledged the problem, but what they gave with the left hand they took back with the right. These films operated dialectically, by first admitting, even accentuating problems like corruption or graft, only to limit and finally transcend them in a dramatic synthesis that is all the more powerful for its frank acknowledgment of blemishes on the face of the body politic.

The third step is to establish the frame of reference within which the problem will be resolved. "Corruption," after all, could be dealt with in any number of ways: moral, psychological, religious, class, existentialist, and so on. Class was a natural candidate in a film that deals with labor conflict, but prosperity, along with the witch-hunt, had made class struggle obsolete. Even so, it was wise to take no chances. The conflict in *On the Waterfront* is not between classes, not labor against management, but within the working class, labor against labor. When those on both sides of the barricades belong to the same class, no class issues can be at stake. And with class thrown overboard, the way is cleared for a priest (Father Barry), the government (the Crime Commission investigators), and a woman (Edie Doyle) to establish the terms that will define and circumscribe the drama: God, country, and family.

The stage has been set, we know which side we're on, we have seen the face of the enemy; the only question that remains is "how?"—how to bring the mob to its knees. The problem faced by the center is that no matter how bad the mob is, if it comes to a choice between the mob and the cops, the longshoremen will choose the mob. "On the docks, we're D and D, deaf and dumb," explains one docker. "No matter how much we hate the torpedoes, we don't rat." In the face of this kind of solidarity, force won't work. The force option is represented by the police, who are helpless. As the dockers crowd around Joey Doyle's dead body, a cop plaintively says, to no one in particular, "I know how you feel about cops, but if you could give us some leads . . ." The men fix him with stony stares, and he lapses into silence.

If the solidarity of the longshoremen is to be broken down, it will be necessary to identify the Third Force, the "responsible leadership" within the dissident community, and use it to drive a wedge between those who can be co-opted and those who can't. Terry Malloy is the character selected for this role. On the face of it, Terry doesn't seem like good leadership material. As he tells the Crime Commission investigators, "I don't know nuthin', I ain't seen nuthin', I'm not sayin' nuthin'." He just wants to be left alone. But Terry has a weak spot, an affection for pigeons, which he raises on the roof of his tenement. Although he's not a natural leader, this glimmer of humanity indicates that he can be "reached," made into a concerned member of society, a leader even, and that is a job for Edie and Father Barry, the agents of Terry's transformation from punk to hero.

Father Barry intervenes decisively at crucial moments to change the course of events. He precipitates the struggle against the mob; he persuades Terry to confess to Edie Doyle that he helped set up her brother, Joey, for his fall from the roof; he prevents Terry from using his gun to avenge the death of his brother, Charlie-the-Gent, at the hands of Friendly; he urges Terry to testify before the Crime Commission; he prevents the dockers from aiding Terry after he is badly beaten up by Friendly and his gang.

All these interventions turn out for the best, but any one could easily have been catastrophic. What emerges is a picture of a ruthless crusader who manipulates others like chess pieces in the name of a higher good for which no price is too high, no sacrifice too great. Why "manipulation"? Despite the fact that Father Barry's interventions are at times direct and forceful (at one point he knocks Terry down), more often they are coyly denied or disguised. On the several occasions when Terry asks Father Barry or Edie outright what he should do, what course of action he should adopt, they insist that it is up to him, to his conscience, that they cannot tell him what to do. When Terry bursts into Edie's flat, in a towering rage after Friendly has killed his brother, but still undecided about whether or not to inform, he yells at Edie, "I'm not going to do what you want me to do." "I don't want you to do anything," she retorts. "You can let your conscience tell you what to do." But invariably, this disavowal is followed by a moral imperative: "Do this or do that." In fact, Father Barry can barely control himself, and he'll have to go back to social-control school if he's not careful. Take this exchange, in which he forcefully, but obliquely, urges Terry to reveal his part in Joey's death to Edie:

FATHER BARRY: What are you gonna do about it? About telling her, the Commission, the subpoena?

TERRY: I don't know . . .

FATHER BARRY: Listen, if I were you, I would walk right—Never mind, I'm not asking you to do anything. It's your conscience that's gotta do the askin'—Edie's coming here. Come on, why don't you tell her.

Ex-fighter Terry Malloy (Marlon Brando), backed into a corner by Father Barry (Karl Malden), who turns him against his pals, dividing-and-conquering the mob.

"I'm not asking you to do anything," Father Barry says one minute, but the next he is urging Terry to confess. But Terry has to feel like his "own conscience" is "doing the askin'," which is to say, he has to internalize social control, experience his choices as coming from within, an expression of his own deepest desires, not imposed from without by moral and psychological pressure. Social directives must be perceived as freedom, not domination. As Charlie-the-Gent says, "This girl and the Father— they got the hooks into the kid so deep he don't know which way is up anymore."

Father Barry succeeds in turning Terry against John Friendly, but his job is not yet done. He has to guide Terry's behavior into acceptable channels. In one scene, after Charlie-the-Gent is killed, Terry goes gunning for Friendly, and Father Barry corners him in a bar. "You wanna hurt

John Friendly? For what he did to Charlie and a dozen other men better than Charlie? You'll fight him in a courtroom tomorrow with the truth as you know the truth. Now get rid of that gun." Terry is threatening to become a Frankenstein, an out-of-control extremist, a vigilante who takes the law into his own hands. But in corporate-liberal films, the arena in which these kinds of issues were decided was not the streets, but the courts, because in the hands of the individual, force is just force, whereas in the courts it is justice, and Terry has to learn this, too.

Revenge was unacceptable for four reasons. First, it was primarily personal, unrelated to the larger goals of society. Second, revenge was a feeling, not a thought. Third, it was genuinely inward, authored by the characters themselves, and therefore it was uncontrollable. And fourth, it was violent, involving force and implying power.

Revenge figures were invariably either villains, or outcasts who had to give up their quest for revenge before they were allowed to reenter society. There was Billy the Kid in *The Left Handed Gun*, whose credo was, "All I know is what I feel." Billy wanted to revenge the death of the man he called his father, and at the end he's shot down by Pat Garrett. When revenge characters were heroes, they had to transform revenge into a socially useful motive, like Terry, or purge themselves of their feelings, like Arthur Kennedy in Lang's *Rancho Notorious* (1952), who forgives and forgets after Marlene Dietrich stops a bullet meant for him. *

When Terry finally defers to Father Barry's wishes and agrees to channel his vengeful feelings, he joins the growing ranks of fifties heroes who plumped for gun control. Westerns in particular were full of tired outlaws who wanted to hang up their guns and settle down. They were afflicted with what critic Michael Wood has called the "anxiety of power." Often, the heroes did, finally, use their guns, but it was an uphill struggle to make them do so. In *Shane*, the eponymous hero is a fighter-who-won't-fight; he has to be insulted, humiliated, and beaten before he can bring himself to use his gun again. He has to be forced to use force, and when he does so, it is not in the interests of revenge.

The ultimate weapon in the arsenal of pluralist social control is the

---

*The uneasiness with which mainstream films view revenge was recently demonstrated when George Lucas had the title of *The Revenge of the Jedi* changed to *The Return of the Jedi* because revenge was a motive unbecoming to his straight-arrow Jedi.

treatment of utopian aspirations, the imagination of alternatives to the as-is. As we saw with sci-fi, in corporate-liberal films, the grass is never greener on the other side of the fence, which is to say, there's no place like the center. *On the Waterfront* presents a good dream and a bad dream, a good alternative and a bad alternative. The good alternative is Father Barry's City of God; the bad alternative is Friendly's mob. *

Friendly's mob is an ethnic grab bag composed mostly of Italians and Irish, with a few Eastern Europeans thrown in for good measure. As an *ethnic* enclave, the mob becomes a crime against the melting pot, against the WASP middle class and the Americanized ethnics aspiring to it. As an ethnic *enclave*, a cohesive subculture held together by strong bonds of solidarity apart from and resistant to the influence of the center, it becomes another affront to consensus, the neighborhood against the city, analogous to the small-town/Washington clash of other films. Ethnic enclaves like Friendly's were an anachronism, a throwback to an earlier period; they were out of step with the present, when immigrant groups were expected to take their cues from the homogeneous national culture transmitted by the media, schooling, and other instruments of social control. Ethnic ghettos were being dispersed by assimilation and upward mobility; the protective reflexes of clan and ethnic loyalty were, it was claimed, no longer necessary. As Christopher Lasch put it, the ethnic family "preserved separatist religious traditions, alien languages and dialects, local lore, and other traditions that retarded the growth of the political community and the national state."[11]

Terry is not too bright, and despite all this evidence to the contrary, he feels that the mob is a family. "They're askin' me to put the finger on my own brother," he complains, and then again, "Uncle" John Friendly "used

---

*The kind of alternative the mob might well have represented in a different kind of film is suggested by comparing *On the Waterfront* with *The Godfather*, made in 1972 after a decade of progressive disillusionment with society, culminating in Watergate. In Coppola's film, the Mafia is a mob very much like the corrupt union in *On the Waterfront* (in fact Marlon Brando's Don Corleone could well have been a benevolent, aging John Friendly), but it is romanticized into a utopian alternative to Nixon's America. Under the benign rule of the Don, people are accorded the justice they don't get from mainstream institutions, not to mention the warmth and nurturance provided by the close-knit, old-world ethnic extended family. But a lot of bombs had fallen on North Vietnam by the time *The Godfather* was made, two decades later, and in *On the Waterfront* the mob is not romanticized and it is not a utopia.

to take me to the ball game when I was a kid." But he's wrong. The mob is a false family; it destroys the family: Friendly first has Joey, Edie's brother, killed, and then Charlie-the-Gent, Terry's brother. Even the marriage ceremony, the celebration of the old-world community that later became the hallmark of ethnic films of the seventies, is a fiasco in *On the Waterfront*. In one scene, a wedding party in a bar degenerates into a brawl.

Far from being a nurturant countercommunity, the world of the mob is dystopic, about as bad as a world can be in a pluralist film: the waterfront is a state of nature, and the state of nature is a jungle, where life is nasty, brutish, and short. Much of the film's dialogue is filled with natural imagery. "Don't fight him like a hoodlum, here in the jungle," Father Barry tells Terry, and Terry himself refers to the waterfront in the same terms. "You know this city's full of hawks," he tells Edie. "They hang around on top of big hotels and they spot a pigeon in the park—bang! Right down on them." The predatory morality that informs the ethics of the mob makes strong claims on Terry as well. "Down here, it's every man for himself. Do you wanna hear my philosophy of life? Do it to him before he does it to you." "Living like an animal," replies Edie in disgust, relentlessly carrying on the jungle metaphor. But there's still hope: the pigeons Terry raises are different. They're the people of the animal kingdom. As Terry says, "They get married just like people and they stay that way until one of them dies." Terry and the pigeons are an alternative to the jungle; as we see, Terry and the pigeons are alike: in one scene he even snacks on birdseed.

If the mob fails to offer any real alternative to whatever shortcomings the center may have, it's not surprising. The center has very few, which is to say, utopian aspirations can only be realized within the existing institutions of society. America's confident sense of grace, its unembarrassed assurance that Americans were the chosen people, is evident in the film's lavish use of Christian iconography. As an alternative to Terry's dog-eat-dog/me-first ethic, it offers Christian compassion. Opposed to Terry's morality, in which the strong (hawks) prey on the weak (pigeons), is Father Barry's New Testament assurance that the meek shall inherit the earth. When the Father tells the dockers in one scene that "Christ is down here, on the waterfront," he's not talking through his collar. He is not speaking rhetorically or metaphorically, but literally. Friendly's victims sprout halos like mushrooms: Joey Doyle's jacket is passed from hand to hand like the Shroud of Turin; Charlie-the-Gent's body is crucified against a wall with a bailing hook. But the figure who really brings Christian transcendence down to earth is, of course, Terry-the-Christ-figure. He is well on his way to crucifixion before he testifies, when he breaks out in stigmata after putting his hand through a plate glass window. The real crucifixion comes at the hands of the mob, when he's beaten senseless by Friendly's boys, and Brando's menacing power is chastised, transfigured, and spiritualized. He becomes a martyr. In a democracy, in other words, power is not confronted with power, but with Christian virtue. When Terry chooses to inform, spiritual values become immanent. In Christian terms, he assumes the role of the dove (the meek); in secular terms, he assumes the role of the stool pigeon (the informer), and the two become one. As Tommy, his disappointed protégé, puts it, throwing a dead pigeon at his feet, "A pigeon for a pigeon." But he hasn't been watching: *On the Waterfront* offers us the informer as saint.

Once informing is linked, nay, equated with a higher morality, it is relatively easy to reconcile the public interest and private life. For a while, when it seemed that the mob was Terry's family, it looked as if public interest and private life were out of sync. To serve the public interest, Terry was going to have to sacrifice private life, his friends and associates. Although pluralist films did on occasion require this, they didn't like to, and in order to make it unnecessary, Charlie-the-Gent has to be killed by Friendly. Had he survived, Terry would have had to make a genuine sacrifice by informing on his own brother.* But pluralist films preferred to show that the contradiction between public and private was only appar-

---

*Kazan, like his fellow pluralists, was a complexity monger. He regarded his transformation from a Red in the thirties to a cold-war liberal in the fifties, from Marx to Freud (he was psychoanalyzed twice), from friendship and artistic collaboration with Arthur Miller to friendship and artistic collaboration with Tennessee Williams (from whom he learned that it is necessary for characters to possess a core of "mystery"), as a journey away from the infantile simplicities of the left to the mature appreciation of complexity characteristic of the center.[12] But, as Victor Navasky points out ironically, "Kazan-Schulberg leave no room for ambiguity in *Waterfront*." If Terry's informing had meant sending his brother to the chair, "then the dilemma posed by the act of informing would have been real." But by killing off Charlie-the-Gent, the audience is denied "any opportunity for genuine consideration of the ambivalent and dangerous complications of the informer issue."[13] So much for complexity.

ent, not real. Once Friendly kills his brother and Terry definitively realizes that the mob is a false family, once he recognizes that the mob has frustrated his dreams of success, sold him a "one-way ticket to Palooka-ville," the way is cleared for the marriage of public and private. Edie, with her promise of kids and a house in the suburbs, is the true representative of private life, and the only way Terry can have Edie is, once again, if he informs. By serving the public interest, in other words, he satisfies his self-interest, his private needs as well. The contradiction evaporates.

Edie incarnates a few utopian aspirations of her own. Most important, she legitimates the private goals thwarted by the mob: personal ambition, self-respect, success. In contrast to Terry's jungle, where hawks snatch pigeons off the streets of Hoboken as if it were darkest Africa, she speaks for culture, not nature. She's been educated in a convent school (the Church again), and plans to be a teacher. Edie represents the process of culturization, presides over the reconciliation of public interest and private life much as Nancy Reed did in *Panic in the Streets*. There, public and private are distinctly out of phase. Dr. Reed is called away from home in the first scene, rarely to return until the last. When he does drop by after a hard day tracking germs, the pressure of his work, his public role, makes him irritable with his wife. He won't let Nancy touch him because his clothes may be contaminated. And if public threatens private, private threatens public as well. Dr. Reed finds that his public-health job pays less money and confers less prestige than comparable work in the private sector. Reed dreams of working for an oil company in Arabia, but Nancy, here the agent of social control, convinces him that by serving the government, by pursuing a career of public service rather than "private" enterprise, he indeed fulfills his deepest, most private aspirations. "You're not a kid any more," she tells him. "You ought to stop thinking like one. Arabian pipelines! You're a pretty lucky guy right this minute. You did exactly what you planned to do when you were a junior in medical school. So stop feeling sorry for yourself." Three things are happening in this speech. First, Nancy tells him to give up his dreams (Arabia) because they're unrealistic. But second, he won't be any the worse without them, because there are other dreams (from medical school) that are being realized right in front of his nose, if he would only look. In other words, as in *On the Waterfront*, there are good dreams and bad dreams. Good dreams can be and are realized within the status quo. Bad dreams are those that make us dissatisfied with life-as-it-is, make us look elsewhere, to Arabia, for example. Third, the distinction between the two is rendered in the therapeutic vocabulary of pluralism. The bad dream is an indication of "immaturity" ("stop talking like a kid"), whereas the good dream shows he's "grown up."

Through Edie, Terry—already in his late twenties—finally "grows up." When Terry testifies before the Crime Commission against his old friends, his "family," it's not presented as informing at all, but rather as an exercise in self-knowledge, a sign of maturity. "I was ratting on myself all them years and I didn't even know it," he shouts at Friendly. Loyalty to friends is presented as an adolescent virtue, the province of Terry's teen-age pal, Tommy, who repudiates him after his appearance before the committee and kills his pigeons.* But Terry has gone beyond Tommy; he's leaving him behind, shedding him like an old skin for Edie, for maturity, responsibility, and adult sexuality. Informing is positively therapeutic.

Once Terry has been convinced that the center incarnates every conceivable utopian aspiration, while the only alternative is unmasked as a morass of violence and criminality, he has only one thing left to learn— that the schoolboy injunction against informing is relative, not absolute. Moral absolutes are, after all, the coin of extremism. Pluralists, more flexible and pragmatic, understood that it's just a matter of where you stand. As Father Barry says, "What's ratting to them is telling the truth to you." But relativism can only go so far, and once the film has relativized the claims of the bad guys, it proceeds to make absolute claims of its own. Church and state can come out of the closet and pit the Big Picture of Father Barry and the Crime Commission investigators against Terry's Little Picture. When Terry objects that he's being asked to "put the finger on my own brother," Father Barry counters with an abstract Christian brotherhood ("You've got other brothers"), while the Crime Commission investigators chime in with the brotherhood of Americans ("The people's right to know"), compared with which local loyalties to neighborhood and friends are narrow and parochial. Since pluralists applauded the state and the public interest in their films, the government could and did make

---

*In terms of the iconography of the fifties, Tommy's execution of Terry's pigeons is curiously fitting. To Riesman, homing pigeons symbolized the old, ethnic, tradition-bound society, which Terry, by informing, destroys.

direct claims on the hero, calling upon him or her to do the Right Thing in the name of civic duty, in turn equated with therapeutic values.

By the end of *On the Waterfront*, Terry has been maneuvered into more than betraying his pals; he has betrayed his own class as well. The values that replace his old ones are mainstream, middle-class values disguised as morality, and the lesson the film teaches is that it is smart to climb out of your class. There's nothing at the bottom except long hours and low pay. Edie will make use of her college education and move up, taking Terry with her. After the spasm of reform has subsided, Terry, if he is still alive, will be unemployable on the docks. He and Edie will follow the working-class migration to the suburbs fostered by postwar tax breaks on loans for single-family dwellings. Their children will grow up breathing clean air far from the smell of the docks. By the sixties, Edie will be teaching English at Forest Hills High and in her spare time will tidy up Terry's diction so that he can become a professional commentator on working-class and urban problems. Like Eric Hoffer, Terry will become a regular on late-night talk shows and sing the praises of labor–management harmony as a guest lecturer in Daniel Bell's classes at Columbia or Riesman's at Harvard.

As we move right to conservative films, social control appears to be more difficult to accomplish. The state can no longer persuade its citizens to do the Right Thing, because the state enjoys less credibility. Conservative heroes were tough and cynical. Even appeals in the name of patriotism and anticommunism often fell on deaf ears. One solution was professionalism. We have seen professionals before, like Captain Warren in *Panic*. He wasn't motivated by any highfalutin sense of duty, like Dr. Reed. He did what he did because he was getting paid for it. Police work was just a job. In conservative films, cops hunted robbers because they were cops and robbers were robbers, not because it was good for society. The code of the professional mediated between society and the self, allowing the hero to fulfill the requirements of the public interest without ever having to acknowledge them. But even professionalism couldn't always do the job. Not everyone was a cop, after all. How could conservatives control men without professions, prevail upon *them* to do the Right Thing?

Underworld USA

The hero of Sam Fuller's *Underworld USA* (1960) is Tolly Devlin (Cliff Robertson). When the film opens, in bravura *noir* fashion, Tolly is a kid, crouched behind some garbage cans in a dark alley. On the wall in front of him is projected a grisly "movie" in which somebody is being beaten to death. All Tolly can see are the shadows of the killers dancing grotesquely before his eyes. When the beating is over, he rushes out to look at the victim's face. It's his father! The police arrive. A man named Driscoll (Larry Gates) asks him if he recognized anybody. "I'm no fink," Tolly says defiantly. "I don't want no help from cops." "I'm no cop," replies Driscoll. "I work for the DA."

Tolly has plenty of time to think about whether Driscoll is a cop or not, because pretty soon he gets into trouble himself and goes straight to jail, where he spends the remainder of his youth. By the time he gets out, he's grown up, and the only thing he has on his mind is revenge.

While Tolly's been inside the Big House, the men who murdered dad, like good, upward-mobile Americans, have risen in the ranks of crime, just as Driscoll himself has moved up from the DA's office to the Crime Commission. They are way up in the syndicate, a highly rationalized criminal empire organized along the lines of the army, on the one hand, and a big corporation, on the other. "Syndicate bosses in the field command the rackets like generals in the army command divisions," Driscoll explains to his anticrime task force. The "chief of staff" is Connors (whom he calls an "animal"), and he is waging war against America's youth, using soda fountains and coffee shops to sell dope. And indeed, we hear Connors, despondent over falling profits, giving marching orders to his army: "There are at least thirteen million kids in this country between the ages of ten and fifteen. Don't tell me the end of a needle has a conscience. Put more men in the field around the schools."

The depiction of the mob as a faceless syndicate—moving the scene of the crime from the streets to the boardrooms—was a common characteristic of conservative gangster films of the fifties (the first to do this was *The Enforcer*, released in 1951) and distinguished them from the films of the thirties, which focused on the rise and fall of an individual gangster. It was prompted in part by the Kefauver revelations, but it also reflected the traditional conservative and right-wing animus toward large-scale organizations. In *Underworld USA*, the syndicate, whose legitimate business front has the innocuous name of National Projects, occupies a downtown skyscraper and even makes philanthropic gifts to underprivileged children.

By way of contrast, in *On the Waterfront*, the mob is just a mob, not a syndicate. It does not have the scope or the resources to infiltrate and overwhelm legitimate authority. Moreover, crime is not only confined to the waterfront, it is confined to only a small part of the waterfront. In

In *Underworld USA*, crime moves from the streets to the boardroom. Here, hit man Gus (Richard Rust) and Connors (Richard Emhardt) relax by the side of the pool.

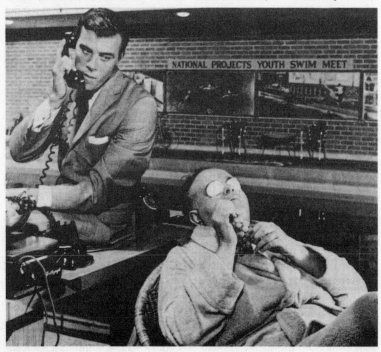

Underworld USA crime is widespread. Mainstream institutions, even soda fountains and coffee shops, have been corrupted. No less than the police commissioner himself is on the mob's payroll. Fuller's is a tabloid vision of reality, with pushers loitering in school yards brandishing Popsicles in one hand and joints in the other. Conservative films like *Underworld USA* are less dialectical and more straightforward than films like *On the Waterfront*. Crime is not a social problem that must be acknowledged, limited, and solved, but a moral blot that must simply be eradicated at any cost. The situation is so serious that only the specially created Crime Commission can deal with it.

But all this doesn't cut any ice with Tolly. He couldn't care less if all the Johnnies in all the schools in the land can't read because they're strung out on dope. He just wants to get even with dad's killers—Gela, Gunther, and Smith—and he needs Driscoll's help to do it. He calls Driscoll and says, "Remember me? I'm the kid who wouldn't fink." A good ten years has passed since Tolly first told Driscoll he wouldn't fink, but scruples like his were so rare in the fifties that Driscoll remembers very well. Now Tolly's changed his mind. He's grown up and realized, as Terry did in *On the Waterfront*, that his distaste for informing is immature. He's high on the joys of finking, doing it himself and making others do it, most importantly his sweetheart, Cuddles (Dolores Dorn), who has information that will send Smith to the chair.

Tolly agrees to work for Driscoll, joining forces with the law. He infiltrates the syndicate and sets one faction against another, dividing and conquering. But unlike *On the Waterfront*, *Underworld USA* has little use for persuasion, few qualms about using force, deploying power when it has to. It does not employ a carrot-and-stick strategy against the enemy. It does not distinguish between good mobsters and bad mobsters. Neither Gela, Gunther, nor Smith is detached from the mob and lured into the fold like Terry Malloy. On the contrary, they are all destroyed.

In conservative films, power was not an occasion for anxiety, nor was it an amorphous, slippery concept; rather, it was simply force, which was not morally questionable, as it was in pluralist films. As we have seen, conservative heroes did not put down the gun; they picked it up. There were any number of films—mostly westerns with titles like *Stars in My Crown* (1950), *Count Three and Pray* (1955), *The Peacemaker* (1956), *The Parson and the Outlaw* (1957), and *The Persuader* (1957)—in which the hero, usually a man of the cloth, discovers he has to use force because trouble just won't go away. Often the preachers in these films were sheriffs as well, which is to say, power is not only morally just, it is institutionalized as well, the prerogative of public officials. When Hawks's *Rio Bravo* (1959) is over and the dusty street is littered with dead Burdettes, Sheriff Wayne doesn't have to move on like Shane does, who is merely a private citizen. Wayne has killed several men, but he can sit tight, because he belongs there. Power is not tragic, nor does it corrupt those who use it. Rather, it is those who refuse to use it, or who are no longer able to use it (like wino Dean Martin in *Rio Bravo*), who are problematic.

Force is necessary because civilian life is not a game but a battleground. If the metaphor of war describes the operations of the syndicate, it applies equally to the operations of the Crime Commission, and contrary to a film like *Detective Story* it is perfectly appropriate. Driscoll's office is a war room, a command center, filled with World War II memorabilia: a Sixteenth Regimental Scroll of Honor, a bronze eagle, and so on. Driscoll is not primarily committed to the rule of law, as men in his position would be in a pluralist film. He is happy to look the other way while Tolly sets up the bad guys for beatings, maimings, and killings. Not once does he speak of getting the gangsters into court, only about "getting them out of the way." Smith is the only one who goes to trial, and this presumably happens after the film is over.

Tolly persuades Cuddles to tell Driscoll what she knows, and Driscoll is effusively grateful. "Thank you, thank you for your courage. There aren't many citizens who would run this risk for society." But she didn't do it for society. "You think I'd stick my neck out just to see Smith burn, do you? I did it for Tolly." Informing is not pitted against loyalty, as it is in *On the Waterfront*; it is precisely loyalty to friends and family that motivates informing. Cuddles finks to Tolly and Tolly finks to Driscoll because they want to, not because they have been made to want to. They have not internalized the goals of others; their motives are authentically their own. *Underworld USA* accepts Tolly as he is, doesn't try to change him the way *On the Waterfront* tries to change Terry. It respects his individualism.

And why did Tolly do it? The invocation of civic obligation, exhortations to abstract principles of social justice, so effective in *On the Waterfront*, here don't work. The state can neither command nor persuade its citizens to act in the way it wishes, just as it cannot override personal loyalties.

Nor is Tolly acting according to a code of professionalism outside himself, as Hawks's heroes often did. He merely wants to revenge his father's death. His motives are purely personal. The women in the film, both Tolly's surrogate mother, Sandy (Beatrice Kay), and Cuddles, moderate voices of the sensible center, urge him to give up his quest for revenge. "You're not a kid any more, you're a grown-up. Act like it," says Sandy, echoing Edie Doyle and Nancy Reed. In a pluralist film, this would be good advice. Here, the women are brought over to his side.

But revenge here is still just too antisocial, too personal, and too erratic to serve as the cornerstone of social control. In one scene, Tolly tells Driscoll he wants out. He's evened the score, having engineered the deaths of two of the men who killed his dad and put the third in jail. Now he wants to marry Cuddles, settle down, and since he doesn't have a personal grudge against Connors, he's content to leave him to the Crime Commission. "With Gela on ice, that wraps it up. You're on your own," he tells Driscoll. But Driscoll says it won't work. "You'll never be able to start from scratch unless you help us get Connors out of the way." And he's right. No sooner is Tolly out of Driscoll's office than he's told that Connors has put a contract out on Cuddles. To protect Cuddles, he's got to kill Connors. *Underworld USA* neither imposes control on Tolly nor entirely yields to his impulses. But it all works out for the best. Luckily appeals to duty and professionalism don't have to work in *Underworld USA*. Tolly's own self-interest coincides with the goals of the government. The miracle of America is that the two coincide. The heart may have its reasons, so long as they are reasons of state. This was precisely the kind of nineteenth-century laissez-faire vision that characterized fifties conservatism. Society is so constructed that public interest and private need coincide. Riesman had written that in the affluent society the invisible hand had given way to the glad hand, but the invisible hand still had a firm grip on films like this.

Many of Fuller's heroes fulfilled public purposes for private reasons. In *Steel Helmet*, Sergeant Zack agrees to lead a platoon of GIs for a box of cigars. In *China Gate*, Angie Dickinson agrees to help a squad of American mercenaries destroy Vietminh headquarters in order to get her Eurasian son an American education. A typical Fuller situation developed halfway through *Hell and High Water* (1954), in a submarine commanded by merc Richard Widmark on its way back from checking out suspicious

Commie activity on an island in the North Pacific. The sub is full of idealistic scientists acting in the public interest. When Widmark finally decides he's had enough and wants out, they appeal to his sense of duty. Had this been a corporate-liberal film like *On the Waterfront*, Widmark would have given in. But it's not, and he thumbs his nose at patriotism. "I'm not sticking my neck out again," snaps Widmark. "I'm a business-man. To a couple of flag-wavers like you, I'm a mercenary, and we're going home."

Later, however, when the Reds treacherously kill Chen-Lee, his loyal, ukelele-strumming "pantry boy," he gets mad. Terry Malloy wants to get even for his brother's death, too, but there, revenge is subordinated to Father Barry's high-minded rhetoric. In *Hell and High Water*, it's the other way around. And now, it's the scientists who want to go home, and Widmark who wants to knock out the Chicom base from which the Reds plan to nuke Korea and blame it on Uncle Sam! "We cannot take it upon ourselves to commit an act of war, no matter what we feel. We are civilians," expostulates one timid professor. But in this film, how Widmark feels is more important than the niceties of international law. "From now on, this is my war!" says Widmark, and suddenly public and private lock into gear.

The snug fit between public and private characterized other conserva-tive films as well. At the beginning of *Clementine*, Wyatt Earp is asked by the citizens of Tombstone to take over the marshal's job, but he refuses. Dodge City was enough. A few scenes later he's asked again, and this time he accepts. What has happened to make him change his mind? In between the two offers, his brother, James, was killed by the Clantons. As marshal of Tombstone, Earp will be able to satisfy his private motive for revenge and fulfill the public interest at the same time. Later, Earp is invited to a dance at the site of the new church, still under construction. It is one of Ford's public celebrations of community, but Earp doesn't know it, so he declines. Next minute, he's changed his mind. The reason? Clementine has asked him to go. Moreover, Earp can easily pass from private to public and back again. Whereas in corporate-liberal films, only by acting in the public interest can the hero satisfy his private needs, in conservative films, only by acting in his own interests can he satisfy public needs.

When Tolly is finally killed, after a marathon run down a deserted street, riddled with lead and weaving crazily across the pavement (this shot was lifted by Godard for the celebrated close of *Breathless*), he collapses amid a clatter of garbage cans in an alley not too different from the one in which his father died years ago. In the last scene, as the camera dollies in on Tolly's corpse, Sandy says to Cuddles, "You gotta sing on Smith. You gotta finish the job for Tolly, or he died for nuthin'." In other words, *Underworld USA* makes revenge work for it. Whereas corporate-liberal films either repudiate or reform revenge heroes, conservative films accommodate them.

Of course, as we have seen, there are limits. Tolly is a little too individualistic, too flaky, too much like Prewitt and Maggio to survive. Some social control is still necessary. After all, it is Driscoll, the special prosecutor, not Tolly the vigilante, who is the moral linchpin, which is why this remains a centrist film. In one shot, Connors's corpse floats facedown in a swimming pool, while next to him bobs a newspaper whose black headline reads, "Connors Defies Uncle Sam." In *Underworld USA*, it is Uncle Sam who ultimately has his way.

The Big Heat

Like Fuller's other films, *Underworld USA* stretches far to the right. It locates authority in a coalition of cops and vigilantes instead of the typical conservative alliance of cops and corporate-liberal experts. As we move right again, still further away from the center's confidence in American institutions, no matter how tenuous, even the fragile alliance between the vigilante and the law in *Underworld USA* breaks down, issuing in all-out war against society and therefore a no-holds-barred attack on the idea of social control. Professionalism can make no claim on the disgusted dyed-in-the-wool individualists who are on the verge of throwing down their badges because the police force is coddling criminals or is mired in red tape, or is corrupt to the core. What then? What will make these heroes do the Right Thing?

When Fritz Lang's *The Big Heat* (1953) opens, Glenn Ford is playing one of his regular guys, a dedicated cop and family man named Dave

Bannion. Bannion has a good job, a wonderful wife named Katie (Jocelyn Brando), and a cute little girl named Joyce. At the end of the film, looking back on his "perfect marriage," Bannion says of his wife, "She used to take puffs off my cigarette, sips of my drink. Sometimes she used to eat food off my plate. I liked that." Bannion's home is his castle, the center of his world, utopia realized in fifties domesticity, an island of peace and calm where his little girl can build castles (of blocks) in the air. But into every utopia a little rain must fall. Bannion begins to get threatening phone calls. One day, while he's playing in the nursery with Joyce, Katie asks him for the car keys. The camera stays in the nursery with Bannion while she gets into the car and turns on the ignition. Bang! Bannion rushes outside to find his car a mangled mass of twisted metal. Inside, he gazes on what is left of Katie. Not much. His pet wife is dead.

Once again, public and private are in disarray. Bannion's job has destroyed his home. Katie is killed because he's been poking his nose into places where it's not wanted. The man who doesn't like Bannion's nose is Lagana (Alexander Scourby), the kingpin of the underworld, the gangster who bombed his wife.

Bannion pays a call on Lagana and finds that he lives on a lush estate in the best part of town. His little girl, Joyce, can build a castle out of blocks, but Lagana has a real one. It is the Laganas of the world who have their hopes and dreams realized in everyday life, not the little people, whose castles collapse, whose dreams turn into nightmares. For them, utopian aspirations are not immanent in society.

Corruption in *The Big Heat* is even more widespread than it is in *Underworld USA*. It is systemic and systematic. In Phil Karson's *The Brothers Rico* (1957), the influence of the syndicate is so pervasive that, as film historian Carlos Clarens has pointed out, even the phone company is suspect.[14] Both films resemble *Invasion of the Body Snatchers* in that normality and business-as-usual become sinister. In *The Big Heat* everyone is corrupt. "Nothing happens in this town without Lagana's okay," says a cop. In one scene the police commissioner, a couple of judges, and a city councilman are all playing poker, not with Lagana himself but merely with one of his henchmen. Lagana's game is the only game in town. There is no recourse to his power, no court of appeal. There are no honest cops, no Driscoll, no Crime Commission. Bannion's extremist view of the society is borne out by the film itself. Crime and the system are synonymous. And, as the titles of films like *The Case Against Brooklyn* indicate, the enemy is not only crime but the city itself, urban life, culture.

As in right-wing sci-fi, films like *The Big Heat* are paranoid and prone to a conspiratorial view of reality, which is presented as commonsensical, while centrists are convicted of refusing to believe what is before their very eyes. Reporters Lee Mortimer and Jack Lait, for example, who parlayed the fifties crime scare into a series of best sellers with titles like *Washington Confidential*, *New York Confidential*, and so on, attacked Democrat Kefauver for whitewashing crime and painted a picture of a "giant conspiracy" that "control[led] practically all crime in the United States," including "negroes [who] have been organized into a ring to steal government checks from mail boxes." To Mortimer and Lait, one conspiracy was very much like another, and they quickly tied Big Crime (particularly drugs) to Big Communism. "Organized gangsters [were] working on one side and the Communists and pinks on the other to turn Americans into addicts," they wrote. "New York dope peddlers are imported from Puerto Rico to sell junk and vote for [American Labor Party Congressman] Marcantonio." Both the Reds and the pushers were aided by corporate and left liberals. "Acheson's dumb daisies" were too inept to stanch the flow of dope from Italy, while "Fiorello La Guardia, New York's pink little stink-weed, commissioned a committee of dizzy do-gooders to report on the reefer situation. They came up with a statement that looked as if they were on hop themselves."[15]

There is still, however, an idea of a public interest in *The Big Heat*, because, as we saw in *Invasion of the Body Snatchers*, right-wing films, despite their fondness for individualism, still cherished the idea of community, only they wanted it on their own terms. Here, too, the public interest lies outside society, and it inheres in individuals, not institutions. In order to fulfill it, Bannion has to work against the system, rather than alongside it as Tolly does in *Underworld USA*.

Like Tolly's, Bannion's motives are genuinely interior. Social control, both persuasive and coercive, is at once bad and unnecessary—bad, because it demands conformity to a corrupt society, and unnecessary, because Bannion intuitively does the Right Thing. In his heart he knows he's right. When Bannion's boss, organization man Wilkes, who has boot-licked his way up the ladder of success, holds out the carrot of promotion and brandishes the stick of dismissal, warning Bannion to lay off Lagana and not rock the boat, Bannion just tells him to go to hell. In order to fulfill the public interest, in other words, he has to become an enemy of society, an outlaw who throws down his badge and picks up the gun.

Bannion is neither an organization man nor a professional. His job is not just a job, but a crusade: he wants to revenge himself for his wife's death. *The Big Heat* is the mirror image of *Detective Story*. Whereas McCloud's vendetta against the "butcher" was loony, here Bannion's similar feud with Lagana is principled. Revenge is a perfectly adequate motive in films of the radical right. It makes a man out of Robert Ryan in *Inferno* (1953), enabling him to survive the desert until he can get even with his wife, and allows Richard Conte to clean up the trucking industry in

In a characteristic extremist gesture, Dave Bannion (Glenn Ford), like Will Kane in *High Noon*, turns in his badge because society is rotten to the core.

Thieves' Highway (1949), where the cops play no role at all until the last scene, when the game's over.

Like *Underworld USA*, *The Big Heat* endorses the use of force, the exercise of power, but it is force deployed against the center. Only by taking the law into his own hands can Bannion purge society, although at the end, the film bows in the direction of moderation by having Bannion repudiate revenge and turn heavy Lee Marvin over to the cops instead of killing him himself. As in many right-wing pro-vigilante films, the people in *The Big Heat* can do it themselves. In *Rio Bravo* we saw that Sheriff Wayne won't let the townies help him. "Most of 'em are well-meaning amateurs worried about their wives and kids. Burdette's men are professionals." In *The Big Heat*, amateurs face professionals once again, but the outcome is different. When the cop detail that has been guarding Bannion's little girl is withdrawn, his brother-in-law recruits some of his buddies to take their place. Bannion isn't so sure they can handle the job. Echoing Sheriff Wayne, he tells them that the mob's torpedoes are "professionals." They "won't be stopped by amateurs whose hearts are in the right place." But here it's enough if their hearts are in the right place, and when one of the "amateurs" mistakes him for a heavy and gets the drop on him, he finds out that he's wrong. They're all war heroes, veterans of the big battles of World War II. And since in this film the war isn't over, these boys are right at home. If they can't protect baby Joyce, no one can. "Amateurs" are okay, whereas "professionals" are gangsters and "experts" are opportunists. * Like Bannion, they act for personal, unofficial reasons, but they cannot act without Bannion, which is to say, they need a leader. Once again, justice is served by a right-wing alliance between superman Bannion at the top and vigilante amateurs at the bottom. It's the law of the excluded middle.

In the final shot of *The Big Heat*, after dispatching Lagana, Bannion is back on the job, answering the phone with the familiar, reassuring, "Bannion, Homicide"; he appears to have rejoined society, having relinquished his extremism, but in fact, as in *Invasion of the Body Snatchers*,

---

The Big Heat attacks professionalism from the right, just as *Panic* attacked it from the left. *Underworld USA* attacked it from the right as well. Fuller, referring to the syndicate's hit man who ends up dead, once said, "He is no psychotic . . . no strange chuckle before he kills. No twitch. A normal young man. He's just a professional executioner."[16]

it is society that has given in. Those who resisted, the business-as-usual organization men and the corrupt professionals, have been either converted or purged.

Force of Evil

As we move to left-wing films, we find two possibilities. On the one hand, the gangster as Robin Hood, distributing his loot among the poor, Jesse James style. This was rare in the fifties, and didn't really make itself felt until the next decade when, in 1962, Al Capone gave away ten thousand Christmas dinners in *The Scarface Mob*, and Clyde Barrow spread the wealth in *Bonnie and Clyde*, five years later. On the other hand, more frequent were films in which gangsters were victimized by class. These take us back to the social-problem genre of the thirties and late forties. In Jules Dassin's *The Naked City* (1948), which spawned a celebrated television series, the class criticism is biting. Rich folk are all neurotic or grasping, and there are several pregnant references to growing up on the wrong side of the tracks. The parents of the girl whose murder provides the focus of the plot live in the country, and when they come to the city to identify their daughter's body, they launch into an attack on urban life and values that pits nature against culture.

Films like this were killed by the witch-hunting frenzy of the fifties. One of the last was Abraham Polonsky's *Force of Evil* (1948). John Garfield plays Joe Morse, a smart lawyer who wants to make it to the top but isn't too particular about how he gets there. He works for the boss of a sprawling numbers empire, who isn't satisfied until he swallows up all the small fry in the city. This would be fine, if one of them weren't Joe's older brother, Leo (Thomas Gomez). Joe tries to save Leo from destruction, fails, and turns on his boss, killing him. At the end, he realizes that he has destroyed himself in the process and decides to spill his guts to the DA.

Although *Force of Evil* is about the rackets, it opens with a shot of Wall Street, and continually equates the syndicate with business. *Underworld USA* did the same thing, but there, this equation did not add up to an attack on business so much as an attack on Big Business, the organization,

If crime is a business in *Underworld USA*, business is crime in *Force of Evil*. Here, John Garfield and Beatrice Pearson at the end of the road.

and the Social Ethic, which trailed in its wake. (Tolly, who has infiltrated the mob, mockingly asks, "What about my future with your organization? I always wanted to have some kind of security.") National Projects was not dangerous because it *was* a business, but because it hid behind business, like Siegel's pods, camouflaging itself in the normal and everyday.

In *Force of Evil*, on the other hand, not only is crime a business, as one character after another repeatedly emphasizes, but business is crime. In a key scene, Leo makes this clear to his wife:

SYLVIA: You're a businessman. . . . You had a garage. You had a real estate business.

LEO: A lot you know. . . . Real estate business. Living from mortgage to mortgage, stealing credit like a thief. And a garage—that was a business. Three cents overcharge on every gallon of gas, two cents for the chauffeur and a penny for me. A penny for one thief, two cents for the other.

Capitalism and crime are the same.

If *Force of Evil* distinguishes itself from films like *Underworld USA*, it also differs from films like *On the Waterfront* as well, mainly by rejecting its reformist framework. Like corporate liberals, the left looked to the environment for the causes of crime, but to them, these causes were part and parcel of the system, not accidents of poor social engineering. Describing the experience of watching Walsh's *White Heat* (1949) in prison, where he was serving a one-year sentence for contempt of Congress, unfriendly witness John Howard Lawson wrote that many of his fellow inmates "recognize that the forces which drove them to vice or crime are inherent in our present social system."[17] *Force of Evil* does the same, or would have, had not its ending been changed in order to win the Code seal of approval. According to Polonsky, he wanted to finish up on a pessimistic note, with Joe's recognition of his own moral disintegration. Polonsky rejected the implication of the upbeat I'll-go-to-the-DA ending ultimately used, that one good man can save the system. More or less like Mr. Upstairs in *On the Waterfront*, the DA in *Force of Evil* is mentioned, but never shown, which is to say, if the concept of structural crime is essentially imaginary to Kazan, the concept of social control is essentially irrelevant to Polonsky, because it implies a society worth salvaging. Despite its jaundiced view of capitalism, however, *Force of Evil* doesn't revert to the rather simpleminded environmentalism of late-thirties films like *You Only Live Once* (1937). The system may corrupt Joe, but it doesn't excuse him.

Wild in the Streets: Juvenile Delinquency

Of all the films of the fifties, it was perhaps the delinquency films that were most thoroughly shot through with omens of things to come: the generation gap and the children's crusade of the sixties.

In 1954, while the Senate Subcommittee on Juvenile Delinquency (like the Crime Committee, also chaired by Kefauver) was holding hearings, sociologist Negely Teeters wrote that "no social problem has wrought deeper concern in the United States" than juvenile delinquency. *New York Times* education expert Benjamin Fine published an influential book called *1,000,000 Delinquents*, and the following year, the *Saturday Evening Post* called delinquency "the Shame of America." Considering that 1954 was the year that Dulles announced the policy of massive retaliation, the year that three Puerto Rican nationalists shot up the House of Representatives, wounding five Congressmen, the year that Ike considered (and decided against) nuking Ho Chi Minh to bail the French out of Dien Bien Phu, and the year the Supreme Court decided that segregated schools were separate but unequal, the fuss over delinquency seems peculiar, to say the least. There was delinquency in the fifties, but the inflation of the problem into a national obsession reflected more than a social reality; it reflected a mood—the first wave of conservative backlash against what William Whyte called the "filiarchy" and what Ehrenreich and English, in their book *For Her Own Good*, later called "the century of the child." When, in 1953, a Boston judge complained that "we have the spectacle of an entire city terrorized by one-half of one percent of its residents. And the terrorists are children,"[18] he identified the real culprits—an autonomous youth culture, not delinquency per se. Kids were aliens, extremists. Fuller's lurid fantasy in *Underworld USA* of danger lurking in school yards, coffee shops, and soda fountains was true, but the threat came from gangs, not mobs.

A number of factors had conspired to create the new youth culture, ranging from World War II, which sent parents off to war or factory jobs, leaving the kids to their own devices; to postwar affluence; the baby boom; the erosion of the authority of the father; and last, but by no means least, the recognition by business that teen-agers would buy everything from records to Clearasil, that they constituted, in short, a market.

Hollywood found itself caught in the middle of the fight over delinquency, torn between the kids and their critics. On the one hand, when the teen-agers who were running wild in the streets paused to catch their breaths, they went to the movies, and Hollywood was understandably loath to bite the little hands that fed it. On the other hand, it could hardly risk offending a large sector of society by seeming to give its imprimatur to the rebellious teen-agers whom so many found frightening. The result was a blizzard of films like *The Wild One* (1954), *Crime in the Streets* (1956), *High School Hellcats* (1958), *Rumble on the Docks* (1956), *The Delinquents* (1957), *Hot Rod Girl* (1956), *Jailhouse Rock* (1957), *High School Confidential* (1958), and *Juvenile Jungle* (1958), that displayed a bewildering array of contradictory attitudes.

In the thirties and forties, the runaway hero of William Wellman's *Wild Boys of the Road* (1933) could say to a judge, "I'll tell you why we can't go home. Because our folks are poor. They can't get jobs, and there isn't enough to eat." Young hoods could say, with John Garfield, referring to society at large, "They made me a criminal," the title of a film released in 1939. Bad kids came from slums on the wrong side of the tracks. They were victims of society, and the causes of delinquency lay out there, in the environment. Since human nature was good, kids were essentially okay. "There isn't any such thing in the world as a bad boy," says Father Flanagan (Spencer Tracy), in *Boys' Town* (1938). In Nicholas Ray's *Knock on Any Door* (1949), one of the last films in this tradition, "Pretty Boy" John Derek was indeed the killer the DA said he was (his motto was "Live fast, die young, and leave a good-looking corpse"), but we felt sorry for him anyway, because his lawyer, Humphrey Bogart, convinced us that he was only "guilty of knowing his father died in prison, of living in poverty, of having been raised in the slums, of the foul treatment of a primitive reform school," and so on.*

---

*Thirties films had to be careful that their stress on the environmental causes of crime did not cross over the line into class criticism. Complaining about the screenplay for *Dead End* (1937), Joseph Breen wrote to Samuel Goldwyn requesting that "you be less emphatic, throughout, in the photographing of this script, in showing the contrast between conditions of the poor in tenements and those of the rich in apartment houses. Specifically, we recommend that you do not show . . . the presence of filth, or smelly garbage cans, or garbage in the river, into which the boys jump for a swim."[23]

By the fifties, the terms of the debate had changed. These kids were no longer criminals—good or bad—they were sick, like young sex maniac John Saxon, who stalks teacher Esther Williams in *The Unguarded Moment* (1956). The causes were still out there, in the environment, but prosperity had become so pervasive that poverty had become obsolete. The new cause was bad families, not bad neighborhoods. Families had occasionally been targeted in thirties and forties films like McCarey's *Wild Company* (1930) or *I Accuse My Parents* (1944), but it wasn't until the postwar period that they routinely took the blame. In *The Unguarded Moment*, the problem is Saxon's misogynist dad, Edward Andrews, who believes women "ought to be wiped off the face of the earth." And we recall that in *12 Angry Men*, Henry Fonda reminds the jurors that the Hispanic defendant was beaten by his father and deprived of mother love at the age of nine, when mom died. If the family was the problem, therapists, once again, were the solution. In *So Young, So Bad*, psychiatrist Paul Henreid wrests control of Elmview Corrective Home for Girls from Superintendent Cecil Clovelly and his sadistic matron, Grace Coppin, whose idea of therapy is to use a fire hose on the inmates. The four JD girls he takes under his wing are Anne Francis, Enid Pulver, Ann Jackson, and Rita Moreno, and they all have family problems.

Teen-agers presented another wrinkle. They ran in packs. But, of course, we've seen peer groups before, and know how easy they are to control. In *On the Waterfront*, the peer group was composed of the longshoremen, both the majority of decent men and the minority of bad apples. As we have seen, authorities didn't so much attack the peer group per se as divide it, using the majority to control the minority. In *12 Angry Men*, the peer group is the jury, and there, too, the majority forced the minority into line.

If the colorful mobs of thirties films were going legit in the fifties, transforming themselves into drab syndicates, gangs of delinquents were filling the gap. They weren't into anything so sophisticated as numbers or prostitution, just good old-fashioned physical mayhem. But gangs weren't dangerous so much for what they did as for what they represented: wholesale disaffection of a major stratum of society. And in the same way that films disagreed on the causes of delinquency, they differed on the best way of handling gangs.

Rebel Without a Cause and Blackboard Jungle

In *Rebel Without a Cause* (1955), James Dean plays Jim Stark, a middle-class rich kid who has gotten into so many scrapes that his parents have been obliged to move from suburb to suburb to stay one step ahead of trouble. When the film opens, they're in a new town, and trouble has already caught up with them. Dead drunk, Jim collapses in the gutter of Mainstreet, USA. He's playing with a little wind-up, doll-like monkey that he gently covers with a piece of newspaper and puts to "bed" before he himself curls up into a fetal ball and passes out. Jim is picked up by the cops and hustled off to the station house, which is busier than Macy's on Washington's Birthday. The rest of the teen-age cast has already arrived: Judy (Natalie Wood), picked up for streetwalking, and Plato (Sal Mineo), turned in by his nanny for shooting a litter of puppies.

What's wrong with these kids? Nothing. They are rebellious all right, but all they want is love, which is to say, the ideology of therapy was undermining the delinquency genre. Judy and Plato are terrified of loneliness. They are street-corner existentialists, filled with angst. They sound as if they spend more time reading Dostoevsky and Kierkegaard than smoking in the bathroom or making out on Lover's Lane. "I'll never be close to anyone," wails Judy. *Rebel* so sentimentalizes its delinquents that although they may be angry and (self-)destructive, they are more moral, upstanding, and law-abiding than anyone else. In fact, it quickly becomes evident that it is not Jim, Judy, or Plato who are the delinquents, but their parents. Jim's dad is weak and indecisive, a poor role model for his troubled son. If Jim's problem is that Mom dominates Dad, Judy's problem is that Dad dominates Mom. Moreover, hobbled by the old-fashioned, Puritan ethic, he can't handle Judy's budding adolescent sexuality; when she kisses him on the lips, he's shocked by the powerful elektrical contact. She's not a teen-age hooker, just a mixed-up kid with a crush on her father. Plato's problem is that he's got no family at all. His parents are divorced, and although he lives in the lap of luxury, his suburban colonial is devoid of parental love. Plato's mom is so bad, she's even put a stop to his psychoanalysis.

With its trilogy of sick families, *Rebel* touches all the bases. Parents are criticized for being too strong and too weak, too authoritarian and too permissive, for being absent when the kids need them and smothering them with affection when they don't. If it's bad to treat teen-agers like children, it's also bad to treat them like adults. In *Rebel*, parents can't do anything right.

If *Rebel* sentimentalizes delinquents and blames the family for the ills of society, if it sympathizes with the misunderstood rebels, appears to back the children against the parents, claims to look with their eyes across the generation gap at the feckless adults on the other side, at the end it delivers these children into their hands, integrates them into the consensus. Before too many frames have passed, it becomes clear that the breakdown of the family does not stand for some larger failure of society; rather, the sick family serves *instead of* the sick society, because in *Rebel*, society is just fine. It is not only fine, it is *better* than the family, better able to carry the ball of socialization that the family has fumbled. *Rebel* attacks the family on behalf not of the kids but of the experts. Child raising is a job for social workers, teachers, psychiatrists, and so on. It is too important to be left to families, which are, after all, staffed by plain old mothers and fathers, the amateurs, for whom pluralists had only contempt. *

Who is the expert in *Rebel*? Jim, Judy, and Plato are minors, so when they get into trouble, they end up in the hands of Ray (Edward Platt), a juvenile officer. Soft-spoken Ray is distinguished from the other cops, who are brusque and surly. He's warm and understanding, more like a social worker than a cop. He wears civilian clothes, while they wear uniforms; he drives an unmarked car, while they drive black-and-whites. Ray confirms Jim's feeling that his problems, like those of *Rebel*'s other rebels, are all in

---

*Experts and families clashed repeatedly in films of the fifties, and in pluralist films the experts won. In *Invaders from Mars* (1953), for example, little David's parents have been "taken over" by means of tiny electrodes implanted in the backs of their necks. David has to be protected not only from Martians, but also from his spaced-out folks—by a woman doctor, who won't let them get near him. "Doctors," David is told, "are sort of like ministers. You can tell them anything." These films might just as well have been scripted by Harry Stack Sullivan, who wrote that "parents must be made to see that children are in no sense their chattels but instead their wards, held in trust as future members of the community."[20]

the family. When Judy complains that her dad doesn't love her, Ray replies softly, "What makes you think he hates you? Maybe you think you can get back at your dad . . . if you're not as close to him as you would like to be." When Jim complains about his parents, Ray is so sympathetic ("Your folks don't understand?") that Jim says warmly, "You see right through me." Transparency is a stepping stone to socialization. The more transparent, malleable, permeable is the mind of another, the easier it is to control. (In *Flying Leathernecks*, the doc who plays Freud tries to get inside Major Kirby's head: "A penny for your thoughts," he says.)

Ray is another agent of the therapeutic state. "The juvenile court movement rested on the belief that juvenile delinquency originated in deformed homes," writes Lasch. "Accordingly, the juvenile delinquent was to be treated not as a criminal but as a victim of circumstances. In order to give him the 'protection' of the law, humanitarian reformers created a new type of noncriminal equity, probation, and endowed probation officers with many of the rights of parenthood. They took a broad view of the state's powers as a surrogate parent."[21] When we recall that Ray's dialogues with Jim and Judy take place in a precinct house, it is an indication of how far we have come from traditional methods of punishment. (The cops even let Jim keep his doll.) Jim has become an outpatient of a therapeuticized juvenile justice system.

Unlike the Baskin-Robbins tough guys in *Rebel Without a Cause*, who look like delinquents-for-a-day on leave from the Actor's Studio, the hoods in *Blackboard Jungle* (1955) feel like the real thing. Led by slouching, snarling Vic Morrow, his mouth twisted in a shove-it-up-your-ass sneer, these boys are mean. And here again is stolid Glenn Ford, fresh from cleaning up the Sodom and Gomorrah PD in *The Big Heat*. This time, he's not a rogue cop, but an English teacher in a big-city vocational high school. From the moment a baseball bounces off the blackboard taking a chunk of slate with it, we know he's in for trouble. The school is North Manual High, Ford's name is Rick Dadier, instantly changed to "daddy-o" by the kids, and in case you haven't guessed, the music blasting over the sound track is Bill Haley's "Rock Around the Clock." (*Blackboard Jungle* was the first film to use a rock-'n-roll sound track, and "Rock Around the Clock," which the film introduced, made the Hit Parade and stayed there for fifteen weeks.)

But ugly as delinquency is, we're reminded that it is still an anomaly, the exception, not the rule. In the same way that Kazan assured us in *On the Waterfront* that "the waterfront . . . ain't part of America," so here we're told early on by Dadier's former professor, standing on an expanse of well-manicured lawn surrounding a posh suburban high school: "For every school like [North Manual], there are thousands like this one." As we follow Dadier and his professor into the auditorium, listen to the stirring strains of the national anthem swell on the sound track, and watch the sea of scrubbed white faces move their lips in sync to the music, we know this must be true. This is the way it should be, and mostly is. (Brooks refused to underline the point by inserting dialogue to the effect that delinquency was worse in the USSR than it was in the U.S.)

Meanwhile, on the other side of the tracks, down in the heart of the inner city, the students are singing a different song. Dadier's class is filled with black and brown faces, and those that are white are also poor. On the first day of school, one boy comes up to Dadier. For a moment, we think we're back at Scarsdale High. But something's wrong. His blue eyes are filled with tears, his tie is askew, and his flaxen hair is all mussed up. He's been beaten up by the toughs in the class, but he's too terrified to name names. The lines have been drawn. It's the black, brown, and white ethnic thugs against the white middle class. It's rock-'n-roll against "The Star-Spangled Banner." Dadier's task is clear enough. He's got to make the halls of North Manual safe for preppies.

Dadier has a difficult job cut out for him, but he's no quitter. He has a strong sense of duty. When the students show up with knives instead of pencils, rather than fleeing to the suburbs he sticks it out, because he wants to bring the light of reading, 'riting, and 'rithmetic to the darkness of the ghetto. His job is to soothe the savage beast, impose culture on nature. As a teacher, he transmits the values of society, and indeed, as he stands in front of the class, an American flag looms prominently over his right shoulder. Explaining why he wants to be a teacher, he says, "I thought I could help to shape young minds, sort of sculpt lives." It would be hard to formulate the goals of social control more succinctly.

If Dadier is culture, the students are nature. In the first scene, they whistle and hoot at passing women, pressing their faces up against the school-yard fence, extruding their arms through the bars like monkeys in a zoo. They are repeatedly compared with animals. "You should have taught me to quiet a class of screaming wild animals," Dadier complains to his former professor. "If I'm gonna be a lion tamer, I should teach with a chair and a whip." Murdock (Louis Calhern), the history teacher, asks Dadier, "Have you got those wild animals trained?" Nature is bad, not good, a jungle, not a garden.

Dadier has the will, but is there a way? *Blackboard Jungle* shows him picking and choosing between methods of social control. The conservative, veteran teachers fight fire with fire. "The first guy gives trouble gets trouble right back," yells one man at the top of his lungs over the heads of five hundred screeching students assembled in the auditorium on the first day of class. Murdock is the spokesman for the conservative position. For him, the only language the students understand is force. "You can't teach an unruly mob," he tells Dadier. "You've got to be a disciplinarian, and that means obedience. Never turn your back on the class." The relationship between the students and the teachers resembles a state of war. Murdock says he has "twelve years of experience and two Purple Hearts," and he and his colleagues repeatedly refer back to World War II.

When Dadier is attacked by his students midway through the film, he gets a chance to implement Murdock's punitive views by calling the cops. "Somebody has to be kicked to death before you'll cooperate? Press charges!" urges the detective. But Dadier won't. He had already sent a student to jail for trying to rape sexy Lois Hammond (Margaret Hayes), a pretty young teacher who made the mistake of exposing a mile of leg to the gaze of the subhuman students by fixing her stocking on the teachers' stairway. But jailing her assailant just made things worse.

Dadier may not want to call the cops, but he's no milksop. If he won't follow the conservative line, he won't buy the bleeding-heart-liberal one either. The latter is represented by Josh Edwards (Richard Kiley), a math teacher. To him, delinquents "aren't bad, they're just ignorant." But we know he's naïve and out of it, because when the camera fastens on the rear end of a curvaceous teen-ager leaning over the bar where he's having a drink, not three inches from his nose, he's cleaning his glasses and doesn't notice. And sure enough, just as he opines that the kids aren't all bad, they jump him in an alley and beat him senseless. In one of the film's most celebrated scenes, Edwards brings his priceless jazz collection to class, only to have the 78s smashed by the rampaging students. Josh is crushed. His bleeding heart is broken.

Later, when the teachers are discussing the record incident among themselves, the conservatives among them toss around phrases like "electric chair," and "clobber'em," while the liberals demur. Dadier has no patience with either side. He rejects the right-wing path, it is important to note, not on principle, but only because it won't work. "They get clobbered at home and in the streets," he points out. "They're used to it." He rejects the left-wing path because it's hopelessly unrealistic. Dismissing both the "clobberers and the slobberers," as he calls them, Dadier seeks a middle way, threading a path between the left and the right.

Dadier realizes that the authorities are not strong enough for a direct assault on the kids—the conservative option recommended by the cops. If he is going to establish his authority, he's got to be more subtle, he's got to turn the peer group to his advantage, make the peer group itself put pressure on the hardcore hoods. As William Whyte explained the pluralist strategy: "The teacher strives not to discipline the child directly but to influence all the children's attitudes so that as a group they recognize correct behavior. If a child falls out of line, he does not have to be subjected to authoritarian strictures of elders; he senses the disapproval of the group and, in that way, the school believes, learns to discipline himself as much as possible."[22]

The major stumbling block in the way of this strategy is the solidarity of the students. Like the dockers in *On the Waterfront*, they are "D and D." When Dadier tries to make one kid call him "Mr.," the response is, "You ever try to fight thirty-five guys at one time, chief?" Therefore, he adopts the now-familiar divide-and-conquer tactics Schlesinger recommended for use against Third World insurgents. Murdock isn't altogether wrong; it is evident that the classroom is indeed a battle zone. His only mistake is that he has the wrong kind of war. It is not a conventional war, and Murdock's tactics, as well as his ideas, are out of date. Rather than calling for main-force troops (the cops), Dadier brings the battle to the enemy, attacking the peer group on its own turf. He's a Green Beret in the blackboard jungle, using guile when he can and his fists when he has to.

In the same way that Father Barry not only identified but created Terry Malloy as a leader, and through him both created and manipulated followers, so Dadier finds his Third Force in Miller (Sidney Poitier), singling him out of the crowd and trying to split him off from his pals by praising him and derogating them. "You're a natural-born leader," Dadier tells him. "You know you're a little brighter, a little smarter than the rest of those guys. Every class needs a leader. You could be that leader. You cooperate [with me], and they'll follow you." Miller wants to quit school to become a mechanic, but Dadier flatters him with personal attention, beguiles him with the sugarplum of college, and paints an endless vista of upward mobility disappearing into the sunset of prosperity: once again, utopia immanent in fifties America. When Miller objects that it is not for him, because he's black, Dadier cries, "You know that doesn't matter, not nowadays. Ralph Bunche proved that. George Washington Carver. Marian Anderson. Joe Louis," and so on and so forth. Dadier convinces Miller that if he fulfills the public interest, society will see to it that he realizes his personal ambitions.

Eventually, Dadier's attentions bear fruit. Miller takes to wearing a shirt with a white collar to class instead of the T-shirt he wore at the beginning of the film, and he agrees to take part in the Christmas play that Dadier is producing. By the time the big showdown comes, Miller is primed to side with Dadier, with "legitimate" authority, and beyond that, with society, against the rebellious delinquents.

Miller's main man, his potential ally, is Artie West (Vic Morrow). The danger here is that Miller and West may act in concert, as Dadier well knows; he complains to Miller that, "you and West ganged up on me." Miller and West, like Terry and Tommy in *On the Waterfront*, are "doubles." Corporate-liberal films often used doubles to dramatize the divide-and-conquer strategy of pluralist social control. The extremist double is detached from the moderate double and jailed or killed, while the moderate is redeemed. West is clearly the extremist here. A good deal more intransigent than Miller, he's an irreconcilable, a *refusé*. He won't join the team, won't play ball. Worse, he is hip to Dadier's tricks. He leads the attack on Edwards's jazz collection because he regards music as an instrument of control. "Haven't you heard? Music is soothing for the savage beasts," he says, tossing Bix Beiderbecke across the room like a Frisbee.

West looks forward to the sixties. His home is in the streets; to him, the streets are what they became to the counterculture flower children of the next generation: a liberated zone beyond adult control. Standing next to a Marine recruiting poster, Dadier warns him that if he continues on his merry way, he'll end up in jail. West says he doesn't care. With a prison record, at least he'll get out of the draft. "A year from now, the army comes along and says, 'Okay, Artie West, you put a uniform on and you save the world and get your head blown off.' Well, with a record, maybe the army won't take Artie West." If Dadier is a Green Beret, West, in 1955, the year Diem came to power and American aid began to flow, is the first draft resister of the Vietnam era. West can't be assimilated to the consensus like Miller. Therefore he must be branded a criminal and destroyed.

If the logic of social control dictates the course of *Blackboard Jungle*, it does the same for *Rebel Without a Cause*. Once it has indicted the parents, *Rebel* moves swiftly to divide-and-conquer its young hoods and deliver them into the hands of its newly rehabilitated adults.

Jim, we recall, is the new kid on the block, and on his first day at Dawson High, the old kids give him a rough time. Buzz (Corey Allen), the leader of the pack, challenges Jim to a "chickie-run," wherein the two rivals drive hot rods up to the edge of a cliff. The last one to bail out wins. But right before they start, Buzz turns to Jim and confesses, "I like you," thereby raising the specter of a united front, an alliance between Jim and Buzz against the authorities. From a social-control point of view, this must not happen, just as it is necessary to prevent Miller and West from joining forces. It's much better by far to keep the kids at each other's throats, and indeed, Buzz is killed shortly after (because?) he offered the olive branch to Jim.

Once Buzz is out of the way, the gang goes from bad to worse. Buzz was no treat, but he was considerably more moderate and responsible than his followers. The top-down hierarchy applies to gangs as well as governments. Under the leadership of his two lieutenants, "Crunch" and "Goon," a few rungs below Buzz on the ladder of authority, the gang descends into overt violence. Deprived of "responsible" leadership, it becomes simply Other. Suddenly we have good delinquents (Jim and Judy) and bad delinquents (the gang). Since there is no particular content to the rebellion of either—they are indeed rebels without causes—it is hard to escape the conclusion that the only difference between the good delinquents and bad delinquents is that the bad ones, causes or no causes, are opaque, beyond adult control, and do not obediently submit themselves to expert scrutiny the way Jim does. Their favorite retort, in this and other JD films throughout the fifties, is, "Nobody tells *me* what to do." Good delinquents are troubled adolescents, mixed-up but essentially decent kids; bad delinquents are portrayed as proto-criminals, which is to say, rebellion against society is criminalized.

Officer Ray has it easy compared with social-control agents like Father

Barry and Dadier, who have to expend considerable energy dividing their hoods into good and bad, keeping Terry Malloy and John Friendly (and Tommy), Miller and West, at odds. Jim is ready and willing to be controlled—even to become a social controller himself, a Quisling, a fifth column within the delinquent underworld. Where Judy and Plato crave love, Jim craves authority too. In the opening scene in the police station, he begs Ray to put him in jail: "Please lock me up. I'm gonna hit someone, do something . . ." he whines. Later, he begs his dad to forbid him to participate in the chickie-run: "Are you going to keep me from going?" he asks desperately, looking for some sense of limits, some sign of parental direction. But Dad is steadfast in his permissiveness. "When did I ever stop you from doing anything?" He doesn't understand that Jim wants to be told he can't go. After Buzz's death, Jim isn't "D and D" the way Terry is after Joey Doyle's; he wants to go to the police. It is not him but his spineless parents who are against it. Jim is an idealist. "We're all involved," Jim screams at Mom and Dad, sketching in the Big Picture. Jim is so eager to toe the line, Ray has almost nothing to do, and his role is consequently much less substantial than Father Barry's or Dadier's.

Jim, Ray's surrogate, goes about gathering the rest of the good delinquents into the fold; first Judy, Buzz's former girl friend, and then Plato. Judy is easy. All Jim has to do is redirect her disruptive Oedipal lustings after her father toward a more socially acceptable object, namely himself. After she falls in love with him, she stops leaning over Dad in her tight sweaters, planting big kisses on his mouth. Next, Jim has to detach her from the gang. At first, he is rebuffed. "Do you want to go with me?" he asks her on his way to school. "I go with the kids," she replies, and runs off to join her peers. But after Buzz is killed, Jim involves Judy in a romantic liaison that supplants her ties to her friends, and she repudiates them: "You shouldn't believe what I say when I'm with the rest of the kids," she confesses.

Once Judy is in the bag, Jim goes after Plato. Plato is a harder nut to crack. He's a puppy killer, after all, more rebellious and neurotic than Jim or Judy, or, to be more accurate, he is more rebellious and is therefore depicted as more neurotic, in the same way that Buzz's gang is more rebellious and is therefore depicted as more criminal. At one point Jim, Judy, and Plato run away from their real families and take refuge in a broken-down, abandoned mansion somewhere in the Hollywood hills,

Plato's fantasy island, where he can pretend that Jim and Judy are his surrogate family. "If only you could'a been my dad," Plato tells Jim wistfully. The mansion is a utopian retreat from the adult world. But it's not very different. So strong is the domestic tug of this film that no sooner do they set foot in the door than Jim and Judy begin to play house, pretending they are newlyweds, and more, prospective buyers of Plato's property, which, in a sense, they are. Their utopian aspirations will be fulfilled, while his won't. "I'm happy here," says Plato. "I wish we could stay here forever." But Plato's dreams quickly collapse around his ears. While he falls asleep, Jim and Judy go exploring. Plato wakes up to find himself surrounded by Goon, Crunch and Co., who've been looking for Jim, thinking he's ratted on them to the cops.

Concluding that Jim has abandoned him, Plato goes berserk, escapes, and holes up in Griffith Park Observatory with his mom's nickel-plated .45. The police surround the place, the headlights of their cars playing over the front of the building. Jim goes in to coax Plato out. By this time, he has come to identify entirely with society. Whereas Plato mistrusts the collection of cops, juvenile officers, and parents ringing the observatory ("Those are not my friends"), Jim trusts them: "These people, every one of them, want to see that you are safe." From society's point of view, and by now Jim's as well, the real danger comes from Plato, not the police. Jim wants to disarm Plato before he hurts somebody. What does Jim do? First, he gives Plato his red jacket. Then he asks Plato to let him hold his gun. "You're my friend, Plato. That means a lot to me. Don't you trust me?" Plato does, and gives him the gun, after making him promise to return it. At this juncture, Jim has three choices: (1) to side forthrightly with Plato against society and help him escape; this would be the left-, or perhaps right-wing solution; (2) to side forthrightly with society against Plato, keep the gun, and force him to surrender. This would be the conservative, coercive solution. But Jim chooses a third course. He surreptitiously removes the clip and returns the gun, meanwhile assuring Plato, "Friends always keep their promises." This is the corporate-liberal, manipulative solution. Jim disarms Plato against the police, leaving him with the form of rebellion, not the substance. Jim has explicitly changed sides, but the film disguises this turnabout by portraying Plato as crazy and Jim's course of action as the only reasonable one under the circumstances. After all, if Plato is crazy, Jim's only alternative is to save Plato from himself.

When Plato finally comes out, he panics in the glare of a spotlight and is shot dead by an overeager, trigger-happy cop. (Remember the low-level eager-beaver cop in *Panic* and the GI in *The Day the Earth Stood Still?*) The use of force is treated as a tragic accident.

Jim's foray into conflict management goes awry. But his failure is inevitable. Plato has to die—he's too rebellious, too disaffected. He's an extremist. Like Buzz's gang, Plato is out of control, opaque, autonomous, beyond the reach of adult authority. Irreconcilable alienation is intolerable and is equated with insanity. Moreover, Plato is Jim's double, an extreme version of Jim, as West is of Miller, Tommy of Terry. He is wearing Jim's jacket when he dies, and Jim's dad momentarily mistakes him for his son. The extremist double is detached from the moderate double and killed, while the moderate double is redeemed. Plato is the scapegoat, Jim's asocial other half that must be exorcised so that Jim can be readmitted to society. Plato's death is the price Jim must pay for the trouble he's caused, for getting his parents out of bed in the middle of the night. Jim's red jacket is the badge, the mantle of rebellion. It is passed on to Plato and with him leaves the picture.

Then, too, there is no room for Plato in the emerging nuclear family of Jim and Judy. "He needs us," Jim tells Judy when she objects to running after Plato. "I need you too," she replies. The nuclear family is exclusive, and Plato has become a liability, a rival to Judy for Jim's affections. Plato's death provides the occasion for the reeducation of the family. His demise makes room for Jim's real son: his father. Jim's father is the most important target of social control. Through Jim, the state, that is, the therapeutic experts represented by Ray, can bring the family into line. Up to this point, Jim has been tutoring Dad in the arts of fatherhood, telling him to be responsible, to stand up to Mom—in effect, playing the role of the father and casting dad in the role of his son. Now it is Dad's turn to show he has done his homework. We know social control has succeeded when patient becomes doctor, student becomes teacher, son becomes father, controlled becomes controller. Controlled and controller change places. In this case, for Dad to become a true father, Jim has to resume the role of son. He has to, as he does, fling himself on his knees, throw his arms around his father's legs, and sob, "Help me!" allowing Dad, finally, to be Dad. And indeed, Dad rises to the occasion, proving that he has been an apt pupil, by mimicking Jim's behavior. He raises Jim off the ground in much the same way that Jim tried to raise him off the floor earlier when he was on his hands and knees picking up a spilled dinner tray. And he puts his coat over Jim's shoulders in much the same way that Jim gave his jacket to Plato. As Dad raises Jim to his feet, he says, "You can depend on me. Trust me." We know that he means it, because when Mom starts to bitch as usual, Dad silences her with a look that could kill, and she clams up with a smile. Like Jim, it seems that she, too, has been looking for authority.

But if Jim's father has learned to be like him, Jim has learned to be like his father too, and this is the most significant lesson the film teaches. It is the parents who have the last laugh, who define the values of the film, not the rebellious children. What are these values, and what does Jim learn? In the final scene, Dad tells Jim to "trust" him, but we have just heard Jim tell Plato to "trust" him at the very moment he was, in fact, betraying him. There is, however, no irony here. Plato's death has inter-

Extremist Plato (Sal Mineo) finds there's no home for him in the vital center, in this case Jim (James Dean) and Judy's (Natalie Wood) nuclear-family-to-be.

vened between the two uses of the word *trust*, and Jim has "matured."
Maturity, in this case, means the recognition that everyone is limited, that
life, like politics, can't always be what you want. Jim now knows that
when Dad told him earlier, "You can't be an idealist all your life," he was
right, and when Dad tells him now, referring to Plato's death, "You couldn't
help it; you did everything a man could," he accepts it. What Jim once
regarded as Dad's expedience, he has now learned is simply "realism,"
acquiescence to the facts of life. With the death of Plato, idealism—
defiance of the facts of life—has been purged for being childish, even
dangerous. And on this basis, the old family is reconstituted, and the new
family, Jim and Judy, is born, literally over Plato's dead body. As Plato's
nanny looks sadly after them, Jim and Judy, Mom and Dad, all pile into
Ray's police car and drive off. The family has been "cured," Jim has
"matured," the body politic has been healed.

Meanwhile, back at rock-'n-roll high school, Dadier is still looking for
a way to "reach" his students. His big breakthrough comes when he shows
the "Jack and the Beanstalk" cartoon cited in the introduction to this
book. Once upon a time Jack's impoverished mother sent her son to sell
the family cow for money to put food on the table. Instead, Jack trades the
cow for a handful of beans. Disgusted, Mom throws the beans out the
window and sends young Jack to his room. The beans sprout a stalk as
high as a skyscraper. When Jack climbs up, he discovers a kingdom inhabited by the very same giant who robbed and killed his own father. After a
series of adventures, including several trips up and down the stalk, Jack
makes off with the giant's goose-that-lays-the-golden-eggs. When the giant
chases him, Jack chops the beanstalk down. The giant crashes to the
earth, and is killed.

"Jack and the Beanstalk" is an eye-for-an-eye revenge fairy tale, in
which Jack slays the giant who slew his father. The official interpretation
of the story, the one that Dadier initially offers, has Jack as the hero and
the giant as the villain. But this moral breaks down in the face of the kids'
street smarts; they think Jack is a jerk for trading his cow for a "mess'a
beans." When the students wander further into heresy, doubting that Jack
was justified in killing the giant at all, Dadier springs to Jack's defense,
reminding them that the giant had, after all, robbed and killed his dad.
But if the kids are going to see Jack as the hero, it will be their own kind
of hero, and they put the most antisocial interpretation on his behavior.
"He got away with burglary three times," says one boy admiringly. West

jumps in, nailing this one down. Jack "took what he wanted," says West, demonstrating that "crime always pays." Another kid calls Jack a "heist man," like the JDs themselves.

While Dadier backs Jack, he can't allow the kids to heroize him in these terms, to make him over into a juvenile Dillinger. To regain some ground, he jettisons Jack and tries to generate some sympathy for the giant, at first without success. "It was only a stinking giant," says one boy, dubious. "Why don't you like the giant?" asks Dadier. "Because he's a giant," comes the reply. Then, the moral: "Is it right to dislike somebody because he's different? There are a lot of us right here in this classroom who are different than anybody else." Through this reading, the giant becomes, if not a hero, at least a sympathetic victim of intolerance, and Jack a racist of sorts. West sees that Dadier's moral is ideology. "Here comes the commercial," he snarls. But he can't put a damper on the ecstasy of the explication. The students are hooked on Dadier's commentary. "That giant—if he done wrong, at least he should'a had a fair trial," says Miller, concluding the discussion with a comment that sounds like it could have come from Father Barry in *On the Waterfront*.

By making the students participate in revising a revenge story into a pluralist fable of tolerance, Dadier has made them vote for the system. He has put some distance between himself and the traditional hard-line interpretation, carved out, with Miller's help, a reasonable middle way between what society says the tale means and what West says the tale means. He has taught the students to be on the lookout for "propaganda," to be skeptical of stories—stories other than his own interpretation, which he does not regard as ideology but as "truth." Although he tells his students his aim is to teach them to "think for themselves," in reality, he has guided their understanding of the cartoon story, chaperoned them through the adventure of interpretation without their knowing it. The "right" reading, after all, appears to be supplied by Miller, not Dadier. It comes from the students and is not experienced by them as an imposition from without. * "So you finally got through to them," says one teacher with admi-

---

*In *Up from Liberalism*, William Buckley attacked pluralist educators for planting their own social agendas in the minds of their students: "In the hands of a skillful indoctrinator, the average student not only thinks what the indoctrinator wants him to think," wrote Buckley, "but is altogether positive that he has arrived at his position by independent intellectual exertion."[23]

ration. "I think so, yes. For the first time," Dadier replies. "But what's the answer? Visual education?" asks another. No, says Dadier. You have to seize their "imaginations." Dadier has succeeded in involving the students for the first time in the learning process. What the students say is less important than what they do, and what they do is give in, cooperate, learn to trust authority (Dadier's), and participate in the ongoing work of the institution (school). They are now ready to recognize leadership (Miller's), and assent to their own role as followers.

Once Dadier has secured the students, he is ready to move against West. He doesn't have to wait long for an opportunity. When Dadier catches one of the boys cheating, West responds by ostentatiously doing it himself. Dadier demands his paper. West balls it up and throws it on the floor. "You talkin' to me, teach?" he says. "Ah, come one, Artie, give him the paper," mutters Miller under his breath, ready to defect to Dadier. Then West makes a big mistake. He has turned a deaf ear to Dadier's attempts to tutor him in tolerance by watching cartoons, and now he will learn the importance of tolerance the hard way. "You just keep your rotten mouth outa this, black boy," he screams, turning Miller irrevocably against him. Now certain of Miller, Dadier can press his attack, isolating West from the others. "We're going down to the principal," Dadier says, advancing toward West's seat. "We are? You gonna make me, Daddy-o? How'd you like to go to hell?" West pulls a switchblade as the rest of the students scramble out of the way. When West's pal, Belazi, tries to jump Dadier from behind, Miller wops him, coming out publicly on Dadier's side for the first time. The one other black student in the class moves up, shoulder-to-shoulder with Miller. It's an alliance between the white corporate liberal (Dadier) and the blacks against the white ethnics. In what may have been the first use of the American flag as a weapon, Belazi is pinned to the wall with the red, white, and blue. As Dadier edges West into a corner, West, like all movie bullies, collapses. "You're not so tough without a gang to back you up, are you?" says Dadier, grabbing him by the shirtfront and banging his head against the blackboard like a Ping-Pong ball. Nobody likes a loser, and as West caves in, the others hasten to demonstrate their allegiance to Dadier. Once again, the coalition of the center takes shape against the dissenters. The peer group expels West.

Dadier has won, but how far can he push it? Looking from one face to another, he says, "I know. You're thinking, 'Why not forget the whole

Glenn Ford *(right)* breaking up the alliance between Sidney Poitier *(center)* and Vic Morrow, so that Poitier, like the majority of students, can be saved.

thing?' No. Not this time. There's no place for these two in your class-room. We've all made a big step forward. There's no sliding back now. Whether you like it or not, I'm taking these two downstairs." But the students are way ahead of him, more completely in his power than he realizes. "I think maybe we'll give you a hand, Mr. Dadier," says Miller, tomming it up. The kids have come 'round, proving that behind their scowling faces, they're just like the boys and girls in *Rebel Without a Cause*. As Dadier's wife, Ann, puts it, "Kids are people, and most people are worthwhile. We all need the same thing—patience, understanding, and love." And the teachers have come 'round, too. Dadier has socialized them as well as the students. He wins over conservatives like Murdock. "I was wrong," says Murdock. "The kids in our school can be taught, if you don't stop trying. All of a sudden, I want to get to them too."

Blackboard Jungle opened to a storm of criticism. Hedda Hopper thought it was the most brutal film she had ever seen, and it was roundly denounced by educators for scaring teachers and encouraging teen-age desperadoes, so that MGM, which produced the film, was forced to run disclaimers in the form of trailers that followed it, letting local schools off the hook. One read:

To our patrons: the school and situations you have just seen are not to be found in this area! . . . We suggest a visit to any of the five schools in our city and county. You will be cordially welcome.[24]

Time magazine wrote that movies like *Blackboard Jungle*, "far more than Communist propaganda," were "responsible for the repulsive picture of U.S. life" abroad. Clare Booth Luce, Ike's ambassador to Italy, saw to it that the film was withdrawn as the U.S. entry to the Venice Film Festival.[25] But when *Blackboard Jungle* was accused in the Kefauver hearings of provoking schoolgirls to set fire to a barn, Ronald Reagan, at that time head of the Screen Actors Guild, sprang to its defense, saying, "Any juvenile seeing it would have to have a feeling of disgust for the bad boy," namely, West.[26]

Reagan was right. Just look at the service Dadier has performed for society. Whereas the cops would have thrown the whole bunch of kids into jail, jamming the court calendar, swelling the prison population, and ultimately costing the taxpayers a pretty penny, Dadier has reduced the number of bad apples to two. He has included the rest, more numerous by far, within society, rather than leaving them to throw stones from the sidelines. And he has trained a leader, passed on the mantle of social control to Miller, molding him in his own image. We know social control is successful when it is internalized, when Dadier and Miller change places, when student becomes teacher; teacher, student. Dadier had once told Miller, who wanted to leave school, that quitting was the "easy way." Now Miller has decided to continue. But he exacts a price. During the first two-thirds of the film, everyone in Dadier's life—from his pregnant wife, Ann (Anne Francis), to West—has been urging *him* to quit school. Dadier has always refused, but when Ann nearly miscarries after receiving anonymous letters suggesting that there is another woman in her husband's life, he's finally had enough. It is his students who give him the strength to go on by demonstrating that he has "reached" them. They, in their newfound maturity, restrain him from his rash course. In the last scene, Miller makes Dadier promise that he won't quit either. They make a pact. Miller shows Dadier what it's like to grow up. As Miller puts it in the final shot, "I guess everybody learns something in school, even teachers."

I Was a Teenage Werewolf

In *Blackboard Jungle*, those who argue, like Murdock, that the kids are "animals" are wrong—kids are "people"—and when all is said and done, it turns out that only a few are bad, and the rest are okay. True, some kids' ids may harbor monsters, but as in the case of Jim, bad parents let them loose. And as we have seen, society doesn't have to be a prison to contain them because groups, therapists, leaders, and institutions (peers, teachers, and schools) can cure or restrain them. In conservative films, however, human nature becomes darker and less tractable, and methods of social control considerably harsher.

The delinquency theme was not confined to its own subgenre, but cropped up in others as well. Gene Fowler's *I Was a Teenage Werewolf* (1957) is a recombinant horror film, in which hood meets monster. It is *Rebel Without a Cause* in wolf's clothing, a film that pits conservative demonology against pluralist ideology, sorcery against therapy, Transylvania against Vienna. *Werewolf*'s teen-age hero, Tony, played by James Dean look-alike Michael Landon (later of *A Little House on the Prairie* fame), is a troublemaker who just can't fit in at Rockdale High. "People bug me," he says, and when the film opens, he's in the midst of a vicious brawl, fighting dirty, throwing sand in the other boy's eyes because he slapped him on the back. "I don't like to be touched," says Tony, twitching angrily. He's a chronic rule breaker who can't even cross the street without being cited for jaywalking. Donovan, the friendly cop, recommends a psychiatrist, Dr. Brandon (Whit Bissell), who's "been working without charge with the police to get kids to adjust." "Adjust to what?" Tony sneers. "To parents, your friends, school—everybody," replies Donovan. "No head shrinker for me," Tony says angrily, but he realizes that something is wrong. "I say things, I do things—I don't know why."

Tony has been raised in a working-class family without a mother, but the point in this film is that his damaged family does *not* account for his strange behavior. His problems, unlike those of delinquents in pluralist films, do not come from out there, from the environment. They are not attributable to any psychosocial matrix outside himself. Conservatives blamed delinquency on the individual, not society. Buckley ridiculed bleeding heart Eleanor Roosevelt for writing, in her syndicated column, "I was shocked to hear that not long ago, in one of our schools, some older boys beat up their teacher. When this happens, you can be sure that the blame does not lie with the young people."[27]

The key film in this mode was, of course, *The Bad Seed* (1956), taken from Maxwell Anderson's Broadway hit, with several illuminating changes. In the play, Patty McCormack plays a homicidal eight-year-old who cuts a swath of murder and mayhem through her friends and acquaintances. There is no explanation for her behavior other than the one alluded to in the title of the play. She's just plain bad. At the end, Mom gives Patty an overdose of sleeping pills, and kills herself. Patty survives, presumably to continue her closet crime spree. In the film, the naughty heroine (also played by McCormack) is similarly motivated by a hereditary flaw, but she's subject in the end to the twin conservative panaceas: divine intervention and old-fashioned discipline. She's struck down by a bolt of lightning—courtesy of the "hand of God"—and in a bizarre epilogue, she's revived so that Mom (Nancy Kelly) can put her over her knee and give her a good spanking.

In Ray's *Run for Cover* (1955), we find John Derek again, a few years older and meaner than he was in *Knock on Any Door*. This time he doesn't come from the wrong side of the tracks or a bad family; he's an orphan, all right, but he's fortunate enough to find an exemplary father figure, James Cagney, who adopts him. Derek's had every opportunity to make good, but he won't. He's not a victim and he's not sick; he's just rotten to the core, and Cagney finally lets him have it: "Why don't you stop being sorry for yourself. There are a lot of people in this world who've had a tougher time than you. It comes with the ticket—nobody guarantees you a free ride. . . . The ones who can't take it, like you—the ones who are looking for a free ride—cause all the trouble, everywhere."

Like Derek's, Tony's problems are inside him; his id is a monster, and he has to shape up. As Tony's girl friend Arlene's dad told him, "You've got to follow authority." But if Tony is born to be bad, therapy is destined to fail, and the only cure is punishment. Dr. Brandon, on the other hand, believes that beneath the verdigris of civilization, people are basically good, nature is better than culture. "Mankind is on the verge of destroying itself. Its only hope is to go back to its primitive dawn and start over again." Brandon is a therapeutic Rousseau seeking to transform Tony into a natural man, a noble savage. For this, the film depicts him as a subversive extremist, which is to say, he is the corporate-liberal therapist depicted as a radical—he thinks nature will redeem culture. And the film condemns him on both counts.*

Brandon shoots Tony full of drugs and hypnotizes him to "release his primitive, savage energies." "Soon you'll be your true self," he assures Tony as his patient floats backward in time. We know no good will come of this, because we have seen Tony get into the habit of wolfing down raw hamburger meat in the days before steak tartare became the bread and butter of singles bars. And sure enough, Tony's true self turns out to be a real savage, not a noble one.

I Was a Teenage Werewolf agrees, in fact, with the conservatives of *Blackboard Jungle*. It imagines concretely what Murdock and his allies were content to leave at the level of metaphor. If the delinquents at North Manual were *like* animals, Tony *is* an animal, a teen-age werewolf, and he spends the rest of the film feeding off his classmates.

Like Dr. Carrington in *The Thing*, Brandon is terminally naïve, so dumb he doesn't recognize the enemy when he sees it. "Tony, Tony, I'm your friend," he cries, as the teen-age werewolf, with its matted dreadlocks and badly occluded fangs, all smeared with yellow plaque, advances upon him, drooling saliva by the bucketful all over his carpet. But Tony doesn't listen. Brandon's success in returning him to a state of nature, that is, liberating him from social constraints, brings disaster. Tony becomes

---

*McGee and Murphy, in the *The J. D. Films*, suggest that interest in regression may have been sparked by the publication, in 1955, of *The Search for Bridey Murphy*. But there were a number of earlier regression films, such as *The Neanderthal Man* (1953), with its "devolution serum," and they can all be interpreted as conservative attacks on the natural utopianism of the right and left, as well as the therapeutic ideology of pluralism.

The werewolf turned on by a nubile bobbysoxer is a monster from the id. Born to be bad, Tony (Michael Landon) cannot be cured, only killed.

dangerous not because therapy has failed but because it has succeeded. Before he sees Brandon, Tony is merely a delinquent; after a few sessions on the couch he leaves a werewolf. The psychiatrist, the pillar of the system of therapeutic control, is simply a mad scientist. "Hugo! Prepare the scopolamine!" he barks at his timid assistant. Hugo remonstrates against experimenting on a human being, but Brandon brushes him off. "You call yourself a scientist," he sneers. "You'll never be more than an assistant." If this were a corporate-liberal film that valued leadership, science, and hierarchy, he would be right, and Hugo would never get his grant from the National Science Foundation. But here it is Hugo who is right to drag his feet, and it is Brandon who is going to lose his license.

Brandon's accomplice in therapeuticizing Tony is the female principal of Rockdale High, Mrs. Ferguson. The school appears to be run entirely by women. (The only teacher we see is a woman gym teacher who wears a suit, always a sign of incipient lesbianism in the fifties.) From a conservative point of view, a female-run institution like the school can expect to have social-control problems, particularly in contrast to a male-run institution like the police department. In *High School Confidential* (1958), directed by Jack Arnold, the high school is a hotbed of liberalism whose personnel have to be given a lesson in the facts of life by the police commissioner. There, the mollycoddling parents, teachers, and principal are shockingly blasé when the kids are discovered smoking marijuana. Teacher: "Commissioner, don't you think you're magnifying the issue?" Principal: "Many of us believe in the progressive theory that there is no such thing as a bad boy or girl." Commissioner: "Well, there's a high school in Indiana . . . out of a total enrollment of 1,200 students, 285 were found to be using marijuana or heroin. This dreadful condition . . . *can happen here!*"[28]

Mrs. Ferguson repudiates the get-tough policy recommended by the authorities. Dangling the same carrot before Tony that Dadier dangled before Miller, she says she'll recommend him for college if he just keeps his nose clean. "I always knew that if we could just get through to you, really get inside you, you'd be a credit to your father." There it is again! Jim, in *Rebel*, had happily told juvenile officer Ray that "you can see right through me," and here, Mrs. Ferguson wants to "get inside" Tony's head the same way Father Your-Conscience-Has-Gotta-Do-the-Askin' Barry got inside Terry's, the same way Rick Dadier "reached" his students, got hold of their "imaginations," the same way Dr. Brandon wants to "enter Tony's mind" with drugs.

Not only does mind management fail, the divide-and-conquer tactic fails as well. Tony and the werewolf are doubles, like Jim and Plato, Miller and West. The strategy of pluralist films, as we have seen, is to separate the good from the bad, the troubled but basically decent folks from the loonies and losers for whom jail or death is the only solution. *Werewolf* sets up this same doubling structure, but only to show that it doesn't work.

Tony and his double cannot be separated. When the werewolf dies, Tony dies too. (In *From Here to Eternity*, another conservative film, both Prewitt and his double, Maggio, die, as do Morbius and his double, the monster from the id, in *Forbidden Planet*.) Conservatives couldn't be bothered with the nit-picking distinctions corporate liberals were always making between foes and potential friends, between revolutionaries and nationalists, Communists and Socialists, fellow travelers, radicals, left-liberals, and so on, and they couldn't have cared less about the Third Force. Everything alien is Other in films like *Werewolf*, and everything Other is alien.

In the same way that conservative films didn't bother to separate good doubles from bad, or if they did, killed them both off, so they didn't go out of their way to manipulate peer groups. Whereas films like *The Thing* cherished small groups of peers, pitting them against large, gangs didn't qualify for small-group treatment, because they were both alien and criminal, offending conservatives' affection for law-'n-order. As Mortimer and Lait put it, speaking for conservatives as well as the right: "Teenagers speak their own mystic tongue, unintelligible to adults but understood by kids throughout the country. Their cells are in juke-box joints, soda dispensaries, and hot record shops. . . . Like a heathen religion, it is all tied up with tom-toms and hot jive and ritualistic orgies of erotic dancing, weed-smoking and mass mania, with African jungle background."[29]

Bad gangs, be they teen-age hoods or the Clantons in *Clementine*, were dangerous. *Village of the Damned* (1960), a British film, showed what a peer group could do when it wanted to. Here it was a whole village of children, products of interstellar insemination, who kept aloof from adults, dressed alike, looked the same, and acted in concert—in short, a conservative nightmare of peer-group power. These kids were literally born bad, and it wasn't they who were the victims, but their parents. When the kids began to give looks that could (and did) kill, with their luminous eyes, it became clear that the only thing they had on their minds (or mind— "What we are dealing with here is a mass mind!" says an alarmed George Sanders) was taking over the world. The solution was conservative too. Sanders simply blew them to smithereens with dynamite.

With the therapeutic option in shambles, with psychoanalysis exposed as the work of the devil, with doubles demolished, the only alternative left is the resort to force, which in the case of *Werewolf* means the police.

Unlike the cops in a right-wing film like *Invasion of the Body Snatchers*, the police here are not narrow-minded dullards, ignoring the pods and blobs under their very eyes. On the contrary, when they come up against the unusual ("Strange—a slice on each side of the throat: Fangs!"), they accept it and act accordingly. They are sympathetic but firm. They don't want to use force unless they have to, preferring milder methods until they don't work. Against their will, in the last extremity, they pick up the gun and kill Tony. But when they do, the lesson is clear: Delinquents aren't sick, they're evil, and the best thing to do with kids who don't like back slappers is to shoot them.

I Was a Teenage Werewolf was a poor but popular film. It grossed over $2 million on a $20,000 investment and gave rise to a spate of imitations, including *I Was a Teenage Frankenstein* (1957), *Teenage Monster* (1958), *Teenage Caveman* (1958), and was remade as *Blood of Dracula*, with a girl instead of a boy, and a vampire replacing the werewolf. Michael Landon reputedly snared his role in *Bonanza* after his convincing performance here. *Werewolf* was not only popular, it was a prescient film as well. By 1957, when it was made, the signs were in the wind, and conservatives saw them first. The peer group, the youth culture that pluralists had midwived, and then fattened with hamburgers, movies, and rock-'n-roll, was, like Tony, about to become a monster. With its long hair and wild, unkempt beard, that monster was a hippy.

Right-wing delinquency films had mixed feelings about their young criminals. We might expect that they would be attracted by the antisocial, vigilante, do-it-yourself ambience of delinquency, somewhat the way that *Underworld USA* glamorized its hoodlum hero. But the right, as we have seen, was more interested in individuals than groups, and besides, they, too, adopted a hard line on crime that canceled out any latent sympathy for the young criminals. For this reason, there were few, if any, right-wing films that heroized delinquents in the fifties. To find one, we have to go all the way back to 1933. In Cecil B. deMille's *This Day and Age*, delinquents are romanticized as vigilantes who do what the authorities should have done were they not so pusillanimous. When the legal system fails, and a murderer is acquitted, five thousand high school students have to take the law into their own hands. They kidnap the killer and hang him over a pit full of rats until he confesses.

Usually, however, the kids are bad, and simply equated with aliens. We only know it's a right-wing film because they are finally cowed not by docs or cops, but by the victim himself, who's finally had enough and fights back, like Regis Toomey in *Joy Ride* (1958). Four punks beat up Toomey's wife and steal the family car. During the wild ride, however, Toomey pulls a gun, forcing punk number one (Rad Fulton) to race along a hairpin mountain road until he bursts into tears.

The Space Children

Left-wing films, on the other hand, were unencumbered by the lust for law-'n-order that shackled their opposite numbers. In the same way that left-wing sci-fi embraced aliens, peer groups or gangs were okay because they formed the core of a potentially oppositional community, and therefore they were entirely justified in their defiance of centrist techniques of social control. In *The Wild One* (1954), a motorcycle gang led by Marlon Brando terrorizes a small town, but the townies are almost as bad as the gang, the adults worse than the kids. It's a bad-town film, in which the sheriff is a twit, and the good citizens become a mob, giving Brando one of the obligatory beatings that have marked his career. McGee and Robertson claim that producer Stanley Kramer's "original intention had been to show the intolerance of middle America to anyone who varied from the public norm, a concept too unsettling for the censors to accept. Emphasis was, instead, shifted to the violence of the gang, and attempts to justify their hostility were blunted. The hypocrisies of the businessmen were similarly downplayed."[30]

In films like *The Blob* (1958), smart teen-agers humiliate their stick-in-the-mud elders, while in Jack Arnold's *The Space Children* (1958) the prepubescent boys and girls form an autonomous kiddie culture that defies adult control. This film pits children against parents, and the children win. In the first scene, a Plymouth station wagon full of Brewsters (dad, mom, and the two boys), stalls on the highway near a California missile base. It is only the boys who see the rainbow and hear the strange whooshing noise like a jet plane. Mom and dad are too busy bickering to notice, which is to say, families here are even worse than they are in *Rebel Without a Cause*.

When the Brewsters finally reach the base, where dad has a job as a technician working on the new doomsday rocket called the Thunderer, we find that most all the parents are bad news, hardline hawks, disciplinarians, and child-beaters. "I don't know how you raise your kids, but I don't like mine to stay up to all hours of the night," says one man gruffly. When Mrs. Brewster mildly questions the propriety of the arms race ("All we do is build them bigger and bigger and blow up more and more"), another parent advocates preventive war: "Down there stands the Thunderer. What are we waiting for? When that [enemy] satellite gets up there we should—bang!!!" Still another man calls his stepson a "spoiled brat" and slaps him hard across the face.

Meanwhile, the Thunderer has attracted the attention of a worried "brain" from outer space. This was not altogether uncommon in the fifties. The invaders from Mars, in the film of the same name, tried to stop U.S. rocket testing and the invaders in *Earth vs. the Flying Saucers* zapped an army missile base. But in all these films, the misguided attempts to interfere with the cold war failed. In *The Space Children*, the outcome is different.

Like the aliens in *It Came from Outer Space*, the brain is benevolent; like Klaatu in *The Day the Earth Stood Still*, it thinks Earth is getting too big for its britches. It glides to Earth on a rainbow, sets up camp in a cave on the beach, and proceeds to "take over" the kids, using them to sabotage the launch. The take-over proves that the kids, like John Putnam in *It Came from Outer Space*, were aliens all the time. The parents are right to be worried; under the influence of the alien brain, their children run in a pack, a tribe, a primitive peer group free from and antagonistic to the adult world. Whereas *Village of the Damned* is alarmed by such behavior from its Keane-eyed kids, this film is pleased.

The Space Children, unlike *Rebel*, goes on to make an explicit link between the politics of the family and those of society at large, in this case the cold war. The parents, of course, are the social-control figures here, but the film takes their kids' side against them. Since the fathers are also arms-race honchos, their definition of the public interest is discredited when we see them beating their kids. Force, so successful in conservative films like *Werewolf*, here doesn't work. In fact, when one dad is about to swat his son with a stick, the brain strikes him dead. But if the conservative fathers fail with their sticks, the pluralist mothers don't do much better with their carrots. When sympathetic Mrs. Brewster tries to reason with her sons, they ignore her—with the film's endorsement.

Social control of all kinds is dangerous. The brain from outer space represents the real public interest, which is to say, the idea of peace, the utopian solution to the arms race, is transcendent, not immanent. It is not a product of everyday life, because most earthlings are too far gone; Earth is dystopic. As in *The Day the Earth Stood Still*, utopianism only exists elsewhere, in advanced civilizations beyond the stars, or within the souls of the outcast kids. And in a dramatic expression of the nature-culture dichotomy, technology is all bad, and nature, conversely, is entirely

In *The Space Children*, the kids aren't bad at all. Here they protect the alien brain from the creepy adults, their puzzled parents and arms-race honchos.

good. The film cuts back and forth between the fathers gathered in the high-tech command center awaiting blast-off and the kids gathered on the beach, the waves crashing majestically behind them. As the countdown proceeds, the brain's convolutions pulse and glow—and the launch is aborted. It's high treason, and in a centrist film, these kids, along with their brain, would have gone the way of the Rosenbergs. But not here. "I don't understand. Why did you destroy the Thunderer?" asks a puzzled colonel at the end. "Because the world wasn't ready for it," comes the reply. "The children all over the world did what we did in every country. The world's been given a second chance." "But are you siding with it against us?" wails one mom. "We're your parents. We love you." The children are mute on this point, while the film leaves us with yet another affirmation of the redemptive power of children: "Verily I say unto you, except ye be converted, and become as little children, ye shall not enter into the kingdom of heaven."

In pluralist films like *Rebel*, the parents and children are reconciled, on the parents' terms. In a conservative film like *Werewolf*, the parents simply kill their children off, in that case, Tony. Left-wing films like *The Space Children*, on the other hand, are metaphorically (and sometimes literally) parricidal. The children defeat the parents, repudiate their values. And like the heroes of other left-wing films, the children are motivated neither by duty, realism, nor the imperative to act with maturity, like pluralist heroes; nor by a suprapersonal code of professionalism, like conservative heroes; nor by revenge, like right-wing heroes. They are motivated by idealism which, like revenge, stands in opposition to centrist social control. They want to change the world, not accept it as it is, grow up, do their jobs, or get even with the man who shot their father. From this perspective, the realism of corporate-liberal heroes looks like little more than opportunism, while professionalism appears parochial, and revenge immoral.

Cochise, Si! Geronimo, No!:
The Limits of Tolerance

Minorities were analogous to delinquent peer groups, in the same way that delinquent peer groups were analogous to mobs of gangsters. They had to be controlled. In *Blackboard Jungle*, it was no accident that the student Dadier chose for the job was black, nor that he turned "Jack and the Beanstalk" into a lesson in tolerance.

Tolerance was a major ingredient in pluralist social control, a pillar of consensus. It was one of the carrots that would make the stick unnecessary. People who came in from the cold, regardless of race, color, or creed, found a warm welcome, a job with an equal-opportunity employer, and shelter from the stormy weather that made life outside the vital center very difficult indeed. While pluralists trimmed their sails when they cruised the choppy waters of civil liberties, they went full speed ahead on civil rights. At the same time that Harry Truman was pursuing his "get tough" policy with the Russians and energetically ferreting out domestic "security risks," he provoked the Dixiecrat defection from his own party by insisting on a strong civil rights plank in the Democratic platform in 1948. "The sin of racial pride still represents the most basic challenge to the American conscience," lectured Schlesinger. "It is fatal not to maintain an unrelenting attack on all forms of racial discrimination."[31] This is not to say that pluralists like Schlesinger were insincere, only that tolerance was useful as well as virtuous.

Films that stressed tolerance for one or another minority formed a sizable subgenre within the social-problem films of the late forties. Dmytryk's *Crossfire*, about Jews, and Kazan's *Gentleman's Agreement*, starring Gregory Peck as a Gentile passing for a Jew, were both box-office hits in 1947, and began the cycle. They were quickly followed by films like *Pinky*, *Home of the Brave*, *Intruder in the Dust* (1951), *Lost Boundaries* (1949), *No Way*

Out (1950), and *The Well* (1951), about blacks; *A Medal for Benny* (1945), *Border Incident* (1949), *A Lady Without a Passport* (1950), *The Lawless* (1949), and *Right Cross* (1950) and *My Man and I* (1952), both with Ricardo Montalban, about Hispanics; and *Go for Broke* (1951), *Japanese War Bride* (1952), *Bad Day at Black Rock* (1954), and *Three Stripes in the Sun* (1955), about Japanese. Most of these films were pretty pale. Blacks, for example, were often played by whites. "There is obviously some murky principle at work that says that we can recognize dignity in blacks," writes Michael Wood, "only when white folks dress up and lend a bit of dignity to them."[32] There is a famous story about *Gentleman's Agreement* recounted by Penelope Houston that goes like this: "A minor technician working on the picture told [the scriptwriter Moss Hart] that being associated with such a film had made a deep impression on him; when the grateful writer asked for details, he said, 'I'll be more careful in the future; I won't ever ill-treat a Jew in case it turns out that he's really a Christian.' "[33]

Nevertheless, their hearts were in the right place. At the time, despite Hart's technician, these films packed a wallop and, like *Blackboard Jungle*, were attacked by the right for helping the Reds knock America. Social-problem films about race and ethnicity stopped making money after the first few blockbusters, and many of those associated with them fell victim to the witch-hunt. (Not surprisingly, it was mostly left-leaning writers and directors who felt strongly enough about these issues to make films about them.) But if the films disappeared, the social problems remained. The earlier films were too topical for comfort, and directors who wanted to examine intolerance turned to sci-fi and to the western, where the conflict between cowboys and Indians became a covert commentary on race relations. Once again, the problem was social control: how to deal with the troublesome groups within society.

Broken Arrow

Delmer Daves's *Broken Arrow* (1950) begins in 1870, during a protracted, inconclusive war between the Americans and the Apaches. It's a nasty war, a "bloody, no-give, no-take war," as the narrator, Tom Jeffords, calls it. As in *On the Waterfront* and *Blackboard Jungle*, force has failed to do the trick. Although the Apaches are outnumbered and outgunned, they're doing a good job of making life miserable for the American settlers of the Southwest. The Butterfield Stage hasn't run in five years, the U.S. mail has been disrupted, and it's not safe to walk on the prairie at night. "He can't read a map, but Cochise and his men know every mountain, every valley in Arizona," says Jeffords. "He can't write his name, but his intelligence service knows when [the colonel] got to Fort Grant and how many men [he] has. For the first time in history, Cochise has the Apaches from all the tribes fighting under one command." Sound familiar? It seemed that the specter of guerrilla war and a general breakdown of "civility" hovered over every film that trundled off the studio assembly line. Hoods and hippies had infiltrated every classroom; Indians were hiding behind every tree.

But there is something different about *Broken Arrow*. When Jeffords (Jimmy Stewart) opens the narration, he says that this story of Cochise is just the way it all happened, except that "when the Apaches speak, they will be speaking in our language." As we have seen, Hollywood rarely respected the Otherness of alien groups, showed little interest, anthropological or otherwise, in different customs or values. Indians always speak English in American films; it's a convention hardly worth mentioning, so that when a film goes out of its way to call attention to it, it's of more than routine interest. *Broken Arrow* sets out to do what conventional westerns don't: not only to acknowledge the autonomy and authority of an alien culture, but to portray it with sympathy. From the earliest westerns on, Indians had been little more than one-dimensional figures, mere savages, rapers of women, scalpers of settlers, the scourge of wagon trains and the

Pony Express. During the forties, there appeared a few films more or less sympathetic to Indians, but it was *Broken Arrow* that forever laid this caricature to rest. Apache civilization is not worse than our own; it is different, and perhaps even a little better. Along with the aloof interstellar visitors in *It Came from Outer Space* and *The Day the Earth Stood Still*, *Broken Arrow* offers us a glimpse of a culture that embodies utopian possibilities outside and against our own society.

Tom Jeffords's education begins in the first scene when he finds an injured Apache boy in the desert. Jeffords is a former cavalry scout and Indian fighter recently discharged from the army and turned prospector. There is no love lost between him and the Apache. "He was something more dangerous than a snake," says Jeffords, when he catches sight of the boy crawling among the rocks. "He was an Apache!" But Jeffords's humanitarian instincts get the better of him; he gives the boy a drink of water, and soon they are fast friends. After a few days, the boy recovers and has to go; his "mother is crying" for him. "It never struck me that an Apache woman could cry like other women," says Jeffords. "To me, they were just animals," which is to say, he begins the film like Murdock, who thought the boys of North Manual were "animals." But while Jeffords is contemplating this novel thought, the tree next to his shoulder is suddenly riddled with so many arrows it looks like a porcupine. The boy's father has come to fetch his son with a hunting party of braves, and he is not pleased to find him with a white man, nor to find a white man on "Apache land." When the boy pleads for Jeffords's life, dad gives in, tying him to a tree instead of killing him. From this vantage point, Jeffords watches the Apaches make short work of a party of prospectors on horseback. Those that are not killed instantly are hanged upside down by their heels, while another is buried up to his eyes in an anthill. This is the kind of Indian massacre that happens regularly in Ford's films, the ones so brutal that they occur off camera, the ones only John Wayne is man enough to see. But here, it is virtually excused. "This was war," Jeffords says philosophically, "with cruelty on both sides." And indeed, one of the slain miners was carrying three Apache scalps in his pouch. Could it be that whites are no different from reds?

Jeffords returns to Tucson a changed man. "I learned something that day," he tells us. "Apache women cried over their sons; Apache men had a sense of fair play." Back at his rooming house, Jeffords encounters a fair sampling of the town fathers over dinner. When Colonel Bernal, who's been sent to "clean out" the Apaches, wants to hire him to "reconnoiter," Jeffords refuses. When he hears the others talking against the Apaches, he can't stomach it. They want to know why Jeffords wasn't killed along with the prospectors. "Maybe you've gotten too friendly with the Apaches," sneers Slade, a rancher. "Maybe you've forgotten which side you're on. If you don't fight against'em, you're with'em. Seems to me a white man like you would want to put an end to this—" "Cochise didn't start this war," Jeffords interrupts hotly, reminding them that it was a nameless American lieutenant who broke the peace. Lowery, a businessman, chimes in. "I know the white men aren't always right, but we're bringing civilization out here—clothes, carpets, boots, medicine—I have a shipment of first-class whiskey waiting for me back East. If it weren't for Cochise, I could [ship it out here and] sell it for a dollar a bottle." Slade demands to know why Jeffords didn't kill the boy. "That's private business, friend," drawls Jeffords. "Not when they're murdering women and kids," replies Slade. "I'll tell you why I didn't kill that boy. I'm sick and tired of killing," Jeffords snaps.

So far, *Broken Arrow* sounds like a left-wing film. If we had any doubts before, it's clear now that the townies are as bad as, if not worse than, the Apaches, and we take Jeffords's side against the crass coalition of business-men and soldiers. The enemy here is the center, not the extremes, not the aliens, who are, as we already begin to suspect, friendly. When Jeffords refuses to answer Slade's questions about why he didn't kill the boy, for "private" reasons, in the face of Slade's invocation of what amounts to a national emergency—the Apache war is equivalent to the attack of the giant ants in *Them!*, the outbreak of plague in *Panic*—he is committing treason in the eyes of the center. In national emergencies, private citizens were supposed to hop to it. But Jeffords is obstructing the public interest with his claims to privacy.

In the context of cold-war politics, if the Apache reds are the Russian Reds (as with aliens in sci-fi, the connection is obvious, if not inevitable), then this film is saying that not only is red better than dead, it's better than white as well. From the point of view of the left, the townies are no-compromise, you-can't-negotiate-with-the-Russians, hard-line hawks, while to the center and right (the film doesn't distinguish between them), Jeffords is the bleeding-heart peacenik, soft on Communism, an unfriendly witness who won't allow inquiries into his beliefs, an Indian-lover and fellow traveler. To them, the war against the Apaches is a Manichean struggle between good and evil, red and white, and in such a war there is no middle ground. When Jeffords says he is "sick and tired of all this killing," he's chucking the martial model of society, saying no to the Murdocks and McClouds. The film levels a radical critique at the hard-liners, portraying them as bigots and bullies. It also attacks the idea that the center is the seat of culture. In the words of Lowery, civilization boils down to a fast buck.

Jeffords, for the moment at least, has been radicalized. When he decided that the Apaches were not animals, he moved from Murdock, in the right lane, to the center with Dadier, who always knew that students are people. But when Jeffords says that he's "tired of being in the middle" and turns left to pow-wow with Cochise, he goes off the road altogether.

Jeffords steeps himself in Apache language and lore and makes his way to Cochise's mountain fastness. As he leaves the town and rides into Apache territory, the critique of American civilization that has just gone down at breakfast is dramatized by the grandeur of the natural setting across which he moves. Like a radical film, this one uses nature to attack culture, uses the primitive to attack the modern. The majestic bluffs and mesas rising starkly from the desert take on the force of a moral critique of the town. All that has transpired within the town has been restricted to the interior of the dining room at the hotel, an enclosed space whose limits reflect the narrowness of the white man's moral vision. Enclosure here is a prison, not a fortress as it is in *The Thing*.

When Jeffords reaches Cochise's camp, we're treated to a large dose of Apache ceremony and ritual, with close attention to the costumes, the body paint, and so on. In Ford's westerns, such as *My Darling Clementine*, the locus of the ritual celebrations of community, the weddings, funerals, and dances that punctuate the action, is, of course, the town; here it is the tribe. Cochise himself turns out to be Jeff Chandler, a handsome, striking man, a noble savage dressed with dignity in simple buckskin and leather. Jeffords tells Cochise what he wants to hear: "My people have done yours a great wrong. . . . Is it not possible for your people and mine to live in peace?" When Cochise sees how much Jeffords knows about Apache lore, his heart is won. Jeffords's heart is won, in turn, by pretty Morning Star (Debra Paget). Cochise agrees to let the mail go

Cochise (Jeff Chandler) and Tom Jeffords (James Stewart) find they have more in common with each other than with the red and white trash in their own camps.

through as a gesture of goodwill, while Morning Star agrees to become Jeffords's bride.

But consorting with the enemy doesn't sit so well with the folks back in town. Jeffords is the natural target for a witch-hunt. He returns with his message of peace and finds a lynch mob waiting for him. No sooner do they string him up to the nearest tree than General Howard intervenes, saving Jeffords's life. Known as the "Christian General," General Howard is, as it turns out, a special emissary from President Grant. His job is to make peace with the Apaches, and since Jeffords is the only white man Cochise trusts, he needs his help.

At this juncture, *Broken Arrow* seems to be as uncompromising as it was in the beginning. But there are some telltale signs, indicating creeping centrism. First, we notice that the film has a distinctly hierarchical view of society, both white and red. At the top of the American heap is President Grant, a man of peace. Ditto General Howard just below him. But as we descend the ladder of rank, things don't look so good. Colonel Bernal is a hawk, and worse is the nameless lieutenant who broke the peace in the first place. At the bottom, of course, are the witch-hunting townies. The same pecking order obtains among the Apaches as well. At the top is Cochise, again a man of peace, but this is not true for the lesser chiefs below him, nor for the hoi polloi, the red riff-raff at the bottom, who can't be trusted not to scalp Jeffords unless he's accompanied by Cochise.

Then, too, we notice that although *Broken Arrow* pits nature against culture, the primitive against the modern, nevertheless it calls a symbolic halt to Jeffords's movement out of society into the wilderness. The key scene in this regard is one in which, standing in a grove of silver birch trees on the bank of a crystal-clear stream, birds trilling away on the sound track, Jeffords is shaving. Shaving scenes in westerns are always an index of the degree to which civilization has taken hold. When the weary cowboy rides into town, grizzled and dirty after weeks on the trail, the first thing he does after attending to his horse is make for the nearest hotel for a bath and a shave. He hangs up his guns and eases himself back into the barber's chair. He's vulnerable here, relaxed, separated from his weapons, his customary wariness momentarily lulled by the ministrations of the barber, who performs the rituals of civility. If he survives this procedure, culture has taken hold, civilization has come to Dodge City, law-'n-order to Deadwood. But if he is interrupted by gunfire or a fistfight, if bullets or bodies come crashing through the plate-glass window, we know that there's still work to be done. "What kind of a town is this?" Wyatt Earp asks about Tombstone in *My Darling Clementine*, as he leaps out of his seat to avoid flying lead. "A man can't get a shave without getting his head blown off." In *Broken Arrow*, paradoxically, only nature is safe for culture, only by the river can Jeffords shave safely. When he goes to town, he's strung up by the mob. But the important point here is that he still shaves; he doesn't abandon the habits of civilization, which is to say, he carries culture with him. Civilization is not thrown overboard in favor of the primitive.

Jeffords brings General Howard's peace proposal to Cochise, and he in turn relays it to an assembly of all the chiefs: "The Americans are growing stronger, while we are growing weaker. A big wind comes and the tree must bend, or it will be lifted out by the roots. Why should not Apaches learn new ways? It is not always easy to change, but sometimes this is required." This means, in effect, face facts, accept reality. Cochise speaks as a realist. "Reality" in this case is the reality of American power, but in westerns, it is generally viewed as History, Progress, the March of Time, Manifest Destiny, and so on. Several chiefs rise to protest the peace treaty and oppose Cochise's policies. Suddenly, where there had been one united Apache nation, now there are two factions, cooperative and uncooperative, peace-loving and warlike, responsible and irresponsible, good Indians and bad Indians: Cochise and Geronimo.

In *Broken Arrow*, Geronimo, leader of the opposition, is depicted in a decidedly unflattering fashion. He's not charismatic like Cochise, but sullen and mistrustful. He doesn't object to peace on principle, as well he might, on the grounds that it will bring a century of slow genocide to the Indians, but only because the treaty will prevent the Apaches from ravaging Mexico, as is their habit. "Where will we get blankets, cattle, corn, if not taking them from the Mexicans as we always have?" he asks. "The American government will give us cattle," replies Cochise. He's fallen for the foreign-aid carrot; he's already on line for the Marshall Plan, a suppliant asking for handouts rather than an equal demanding his rights. Geronimo, on the other hand, is the sad-sack Eeyore who rejects the carrot and finds that it is his lot in life to be endlessly pursued by the cavalry.

Cochise is not one to brook contradiction, and he expels Geronimo from the Apache nation. "Take your women, your children, and leave our territory. If Geronimo and his followers come to this territory again, let them come with weapons." It's Terry and Tommy, Miller and West, Tony and the werewolf all over again. An important goal of social control has been achieved. Cochise was particularly dangerous, we recall, because "for the first time in history he has all the Apaches from all the tribes fighting under one command." They were dangerous because they were united, in the same way that the dockers in *On the Waterfront* are "D and D," in the same way that Dadier knows he'd have to fight "thirty-five guys" if he messed with West. But now that the Apaches are divided into opposing factions, conquering can't be too far behind.

Cochise, si! Geronimo, no! This refrain echoed throughout fifties westerns. For every good Indian there was a bad Indian, for every Cochise there was a Geronimo to throw a tomahawk into the works. The war

between the two had a long history in the western. Geronimo first put in
an appearance in 1912. In 1939, he was played by Chief Thunder Cloud,
a genuine Cherokee who nevertheless required sessions under a sun lamp
because the studio thought he was too light for the role. But in the fifties,
Cochise and Geronimo played their good-guy/bad-guy routine more fully
and more frequently than ever, in films like *Fort Apache*, *Battle of Apache
Pass* (1952), *Conquest of Cochise* (1953), *Indian Uprising* (1952), *Taza,
Son of Cochise* (1954), and *I Killed Geronimo* (1950). (Actually, Geronimo died of pneumonia in 1909, after twenty-three years as a prisoner of
war at Fort Sill, Oklahoma.) Even when they were called by other names,
the Cochise/Geronimo dyad was central. In Rudolph Maté's *The Far
Horizons* (1955), it was Wild Eagle against Chief Camillo; in Fuller's *Run
of the Arrow* (1957), it was Crazy Wolf against Red Cloud; in Ford's *Two
Rode Together* (1961), it was Stonecalf against Chief Quana Parker. What
was the difference between the good Indians and the bad Indians? In *Two
Rode Together*, Jimmy Stewart and Richard Widmark have been sent into
Indian territory by the army to rescue some whites captured by the
Comanches many years ago. They find that Quana Parker speaks English
and is dressed modestly in a blanket, like a cigar-store Indian. No rube,
he is eager to learn "new ways." Like Cochise, he's a "realist," a "modern-
izer," who wants the white man's up-to-date weapons. Stonecalf (Woody
Strode), on the other hand is not. He grunts in Comanche, is covered
with war paint, and looks decidedly fierce and alien. "Stonecalf! He still
says words over shield to turn away bullets," Quana Parker says disdainfully, as he watches Stonecalf jump around the fire pounding his chest
like a madman. Stewart leaves Chief Parker alone, but kills Stonecalf a
few scenes later. Why? "We can come to terms with [Quana Parker], but
there was no reasoning with hotheads like Stonecalf," says a cavalry officer, congratulating Stewart, "His death is most timely."

In *Broken Arrow*, Cochise not only banishes Geronimo, but he does
the work of the cavalry for them. In defiance of the three-month armistice,
Geronimo's rebels attack the stagecoach, at the very moment that Jeffords
happens to be riding alongside it. "This can't be Cochise and his men,
but a band of renegade Indians," cries Jeffords. And while the driver and
the passengers are pinned down by a hail of arrows, he rides off for help.
From the cavalry—as in a traditional western? No—from Cochise! After
a band of good Indians has chased off the bad Indians, the driver, shaking

his head in disbelief, says, "Apaches protecting Americans! And I've lived to see it." It's no accident either. "From now on," announces Cochise, "we will protect all whites entering or leaving Tucson." Indians killing Indians for Americans! In the sixties, they had a name for it: Vietnamization.

Broken Arrow is not a film like *Attack!*, which scampers back to the center at the last moment because it lacks the courage of its convictions. Rather it works by intentionally giving full rein to values antagonistic to consensus, extending sympathy to radical attacks on the center, portraying vigorous utopian alternatives to pluralism, and then, once we're hooked, taking us back to the center.

The dialectic of Indianization has two steps: first, the creation of sympathy for the Apaches rather than the whites. At this stage, *Broken Arrow* turns *On the Waterfront* and *Blackboard Jungle* on their heads. It sides with Friendly against Father Barry, West against Dadier. The bad guys in those films are the good guys here. Second, rather than staying with the Us/Them format, as a left-wing film might, siding with Cochise and Geronimo, say, as they burned Tucson to the ground, slaughtering the Slades and Lowerys and sending the cavalry packing back to Washington with its tail between its legs, it jettisons the color war and uses Cochise to bridge the gap between red and white. Suddenly the town is not all bad, just as the Indians are not all good. There are good townies (although we virtually never see any) as well as bad Indians. "All Americans are not like the lieutenant who broke the last peace. There are Americans I trust," Jeffords tells Cochise. "Me too, me too," replies Cochise sagely. Complexity is back in the saddle. What this all boils down to is that, like the corporate liberals and conservatives who discovered that they had a lot more in common with each other than with the left-wing and right-wing on their flanks, Jeffords and Cochise forge an alliance of moderates against extremists, both white trash and red trash, Slade and Geronimo—they are equated.

Humanism is the opening wedge in the destruction of Apache resistance to the white man. Although the film opens by indulging the Otherness of the Apaches, it ends by showing that for all their basic differences, reds and whites, Apaches and Americans, are basically the same, just human, and therefore they have common interests that transcend the abyss that appears to separate them. These common interests, however, are not the interests of humanity; they are the interests of the center.

The new alliance of moderates is based on tolerance. Jeffords is such an effective social-control agent *because* he is a liberal, an Indian-lover, ready to learn the Apache language and love an Apache woman. A conservative would have failed where Jeffords succeeds. *Broken Arrow* is a pluralist critique of conservative methods of social control. It pits tolerance against force and then uses it to erode the solidarity of the Apaches. If Cochise agrees to stay on the reservation, not only will he be secure from attack but he will get free Hershey bars from the government, and every once in a while, maybe he will have his picture taken with President Grant. This is the same "utopia" of security and upward mobility that awaits Miller and Terry Malloy. If collaborators like Cochise can't expect better treatment than resisters like Geronimo, why play ball? If he has no incentive to make peace, he might as well fight to the death.

Not only has Jeffords succeeded in dividing and conquering the Apaches, single-handedly doing what the United States Cavalry failed to do in ten years of warfare, he has "turned" Cochise's head as well as his heart. Jeffords has got his hooks into the chief so deep he doesn't know which end is up. Cochise has begun to use white man's reasoning as his own. His speech about the realities of power ("A big wind comes and the tree must bend or it will be lifted out by the roots," and so on) is cribbed word for word from the lecture Jeffords gave him earlier in the film. He adopts the white man's distinction between good and bad Indians. "If this peace is broken, it will not be by Indians—not even bad Indians." He is "possessed" by Jeffords, and were this a sci-fi film, he would be "taken over" by aliens from outer space. Like Terry, whose "conscience has gotta do the askin'," Cochise has internalized social control.

Slade concocts a plan to ambush Cochise. Jeffords doesn't see the trap and foolishly advises Cochise to take Slade's word. In the ensuing gun battle, Morning Star is killed. * Most of the bushwackers are slain along with her, but some survive. Cradling her dead head in his arms, Jeffords

---

*The reason why Morning Star is killed, of course, is that she has married a white man. Hanky-panky between whites and reds was all very well on the reservation, but not in Lake Forest among the organization men. In *Broken Arrow*, as well as films like *Across the Wide Missouri* (1951) and *Last Train from Gun Hill* (1959), squaws who marry white men sooner or later find their way to the Happy Hunting Ground, or else, as in *Distant Drums* (1951), they are already dead when the film begins.

cries, in anguish, "The peace is a lie. They don't want peace." He demands a knife to kill the surviving whites. Cochise refuses. "The peace is not a lie, and I will not let you make it so, you who have taught me so well." Once again, we know that social control has worked when controlled and controller have changed places. Here, Jeffords makes an error in judgment that allows Cochise to make the transition from the one to the other. Like Jim and his dad in *Rebel*, like Miller and Dadier in *Blackboard Jungle*, the student has become the teacher; the teacher, the student.

Broken Arrow was parlayed into a popular radio serial and a television show. It made Jeff Chandler a star. (He was nominated for an Academy Award for his role as Cochise.) It was followed by a slew of westerns in which unscrupulous traders, greedy cattle barons, and psychotic officers tormented more-sinned-against-than-sinning Indians. *Broken Arrow* itself spun off an extraordinary number of films featuring a Jeffords-like character trying to keep the peace between whites and reds. In *The Great Sioux Uprising* (1953), it is Chandler himself who finally gets a crack at the Jeffords role he was trained for in *Broken Arrow*. In *Tomahawk* (1951), it is Van Heflin who tries to pacify the Sioux after a lieutenant murders an Indian boy; in *Apache Woman* (1955), a fed falls for the eponymous heroine, Jeffords-style, and comes to the aid of her beleaguered tribe, falsely accused of murder and mayhem by scheming whites. In *The Battles of Chief Pontiac* (1953), Lex Barker tries to keep the peace after a bad army officer sends blankets infected with smallpox virus to good Indians; and on and on and on. Some films picked up on the Indianization policy recommended by *Broken Arrow*. In *War Arrow* (1954), a cavalry officer (Jeff Chandler—who knew better?) trains friendly Seminoles to make war on unfriendly Kiowa. In other films, such as *Broken Lance* (1954), *The Unforgiven* (1960), and *Flaming Star* (1960), whites defend full- or part-blooded Indians whom they have married, sired, or adopted. (Oddly enough, blacks, the covert subjects of these films, who had been common enough in westerns, especially the Civil War variety, of the twenties, thirties, and forties, dropped out of fifties westerns altogether.)

The Searchers

Despite the tolerant thrust of most of these films, there were exceptions. It is in the shifting balance of power in the Cochise-Geronimo-Jeffords trio that the political inflections make themselves felt. In John Ford's *The Searchers* (1956), a conservative film, the central role is played by an Indian-hater, not an Indian-lover. The model for this character was Al Sieber, a real-life Indian hunter who, like Cochise and Geronimo, crops up over and over again. Here, Sieber is called Ethan Edwards, and he's played by John Wayne. Geronimo is a renegade Comanche chief named Scar, who has slaughtered Ethan's family and captured, raised, and married his niece, Debbie (Natalie Wood).

Edwards is the mirror image of Jeffords. Instead of forgiving and forgetting, he vows revenge, and most of the film is devoted to showing us how he gets it. Ethan is a vigilante, a hard-liner. He does what the townies want Jeffords to do in *Broken Arrow*. "Tolerance" is not in his vocabulary. He's so vindictive that he shoots out the eyes of dead braves so that their spirits, so the Comanches believe, will "wander in the wind" instead of settling down where they belong. He doesn't wish to reason with Scar, only to kill him. Nor is he really interested in rescuing Debbie. To him, she's defiled beyond redemption. She's better off dead than red.

Ethan is too tough a nut, even for a film like this one. He's a right-wing extremist, a radical individualist ("I'm going on alone," he snaps), a fanatic motivated solely by revenge. Ethan is so far gone he's even equated with Scar. He knows the Comanches' customs and speaks their language. At the end, he relents, rescuing Debbie instead of killing her, but he hasn't mellowed enough. In the last shot, he rides away from the community of friends and kin once more, destined, like the Comanche spirits, to wander forever.

But if *The Searchers* attacks the far right, it also attacks films like *Broken Arrow*. In Ford's film, Jeffords becomes Martin Pawley (Jeffrey Hunter), Ethan's young, bleeding-heart sidekick, a secondary role. He wants to save

Debbie; to him, she's better red than dead. But there, the resemblance ends. Although Martin is Ethan's foil throughout, he is also his heir apparent, and this film will accomplish his education. It is Martin who actually kills Scar. After an hour and a half of dragging his feet, of restraining Ethan and shrinking from violence, he encounters, in his moment of truth, the imperatives of power. Whereas Jeffords never uses force and is wrong when he tries, Martin has to learn to pick up the gun. The vigilantes have brought the bleeding hearts around, toughened them up, and made them good conservatives.

Since it prefers the stick to the carrot, *The Searchers* has little use for tolerance. It does not employ a divide-and-conquer strategy against its Comanches. There are no doubles, no Cochise to balance Scar's Geronimo, no good Indians to offset the bad. Actually, this is not strictly true. In one scene, we encounter a band of harmless Indian refugees. When conservative films did present a good-Indian/bad-Indian pair, they foregrounded the bad Indian instead of the good—Stonecalf instead of Quana Parker in *Two Rode Together*—whereas films like *Broken Arrow* do the opposite. Of course, if the bad Indian is more prominent, force is more plausible.

Generally in Ford's westerns, the good Indians were tolerated by whites but forced to live outside society on reservations, like Cochise or, less luckily, the drunk in *My Darling Clementine*, to whom Marshal Earp says simply, "Indian, get out of town and stay out," as he kicks him in the butt. The bad Indians, the Geronimos, must be hunted down and exterminated. Here, for example, is Jimmy Stewart, in *Two Rode Together*, describing to a white woman the probable fate of her kid brother, captured by the Comanches when he was a little boy: "That kid's got braids down to here, now. Stiff, stinking braids, filled with buffalo grease. . . . He forgot his English. He just grunts Comanche now. And he's killed. He's even taken scalps. White men's scalps. And given the chance, he'd rape you. And when he's finished, he'd trade you off to one of the other braves for a good knife or a bad rifle."*

---

*In justice to Ford, *Fort Apache* presents a much more positive picture of Indians. Why? In this case, the temptation to sentimentalize outcasts as natural men and noble savages so that they can be used as a club with which to batter the corporate liberals outweighs the punitive and racist inclinations of conservative films.

In *The Searchers*, the good Indians play such a minor role, they are insignificant, at best victims and at worst buffoons. At one point we are supposed to be amused by a squaw who believes she has become Martin's wife by trading him a couple of blankets. When Martin, disgusted by her attempts to sleep next to him, kicks her down a small hill, it's supposed to be funnier still. Martin himself is part Indian—films like this can have red-blooded heroes—but when it turns out that the part is no more than an eighth, the film's commitment to tolerance is reciprocally diminished.

The Searchers accurately reflected conservative attitudes toward issues of race. Buckley referred repeatedly (and nastily) to Mrs. Roosevelt's "hyper-toleration,"[34] and many conservatives, in fact, opposed the Supreme Court's 1954 *Brown* v. *Board of Education* decision, which integrated the public schools. "The central question," editorialized the *National Review*, was "whether the White community in the South is entitled to take such measures as are necessary to prevail, politically and culturally, in areas where it does not predominate numerically. The sobering answer is *Yes*."[35]

Right-wing westerns either heroized Indians, attacking the center for decadence or corruption, or since tolerance for minorities was not a major item on the right's agenda, more commonly they villainized both Cochise and Geronimo, portrayed peacemakers like Jeffords as traitors, and lauded hard-liners like Sieber, Slade, and Ethan Edwards. Either way, right-wing, like left-wing, westerns were rare. In one, Charles Marquis Warren's *Arrowhead* (1953), the hero is Charlton Heston, a venomous Indian-hating scout whose character was also based on Sieber's life. The villain is a Geronimo-like eastern-educated Apache chief played by Jack Palance, whose first move on returning from college is to murder his brother, an assimilated Uncle Tomahawk (Cochise) who works for Wells Fargo. At the end, with the film's approval, Heston simply breaks Palance's neck with his bare hands.

Apache

The left had a much larger appetite for tolerance than even pluralists did. It was ideologically committed to minorities and backed them in their defiance of the center, much as it pitted peer groups against parents. It set nature against culture, romanticized outcasts, and attacked social control.

In Robert Aldrich's *Apache* (1954), the hero is Massai (Burt Lancaster), an Indian rebel who is persecuted by the white man. When Geronimo surrenders at the beginning of the film, Massai keeps fighting. The Coch-

Massai (Burt Lancaster) is a noble savage who keeps on fighting when Geronimo gives up. To the white man, however, he's a dangerous red who's better off dead.

ise figures are no more than collaborators, in contrast to which Massai is virtuous and principled. On the run from the whites, he is stalked by—guess who?—Indian-hater Al Sieber, who turns up again under his own name, this time played by John McIntire. Sieber is obsessed with Massai, in much the same way Edwards is obsessed with Scar, Heston with Palance, but this film is told from the Indian's point of view, and Sieber is certainly no hero.

Like Aldrich's *Attack!*, *Apache*, made two years earlier, veers back to the center at the end. Massai eventually heeds the advice of a wise Cherokee (a "realist," of course), who tells him that "the days of the warriors are over" and gives him a handful of maize to plant. At the end, Massai outwits Sieber, but instead of killing him, he just walks away into a happy ending. Aldrich complained in an interview, sometime later, that he would have preferred a grimmer, less compromising ending, with Massai killed by Sieber, but the producers wouldn't have it: "Hecht and United Artists wanted Lancaster to be able to live, but it made a joke of the whole film."[36]

In all films we have examined so far—war films, sci-fi, westerns, gangster, and JD films—women play a key role, either facilitating social control, like Edie Doyle, Nancy Reed, and Pat Medford, or obstructing it, like Becky in *Invasion of the Body Snatchers* or Helen Benson in *The Day the Earth Stood Still*, who encourage the heroes to defy the center. Men and women are often examined separately, but they are so intimately related—this kind of man calling for that kind of woman, and vice versa—that the role and function of one can be properly understood only in relation to the role and function of the other. What were the sexual politics of films of the fifties?

PART THREE

MALE
AND
FEMALE

ALL IN THE FAMILY

Coming Home

Johnny Ringo is the fastest gun around. But when he rides into town at the beginning of Henry King's *The Gunfighter* (1950), he's a changed man. As the marshal says, he's "a little older, a little quieter, not as cocky as he used to be." Ringo (Gregory Peck) is a tired outlaw who wants to retire, settle down with his wife, Peg, the town schoolteacher who left him years before because she didn't like bullets bouncing off her blackboard. But now Ringo's also had enough. He's fed up with squatting before campfires; he wants to sit in front of the television, trade his horse for a station wagon, his gun for a pipe.

We also want Ringo to get these goodies. The only question is, Is it too late? In *The Gunfighter*, it is. At the end of the movie, his reputation catches up with him. He's shot in the back by a young squirt who wants to be known as the baddest man in town, the "man who shot Johnny Ringo."

Ringo couldn't come home because he was out of step with the lonely crowd; he was an individualist in a world of organization men. But there was another reason why Ringo couldn't come home: he was the wrong kind of man. It wasn't enough for him just to want to come home; he would have had to transform himself, take a course in human relations, read Erich Fromm's *The Art of Loving*, acquire a whole new personality. While he was out on the trail, the name of the game had changed. It was no longer "cowboys and Indians"; it was "house." His wife didn't believe he could change, and neither do we, and his death underlines the magnitude of the transformation that would be required of the American male, and the pathos of failure, of exclusion from the paradise of domesticity.

The millions of American men who were coming back from Europe and the Pacific in 1945 found, to the surprise of many, that man's place was in the home. Home was more than a pipe, slippers, and a warm bed.

For one thing, it was the seat of the family, the domestic version of the group so favored by pluralists. "Whether you are a man or a woman," as *The Woman's Guide to Better Living* put it, "the family is the unit to which you most genuinely belong."[1]

For another, it was the key economic unit of the affluent society, dependent as affluence was on a high rate of domestic consumption, and therefore most men, unlike Johnny Ringo, got the chance to go home whether they wanted to or not. In 1945 it was John Garfield's turn in *Pride of the Marines*. Garfield had been blinded during the war, and what's more, he felt that America "isn't my home any more." Too bad. His nurse tells his sweetheart, Ruth, that she has to "bring him back home where he belongs." At the end, Ruth succeeds in carrying him off from the hospital and packing him into a taxi. "Where to?" asks the driver. "Home," replies Garfield.

Home was all very well for women. When David Riesman discussed sex roles, he didn't even mention them, because they were presumably already where they belonged. Women didn't have to change to fall into step with the lonely crowd; they were already at the head of the parade. But men had a harder time. Garfield could be assimilated to the home because he was half dead anyway. And so were the other war heroes who came home with him, maimed (*The Men, The Best Years of Our Lives* [1946]), crazy (*Crossfire, Home of the Brave*), and amnesiac (*Random Harvest* [1942], *The Chase* [1946], *Somewhere in the Night* [1946]). While their assorted disabilities appeared to make it difficult to integrate themselves into postwar life, they actually made it easier. The war wound was the ticket to the new world of domesticity, the symbolic castration that guaranteed that returning vets wouldn't throw over the traces, break the crockery, or run away from home.

But Johnny Ringo had no disabilities, was not in need. He was what Riesman called an "inner-directed" individualist. The inner-directed man, Riesman wrote, has a "tendency to acquire early in life an internalized set of goals," a "psychological gyroscope."[2] He is dominated by the Protestant Ethic of hard work, thrift, discipline, delayed gratification, and competitiveness. The old-fashioned American male was a striver, an achiever, hard as nails; he wasn't cut out for mowing the lawn or playing Ping-Pong with junior in the game room. He didn't even like women all that much.

We knew the tough guys were tough because they were misogynists.

They would trample mother if she stood in their way, and they wouldn't hesitate for a moment to send Mary Astor up the river, as Humphrey Bogart did in *The Maltese Falcon* (1941): "Maybe you love me, maybe I love you. . . . [But] I won't play the sap for you." A smart move, because, as Barbara Deming points out, the weaklings in films of the forties, the men who plunge headlong to their own destruction, are the ones with a sweet tooth for women, men such as Burt Lancaster in *The Killers* (1946), who just can't keep his hands off Ava Gardner, Lancaster again in *Criss Cross* (1949), who can't live without Yvonne de Carlo, or Brian Donlevy in *The Glass Key* (1942), who says, "I want Janet Henry more than anything in life."[3]

Inner direction was fine for the frontier and the heroic days of cutthroat, competitive capitalism. But not now. In *Shane* it doesn't win the hero any awards. Jean Arthur may have fallen in love with the itinerant gunfighter, but when he rides off into the sunset, she stays with hubby, Van Heflin. The kind of man who is suitable to the new society of settlers or consumers is the unheroic "sod-buster," the domesticated family man who is better with a hoe than a gun.

By the fifties, the tough, hard-boiled Hemingway male of the thirties and forties, the man who hid his feelings, if he had any, behind a façade of glacial indifference, the man who endured adversity alone with proud, stoic silence or wooden unconcern, had seen his best days. Like Shane, the tough guys were on their way out of town or, like Ringo, destined for Boot Hill.

Almost every major male star of the thirties and forties associated with this version of masculinity took the roles with which he was synonymous and transformed them, in the fifties, into neurotics or psychotics. James Cagney took his public enemy and made him into a nut in *White Heat* (1949). Gary Cooper took his laconic loner and made him over into a neurotic in *The Bright Leaf* (1950). Humphrey Bogart played a psycho artist in *The Two Mrs. Carrolls* (1947), a neurotic, perhaps homicidal writer in *In a Lonely Place*, and crazy Captain Queeg in *The Caine Mutiny*. Jimmy Stewart was invariably unbalanced in Anthony Mann's westerns, such as *Bend of the River* (1952) and *The Naked Spur* (1953), and he played a certified loony in Hitchcock's *Vertigo* (1958). Even John Wayne took his cowboy and made him into an obsessive in *The Searchers*. Clark Gable played, if not a neurotic, at least a deeply troubled loner in

The Misfits (1961). Peck tried to play a traditional leader in *Twelve O'Clock High*, but it was too much for him, and he had a nervous breakdown. Then he gave up and played mad Captain Ahab in *Moby Dick* (1956). Even when these actors weren't playing psychos, it was clear that they were getting old, slowing down, and their tired, worn faces showed, to all who cared to see, that when they went, they were going to take inner-direction with them. In geriatric westerns like *High Noon*, it seemed that Gary Cooper was just as likely to be taken off by cardiac arrest as a bullet in the gut.

Then there was a cycle of films that made villains out of hard-driving industrialists, self-made men such as Edward G. ("Play to win: that's my motto") Robinson in *All My Sons* (1948); Robert ("Only nice people lose") Ryan in Max Ophuls's *Caught* (1949); Gary ("I get what I want") Cooper in *The Bright Leaf*; Ryan again ("People only envy a successful man; they envy a failure nothing") in Raoul Walsh's *The Tall Men* (1955).* Sometimes, as in Douglas Sirk's *Has Anybody Seen My Gal?* (1952), the capitalist is benign, but the message is the same: Don't follow in his footsteps. Here, the self-made millionaire is the "richest man in the world," having made a fortune in Alaska after being disappointed in love. But when the film starts, he is many years older and wiser, and tells young Rock Hudson, a soda jerk, "It's not money that makes a person happy, but what you do with it." He'd trade money for love any day and advises Rock to do the same, *not* to "go West," but to stay put in Smalltown, give up his plans to strike it rich, and marry the girl next door instead.

Closely related to the rogue capitalist films was the cycle of late-forties antisuccess films, such as *Rhapsody in Blue* (1945), *Humoresque* (1947), *Body and Soul* (1947), *Champion* (1949), and *Force of Evil*, that continued into the fifties and early sixties with films such as *The Harder They Fall* (1956), *The Sweet Smell of Success* (1957), *The Hustler* (1961) and, in a lighter vein, *Will Success Spoil Rock Hunter?* (1957). They not only portrayed achievers as villains, but mercilessly dissected the methods their

*Other figures in the same mold were industrialist Robert Taylor in *Undercurrent* (1946), who stole the invention on which his fortune rested and murdered the inventor; film mogul Rod Steiger in *The Big Knife* (1955); another film mogul, Kirk Edwards, in *The Barefoot Contessa* (1954); media king Charles Laughton in *The Big Clock* (1948); and Zachary Scott in *Ruthless* (1948).

"heroes" used to reach the top. In these films, men who were ambitious, attractive, and talented turned out to be heels. When they succeeded in clawing, kicking, and gouging their way up the ladder of success, they were likely to find that winning wasn't much different from losing. They found success, but lost themselves.

The antisuccess films were leftist in inspiration. The formula they all followed was first rehearsed by John Howard Lawson in his play *Success Story*, put on by the Group Theater in 1932. The liberals who produced the films doubtless thought they were making a progressive attack on some of the worst aspects of competitive individualism and capitalism itself. But for the most part, these films merely kicked a dead horse, sniped at an ideology that was on its way out anyway, and therefore they did little more than pave the way for a new one, the ideology of affluence, which also knocked ambition, but for different reasons, not because it was immoral but because it was unnecessary. In the fifties, one got ahead virtually without trying. Moreover, on seeing one businessman after another struck down by heart attacks, it was hard to avoid the conclusion that inner-direction was bad for their health as well.

Then there were the bad-dad films, which attacked a strong, inner-directed father figure, a patriarch who was depicted as corrupt or tyrannical, such as Lee J. Cobb in Vincent Sherman's *The Garment Jungle* (1957), and again in Anthony Mann's *Man of the West* (1958); or Raymond Massey in Kazan's *East of Eden.** In *Invaders from Mars*, no sooner is dad taken over by Martians than he's peremptorily demanding a cup of coffee from mom and knocking little David to the ground with one blow. And in *Conquest of Space*, when bad dad goes crazy, his astronaut son has to take over and bring the ship in safely.

What was wrong with these fathers emerges from this exchange in *12 Angry Men* between Henry Fonda and Lee J. Cobb. As we have seen, Fonda blames the defendant's criminal record on his bad dad: "Ever since

---

*Other bad dads included Donald Crisp in *The Man from Laramie* (1955); Pat Hingle in Kazan's *Splendor in the Grass* (1961), and again in *A Taste of Honey* (1962); Edward G. Robinson in *All My Sons* (1948); Karl Malden in *Fear Strikes Out* (1957); and Fredric March in *The Man in the Gray Flannel Suit* (1956). Bad dads appeared in B-films as well, such as *Rogue River* (1950), Phil Karlson's *Kansas City Confidential* (1952), and Joseph Lewis's *The Halliday Brand* (1957).

he was five years old, his father beat him up regularly." Cobb, on the other hand, blames the kid: "It's the kids, the way they are nowadays. Listen, when I was his age, I used to call my father 'sir.' You ever hear a boy call his father that any more?" "Fathers don't seem to think it's important any more," replies Fonda, mildly.

The revenge characters of the fifties, such as Tolly or John Friendly, were yet another negative embodiment of this version of masculinity. They were typical inner-directed types, rigid, obsessed, fanatical men, altogether at odds with the prevailing attitude of relaxed tolerance. Rather than being open, sensible, and pragmatic, they were closed, irrational, and dominated by some past injury.

Since men belonged at home, not on the streets or out on the prairie, most films wanted them married, not alone or hanging out with other men. Men without women, men in groups, were usually bad, except in circumstances where it couldn't be helped, such as war, and even there, as we have seen, life in combat was punctuated with heterosexual interludes, flashbacks to civilian life before the war, or glimpses of the family on the homefront. Outside of war, however, men in groups fared badly. In gangster films, men in groups were the "mob"; in delinquency films, the gang. In westerns, if villains weren't loners or Indians, they were male clans, the brothers in *The Gunfighter*, the Rikers in *Shane*, the Faskins in *Vengeance Valley* (1951), and Doc Tobin's gang in *Man of the West*. These clans were in triple jeopardy. They not only had the misfortune to be male groups, they were also frequently motivated by revenge and were presided over by tyrannical patriarchs. And it wasn't only gangster films, delinquency films, and westerns. In Delbert Mann's *Marty* (1955), a critically acclaimed "adult" film, the guys on the block were immature and emotionally retarded, and Marty had to escape from them into domesticity.

Not only were particular kinds of men obsolete, heroism itself was done for. In the matter-of-fact, business-as-usual world of the fifties, traditional heroes, like tough guys, were an embarrassment. They were extremists, the next thing to totalitarians. Daniel Bell ridiculed "conceptions that derive from 'heroic' and ultimately romantic images of life and man's place in it." For this generation, he continued, "a 'heroic' life" is "truly 'quixotic.' This is, as for Cervantes' Don, the end of an age."[4] And so it was that heroic gestures were often only that—"gestures"—futile, destined to fail. A favorite choice for the Last Hero was the Southerner, a romantic hangover from an earlier, more glorious age. In *Shane*, Elisha Cook, Jr. plays a character named Stonewall Jackson Torrey. He is a Southerner, from Alabama, and he makes one last gallant but foolhardy gesture, going up against Jack Palance, a "professional" gunfighter. Palance calls him "Southern trash," and as the sounds of "Dixie" fill our ears, Palance casually plugs him three times before Torrey can get off a single shot, and the little man collapses in a puddle of water. Romantics lose out to realists. These films marked the passing of the hero, and although they shed a few crocodile tears at his demise, they were in the business of liquidating the past, not mourning it.

All these men—the last heroes, the bad dads, the self-made men, the revenge figures, the men in groups, the crazies of various sorts—had to "relax." They had to calm down, take life easier, ease themselves into the warm bath of pluralism. They were Type A personalities, asking for a coronary, and their friends and acquaintances begged them to be B's. In *Detective Story*, easygoing William Bendix tells McCloud to "relax," while in *Twelve O'Clock High*, Doc Kaiser tells General Savage the same thing: "Ease up." And in *Giant* (1956), Rock Hudson's son tells him to "relax, your blood pressure's too high." Like Cochise in *Fort Apache* and *Broken Arrow*, they have to bend with the wind or break.

Realism, compromise, accommodation, flexibility, were at once political and psychological necessities, keys to bringing competing groups to the bargaining table, and men into the home. The characteristics that made such emotional elasticity possible were supplied by the psychology of pluralism. Riesman called the pluralist personality "other-directed." Other-directed men had "a social character whose conformity is insured by their tendency to be sensitized to the expectations and preferences of others."[5] They were characterized by a post-Protestant, postscarcity ethic of cooperation. Their rough edges were rubbed smooth; the new men were altogether more gentle, mild, and sensitive.

Like *Shane*, many films made their point by presenting two alternative models of masculinity and helping viewers to select one. In *Sands of Iwo Jima*, we have to choose between John Wayne, once again a tough Marine sergeant, and John Agar, a softer, younger, gentler man, the liberal to Wayne's conservative. Agar's dad, known as "Screamin' Sam," had been Wayne's commanding officer; Wayne admired him, but Agar didn't. "I embarrassed my father. Too soft," he says, bitterly. Now, Wayne, "He's the kind of man my father liked. A real man. With a ramrod up his back. Not me. I'm a civilian, not a soldier." Speaking of his own son, Agar adds, "He won't have to be tough; he'll be intelligent. He'll read Shakespeare and be cultured." By the time it's time to raise the flag over Iwo Jima, of course, Wayne and Agar are fast friends, restoring the coalition of the center. Wayne has softened, and after he saves Agar's life, Agar acknowledges that in time of war, toughness has its place. But the war will be over soon, and it's clear that Wayne's days are numbered. The qualities that made him a good soldier will make him a bad civilian. The turning point comes when, on leave, he picks up a woman. He doesn't know how to talk to her, ends up insulting her, apologizes ("I didn't mean to sound so tough"), and goes home with her. While they are relaxing in her living room, he hears a sound in the next room. In a flash he's up on his feet, grabbing a bottle to wop the Jap behind the door, just as Shane had instinctively drawn his gun on ten-year-old Brandon de Wilde when de Wilde tiptoed up behind him. Here, as in *Shane*, the offender is a child, this time a baby in a crib. Wayne would be a menace in Scarsdale or Evanston, less an Audie Murphy than a Richard Speck, and at the end, he's killed off, while Agar is left in peace to bring up his son to read Shakespeare.

The new generation of actors who came to age in the late forties and early and mid-fifties were well suited to the new masculinity. Men like Montgomery Clift, James Dean, Tony Perkins, Rock Hudson, Sal Mineo, Warren Beatty, and to a lesser extent Marlon Brando and Paul Newman, were sensitive, in close touch with their feelings (or could be made to be); they cooperated rather than competed; they put family ahead of career, were moderate in their ambitions, attuned to the needs of others, were not afraid or reluctant to ask for help, and some even had an inner life, heretofore the prerogative of women. The sex that had historically been regarded as flexible, pliant, and sensitive, in touch with their feelings, apt to cry, nurturant, and expected to compromise at the drop of a hat was, of course, female. Men, in other words, were becoming more like women. They were becoming "feminized." When they put down the gun, they put on the apron.

In *The Man Who Shot Liberty Valance*, Jimmy Stewart teaches school, repudiates violence, and in fact wears an apron. In *Broken Arrow*, it is Stewart again, nursing the Apache boy back to health. He is accused of being a "woman" for his pains, but there that's all right. Colonel Davenport removes General Savage's shoes in *Twelve O'Clock High* and covers him with a blanket. Conversely, McCloud denounces "softness" in *Detective Story*, but in that film he is wrong, because being soft is just being human.

Even the biblical epics that sprawled across the screens of the fifties were crawling with feminized men. The new masculinity meshed well with their turn-the-other-cheek Christianity. In *Quo Vadis?* (1951) Robert Taylor plays Marius, a proud Roman general. One day, he hears Simon-called-Peter telling a crowd that "blessed are the meek, for they shall inherit the earth." This is too much for Marius. He makes fun of the disciple, calling him "womanish," and rides off in a cloud of dust. Before he has traveled a great distance, he comes upon a boy sitting by the side of the road, sobbing his heart out. Come, come, says Marius, pausing to give him a word of fatherly advice. He'll have to dry his nose and stand up straight if he expects to become a centurion when he grows up, Marius tells him heartily. But the boy doesn't want to become a centurion when he grows up. He wants to be like the fisherman, Simon-called-Peter, whom Marius had mocked. And before long, so does Marius. He becomes a "woman" himself, and in the last scene, we leave him sitting beside his beloved Lygia in a donkey-drawn cart, on the road out of Rome. The cart is equivalent to the buckboard in westerns, which in turn was equivalent to the family station wagon. When a man gets off his horse and into a cart or a buckboard, we can be sure he's settling down.

Fifties films were full of men who, borrowing a leaf from Johnny Ray, whose novelty hits "The Little White Cloud That Cried" and just plain "Cry" headed the hit parade in 1952, wept and sobbed with such abandon they made Stella Dallas, Ma Perkins, and the second Mrs. Burton seem like tough guys in comparison. Burt Lancaster cried in *The Rose Tattoo* (1954), Montgomery Clift wept in *Raintree County* (1957), and so did Ernest Borgnine in *Marty*. James Dean cries so much in *East of Eden* that Julie Harris has to ask him to stop: "Are you going to cry for the rest of your life?"

Take Rock Hudson, who starred in innumerable fifties "weepies," such as Sirk's *All That Heaven Allows* (1956), and *Written on the Wind* (1957). He made an excellent feminized man, because he was manly and tender at the same time. Rock was sweet-tempered and romantic, a gentle giant who got his kicks from helping old ladies across the street or tending blind widows, as he does in Sirk's *Magnificent Obsession* (1954). Whereas other feminized fifties actors, such as Clift and Dean, were short and slight, Rock was as tall as an oak; his very height guaranteed that a man who sounded like Liberace wasn't a sissy.

Another fifties favorite was shy, diffident Tony Perkins. Perkins had a tense, nervous edge that often led him to play disturbed adolescents. A typical role was that of Jimmy Piersall, the neurotic baseball player in Richard Brooks's *Fear Strikes Out* (1957). Tony is a Boston Red Sox outfielder who is hounded by his bad dad, Karl Malden. Nothing he does is good enough for dad. His whole life is baseball, and when he isn't on the field, he is working at odd jobs trying to help his family make ends meet. His normal pals invite him to go drinking or dancing, but his answer is always no. Tony is a party pooper, an old-fashioned, inner-directed striver, delaying gratification with a vengeance. "You gotta relax once in a while," his buddies tell him, but he can't. Flying in the face of *The Power of Positive Thinking* ("There is no virtue in overtrying," counseled Norman Vincent Peale), Tony mutters to himself, "I gotta work, I gotta work."[6]

Tony is still Tony, nevertheless. There's a feminized man inside him waiting to be born. He's shy, awkward, and speaks with a slight stutter. On his first date with his wife-to-be, he does the cooking and the dishes, and, yes, ties on an apron. Indeed, Tony's having trouble making the Red Sox because he can't hit; he doesn't have enough "power," which is to say, he has to struggle against feelings of effeminacy. He does make the team, finally, but the collision between the demands of his father's old-fashioned Protestant ethic and his own feminized personality drives him crazy. He becomes paranoid and violent. Mary, his wife, wants to send him to a shrink, but dad says no. "We don't go for that kind of thing, do we? You don't want'em to call you yellow, do you? Then you're no son of mine." (Only middle-class liberals were hip to therapy; this dad is a jerk because he's a foreman of a factory.) A potential parricide, Tony turns on Malden: "I want to kill him," he says angrily, and lands in the hospital. Once safely in the hands of the experts and away from his bad dad (the docs won't let Malden near him), he speedily recovers. "What about baseball?" Tony asks the doc. "That's up to you," Doc replies, bouncing the ball back, so Tony can be sure the answer comes from inside him, not from somewhere else. "It won't be easy to go back," warns the doc, but Tony is only one cut away from Fenway Park, and when the cut comes, he's there, shaking hands with Joe Cronin, the Sox's owner. The moral? You don't have to be a workaholic to make the team, and if soft-boiled men occasionally go crazy too, it isn't their fault. Their bad dads drove them to it.

The power, strength, and sexual energy that were drained off soft-boiled middle-class males like Rock Hudson and Tony Perkins ended up in outsiders like Marlon Brando, where they were all the more seductive for being faintly illicit. The men Brando played, such as Stanley Kowalski in Kazan's *Streetcar Named Desire* (1951), instead of becoming more like women, destroyed women; they were inimical to women's world, as Stanley is to Blanche's. Yet, macho man had to take his lumps. Brando was punished for his raw power and masculinity in almost every film he ever made, being badly beaten in films as different as *The Wild One, On the Water-*

Marlon Brando was too powerful for his own good and therefore he was humiliated in most of his major films. Here, he's battered in *The Wild One*.

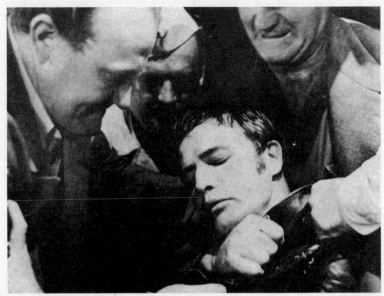

front, One-Eyed Jacks (1961), *The Chase* (1966), and *The Appaloosa* (1966).

Brando inherited John Garfield's slum-kid roles, but he cleaned up Garfield's act, laundering his working-class Jew-boy *shtick* into the existential anguish of the outsider, which was more in keeping with the fifties fondness for *angst*. In Brando, class was inflated to alienation or reduced to mental illness. Beneath the muscles and torn T-shirt, Brando was screwed up, too, just another neurotic tough guy. His bravado masked the pain inside; he wouldn't talk because he couldn't, and even he cried in *The Wild One*, while in *The Men* he stopped mumbling long enough to beg his wife, "Help me!"

But there was still something a little old-fashioned about Brando. Maybe it was the lingering touch of class, the whiff of the thirties. Pauline Kael, comparing *On the Waterfront* and *East of Eden*, put her finger on the problem.

The mixed-up kid has evolved from the depression hero, but the explanation from the thirties (poverty did this) no longer works, and the refinement of it in *On the Waterfront* (corruption did this) didn't work. It gives way in *East of Eden* to something even more facile and fashionable: the psychiatric explanation (lack of love did this). . . . The concept of Terry was a little behind the times: he was posited as heroic because he acted for the social good. Cal is the hero simply and completely because of his *need*, and his frenzied behavior, the "bad" things that he does.[7]

Kael was right. It was James Dean, more than Brando, who hit a nerve. Dean was the Dead End Kid of the therapeutic fifties, the ideal hero, the perfect patient. As with Perkins, trying to be tough drove him crazy. If the teen-ager in *Werewolf* was born to be bad, Dean was born to the couch, a sick boy, not an evil one.

In *Rebel Without a Cause*, we recall, Dean played Jim Stark, one of a trio of delinquents, the others being Judy and Plato. Plato has a pinup of Alan Ladd taped to the inside of his locker at school. Ladd was a forties tough guy, and as critic Joan Mellen has pointed out, Dean replaces him in Plato's eyes. But Ladd's was a hard act to follow; it was difficult to be a hero in the fifties, and Jim's problem in *Rebel* was that he didn't know how to be masculine. Explaining his participation in a hot-rod race to his dad, he says plaintively, "What can you do when you have to be a man?

It was a matter of honor. They called me a chicken. You know, chicken? I had to go." But then he confesses, "You can't keep pretending you're tough, you know?" and before he knows it, he is nurturing Plato. But Jim's masculinity is precarious. He is, after all, a young man who plays with dolls, twice hungrily drinks (mother's) milk from a bottle, and on the first day of school we see him push open the door of the women's bathroom by mistake. When he realizes his error, he makes for the men's room instead, but he has to look up at the sign to make sure he has it right. Masculinity, in other words, cannot be taken for granted. Men are made, not born. Jim is uncomfortable with macho, but where does that leave him? Is being a girl the only alternative to being a boy?

It is Jim's sweetheart, Judy, who articulates what it was to be a man. "What kind of a boy do you think a girl wants?" she asks Jim. "A man," he replies. "But a man who can be gentle and sweet," she goes on. "Someone who doesn't run away when you want them. Like being Plato's friend when nobody else liked him. That's being strong." When she compliments Jim for having "soft lips," we know we are a long way from Philip Marlowe and Sam Spade.

And it wasn't only Judy who felt this way. The reassuring moral of many of Marilyn Monroe's films was that you didn't have to be a Clark Gable (except in *The Misfits*) to win her favors. In fact, she preferred Average Joes, like the bland John (David Wayne) she was coupled with in *How to Marry a Millionaire* (1953) and again in *We're Not Married* (1952). In *The Seven Year Itch* (1955), she tells Tom Ewell that she wanted a man who would be "gentle, tender with you, nice and sweet." She tells Tony Curtis in *Some Like It Hot* (1959) that she likes men with glasses ("men who wear glasses are so gentle, weak, and helpless"), and sure enough, her boyfriends in *Gentlemen Prefer Blondes* (1953) and *How to Marry a Millionaire* both wear them. When Marilyn told men what she liked, they listened, and the message was that she liked feminized men.

The fifties are popularly known as the Dark Ages of sexual ideology, a time when sex roles were polarized into incompatible stereotypes, a time when men were men and women were women, and never the twain did meet, except in the missionary position. We have seen that at least as far as men were concerned, this was not entirely true. Men were becoming more like women. What was happening to women? Were they becoming more like men?—or more like women, that is to say, still more "feminine," seductive, mothering, and so on? On the face of it, it seemed like the latter was the case. In *The Feminine Mystique*, Betty Friedan wrote that "in the second half of the twentieth century in America, women's world was confined to her own body and beauty, the charming of man, the bearing of babies, and the physical care and serving of husband, children, and home."[8] The "experts" on sex roles who filled the women's magazines with advice to housewives put family first and equality second. "Absolute equality of opportunity is clearly incompatible with any positive solidarity of the family," wrote Talcott Parsons.[9] Women were supposed to have babies instead of careers.

And, indeed, many films punished ambitious women for their independence, to such an extent that Friedan argued that the career woman had replaced the vamp as the *femme fatale* of the fifties; the scarlet letter stood for ambition, not adultery. When women in these films competed directly with men, it suddenly turned out that the pie wasn't big enough to go around after all. Women succeeded, but only at men's expense. In Cecil B. DeMille's *The Greatest Show on Earth* (1952), Betty ("The-only-net-I-use-is-in-my-hair") Hutton plays a glamorous high-wire artist vying for the center ring with acrobat Cornell "King-of-the-Air" Wilde. Cornell can't take the heat, and in an effort to go Hutton one better, he falls from the high wire and is crippled for life. In George Cukor's *A Star Is Born* (1954), Judy Garland is allowed her career, but she pays a high price. As Judy's star goes up, husband James Mason's star goes down, and he becomes a hopeless alcoholic. She's ready to give it all up to look after him, but once she's decided to sacrifice her career, she doesn't have to (it's the thought that counts), because he considerately commits suicide so that her star can twinkle on.

Career women ran the risk of being criminalized, neuroticized, failing, falling ill or under cars. Or, being just plain unhappy. Ava Gardner in *The Barefoot Contessa* is a wildly popular movie star, but her private life is a shambles, and she ends up shot dead by her husband. Jennifer Jones, a successful doctor, falls in love with correspondent William Holden and loses both Holden (killed by a North Korean bomb) and her career in Henry King's *Love is a Many Splendored Thing* (1955). In *The Other Love* (1947), Barbara Stanwyck plays an accomplished pianist afflicted with a deadly disease-without-a-name that lands her in a sanatorium under the care of Dr. David Niven. She's desperately in love with him, and he loves her too, but he also loves the sanctity of the doctor-patient relationship, and the more she throbs with passion, the more he retreats into the folds of British reserve. Stanwyck grows impatient and takes up with Brand X, Richard Conte, a playboy racing driver. But in the midst of a whirlwind romance among the gambling tables of Monte Carlo, she starts to cough blood, has to renounce fast-lane Conte, and ends up back where she began, in the hands of feminized Niven. This time he's willing, and they settle down in a cozy cottage high up in the Alps. Her brilliant career? Forgotten.

The classic study in the villainy of career women was, of course, Joseph Mankiewicz's *All About Eve* (1950). Bette Davis, the "first lady of the stage," is the good career woman, because she acknowledges the importance of men, and better, is getting married, and better still, is giving up her career. "A funny business, a woman's career," she muses. "You forget you'll need [men] when you start being a woman again. You forget you'll have to turn around in bed and see him—and if he's not there, you're not a woman." After she's married, she rejects a part she's wanted desperately, because "I've finally got a life to live. . . . I have things to do with my nights." The heavy of the piece is Anne Baxter, the ambitious understudy who scratches and scrambles her way to the top. She is the bad career woman because she actually wants a career, and instead of loving men, she just uses them.

By the high fifties, the ideology of domesticity had become so pervasive that the Anne Baxter figure had virtually ceased to exist. In *The Tender Trap* (1955), Debbie Reynolds has just successfully auditioned for her first part on Broadway. "Aren't you excited?" wonders Frank Sinatra. "The theater's all right, but it's only temporary," replies Reynolds. "Are you thinking of something else?" asks Sinatra, incredulously. "Marriage, I hope," she replies. "A career is just fine, but it's no substitute for marriage. Don't you think a man is the most important thing in the world? A woman isn't a women until she's been married and had children."

Women didn't necessarily have to pursue a career to run afoul of the cult of domesticity. Any form of resistance could lead to trouble. Look what happened to poor Olivia de Havilland in Anatole Litvak's *The Snake Pit* (1948). Had her husband, bland, normal Mark Stevens had a little more on the ball, instead of dreaming about babies and formulas as he does, he would have recognized a long time ago, when they were courting in Chicago, that there was something weird about Olivia. She smoked, never went out with boys in high school, was pursuing a career as a novelist, and "didn't want to be pinned down" to marriage. When Mark pressed his attentions, she disappeared without a trace, turning up six months later in New York, where they met accidentally and finally married. Surely she was trying to send him a message, but Mark wasn't listening. When he wakes up, it's too late. Olivia has become aloof and withdrawn. She spends most of the time staring out the window. "You can't make me love you," she says distantly, as if he's not there. She hears voices, speaks irrationally, is subject to lapses of memory, and doesn't want him to touch her.

Olivia was wrong when she said that Mark couldn't make her love him. He could. Rejecting her husband leads directly to the loony bin. If she doesn't like the company of men, she can spend the rest of her life in the company of women, crazy ones at that. But Olivia is unfazed. She adds insult to injury by insisting on using her maiden name, removing her wedding ring, and denying she is married. In other words, behind the exotic symptomology, the ideological content of Olivia's illness is merely that she has no use for domesticity. She is a premature feminist, and her rebellion is perceived (and presented) as lunacy.

Olivia constitutes a fundamental challenge to the family, and therefore she has to be "cured." Several thousand volts later, after she's absorbed enough electricity to light up a Christmas tree, and spent countless hours on the couch, she is. We know this because as she leaves Frances Farmer Memorial Sanitarium with Mark, she asks him to replace her wedding ring.

The lesson of *The Snake Pit* is that women have to be controlled. They take their place alongside gangsters, delinquents, minorities, and Commies— and the other enemies within. It wasn't only a question of encouraging women to leave their wartime factory jobs and reenter the home; even when they were in the home, they were difficult. Hysterical, emotional, irrational, they were, as we have seen, potential extremists. Olivia was cured by a stiff dose of therapy, but therapists weren't always around when you needed them. Another solution would have to be found, namely, allowing women to function as social-control agents themselves.

See how this worked in *Blackboard Jungle*, where Dadier's pregnant wife, Ann, has become a serious problem herself. We recall that she wants Dadier to quit his teaching job at North Manual High. He refuses, she pleads, he's adamant. But she won't give up. "You're not going back to school again," she says firmly. West, too, wants Dadier out of the school, and in a way, she and West are allies, partners in extremism.

Things come to a head when West starts writing Ann those anonymous letters suggesting that Dadier is in love with another woman. The shock sends her into premature labor, and she has to be rushed to the hospital, where she delivers two months early. When Dadier finds out about the poison-pen letters, it's the last straw. He's finally ready to quit. By changing his mind and agreeing to obey his wife, he allows her to play his role, just as Jim has allowed his dad to play his role in *Rebel*, just as Jeffords had allowed Cochise to play his role, control him in *Broken Arrow*. Here, as there, controller and controlled trade places. This is the deal. She agrees to become an *object* of social control in exchange for becoming an *agent* of social control. In other words, as soon as he acknowledges her power, she turns around and gives in. All of a sudden she is urging him to stay, taking her place with Edie Doyle and Nancy Reed, women who use their power to get their men to do the Right Thing. *

There were a number of practical reasons for bestowing power upon housewives. One of them was that weak women made poor consumers. Hidden persuader Ernst Dichter told Betty Friedan that the passive, conservative "True Housewife" was threatened by modern, labor-saving products. He advised his clients to steer a centrist course between her and the "Career Woman," who was an equally bad bet because she didn't spend enough time in the kitchen. Preferable to both was the middle-of-the-road "Balanced Homemaker." Dichter's report suggested that ad copy should "emphasize her Kingpin role in the family . . . help her to be an expert rather than a menial worker."[10] In other words, women were to be made to believe that they were "experts," "managers," "executives," and that the home was a business or factory. The managerial mother was a career woman after all; it's just that her career was the home and the family.

Friedan to the contrary, families in fifties films were very often matriar-

---

*This solution to the problem posed by women is similar to the one proposed in *Them!*: Give an inch to Pat Medford or lose a mile to the queen.

chies. Within these families, women were charged with no less than the task of transmitting the values of civilization. As Dorothy Thompson counseled housewives in *The Ladies' Home Journal* (March 1949), "The homemaker, the nurturer, the creator of children's environment is the constant recreator of culture, civilization and virtue." Adlai Stevenson repeated the lesson to Smith College graduates in 1955: Woman's role was to "help her husband find values."[11]

Since women were identified with the system, films that liked the system liked women too. They depicted women as priestesses of principle, keepers of the flame, custodians of conscience, which is another way of saying that they were agents of social control. They defined and confirmed the value systems embodied in the narrative, culturized or civilized men who, as rebels, delinquents, revenge heroes, alcoholics, sickies, bad dads, old-fashioned pioneers and capitalists, or even bachelors, were outside society, and therefore equated with nature. In *On the Waterfront*, it was Edie Doyle who brought Terry out of the jungle; in *Spellbound*, it was Ingrid Bergman who brought Gregory Peck in from the cold, and in *The Man in the Gray Flannel Suit*, it was Jennifer Jones who urged him to be straight with his boss; in *Somebody Up There Likes Me* (1956), it was Rocky Graziano's mom who urged him to get a job. In *Raintree County*, it was Eva Marie Saint who urged Montgomery Clift to do his best, run for Congress. "I want you to do something you're capable of doing. You cannot escape responsibility," she told him. In *On Dangerous Ground* it was Ida Lupino again who socialized rogue cop Robert Ryan. Marilyn Monroe made Clark Gable stop "mustanging" in *The Misfits*, while in Joshua Logan's *Bus Stop* (1956), she civilized wild Don Murray, another "cowboy." Both Gable and Murray were natural men (Murray's pal Arthur O'Connell called him a "barbarian" and had to remind him, "You're in civilization"), but before Marilyn's finished, both cowboys are ready for the last roundup. In *The Lost Weekend* (1945) Ray Milland went on the wagon for Jane Wyman, while in *The African Queen* (1951), Bogart made war on the Germans for Katharine Hepburn.

When there are exceptions to the rule that good women transmit cultural values to men, that is, when men do this to women, they are our old friends, teachers, social workers, but most often doctors, like Dr. David Niven in *The Other Love*, ministering to poor Barbara Stanwyck; Dr. Leo Genn in *The Snake Pit*, psychoanalyzing Olivia de Havilland; Dr. Widmark in *The Cobweb* (1955), soothing his high-strung wife, Gloria Grahame; and Dr. James Mason in *Caught*, educating Barbara Bel Geddes in a career of service to the poor. This collection of male doctors might as well have been women, because they stand for nurturant values that these films ascribe to women. And even in these instances, women doctor the doctors, teach the teachers. In *Panic in the Streets*, it is Nancy Reed who persuades Dr. Reed to stay at his job, instead of dreaming about the private sector. When feminized men play a socializing role with regard to macho men, women are better at it and take over after they enter the picture. In *Bus Stop*, Marilyn Monroe supplants Arthur O'Connell as Don Murray's socializer. "You don't need me to look after you," says O'Connell, saying good-bye. And Dick Powell's man Friday says good-bye to him when Debbie Reynolds takes over in *Susan Slept Here* (1954): "I'm leaving him in your hands," he says to her, and exits.

Often, women literally are, or are about to become, schoolteachers in these films, like Edie Doyle or Ringo's wife in *The Gunfighter*, but sometimes the lessons are administered informally, at home. In Stanley Donen's *Seven Brides for Seven Brothers* (1954), set in Oregon circa 1850, Jane Powell has to impose culture on nature, educating and socializing her husband, Howard Keel, and his six wild brothers, so that they can be suitable matches for the refined ladies in town. The seven brothers live in the wilderness and act like it. Powell has to make them wash, shave, say grace before dining and "please" when they want the salt and pepper. The film pits her values against Keel's, the townies against the mountain boys, women against men. In one celebrated scene, the "barn raising," the Keel brothers compete against a team of townies to see who can get their side of the barn finished first. The townies cheat, bopping the Keels with two-by-fours at every turn, tripping them up and pushing them down, but the brothers, good students of Powell, turn the other cheek, until Keel taunts them with "momma's boys." During the free-for-all that follows, the walls they raised come crashing down, and the new barn is demolished. In this film, in other words, it is momma's boys who create culture, build civilization; when they listen to dad (or big brother), they destroy it.

Keel thinks women are no better than cows, and he has to be taught a lesson. When the film opens, he's in town, "shopping" for a wife "who's not afraid to work." "Any particular brand?" asks a storekeeper wryly. "You figger you can trade for a wife like she was a bag'a meal?" chimes in his spouse. "None of our gals is gonna go off to bear country with you to cook and wash and slave." Powell does, but she has a surprise in store for Keel. She quickly realizes that he doesn't "want a wife, but a cook, a washer-woman, a hired girl." When Keel eggs on his brothers to kidnap, not court, the girls they want, Powell is furious. She puts the girls in the house and makes the brothers, who have reverted to a state of nature with their uncivilized behavior, live in the barn "with the rest of the livestock." She kicks Keel out until he repents, accepts Powell's values, and agrees to take the girls back to town. By this time, of course, they want to stay, and the film ends with a mass wedding. In a sense, culture defeats nature, women defeat men. (When Powell has a baby, it's a girl, a slap at Keel. "I might'a known she'd have a girl," he grumbles.) But the townies, unalloyed culture, turn out to be snobs, just as bad in their way as the brothers, unalloyed nature, are in theirs. The ideal, in other words, is nature civilized, nature and culture combined.

The films in which women snare reluctant bachelors, legion in the fifties, embodied an inflection of women's role as culturizers. Debbie Reynolds was a specialist at this, and in *The Tender Trap* she snares Frank Sinatra, a bachelor spoiled by a surfeit of willing women. (The bachelor, of course, was the urban version of Johnny Ringo, the loner.) To him, they are only "trophies hanging in [his] game room," but he's mistaken as to who are the hunters and who are the hunted. Reynolds reads him the riot act. "Listen to me," she snaps. "From now on, you're gonna call for me at my house, ask me where I want to spend the evening, and you're gonna meet my folks and be polite to them and bring me candy and flowers. . . . I've got to make a man out of you." In this film, a "man" is a man who abides by the rules laid down by women.

The control women exercise is internalized, just as it is in *On the Waterfront*. They play the role of therapists, getting inside men's heads. In *The Seven Year Itch* (1955), Mr. Milquetoast Tom Ewell is a "summer bachelor" whose wife is away in the country, and his job is to keep the lid on his id, which lusts after nextdoor neighbor Marilyn Monroe. One look at Marilyn is enough to turn even Ewell into a primitive, natural man. He works for a publishing company and he's editing something called "The Repressed Urges of the Middle-Aged Male," a chapter from a book entitled *Man and the Unconscious*. He compares himself to the creature from the Black Lagoon, and says at one point that "under the veneer of civilization, we are all savages." His monster from the id is not a planetary force, but a working-class janitor who pops up every so often at inconvenient moments, unshaven and shirtless, making lewd jokes. It's touch-and-go for a while, but Ewell has so successfully internalized his wife's injunctions that we even hear him hearing her voice in his head ("Use the can opener, Tom"), so we know his id will stay where it belongs. He's so wracked with guilt ("Relax," Monroe tells him) that he can barely stand to look at her. There's a running joke about little Ricky's kayak paddle that he forgot and left with dad. Ewell repeatedly neglects to send it, until at the end, still chaste, he leaves Monroe to join his wife in the country, bringing the phallic paddle with him home to mommy, where it belongs.

Mothers disciplined and educated children while men spoiled them. In *The Man in the Gray Flannel Suit*, for example, mother punishes Petey; father comforts him afterward: "Petey boy, have you forgotten that you and I are buddies?" says dad, a pal, not a patriarch. In *Panic in the Streets*, mom gets angry when Dr. Reed supplements Tommy's allowance with a quarter. In *The Big Knife*, the education of Lupino and Palance's son is Lupino's job. "Billy musn't grow up to be a rich man's son," she says. "They're made of sponge cake." If men allied with children against women, this was because men and children were essentially the same. Strong mothers allowed men to be boys. As Robert Warshow put it, "in the American mind, refinement, virtue, civilization, Christianity itself, are seen as feminine, and therefore women are often portrayed as possessing some kind of deeper wisdom, while the men, for all their apparent self-assurance, are fundamentally childish."[12] Or, as Friedan pointed out, "men re-created their own childhood in suburbia, and made mothers of their wives."[13] Watching James Mason sleep one off in *A Star Is Born*, Judy Garland says, "He looks so helpless lying there smiling in his sleep just like a child," and she blames herself for not mothering him enough. "Maybe if I'd had a chance to be with him more, some of these things wouldn't have happened." It was all right for men to be momma's boys, and in these films bad moms were those who rejected their children instead of loving them enough. Even the infantilization of men was acceptable, if not desirable. When Frank Sinatra gets his first dinner date with Debbie Reynolds in *The Tender Trap*, she feeds him like a baby, while in *The Rose Tattoo*, Burt Lancaster tells Anna Magnani that "I'm looking for an older lady. She has to be understanding." In *Rhapsody in Blue*,

Gershwin's ex–girl friend sings, "Don't be a naughty baby, come to momma, come to momma, do." In *The Misfits*, Montgomery Clift puts his head in Monroe's lap, complains that he's been abandoned by mom, and calls her "ma" when she covers him with a blanket. (All three men in this film are basket cases.) At one point in *Will Success Spoil Rock Hunter?* Jayne Mansfield says to Tony Randall, who has soiled his clothes, "Why don't we let baby dress in momma's bedroom?"

The civilizing, nurturing role assigned women in films of the fifties required strenuous efforts, so that we find in them strong-willed heroines who do not resemble the passive and pliant cream puffs described by Friedan. If men were feminized, women were masculinized. They kept their hair up or short, often wore pants, and drove cars, while their men sat placidly at their side, or, on the contrary, drove wildly until they had accidents. This tendency is evident in the vogue of asexual female stars like Jean Simmons, girl-next-door Doris Day, tomboy Debbie Reynolds, or Grace Kelly and Audrey Hepburn, whom critic Molly Haskell called "boyish" and "androgynous."[14] They made the safest mothers, even though they rarely had babies other than the men they nurtured.

The need for strong women and constant mothering evident in fifties films was contradicted by the fear of the monster from the id, and created a sexual dualism between the good woman and the bad, schoolteacher and seductress, mother and whore, culture and nature. In fact, when Friedan remarked that the career woman had replaced the vamp as the villain of fifties films, she was only partly right, just as Susan Sontag had been only partly right when she said that the fear of dehumanization had replaced the fear of the primitive in fifties science-fiction films. Although most films didn't like career women, there were plenty of vamps around, and these films liked them even less.

When actresses like Monroe, Mansfield, and Jane Russell appeared in films other than comedies, where the threat they posed was neutralized by laughter, they were often troublemakers, monstrous mothers against whom men played out their mixed feelings of fear and dependence.

Infantilization was seductive, but it was frightening too, especially at the hands of Monroe and Mansfield. It takes only a glance at men and milk in American movies to recognize how conflicted the relations between men and women really were. In *Bus Stop*, Don Murray, who follows Monroe and her mammaries around like a lapdog, gulps milk by the bottleful, but switches to whiskey when she momentarily rejects him. In *Rebel Without a Cause*, Jim is drunk in the first scene, but before too long he switches to milk, and in one scene, caresses his face with the cool neck of the bottle. In *I Was a Teenage Werewolf*, Tony, more deeply disturbed than Jim, throws a bottle of milk against the wall of his motherless home. There's one celebrated scene in *The Girl Can't Help It* (1956), where Jayne Mansfield, just back from the grocery store, stands in the kitchen clasping two bottles of milk in front of her pneumatic breasts, to the astonishment of Tom Ewell.

Both Ewell and Randall were visibly terrified by Mansfield, and in *The Girl Can't Help It*, her boyfriend is a gangster, so that the fear she inspires has a basis in the plot. But Mansfield and Monroe were invariably dumb blondes; sex and brains, head and heart, both in the same body were evidently too hot to handle. It's the same principle that required Brando to be beaten senseless so often, at work in the opposite sex. These films, in other words, frightened men only to reassure them. Monroe and Mansfield were too dim to hurt a fly, unless you bumped into them in the dark and put an eye out.

If good women were identified with civility, bad women were voluptuous, sensual animals. Their habitat was the jungle, not the kitchen, and they lured men away from culture into nature, naturalizing them instead of culturizing them. Women like Ava Gardner, in many of her films, Carroll Baker in *Baby Doll* (1956) and again in *The Fugitive Kind* (1959), Jennifer Jones in *Duel in the Sun* (1947) and again in *Ruby Gentry* (1952), were "nymphomaniacs," women whose promiscuous behavior threatened the sexual center. In many films, desexualized good women, analogous to the Robby-the-Robots of sci-fi (someone says that "Robby looks after us like a mother"), are pitted against hypersexual bad women, the monsters from the id, and like the films that offered up two alternative definitions of masculinity, these films asked us to choose one, or watch while they chose for us. In *Don't Bother to Knock* (1952), Marilyn Monroe played a psycho, while Anne Bancroft played the good woman. In Henry Hathaway's *Niagara* (1953) it was Monroe again, this time plotting to kill her husband, while straight-arrow Jean Peters played the wholesome housewife. In Mervyn LeRoy's *East Side, West Side* (1949), mealymouthed James Mason is torn between his noble, wealthy, and refined wife, Barbara Stanwyck, and his sultry mistress from the wrong side of the tracks, Ava

Gardner. In *The Best Years of Our Lives* (1946), Dana Andrews has to choose between the good girl—pure, innocent, and middle-class, a banker's daughter, and the bad girl—sexy, ambitious, and working-class. Sex and ambition (and class) often went together, particularly in the *femme fatales* of *film noir*; one derogated the other. In *A Lion Is in the Streets* James Cagney, who plays a Huey Long–type demagogue, can't decide between good Barbara Hale and bad Anne Francis, who explicitly present a choice between culture and nature. Hale, his wife, is a schoolteacher, while Francis, his mistress, is a sort of natural woman, a swamp girl raised in the bayou who is on a first-name basis with alligators and flamingoes. In fact, her name is Flamingo.

In some films, the mother/whore, tomboy/sexpot clash was transformed into a battle of actresses, pitting Day or Reynolds against a Monroe type. In *Singin' in the Rain* (1952), for example, the blond bombshell silent star, an MM look-alike, was exposed as a talentless washout and replaced by pert Debbie Reynolds. Similarly, in *The Thrill of it All* (1963), a breathless blond starlet makes a fool of herself in a TV soap commercial posing in a bubble bath and is replaced by Doris Day, who is a hit when "her fumbling, improvised performance charms the televiewers."[15]

These films were sexually repressive, punishing (or mocking) sexually active women, depicting them as bad (or foolish). Nevertheless, they tried to reconcile culture with nature. Although the whores were killed off, like Monroe in *Niagara*, the neutered mothers who survived them were loosened up, like Peters in the same film, or the rigid, puritanical wife and mother who relents and takes a turn in the hay with Gary Cooper in Wyler's *Friendly Persuasion* (1956).

Although many films empowered women, depicted families as matriarchies dominated by strong females who both culturized and mothered men, it is important to remember that the authority of women was derivative. Women were junior partners in the patriarchy of the center and were allocated the role of culturizer by men. Often the alliance between women and male authority figures from whom they derive their power was explicit. In *Seven Brides for Seven Brothers*, Jane Powell's values may triumph, but they operate in the service of Keel's. Powell is the Cochise of the kitchen, acting for Keel, teaching the brothers how to manipulate the girls when force won't work: "If you want to get a girl, you've got to learn how to talk to them," she explained. "You've got to act gentlemanly and well-spoken." Edie Doyle was allied with Father Barry in *On the Waterfront*, who in turn does the work of the police. But, as we saw in *Blackboard Jungle*, the relationship between the dominant patriarchy and the subordinate matriarchy is dialectical. Patriarchy is strengthened by strengthening, not weakening, matriarchy. Men were strengthened by strengthening, not weakening, women. Still, power over home, family, and quality of life may have been delegated power, but it was power nonetheless.

The transformation of the American character that preoccupied the fifties, the feminization of men and the masculinization of women, was clearly evident at the time. Everyone, all across the ideological spectrum, agreed that sex roles were changing. Mortimer and Lait, speaking for conservatives as well as the right, ridiculed the masculinization of women in *U.S.A. Confidential* and even blamed Hollywood. "America has become a matriarchy. Women own and run it," they wrote. "Under a matriarchy men grow soft and women masculine. The self-sufficient girl who doesn't want to become an incubator or 'kitchen slavie' for a man is a push-over for a predatory Lesbian. . . . Marxian teachings, the examples of women in high political and social places, and the propagandized knowledge that many of the movie set prefer it that way are contributory."[16] As these sentiments indicate, whereas pluralists applauded these changes, competing ideologies resisted them. Conservatives, for example, would have nothing to do with either feminized men or managerial mothers. The tried and true were good enough for them. While corporate liberals were softening up men who were too hard, conservatives were hardening men who were too soft, callow youths who had to be initiated into manhood or domesticated husbands who had mowed too much grass to get it on when the moment of truth arrived. In conservative films, feminized men were either psychos, or weak and vulnerable, like young James Earp in *Clementine*. James cooks for his brothers, and in one scene, one of them comments, "Mighty fine chow. One of these days you're gonna be as good a cook as Maw." Brother Verge kids him about being "pretty," and he even wears jewelry, an ornate cross given to him by mom. It's no wonder that when the Clantons kill an Earp, James is the one who has to die.

Thus, conservative films were more concerned with shoring up traditional sex roles than with transforming them. The heroes of these films, like John Wayne in *Rio Bravo*, didn't cry and didn't ask for help. Conservative families were strictly patriarchies in which women, not men, were infantilized. Dads were bad because they were too weak, like Tony's father in *Werewolf*, not too strong. Typical in this regard were Lang's *While the City Sleeps* and Sirk's *Written on the Wind*. Both feature dying patriarchs, one a newspaper tycoon and the other an oil baron. These men are not cutthroat capitalists, but benevolent dictators, and if they are lacking, it is once again because they are too soft. They've spoiled their sons, insecure Vincent Price in one case and alcoholic Robert Stack in the other. The erosion of patriarchy was no laughing matter, and these films worried that the sons weren't big enough to fill dad's shoes.

While bad moms in pluralist films were likely to be "rejecting" moms, who didn't love enough, bad moms in conservative films loved too much. They were smothering, possessive, castrating, and the momma's boys they produced were liable to be psychos. Moreover, if sons who avenged their father's deaths were crazy in pluralist films, such as *The Left Handed Gun*, in conservative (and right-wing) films like *Underworld USA*, *Thieves Highway*, *Johnny Angel* (1945), and *Winchester 73* (1950), loyalty to dad was *de rigueur*. Often, male-centered conservative films symbolically revealed their gender preferences through the sex of babies. In pluralist films like *Strategic Air Command* and *Seven Brides for Seven Brothers*, babies tended to be female, while in a film like *Battle Hymn*, husband says to wife, hopefully, "It will be a boy, won't it?" Wife: "If that's what you want— anything you say, dear."

Both kinds of centrist films, corporate liberal and conservative, dramatize the process of culturization, but in the former, men were culturized by women, while in the latter, women were culturized by men. Men, not women, represent the system; authoritative (as opposed to authoritarian) good dads had the Big Picture. They educated, molded, passed on the values of society to weak men, children, liberals, and women, who were naïve and parochial, like nature-girl Alta in *Forbidden Planet*, who is taught the facts of life by the Skipper. Men, in short, were culture, while women, both good and bad, were associated with nature, promiscuous, sensual creatures (like Alta) who had to be desexualized. Often, too, natural women were aggressive and domineering, and men had to "tame" them. *The Taming of the Shrew* was made into *Kiss Me Kate* in 1953.

Since women were stripped of their value-bearing function, they were generally less important in these films than they were in corporate-liberal films. They often did no more than endorse the values of men. Far from being their conscience, they were "yes-women," liberals who finally recognized the virtues of conservatism. In *One Minute to Zero*, Ann Blyth, who works for the UN, doesn't believe Col. Robert Mitchum when he warns her that the North Koreans are planning to attack the South. "Strong-minded," says one of Mitchum's pals. "I wonder what her husband does." "Probably stays home and watches the baby." She doesn't have a husband, however, and by the end she's learned which way is up. "Forgive me!" she implores Mitchum. "I want to be your wife."

Women deferred to men, who instructed them and children in both right- and left-wing films. Like conservatives, the right wanted no part of feminized men and masculinized women. The feminization of men was the result of a set of economic facts and social and ideological practices— pluralism, consumerism, and bureaucratization—that right-wingers resisted. For them, the age of heroism had not ended. On the contrary, heroes were more necessary than ever, to set society right. Buckley complained that "the tendency, these days, is to yield to the passion for modulation. Even in literature, one does not often find oneself concerned with kings and knaves, fair maidens and heroes, treachery and honor, right and wrong; one speaks in greys, and muted hues, of social problems, and life adjustment, and coexistence and inter-credal amity."[17] To the left, on the other hand, pluralists did not go far enough. The left embraced and exaggerated the feminization of men, used it as a fulcrum to turn the center upside down and challenge prevailing definitions of sexuality, work, and authority.

As far as women were concerned, radicals accepted pluralists' equation of the female principle with society, but since they didn't like society, they attacked it by attacking the center's conceptualization of women, much as they did in the fifties novel, James Jones from the right, Norman Mailer from the left. Since, as we have seen, radical films did not fear nature so much as culture, their good women were mirror images of the center's ideal, more sensual than neutered, while their bad women were emotionally repressed. In the vernacular of the fifties, they were "frigid," not promiscuous; they were poles apart from the nymphomaniacs who terrorized the men of centrist films. They were masculinized automatons driven by career ambitions or social conventions, analogous to the bad robots or pod-people of radical sci-fi. We recall that the fear of machines Sontag saw superseding the traditional fear of the id in fifties sci-fi really characterized only radical sci-fi. In the same way, although the fear of ambition in and domination by women that Friedan saw superseding the traditional fear of the vamp characterized all films, it was much more emphatic in radical than in centrist films, in which men continued to be threatened by sexually active women. Uptight women in radical films had to become more natural, more in touch with their feelings, in short, more feminine. They had to get out of their pants and into dresses, let their hair down, and stop driving cars. They had to learn to throw off the constraints of a corrupt and stultifying society. Teaching them to do so was the job of men. Generally speaking, however, women were even less prominent in these films than they were in conservative films.

Despite the fact that radical films, like conservative films, presented a man's world, they should not be confused. Patriarchy was no better than matriarchy if it embodied the values of the center. In radical films, men played nature to women's culture, and when women deferred to men, they were drawn outside society altogether, out of culture into nature. Right- and left-wing films cannot be distinguished through their portrayal of women, only men or couples. In right-wing films, the couple yokes polar opposites, hard men to supersoft women. In left-wing films, soft men and soft women are partners in a feminized marriage.

What will we be looking for in these films? First we must ask, Who's in the driver's seat, a man or a woman. Do women wear their hair up or down? Do they wear pants or dresses? Do they have a career or run a household? Is the family broken or whole, and if broken, who is absent, mom or dad? Is the family a matriarchy or patriarchy? In other words, who knows best, father or mother? Who educates the kids, mom or dad, or do the kids tell the parents what's what? Is junior a momma's boy or a poppa's boy? Is he following in dad's footsteps or does he rebel? Finally, who is culture and who is nature, and which is dominant?

Bringing Up Father
Red River and the Feminization of American Men

A wagon train is slowly making its way across the Chisholm Trail from
Saint Louis to California, and now it has reached dangerous ground,
Apache territory. Among the settlers are Tom Dunson (John Wayne) and
his sweetheart, Fen. Dunson has spotted some "good land south'a here,"
and he wants to strike out on his own. "I'm starting my own herd," he
tells the others. But the settlers are expecting an Indian attack and implore
him to stay behind because he's good with a gun. Dunson refuses. Not
only is he determined to go, but he's leaving Fen behind. "It's too much
for a woman," he says. This is what we've come to expect from John
Wayne, and we're not disappointed. "I've made up my mind," he says,
and with no more ado, he hops on his horse and rides south with his
sidekick, Old Groot (Walter Brennan). No sooner is he over the horizon
than the Apaches attack and slaughter the settlers, Fen included. Dunson
is too far away to help.

Dunson is a rugged individualist, and when he defies the group, aban-
doning the wagon train to its fate, it's okay. After all, it's 1851, Dunson is
a pioneer, and rugged individualism is the order of the day. Individualism
and culture are not antagonistic, as they will become later; here, they are
synonymous. Dunson tames nature and brings civilization to the West.

Minutes later, as Dunson surveys the vast expanse of land south of
the Red River, Fen is all but forgotten. "Everything a man could want,"
he drawls. After all, to John Wayne, what is a woman compared with
a few hundred head of cattle? Fourteen years later, he owns the "biggest ranch in Texas," and the few hundred head of cattle have grown to
ten thousand. "I built something," he says proudly, "I built it with my
own hands."

But times have changed. The Civil War has come and gone, draining capital out of the South. Texas is rich in commodities, but unless they can be sold, they're useless. Dunson has to move his herd to market or lose his shirt. It's also 1948, the year *Red River* was made. World War II had come and gone, and the American economy, now producing cars instead of cannons, was finding it hard to unload its consumer goods on its prewar European customers, still in ruins. There had been a recession in 1947, and many heads were still wondering whether the domestic market was going to be able to take up the slack or whether the country was headed back to the Great Depression. The problems of production had been solved to such an extent that production itself had become a problem. The drama had shifted from production to marketing, from marketing to consumption.

Dunson hires a bunch of cowpokes and begins the cattle drive from Texas to the railhead in Kansas City. But the ruthless determination that served him so well when the job was building a cattle empire becomes a liability when the job is managing men, not producing things. As the long trek stretches out from weeks to months, Dunson pushes his men too hard. Although the war is over, he is still wearing his army pants along with his buckskin shirt; he's still half officer, and like McCloud, he treats peacetime like wartime, his cowboys like soldiers. He's too stubborn and inflexible to succeed as a personnel manager. "Nothing you can say or do will make me change my mind," is his constant refrain. As someone says, "He started thinking only one way—his way. He told the men what to do and made them do it." But force backfires, and the men turn against him. The moment of truth comes when three cowpokes steal away during the night. Dunson has them brought back and plans to hang them. "I don't like quitters," he says angrily and, using the language of war, accuses them of "deserting." "I'm the law, and you're thieves," he adds. But we know that corporate-liberal films don't like to hear people say that they are the law. As soon as Dunson says it, he becomes a marked man, a proto-vigilante. When he reaches for his gun to plug Teeler, the ringleader of the rebels, it's shot out of his hands by someone who is better fitted to the requirements of the postwar period: Montgomery Clift, the right man for the right job.

Clift plays Matthew Garth, whom Dunson had taken in as a youth and raised as a son. Although Matt loves Dunson as a father, he knows he's wrong and sides with the men.* *Red River* offers us a choice between two different definitions of masculinity, old and new, father and son, hardboiled and soft-boiled.

We see that Dunson's problem is that his historical role as pioneer, as civilizer, is over. He has now become an obstacle to civilization, an Indian himself, like Ethan Edwards, a primitive, an asocial savage. There is a hint in the beginning that this will come to pass. The fact that Dunson leaves Fen behind, knowing that the Indians might attack, the fact that they do so as soon as he does leave, and the casual way that he accepts the fact that he's too far away to help her suggest that there is a sense in which he may have wanted her and the settlers dead. From the pluralist point of view, he and the Indians, the white man and the red man, the pioneer and the savage, are two sides of the same coin, doubles, in fact, unconsciously allied in their hatred of the bleeding-heart center: the women and children, with their baggage of civilization and its restraints, its softness, its legalisms—the ultimate suffocation of the individual. The Indians carry out Dunson's secret desires, and although he stabs an Apache to death in a violent struggle in a pool of water, he can't quite get him out of his system. There is even a suggestion that Dunson is unbalanced; several of the trail-hands call him "crazy," so that he joins the ranks of the other hard-boiled men seen as neurotics in the fifties. By the end of the film, he degenerates into a revenge figure, consumed by hatred: "I'll catch up," he vows, as the cattle drive leaves him behind. "Every time you turn around, expect to see me. One time I'll be there. I'll kill you, Matt."

We've seen all this before, the rugged individualist going down the tubes, but what this means in terms of sexual politics is that Dunson is too macho. He devalues the feminine. This is evident from the start, of course, when he cuts himself off from Fen. "You'll need what a woman can give you to do what you have to do," she reminds him as she presses her body to his. "The sun only shines half the time." But it's no go. In

---

*What is at issue here is not the legitimacy of the group itself, but merely how the group is to be governed. *Red River* supports the cowhands' mutiny because Dunson's group is a bad one, governed by conservative or right-wing authoritarian principles, like the initial majority in 12 *Angry Men*. But there is no question that the group comes before the individual. The weakness of a single man can jeopardize the entire enterprise, as we see in one scene where a cowboy with a sweet tooth reaches for a lump of sugar and upsets a chuck wagon full of pots and pans, causing a stampede that takes another cowboy's life.

one scene, when a cowpoke says he's heard there's a railhead in Abilene, hundreds of miles closer than Kansas City, Dunson is skeptical. "Did you see it with your own eyes?" he asks. "No. A girl told me," comes the reply, and that's enough for Dunson. The trek to Kansas City continues.

We've met Matt before, too. He's an organization man, but what this means is that he's feminized. Although Dunson raised him from childhood, he's more a son of Spock than of Wayne. After the Indians kill Dunson's cows in the first scene, sparing only his bull, Matt, the sole survivor of the massacre, appears with his cow. "That was the meeting of a boy with a cow and a man with a bull," goes the narration, and it was on the issue of this union that Dunson's empire was built. Film historian Robert Sklar has gone so far as to call Matt "androgynous," citing a line from Borden Chase's script that never made it into the finished film, in which Matt is told that he is "as tender as a mother and child."[18] And

Sensitive Montgomery Clift was one of the leading feminized heroes of the fifties. Instead of shooting Indians, he's pulling arrows out of Joanne Dru.

indeed, there is a good deal of truth in this. When he rides to the rescue of a wagon train under attack by Indians, he finds Tess Millay (Joanne Dru) impaled by an arrow, and sets about dressing the wound, playing the nurse. He is so solicitous of his men that at one point he actually gets up in the middle of the night to comfort a cowpoke who is having a nightmare.

Since Matt is softer, more pliable, than Dunson, his style of leadership is altogether different. Like a good other-directed man, he takes his cues from his peers, not from his "psychic gyroscope." Matt is the captain of a team, whereas Dunson is the general of an army. Matt's model of society is civil, whereas Dunson's is martial. Matt is rarely photographed alone; he is always the center of a group. He rules by consensus, whereas Dunson rules by force. Rather than expelling Teeler and the cowboy who caused the stampede from the group, Matt allows them to rejoin the cattle drive, much as Fonda in 12 Angry Men extended the hand of reconciliation to his opponents on the jury. It is Matt's job to suppress conflict between factions, prevent the antagonism between Dunson and the men from getting out of hand. He restrains Dunson in the same way that Dr. Medford restrained the army in Them! Matt is open and relaxed where Dunson is closed and tense. When the men gripe about the hardships of the grueling trek, Matt listens. Where Dunson shrugged off talk of a new railhead in Abilene as idle gossip, rigidly adhering to his plan, Matt acts. He's flexible, capable of adapting to new circumstances, adept at living with uncertainty, as Schlesinger prescribed. He turns the herd north, toward Abilene, the birthplace of Dwight D. Eisenhower.

The conflict between Dunson and Matt, the generation gap of the fifties, was a result of the collision of the Protestant Ethic of the older generation and the consumer ethic of the younger, or, in terms of Riesman's characterology, of inner-direction and other-direction. In most films, other-direction was in the ascendancy, which is why son must raise father, student teach teacher, in films like Rebel Without a Cause and Blackboard Jungle. "The child consumer trainee becomes a consumer tutor in the home circle, 'bringing up' mother as well as father," wrote Riesman. "Teen-agers must initiate adults rather than vice versa."[19] These films fostered Oedipal conflict, which became a natural outlet for the social antagonisms that bubbled just below the surface. Sons had to rebel against fathers in order to bring them into the postwar era with its new, unfamiliar values.

What did these feminized heroes want? Rugged individualists like Dunson wanted the world. They were builders, and Dunson wanted to create a kingdom. "I built something, I built it with my own hands," he says, referring to the Red River D. In *The Big Knife*, film mogul Rod Steiger says the same thing in almost the same words: "I built this studio with my brains and hands. I tore it out of the world." Girdle king Lee J. Cobb repeats the same refrain in *The Garment Jungle*: "I built this place with my own hands." Terry Malloy, on the other hand, in *On the Waterfront*, set his sights lower. He only wanted to build a career. He wanted to be a "contendah," and when he couldn't he was disappointed. "I could'a been somebody," he complained to his brother. But Johnny Ringo in *The Gunfighter* wanted to create neither a kingdom nor himself. He didn't want to build something or be somebody; he already was somebody, and he knew that all it would get him was a bullet in the back. He wanted to be "somewhere," to have security, be rooted, stay put. Clark Gable, in *The Tall Men*, agreed. All he wanted was "a little ranch . . . a corner for myself with the right kind of woman." And Joel McCrea, in *Colorado Territory*, agreed with Gable: "I've been thinkin' 'bout settlin' down, buyin' me a farm someplace." Jim Stark in *Rebel Without a Cause* throws in his lot with Ringo, not Terry. He wants to be someplace, not somebody. "If only I had just one day when I felt I belonged someplace," he says, "everything would be all right." According to William Whyte, Jr., college seniors in 1949 were looking for security more than anything else. "I heard one recurring theme: adventure was all very well, but it was smarter to make a compromise in order to get a depression-proof sanctuary."[20]

Although *Red River* feminizes Matt, it is careful not to go too far. In *Rebel Without a Cause*, it was the bad luck of Jim's pal Plato to illustrate the pitfalls of too much feminization. (There is an undertow of eroticism in his relationship with Jim that adds a sexual dimension to his rivalry with Judy. Plato is a borderline homosexual, another reason he has to die.) *Red River* makes sure that we know Matt is a red-blooded American boy, and fast on the draw to boot. Although Dunson repeatedly calls him "soft," and at one point says, "Won't anything make a man out of you?" we know he's wrong. Matt already is a man. *Red River* doesn't throw heroism and masculinity out the window, it just redefines them. Matt represents the heroism of the center, the heroism of moderation, the moderate as hero. The fact that Matt is feminized doesn't make him any less heroic, because in these films, women were more principled, more ethical and civilized than men.

Still the imperative to feminize men, compromise, reach consensus was so strong that it makes mincemeat out of the climax of *Red River*, the final confrontation between Matt and Dunson. Dunson finally catches up with Matt in Abilene, and we know there's going to be a showdown because Dunson has vowed to kill him. But Matt refuses to fight back, refuses to draw his gun or throw a punch. * Of course, there comes a point when Matt has to, and the job of dampening conflict is passed along to his sweetheart, Tess Millay. It's woman's work anyway. She presides over the restoration of the center, imposes her feminine values on the men, making them subordinate conflict to consensus. She facilitates the transition from the older generation to the younger, guarantees that the change-over is a smooth one. As Matt and Dunson roll about in the dust, beating each other senseless, she breaks it up. "Anybody can see you love each other," she tells them, and she's right, they do. Matt looks at Dunson, Dunson looks at Matt, they grin sheepishly, and suddenly they're friends again. Dunson relinquishes his obsession with revenge and, like Johnny Ringo, decides to hang up his gun. Power and nurture are reconciled. As we have seen repeatedly, corporate liberals and conservatives often squabbled, but when the chips were down, it quickly became clear that they cared more for each other than they did for anyone else. Dunson cements the coalition of the center by adding Matt's initial to the Red River D. The resolution of *Red River*, the shoot-out that didn't happen, made good ideology, but a bad ending; it displeased reviewers at the time and has never found favor with traditionalists. In the same way that the therapeutic was undermining delinquency films like *Rebel Without a Cause*, consensus was destroying the western.

---

*The prohibition against conflict is so powerful that it suppresses a secondary conflict as well, the potential one between Matt and a gunslinger named Cherry (John Ireland). Cherry is fast on the draw like Matt, and when he sees Matt shoot, he drawls, "You're as good as they say you are," and then adds, ominously, "Maybe as good as me." "Them two's gonna tangle for certain, and when they do, it ain't gonna be pretty," observes Old Groot, who's overheard this exchange. But Matt and Cherry never do "tangle"; they become friends instead.

Mother Knows Best

Giant and the Decay of Patriarchy

George Stevens's *Giant*, released in 1956, could well have been the sequel to *Red River*, a big, sprawling *Red River II*. It is more than half a century later now, the 1920s, to be exact. As America prospered, the Red River D prospered with it. The ranch has grown bigger and richer—half a million acres and fifty thousand head of cattle, only now it's called Reata. Matt Garth is no longer a kid; he's a wealthy rancher, and as the years have passed, he's become more like Dunson, more set in his ways. His name is Bick Benedict, and he's played by Rock Hudson, not Montgomery Clift. There are no cattle drives any more; the railroad comes right to the ranch, to a stop called Benedict. Despite these changes, the message is the same; the whole cycle is about to start over, only there's no young Matthew Garth to play against Bick's Dunson. There's Bick's future son, Jordy, and a surly ranch hand named Jett Rink (James Dean, in his last role), but neither is quite right. Jordy is too young, and Jett Rink too mean. But maybe we're looking in the wrong place; after all, Matt was a feminized man; perhaps we should be looking for a woman.

When *Giant* opens, Bick's coming East on the train. He is on his way to purchase a black stallion called Whirlwind from a Maryland doctor named Layton, who seems to raise fine thoroughbred horses on the side, between house calls (it's the new medical aristocracy). Dr. Layton picks him up at the station and drives him out to the Layton estate. Bick can't wait to get a look at Whirlwind, but when he does, he gets a surprise. Guess who's perched on Whirlwind's back? Montgomery Clift's good friend Elizabeth Taylor, and compared with her, the stallion runs a poor second. She's Dr. Layton's daughter, Leslie, and she will turn out to be Bick's Matthew Garth, destined to civilize and domesticate him. She's engaged to elegant Rod Taylor, an Eastern thoroughbred in the diplomatic service, black tie, impeccable manners, and all that. But when Leslie sees Bick, who's handsome enough to stop a clock, and so tall he almost cracks his head on the crystal chandelier in the Laytons' drawing room, it's love at first sight.

Bick buys Whirlwind and wins Leslie too (it's hard for him to tell the difference—he calls her a "filly"); he returns to Texas with both, but it is far from clear who's in the saddle. When Bick's private railroad car is deposited on a siding in Benedict, and Leslie gets her first glimpse of the Benedict house, she sees an enormous four- or five-story mansion stuck out in the middle of nowhere, and she realizes she may have bitten off more than she can chew. The next moment Leslie runs smack into Luz, Bick's tough, foul-mouthed, cowgirl sister, played by Mercedes McCambridge, fresh from a stint as Emma, the masculinized, proto-lesbian villain of Nicholas Ray's *Johnny Guitar*. It quickly becomes clear that before Leslie can take on Bick, she's got to dispose of Luz.

Luz is a woman who is like a man. "Everybody knows you'd rather herd cattle than make love," somebody tells her, and it's true. She's more at home on the range than in the house, although she runs that as well, "and the ranch too, some say," observes Bick. Luz thinks Leslie is just a marshmallow from back East, and she resents her for coming between herself and Bick. But Luz underestimates the competition. Leslie trades in her Abercrombie and Fitch riding togs for Levis and lays down the law to Luz: "I don't want to take your place, but you can't take mine either," she tells her firmly. "I can't be a guest in my husband's house." Just as it seems that Bick will have to make a choice between his wife and his sister, "fate" steps in. Against the advice of the hired hands, Luz saddles up Whirlwind and hops aboard, viciously digging her spurs into his sides in big, bloody close-ups. If she can't master Leslie, she'll master Leslie's horse, but it turns out that she's the one who can't ride, not Leslie. Whirlwind throws her for a nasty fall, and she's killed.

Luz has made a lot of mistakes, and the retribution is swift. She has to die because she's too independent, too masculine, too indifferent to the pleasures of domesticity. She's a Career Woman, and pays for it. It is a simple horse trade, Whirlwind for Luz. Leslie gives up her horse, the symbol of her independence (Bick shoots him after the accident), while Bick gives up his sister. But just because *Giant* lops off Luz, a strong woman, doesn't mean it opts for a weak one. Quite the contrary. With Luz out of the way Leslie, the Balanced Homemaker, can take over.

Leslie agrees to remain in the house, but only if she can run the home. Even so, it's far from smooth sailing. Before long, Bick and Leslie begin to disagree on just where the limits of the home are, where women's world ends and men's begins. Leslie has noticed that the ranch is surrounded by squalor, that everyone who is not white lives in dire poverty, and she begins to take an interest in the Mexicans, the people who clean the stables, do the cooking, and perform the disagreeable odd jobs around the grounds. To Bick, they are little better than beasts of burden, the poor who will always be with us. "Those people never learn," he mutters to himself in disgust. But to Leslie, they are objects of pity and charity. "Why don't you do something about it?" she demands of Bick, pointing to the tar-paper shacks. "I'm not the Red Cross," he retorts. "I'm a cowman. Stop trying to make a fuss over those people. You're my wife; you're a Benedict." But Leslie won't stop making a fuss. While Luz is off digging her spurs into Whirlwind, Leslie is attending to Angel, the Obregons' sick baby, and the film intercuts the two scenes to underline the different roles the two women play. Leslie nurtures while Luz injures. The conflict between Maryland and Texas, East and West, culture and nature, has taken on a more specific ideological dimension. Leslie is a liberal, and Bick is a conservative. And this in turn is quickly transformed into a battle of the sexes, a fight over turf: What is woman's place and what is man's? And values: What are woman's, what are man's, and which will prevail?

After dinner, Bick retires to the den with his cronies to discuss politics. The women go one way, and the men go another. This is custom, tradition, the way it has always been done, but we know there's going to be trouble, because the men form a male group. Instead of going quietly with the wives, as she's supposed to do, Leslie walks up behind Bick and embarrasses him by whispering loudly in his ear that she loves him. The conversation abruptly ceases as the men wait for her to leave. "Don't mind me," she says, but they do. "We're talking about politics. This is man's stuff. Don't bother your head about it." "You mean my empty head," Leslie retorts, growing angry. "Set up my spinning wheel, girls," she cries to the other wives, "I'm joining the harem section in a minute." "You don't feel well, do you, Leslie," Bick says tensely. But she's not to be

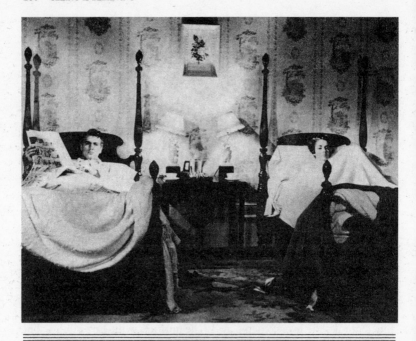

The master and the matriarch—separate but equal. Elizabeth Taylor may be excluded from Rock Hudson's world of business, but the values she stands for win the West.

deterred. "You gentlemen date back one million years. What is so masculine about a conversation that a woman can't enter into it?" she asks, and then stomps out, with one parting shot: "Send the children up to bed so the grown-ups can talk." Up in the bedroom, later that night, the argument continues. "You're my wife. When are you gonna settle down and behave like everybody else? Who do you think you are? Joan of Arc? Carryin' on like Carry Nation, mixing in with stuff that's none of your business. I want you to understand this: I run Reata." "Does that include me?" she asks hotly. "That's the way my grandfather and my father ran it," he continues, ignoring her. "I'm keeping it together for my son." "You could at least say 'our' son," she replies. He's about to storm out, but she gets the last word with the unbeatable conversation stopper of the fifties. She's going to have a baby, she tells him. His eyes glaze over. "Our baby is going to be a boy," predicts Leslie, throwing him a bone, in case she'd gone too far, become a veritable Carry Nation, as Bick said. It does turn out to be a boy—and a girl, twins, in fact, so that the battle of the sexes is handed down to the next generation.

Up to now, it is in fact Leslie who has made most of the compromises, Leslie who has had to change, to discard her Eastern clothes and habits. But Bick has to compromise too. Like Dunson, he has to change with the times. The ways of his father, and his father's father before him, are no longer the right ways. But Bick won't change willingly, and Leslie has to leave him.

Controlling men wasn't easy, and occasionally required drastic measures. Relations between Bick and Leslie deteriorate to the point where she returns to her parents in Maryland, just in time to see her kid sister marry her old boyfriend, Rod Taylor. But right in the middle of the wedding, who should pop up, hat in hand, tail between his legs, but Bick, come all the way from Texas to win his wife back. Just as the minister says, "Those whom God hath joined let no man tear asunder," the organ music, beefed up by the Warner Brothers orchestra, swells up like a heavenly chorus, and Leslie, sensing Bick's glance, turns and throws her arms around him. This marriage, like all marriages, can be saved—but on Leslie's terms. "I'm no different than when I left," she warns him. Bick gives in. "We Texans like a little vinegar on our greens. It gives 'em flavor."*

Leslie has won the war between the sexes, but what, precisely, has she won? Despite her independence, her role outside the home remains limited. She never participates in Bick's cattle business. She does continue and even extend her "work" with the poor, against his wishes, but for this there was ample precedent; if women had to do something, clubwork or charity work couldn't get them into much trouble. In the home, however, it is another story. If the business world belongs to Bick, Leslie is Queen of the Hearth. Separate but equal. This would seem like small solace, but appearances are deceiving. Leslie's power starts with the physical decor. She sets the scene. In her hands, the furnishings of the ranch evolve from

---

*Like Leslie, women in films of the fifties didn't just sit around and take it; they fought back. In the same way that Johnny Ringo's schoolteacher wife left him in *The Gunfighter* and Leslie leaves Bick, so Jane Powell left Howard Keel in *Seven Brides*, Ida Lupino left Jack Palance in *The Big Knife*, Judy Holliday left Aldo Ray in *The Marrying Kind* (1952), and Greer Garson threatened to leave Clark Gable in *Adventure*.

"masculine" to "feminine." Dark earth colors, tans and browns, give way to pastels, pinks and greens; stuffed moose heads mounted on the walls give way to stuffed teddy bears scattered about the brightly colored sofas. Chuck's Steak House becomes Neiman-Marcus.

Moving around the furniture may not seem like much, but there's more here than meets the eye. In *Pillow Talk* (1959), Rock Hudson plays one of those fifties bachelors besieged by women. He wants a wife as much as a hole in the head, but that's before he gets a look at Doris Day, an interior decorator. No sooner does she flash her Pepsodent smile than he's in love, and he hires her to redecorate his bachelor's pad, telling her, "That bed is the first thing I want you to get rid of. And anything else you think is in bad taste. I want this to be the kind of place you'd feel comfortable in." Once again, female molds male. Interior decoration becomes a metaphor for woman's power to make over man's world, his values, in her image.

Not only does Leslie get her way with the physical decor of their home, she takes over child rearing from Bick. It is she, not he, who guides the formation and determines the values of the next generation. Bick naturally wants his son to follow in his footsteps, run the ranch when he retires. On little Jordy's fourth birthday, Bick presents him with a pony, while his twin sister, who also has a birthday, gets nothing, merely watching the festivities unhappily from her mother's lap while all the attention is focused on the male child. "This boy's gonna be the best,' says Bick proudly, dressing Jordy in toddler chaps and a baby Stetson. But when Bick puts him in the saddle, he begins to wail mournfully. He's afraid of horses. "I rode before I could walk," says Bick in disgust. "He's another person entirely," snaps Leslie, sweeping her son into her arms and briskly carrying him into the house, where he seizes a toy stethoscope. Could it be that Texas, too, has fallen to the therapeutic?

Later, as Leslie stands moodily looking out the window, sympathetic Uncle Boyd (Chill Wills) ratifies what we have just seen: "Bick doesn't know a damn thing about raising kids," he says. "You stick with it and raise those kids so they grow up to be what they want to be," which is to say, *Giant* not only decides whose province child rearing is, mom or dad's, it favors a particular kind of child rearing: progressive, permissive child rearing. As we saw in *Red River*, parents weren't supposed to teach children, but to be taught by them instead. The earlier, behaviorist methods of child rearing, popular in the twenties and thirties, regarded baby as a presocial savage who had to be tamed. According to Mary Ryan, "the major objective" was to "foster the child's independence and individualism."[21] Both were jeopardized by too much mother love, which threatened to produce "momma's boys." In the early forties, the experts made an about-face. Drs. Benjamin Spock and Arnold Gesell held that baby was essentially good and that baby's whims had to be nurtured, not curbed. Parents were not supposed to impose their wishes from without. The goal of child rearing was no longer individualism, and consequently both mother love and momma's boys lost their stigma, although "overprotective" mothers still occasionally got their lumps.

If the theory behind progressive child-rearing theory sounds familiar, it's because it is our old friend, noncoercive, manipulative social control. Gesell made the emphasis on manipulation explicit. Calling for a little "household engineering," he and his associate, Louise Bates Ames, wrote, "A factory manager doesn't simply tell his workers that they ought to produce more. Instead, he tried to arrange things so that higher production is possible. Similarly, a little creative thinking about some of the ordinary household routines can often result in improved behavior on the part of the child."[22] Bick would prefer force to manipulation; he is too authoritarian, a conservative parent; almost, but not quite, a bad dad. Leslie, who knows that love is the secret to winning her babies' hearts and minds, is, conversely, a good mom.

Years later, when Bick gives Jordy, now grown up into Dennis Hopper, a man-sized Stetson for Christmas, it still falls down over his eyes. You don't have to be Roland Barthes to know that Jordy will never follow in daddy's footsteps. He doesn't want to be a rancher; he wants to be—guess what, a doctor! And that's not all. Bick has another bitter pill to swallow. Jordy marries a Mexican nurse named Juana, who bears a cute little brown-faced baby. (The Code prohibition against depicting miscegenation was dropped in 1956.) Jordy, in other words, is the son of his mother, not his father. He's a momma's boy, but in this film, that's okay. *Giant* applauds the decay of patriarchy. "Have it your own way," Bick grumbles. "Everybody else does around here," and they do.

If Jordy, the boy, disappoints his father, Judy, one of the two girls, disappoints her mother. Leslie had all but signed her up for a finishing school in Switzerland, but she wants to go to Texas Tech and learn animal husbandry so that she can be a rancher, like her dad. Both parents appear to get their comeuppance, both see their plans for their children confounded. But in reality, it is Leslie who, once again, wins. At issue is not so much what Jordy and Judy do with their lives as the principle that what they do is what they want.

Giant depicts the erosion of sexual stereotyping. Leslie is more assertive, more a man than her mother back in Maryland, and she feminizes Bick, sees to it that he becomes more a woman than his father. With their children, this exchange of roles goes further: Judy is the rancher, while Jordy is the doctor, the profession of choice for the nurturing, feminized man. Moreover, if Leslie and Rick's generation is more liberal than their parents', if their children are more liberal than they, their children's children will be more liberal still. In Jordy and Juana's brown-faced baby, the contradictions that bedeviled the parents are overcome. In the consensus of the center there is room for (almost) everybody. The utopian transcendence of dualism is immanent in the family, and in history as well, which is, quite simply, progress.

All that remains is to put the finishing touches on the new Bick. Near the end of the film, Leslie, Bick, Juana, and her baby end up in Sarge's Diner, a greasy spoon by the side of the highway. As soon as they set foot inside, every eye turns toward Juana, and we know that Sarge isn't in the habit of serving Mexican Americans. When they order ice cream for the baby, the hulking six-foot-four-inch redneck who runs the place drawls, "Ice cream—I thought the kid would want a tamale." Bick hauls himself out of his chair so that he's nose to nose with the cracker, two giants facing off in the tiny diner, and the next thing you know, they're fighting like bears, rolling around on the floor, with dishes, food, and garbage flying in all directions. It's all handled in a faintly comic vein; they're just grown-up children letting off some steam.

Bick loses the battle; Sarge finally decks him, but physical force proves nothing in a film like this, and he wins the battle of the spirit. A few reels back, Leslie had angrily accused Bick of treating her like a child. Now, as in *Blackboard Jungle*, the roles are reversed. At home, Bick lies with his head in Leslie's lap, a baby, finally, and happy about it. Mother explains to him what was won and what was lost in his fight with Sarge: "You know all that stuff you used to do to dazzle me? But nothing made you as big a man to me as when you were on the floor of Sarge's hamburger joint. When you got toppled over that pile of dirty dishes, you were, at last, my hero. You wound up on the floor, on your back, and I said to myself, 'After a hundred years, the Benedict family is really a success.' " As in *Red River* and *Rebel Without a Cause*, male heroism has been redefined—by a woman. It is Leslie who decides what is heroic and what isn't.

By the time the final shot fades out, we see that although woman's place is in the home, the home is truly vast; it encompasses a good deal more than the four walls of the Benedict mansion. Woman's world has been equated with the aggregate of pluralist values: tolerance, compromise, flexibility, civility; and since pluralists identified their values with the highest aspirations of society, of civilization, woman's world comes to be equated with nothing less than culture itself.

Giant was a big-budget, A-picture, stuffed with stars and packed with production values, and a top grosser as well, third in line in 1956 behind *The Ten Commandments* and *Around the World in Eighty Days*. Consequently, it would be fair to say that its ample definition of woman's world was no fluke, but on the contrary, generally characteristic of the dominant cinema of mainstream culture. The relation of women's world to men's was examined explicitly and repeatedly throughout the fifties. Take Joseph Pevney's *Foxfire* (1955): Jeff Chandler (Jonathan "Dart" Dartland) is a half-Apache mining engineer in Arizona, while Jane Russell (Amanda Lawrence) is a newspaper heiress from back East. It's love at first sight, but it is evident that there are storm clouds on the horizon. Amanda is a handful, decked out in fifties proto-punk tight black black pants, bright pink blouse, and butch haircut, not to mention Jane Russell's Big Bertha breasts. She's socially facile, a thoroughly modern woman, at home in groups, relaxed and other-directed. Dart, on the other hand, is the strong and silent type, rigid, proud, and old-fashioned. When he has to talk to more than one person at a time, he breaks out into a cold sweat.

Amanda and Dart marry, but right away they fall to fighting. One day Dart leaves for work without his lunch bucket. Amanda follows him to the mine and gives it to him. He's furious. The mine is his world, man's world, and she's not welcome. "You mind your business, and I'll mind mine," he snaps. But just what is Amanda's business? Like *Giant*, *Foxfire* asks the question: How wide is woman's world? Or, put another way, are men's and women's worlds mutually exclusive, as Dart suggests? Women who ventured from the home like Amanda were often made by men to feel like trespassers on alien territory. In *Strategic Air Command*, Sally is continually intruding on Dutch's world, phoning him at the base in the middle of his physical, then again interrupting him while he's taking an altitude test, then bursting into General Hawkes's office to give him a tongue-lashing. If these women kept to their own worlds, they complained that they were superfluous people, mere spectators watching men act, the way Tony Perkins's wife sat in the stands and watched him play baseball in *Fear Strikes Out*. In Nunnally Johnson's *Oh Men! Oh Women!* (1957), Ginger Rogers complains to Tony Randall that the spark has gone out of their marriage. "I want to be needed, I want to be necessary," she complains. "It's your world. It used to be ours. Now I'm just looking on. Just a sidewalk superintendent."

But Amanda has been reading the 1954 issue of *McCall's* on "togetherness," which more or less acknowledged that woman's world was not enough, and called on men to share the housework and let women have a peek at the big world outside the home. "I thought mine was yours and yours was mine," she says, but she can't make a dent. Maybe Dart's mom, on the Apache reservation, can tell her what makes him tick.

Apaches bring up their sons differently from white folks, mom explains. "A boy of twelve does not cry or ask help from a woman. He will rely on his own strength and independence and never need help from anyone." Dart has to learn that it's all right for a man to ask for help. He has to become more like Amanda, but before he does, like Leslie and the other scrappy wives of fifties films, she has to leave him. He tracks her down to a dude ranch, where she's gone to recover from a miscarriage, but it's still no dice. "You don't need me," she tells him. "You treat me like a squaw. When you don't want me for anything, I walk twelve paces behind. I can't live that way. I don't want to be married that way. Good-bye, Dart." He exits, with heavy heart. But it's not his heart he'll have to worry about; it's his hands. There's a mine cave-in, and it's his turn to go to the hospital, with crushed fingers. (Stints in the hospital or catastrophic illness in films like this served the purpose of therapeutic lessons.) Amanda rushes to his side. "I wondered how long it would be before you hollered for help," she says, bursting into his hospital room. "I did holler for help," he replies. "I called you this morning. I need you," and sure enough, he does—to make coffee. "Come with me and see the mine," Dart offers, inviting her to enter man's world, where once he made her fear to tread. Off they go, in his jeep, but since his hands are still bandaged, she's in the driver's seat. In all these films, women who enter men's world, like Sally on Dutch's air base or Tony Perkins's wife in the Red Sox dressing room, come to be welcome guests, not intruders, whereas men who try to exclude their wives from their world ("A wife must stay out of a man's life when it concerns his bread and butter," bellows Rod Steiger in *The Big Knife*) are wrong or villains or both.

The Taming of the Shrew
<u>Mildred Pierce</u> and the Feminist Mistake

Michael Curtiz's *Mildred Pierce* (1945) is a rags-to-riches Horatio Alger story. Mildred (Joan Crawford) begins as a waitress and ends up a wealthy woman. She works hard, makes sacrifices by the dozen, and delays gratification with the best. Hers is the kind of success story that would have been applauded in most conservative films, like this one, had Mildred been a man. But what was good for men was rarely good for women, and Mildred is punished for her career.

Conservative films didn't like career women any better than pluralist films did; in both, women had to return to the home. The difference was that once they did return to the home, pluralist films rewarded women with power. In conservative films, on the other hand, there was no difference between outside and inside; women were not lured into the home with a "deal," which allowed them to exercise social control over men. Rather, they were expected to subordinate themselves to men inside the home as well as outside, and not just to any old men, but to traditional, strong, conservative men.

Mildred's is a child-centered family, one that would have done Dr. Spock proud. She has two girls, Veda, the elder, and Kay, the younger, and she fills their time with ballet, piano, and singing lessons. "I'll do anything for those kids, including their crying, if I have to," she says angrily, arguing with her husband, Bert (Bruce Bennett), about how to raise the kids. "You might as well get one thing straight. Those kids come first in this house, before you or I." Like Leslie in *Giant*, she is in charge of child rearing, and the values transmitted in this process are hers; but unlike Leslie, she commits all the sins in the book or, rather, in this film Leslie's virtues are Mildred's vices. The progressive methods that worked so well with the Benedict kids make a mess of the Pierce kids. When Leslie let her children do what they wanted, it was all for the best; when Mildred does the same thing, she's "spoiling" her kids.

Ambitious, overprotective Mildred was a case study in "momism," a phrase coined by conservative social critic Philip Wylie in his 1942 best seller *A Generation of Vipers*. "Megaloid momworship has got completely out of hand," Wylie wrote in his inimitable style. "Our land, subjectively mapped, would have more silver cords and apron strings criss-crossing it than railroads and telephone wires. Disguised as good old mom, dear old mom, sweet old mom, your loving mom, and so on, she is the bride at every funeral and the corpse at every wedding.'²³ Conservatives didn't like mother love. They clung to the behaviorist child-rearing theories of the twenties and thirties that had been discarded by Spock and Gesell, theories that argued, as Peter Viereck put it, that "every modern baby is still born a cave man baby. What prevents today's baby from remaining a cave man is the conservative force of law and tradition,"²⁴ not coddling and candy. We saw that momma's boys like Jordy in *Giant* were fine, but in conservative films they were not. In *White Heat*, momma's boy James Cagney was a psycho. He was trained as a criminal under her tutelage, and he internalized her directives. Robert Walker was the nut who danced to his mother's tune in Hitchcock's *Strangers on a Train* (1951), and again the Commie/fag/egghead whose mind rotted on mommy's breast in *My Son John*, which, in typical conservative manner, pillories poor John for being an intellectual with a college education. Then there was the loony killer in Lang's *While the City Sleeps*. "He's a momma's boy, unless I'm mistaken," says ace reporter Dana Andrews. He's right. As the killer sits in his pj's watching Andrews bait him on TV, he complains to mom: "When you adopted me, you wanted a girl, and [Dad] wanted a boy—neither of you was satisfied. I remember when I was a kid—I was dusting the house, and a neighbor came in and said, 'You have such a nice little girl!' " "You've never been happy since your father died," replies mom sympathetically. This momma's boy is known as the Lipstick Killer, and goes about bludgeoning young women to death. Whose fault is it? "ASK MOM" are the words he scrawls with lipstick at the scene of the crime.

Bert, like Bick, is excluded from child rearing, but here that's bad, not good. Ultimately, Mildred throws him out of the house altogether, confirming dad's irrelevance to the matriarchal, corporate-liberal household, the fulfillment of dad's worse fears. Stung by Mildred's neglect, Bert has picked up a mistress somewhere along the way, Mrs. Biederhoff, and Mildred, in another, we feel, unreasonable display of female pique, forbids him to see her. "I go where I wanna go," Bert says, making a stand. But it's his last one, and Mildred calls his bluff. "Then pack up," she retorts. Bert does, and Mildred is on her own.

For all Mildred's dislike of domesticity she's a whiz at cooking, and before long she starts a restaurant, which becomes an instant success. On her way up, she falls for Monty Beragon (Zachary Scott), an indolent playboy on his way down. Monty lures Mildred to his beach cottage, where he tells her that when she's close to him "there's a sound in the air like the beating of wings," and gets her, presumably, into bed. Mildred is becoming more sexual, more natural. The monster from the id is raising its ugly head, and this film links female ambition, permissiveness, and sex. Each is bad and tars the others with guilt by association.

Meanwhile the kids, Kay and Veda, are spending the weekend with Bert and Mrs. Biederhoff. When Mildred returns home, she finds that Kay has fallen seriously ill with pneumonia. The doctor can't help her (no miraculous cures here, as there are in therapeutic films like *The Other Love* and *Magnificent Obsession*), and straightaway she dies. Mildred is being punished for breaking up her home and having a fling with Monty. This may seem like strong medicine, but women like Mildred were dangerous, and if the death of her child was needed to steer her back on the straight and narrow, it couldn't be helped. *

Kay's death is a danger sign. It tells us, and should have told Mildred, that she has taken a wrong turn, wandered onto dangerous ground— female sexuality, on the one hand, and man's world, on the other. But

---

*Children's deaths were often used in films of the fifties to underscore parental derelictions. In *Foxfire*, we recall, Amanda had a miscarriage, while in Joseph Pevney's biography of Lon Chaney, *The Man with a Thousand Faces* (1957), little Creighton Chaney fell ill because his mom wanted a career of her own. In *The Marrying Kind* (1952), Judy Holliday and Aldo Ray go at it so often and so furiously that it begins to have a deleterious effect on their kids, who wander in, teddy bears in tow, to stare forlornly into space while mom and dad chuck lamps at each other. After an hour or so of family feuding, their son drowns. In *The Country Girl* (1954), when Bing Crosby, an alcoholic singer, lets go of his son's hand for an instant to reach for a record in a publicity shot, the boy promptly runs in front of a car and is killed. And Captain Holmes lost his baby in *From Here to Eternity* because he was cheating on his wife.

she ignores it, throwing herself ever more energetically into both her affair with Monty and her career. Her business, like her love affair, we are meant to see, is built over Kay's dead body; her success at both does not enhance the fortunes of her family; rather, it is achieved at their expense.

One restaurant leads to another, and soon Mildred is a rich woman. But she becomes masculinized in the process. She begins smoking cigarettes, wears suits with wide, padded shoulders, and starts to drink. "It's a habit I picked up from men," she says, pouring herself a stiff one. As she becomes a woman who is like a man, she is more dangerous to men than ever. Not only does she kick Bert out of the house, she demands a divorce. She rejects her pal Wally (Jack Carson), who wants to marry her, manipulates him into doing her financial dirty work ("Oh, Wally, you're so wonderful!"), and in one scene, has him doing the dishes in an apron, in this film a sign not of the new male sensitivity but of castration. She

Career woman Mildred Pierce (Joan Crawford) emasculates every man in sight. Here, in her new restaurant, she ties an apron around Wally (Jack Carson).

"keeps" Monty, lets him go when she's tired of him, and makes him propose to her when she wants him back. Finally, of course, she tries to frame Wally for murdering Monty.

Mildred is asking for it, and it is only a matter of time before she gets it. Her Achilles heel is her daughter Veda. Mildred gave Veda everything she never had herself, and what she never had is not only money but freedom from the traditional constraints that mold women's roles. "I was always in the kitchen," she explains. "I felt like I'd been there all my life except for the two hours it took to get married. I got married when I was seventeen. . . . Cooking, washing, mending, I never knew any other kind of life." Mildred saw to it that this didn't happen to Veda, but her permissive overprotectiveness backfired and now Veda is a stuck-up snob. She is a chip off the old block, her mother's, not her father's, child. Played by Ann Blyth, Veda even looks like her mother, dresses like her in suits, and like her victimizes men. At one point, she marries a callow youth named Ted for the sole purpose of blackmailing his family into a $10,000 annulment by pretending to be pregnant when she's not. In the negotiations, Ted is represented by his mother, another specimen in the film's rogues' gallery of domineering women. Ted's dad is nowhere to be seen, and when Ted is incautious enough to venture a remark of his own, mom says, "Theodore, will you be good enough to keep quiet." "Yes, mother," he replies, and lapses into silence. Ted is another momma's boy.

One day Veda shows her true colors. Why did she want the $10,000? Mildred asks her. "With this money I can get away from you, from your chickens, your pots and pans." Mildred tears the check in two; Veda slaps her across the face, and Mildred throws her out. She has been deeply hurt by Veda's perfidy, but she can't bear her daughter's absence, and since the only way to get her back is to marry Monty, with whom Veda is infatuated, she does. Veda indeed returns, but keeping Monty and Veda in the styles to which they are accustomed is expensive, and Mildred loses her restaurants. Betrayed by the men she pushed around, she learns that it's a man's world after all; if she can't stand the heat, she had better get out of the kitchen. Arriving at the beach house to have it out with Monty, she sees him and Veda kissing passionately at the bar. "He never loved you; it's always been me," shrieks Veda triumphantly. Mildred pulls a gun from her bag, but she can't pull the trigger, drops it on the floor, and rushes out. Veda has no such inhibitions. When Monty calls her a "rotten little tramp," she plugs him. The ultimate crime at the heart of *Mildred Pierce* is a crime of a woman against a man. The unnatural fruit of Mildred's momism is a crime of passion and (figurative) incest, nature run wild.

Hearing the shots, Mildred returns, and subsequently tries to protect Veda by first framing Wally, and when that fails, confessing to the murder herself. But the cops are too smart; it won't wash. They know Veda did it, and as she is hauled off to jail, where she'll get a taste of the discipline she didn't get at home, Mildred walks off into the rising sun—with Bert!

Why Bert? Because Bert is the conservative ideal midway between the extremes of Wally and Monty. Once again, we are given our choice from a smorgasbord of male alternatives. Wally, the loud, backslapping businessman, the man with the polka-dot bow tie and a million laughs, is the harbinger of the other-directed personality to come. If Wally is the future, Monty is the past. He has nothing but disdain for the Protestant work ethic that this film cherishes. When Mildred asks him what he does, he replies, "Nothing." His occupation? "Loafer." He's an idle rich affront to middle-class hegemony. James M. Cain's novel, on which the movie was based, was published in 1941, and *Mildred Pierce*, released four years later, already feels a little dated when it portrays leisure as decadent and consumption as conspicuous, instead of routine and patriotic, as they would become in the hands of the affluent middle class of the fifties, but it was typical of backward-looking conservatives, who never bought the "affluent society" to begin with.

Bert has all that Monty and Wally lack. If Monty disdains work and "drinks too much," Bert declines to drink at all, because his "hours are too long." While Wally is easygoing, relaxed, and morally suspect, Bert is grim, rigid, and moralistic. He disapproves of the way Mildred has brought Veda up, and he's right; he's been right all along. Mildred has learned the hard way that she made a mistake when she kicked Bert out those many years ago ("I was wrong," she confesses), and now that Veda is out of the way, she can retrace her steps and pick up where she left off. She must subordinate her judgments, her perceptions of the world, to his, because his are superior. She must recognize that he, not she, represents culture, that is, the values of society. Culture and patriarchy are synonymous; the relation between patriarchy and the family is direct, not dialectical as it is in corporate-liberal films. *Mildred Pierce* allows for neither career nor the power of the managerial mom ceded Leslie in *Giant*. The family simply replicates the patriarchal structure of society. If Mildred, in her behavior, defied patriarchy, she must, in the end, acquiesce. It is Bert, not Mildred, who rules the roost. It is in this sense that Mildred has to learn to be like him, accept his values. Finally, she learns that women's world and men's are mutually exclusive. Had she stayed in the kitchen where she belonged, she could have saved herself a lot of trouble.

Why does eliminating Veda allow Mildred to return to Bert? She is Mildred's bad nature, her monster from the id. She acts out Mildred's secret desires. She fires the gun that Mildred drew and dropped; she kills Monty, whom Mildred wished dead. Mildred has lost both her business and her daughters; doubly castrated, she can only return to the home she once scorned and lick her wounds under the protective wing of her former husband. Women, not men, are domesticated (read, punished and infantilized) in conservative films.

The masculinization of women was fine in pluralist films, but conservative films called a halt. Their women were supposed to become like men too, but only, as we have seen, in the sense of accepting a place in men's world, where, as critic Leo Braudy, referring to Hawks's films, put it, "the woman can adopt the male point of view and its value system."[25] This value system, of course, puts women in the home. Conservative films specialized in transforming strong women into weak ones, whores into mothers. In *Rio Bravo*, for example, Angie Dickinson is transformed from call girl to housewife. Like pluralist films, conservative films made their heroes choose between a good woman and a bad one. And likely as not, these heroes, required to culturize natural women, chose the "bad" over the "good," the little lady of shady lane over the prim proprietors of the little red schoolhouse, to prove male strength and power. Clark Gable chooses exotic Ava Gardner over proper but bland Grace Kelly in Ford's *Mogambo* (1953), Rock Hudson chooses hard Julie Adams over wholesome what's-her-name in Walsh's *The Lawless Breed* (1952). Since these women were tougher, wilder, and free from the baggage of culture that weighed down their gumdrop-sweet pluralist counterparts, they were often more appealing as well, but once they entered the kitchen, they were rarely heard from again.

In Ray's *Johnny Guitar*, Joan Crawford plays another self-made woman very much like Mildred. Her name is Vienna, and she runs a saloon in a dusty, two-bit town out West. "I never seen a woman who was more a man," says one of her male employees. "Thinks like one, acts like one, and sometimes makes me feel like I'm not." Here, wrote critic Raymond Durgnat, "is your American matriarch, woman as owner and boss, wearing not only the pants but the six-shooters. She and the hero have exchanged roles."[26] The hero in question is Johnny Guitar (Sterling Hayden), a feminized ex-outlaw who now prefers a guitar to a gun and has nothing on his mind but marriage to Vienna. Vienna tells Johnny to get lost, but before the end, Vienna has been punished for her independence, and the role reversals with which the film begins are undone. When her saloon is burned to the ground, it marks something of a turning point; from then on, Vienna becomes more feminized and Johnny becomes more masculinized. She learns to cry, and he learns to pick up the gun, save her life, and tell her what to do. As they're scampering across the rocks one step ahead of the posse, he helps her so she won't lose her footing. By the end of the film, she can't even buckle her belt without his help, and he even manages to get her into the kitchen, where she rustles up his breakfast, although she does make him fetch the eggs. By this time, Vienna is playing the peacekeeping role Johnny played in the beginning, but she is allowed one last shot, to purge herself of her masculinized double Emma (Mercedes McCambridge). At the end, she throws her gun away and herself into the arms of Johnny Guitar.

Mildred is not only put in her place by Bert, she is subordinated to a cop as well, Inspector Peterson, who ultimately gets his man, or in this case, his woman. Most of the film is devoted to a flashback narrated by Mildred, but the cop's narration frames hers, in the same way that her view of the world ultimately makes way for Bert's. From the beginning, the cops have played cat and mouse with Mildred, and it turns out that her feminine subterfuges are nothing to their masculine professionalism. Moreover, the film insists on a conservative, punitive framework, not a therapeutic one. Mildred "confesses" to a cop, not a doc, and when she doesn't tell him the truth, it's not because she's neurotic, it's because she's lying. Mildred explains to the cops that Veda had persuaded her to cover up the truth by appealing to her maternal instincts, by luring her into a therapeutic quicksand of guilt and anxiety where she quickly loses her footing. "It's your fault I'm the way I am. Help me!" pleads Veda, insisting that she's sick, not criminal, and that Mildred has made her a killer. In a corporate-liberal film like *Rebel Without a Cause*, Veda would be right, but here, that's no explanation, no excuse. Her mother may not have helped matters, but evil lies within the self, not outside in the family, and Veda is naturally bad. With its spare-the-rod-and-spoil-the-child attack on permissive child rearing, *Mildred Pierce* takes a hard line against children. It is Mildred's pal Ida (Eve Arden) who sardonically delivers what may well be this film's verdict on youth: "Veda's convinced me that alligators have the right idea—they eat their young." (Fearing parricide, it endorses infanticide.) The cops brusquely reject Veda's formulation, and it is their point of view that prevails. When Mildred, on the verge of tears, explains how Veda convinced her ("I thought it was my fault"), Inspector Peterson replies, "Not this time, Mrs. Beragon. This time your daughter pays for her own mistakes."

Like so many conservative films, *Mildred Pierce* is AC/DC, torn between left and right, and therefore Mildred gets it coming and going. The film attacks her for spoiling her children, putting them first, but when she puts herself first, as she does when she takes a few moments out from running a home and business for a couple of kisses, she is punished with the loss of her daughter. On the one hand, it chastises Mildred for her sexualization, for giving way to her libido, nature within. On the other, it attacks her for being too hard, tough, masculine, insufficiently feminine and natural. Ultimately the film opts for rigid gender distinctions, the traditional family, and rejects the therapeutic.

But we can see pluralist ideology nibbling away at the edges. The detective work in the film consists solely of listening to Mildred's story, peeling away the layers of evasion and half-truth that, for whatever reasons, disguise the full truth. The process of detection, in other words, is very much like psychoanalysis; Inspector Peterson might very well have been Dr. Peterson. Moreover, for all his closed, stiff-upper-lip rigidity, Bert plays the feminine role to Mildred's male one. When Mildred divorces him, he doesn't remarry, but suffers, watches, and waits, until his passivity is rewarded and Mildred returns. He's like the Nice Girl next door in the antisuccess films of the late forties whom the hero-on-his-way-up leaves behind. *Mildred Pierce* is *Body and Soul* in drag, and even for men like Bert, feminization is just around the corner.

I Remember Poppa

Executive Suite and the Persistence of the
Protestant Ethic

Both *Red River* and *Giant* contemplated generational change with equa-
nimity. When dads grew bad, as they tended to do in these films, it was
time to let the kids take over. In conservative films, it is no longer dad
who is the problem, but junior. Robert Wise's *Executive Suite* (1954) is
concerned with a crisis of dynastic succession. In the very first scene,
Avery Bullard, head of Tredway Enterprises, a large furniture manufac-
turer, drops dead in the street of a heart attack. In another kind of film,
this would have been a therapeutic warning to his colleagues, but here it's
only the catalyst for a furious fight for control of Tredway. Although no
longer a family firm, Tredway is not a modern "managerial" corporation
either, but an old-fashioned company whose every product is stamped by
the vision of one dominant personality: Avery Bullard. His death is consequently a serious blow to Tredway, leaving it, as someone says, "a one-
man company without its one man." Unlike similar figures in corporate-
liberal films, Bullard was not a bad dad; "he was a great man, the greatest
man I ever knew," as someone else says, and this stands as the film's
verdict. Bullard taught the next generation; he did not have to learn from
it, as Dunson had to learn from Matt. Consequently, his successor must
live like him, emulate him, not differ from or rebel against him. Conservative films did not encourage Oedipal rivalry; they suppressed it. As the
vice-presidents scramble to fill the old man's shoes, the question becomes,
Who is most like Bullard? At the same time, the competitors offer not
only alternative ways of running a business, but alternative ways of being
men.

The logical successor to Bullard, his right-hand man, is an executive named Alderson (Walter Pidgeon), but he's lived in Bullard's shadow for so many years he no longer has what it takes. "I thought I could do it, but I can't," he says sadly. "Bullard didn't want me to be president, more or less than what I am: number-two man." Alderson is the son who is not man enough to follow in his father's footsteps. Jesse Grimm (Dean Jagger), vice-president in charge of production, doesn't want the job. He's too old-fashioned, and he knows it. He's retiring. J. Walter Dudley (Paul Douglas), vice-president in charge of sales, the Wally of this film, won't do either. "He's a damn good salesman. That's all," someone says. "Bullard didn't build this company on being popular." The attack on popularity, of course, is the tip-off. We heard both General Savage and Major Kirby scorn popularity in *Twelve O'Clock High* and *Flying Leathernecks*, and we know that it was one of the hallmarks of the new, postscarcity managers, for whom handling people was just as important as producing things.

The leading contender for this job, and at the same time the worst alternative, is Loren Shaw (Fredric March), the comptroller. He is an out-and-out villain, a heartless and unscrupulous manipulator. He is the corporate-liberal organization man, the manager/administrator. He represents the triumph of Wall Street and corporate capital over the old-fashioned family business. "Efficiency today has become a dirty word; budget control has a bad odor," Shaw sneers, making his pitch to the other directors. "You know why more and more corporations today are drawing their leaders from the ranks of comptrollers and investment bankers? Because the problems that come to the president's office today are predominantly financial." But his enemies won't buy it. "Improve the process, but never the product. That's Shaw's philosophy. To him, the whole company is just a curve on a chart," says one man in disgust.

Finally, there is Don Walling, a design engineer and dark horse. As soon as we see that he is played by William Holden, we know he's the right man for the job. As an engineer, Walling qualifies for the role of expert, but it quickly becomes clear that his notion of leadership is more conservative than Shaw's, which is to say, he's more of an old-fashioned rugged individualist. Walling ridicules Shaw for "grabbing for the sure thing, the quick and easy way a lot of people are doing these days." To Shaw's narrow emphasis on making money ("return on investment"), he counterposes the tradition of quality. Pulling a new Tredway chair to pieces with his bare hands, Walling castigates "a management that's willing to stoop to this kind of junk in order to add a dime a year to the dividend." He articulates a conservative critique of big business, charging that the cash nexus has eroded traditional values. When Walling does mildly criticize Bullard's leadership, he merely suggests that Bullard fell short of his own goals. Of all the candidates for the top spot, he is most like Bullard.

Not only is Walling more suited than the others to run Tredway, he's also more of a man. When Alderson initially objects that Walling is too young and inexperienced for the job, Walling fires back, "You mean I'm not old and tired and weak and afraid," like the others. And again, "I'm not going to stand by and see the company fall into the hands of a weakling like Dudley."

In *Executive Suite*, the only people who don't like Bullard are women. Bullard was like a father to Julia Tredway (Barbara Stanwyck), the daughter of Tredway's founder, whom Bullard succeeded, but Julia thinks he's been a bad dad. Julia complains bitterly, "I gave him ten years of my life and all my love; what did I ever get out of it but loneliness and sudden death?" The film never clarifies exactly what their relationship was, but what is clear is that if it was unsatisfactory, it was Julia's fault, not Bullard's. She is portrayed as a neurotic, hysterical spinster.

Mary (June Allyson), Walling's wife, is almost as bad as Julia Tredway. Walling had a dream when he came to work for Tredway, and Mary casts herself in the role of the guardian of his dream, the woman who sees to it that the man does his best. She's felt for some time now that Walling's dream is dead. He had never been given the opportunities he expected. "Bullard made you a promise," she tells him. "Plan what you want, design what you want, develop new ideas, but it's over with." (Such were the fifties that she makes *Executive Suite* sound like *Arrowsmith*; Walling is not on the verge of discovering a cure for polio, however, he's only designing Castro Convertible sofas.) With a promotion, it can merely get worse. He'll be more of a company man than ever. But Mary makes one mistake. Dreams were disruptive to the status quo, utopian, and therefore dangerous. Mature women like Nancy Reed, who trafficked in dreams, were realists, always arguing that their husbands' aspirations could be met by the as-is. Mary, on the other hand, tries to get Walling to leave Tredway, in much the same way as Ann Dadier tried to get Rick to leave the blackboard jungle. She's a troublemaker, a proto-extremist.

At first, Walling listens. He doesn't, he says, want to follow in Bullard's footsteps: "I'm not going to die at the top of the tower worrying about bond issues and stockholders' meetings." But soon he changes his mind, and when he does so, he makes the decision on his own, without consulting Allyson, the same way Dutch Holland decided on his own that he wanted to stay in the Air Force in *Strategic Air Command*. Mary objects to Walling's decision to go for the top, and they fight about it. She thinks' he is becoming too much like Bullard: "Avery Bullard has to be kept alive, is that what you mean? You want to sit in his chair, be his ghost? You're even beginning to sound like Bullard," she says, echoing Sally, who accused Dutch, in almost the same words, of beginning to sound like General Hawkes. Besides, she doesn't think he can mobilize enough board members behind him to get the job. She continues, "I love you, and I wouldn't want you to hurt that lovely head of yours against a stone wall trying to do the impossible." "Nothing's impossible," snaps Walling, determined to challenge Shaw for Bullard's job. Walling is a risk taker, a gambler who resembles right-wing heroes like Billy nothing's-impossible Mitchell, for whom no challenge is too great.

As things get hot and heavy between Walling and Mary, it looks as though he may have to choose between his career and his family, like Dutch and Dadier before him. But as we have seen, films like *Strategic Air Command* and *Blackboard Jungle* didn't like to be forced to choose between either/or, mutually exclusive alternatives. Both Dutch and Dadier chose wrong, career over family, and were punished for it, Dutch by his bum shoulder and Dadier by poison-pen letters that led to the premature birth and near death of his baby. But they were punished only for a moment and only so that, once the lesson was learned, they could be rewarded by getting it all.

In another corporate-liberal film, *The Man in the Gray Flannel Suit* (1956), adapted from Sloan Wilson's best seller in 1956 by screenwriter/director Nunnally Johnson, Tom Rath also has to choose between his family and his job. When Rath (Gregory Peck) gets a position at United Broadcasting, Mr. Big (Fredric March) at the top of the tower takes a liking to him. Mr. Big is an inner-directed striver of the old school, but he has gotten to the top at the expense of his family. He and his wife are separated, and his teen-age daughter is a borderline delinquent. *

Mr. Big offers to groom Rath for the executive suite, everyman's dream, we should have thought, but not this one's. Rather than burn the midnight oil at the office every day to climb the ladder of success, he preferred to spend those evenings with the kids and the missus, watching Milton Berle and Jackie Gleason on the tube. Peck saw what had happened to Johnny Ringo. He knew. Pluralist men would rather be weeding the backyard than making the important decisions in the boardroom. And like Sirk's millionaire in *Has Anybody Seen My Gal?*, Mr. Big concurs: "Don't let anybody keep you away from your family," he counsels Rath. "You know where I made my big mistake? Big successful businesses just aren't built by men like you—nine-to-five and home and family. Big successful businesses are built by men like me, who give up everything they've got for it—love it body and soul. My mistake was in being one of those men." "I'm afraid I'm one of those nine-to-five fellas," confesses Rath. "That's okay," Mr. Big reassures him, ratifying his choice. "We need both kinds. If I had my choice again, that's what I'd be. Nine-to-five, home, and family." Ultimately, Rath isn't really sacrificing very much by repudiating the buccaneer model of capitalism; he can make quite enough as a middle-level executive to get along, not to mention the fact that his grandmother has just left him a parcel of prime real estate in a much-coveted suburb that his wife is itching to convert to condos. In the characteristic centrist conclusion, Rath gets to be right and rich at the same time. He chooses family, but a nice career comes along with it. †

---

*Mr. Big's rebellious daughter makes a postscarcity, fifties-going-on-sixties attack on the Protestant Ethic: "It's really stupid the way you live, working all the time," she says, but then she goes too far, adding, "I don't want to work at all." Workaholics in films like this were heading for a fall, like George Gershwin in *Rhapsody in Blue*, who found that writing too many symphonies was no good for his health. But rejecting work altogether was bad too. How much work was enough? Somewhere between too much and too little.
†"In [Fiedler Cook's] *Patterns* (1956)," Whyte wrote, "another, equally curious business tale, the hero doesn't mind work so much but he is similarly sanctimonious. He is appalled by the ruthless tactics of the industrial buccaneer. When the buccaneer offers him a top spot the hero says he wants no part of it. He is a moral man and he gives the boss a tongue-lashing. Having thereby saved his soul, he takes the job (at twice the salary). [Once again], in a masterpiece of the have-your-cake-and-eat-it finale, he tells the boss he'll punch his face if he doesn't act right."²⁷

Like *The Man in the Gray Flannel Suit*, *Executive Suite* pits business against family—with precisely the opposite results. Walling's son, Mike (Tim Considine), is a pitcher in the Little League, and at one point they are playing catch in the backyard when dad gets a call from the plant and abruptly departs, leaving little Mike near tears. He's the reverse of Tom Rath, who put family first. Later, not only does he miss junior's big game, but the game is intercut with the decisive scene in which he decides to run for Tredway president, emphasizing the precedence of business over family. After Mary and Walling fight, Walling walks out. "Hey, pop—cries Mike. "Later, Mike," replies dad, brushing him aside. "Gee whiz, he didn't even ask me who won the game," complains Mike.

When Walling slams out of the house, it's a miniaturized version of the scenes in *Giant* et al., where wife leaves husband. But here, the shoe is on the other foot, and it is Mary who gives in, not Walling. She bursts into the boardroom during a break in the meeting—to apologize. "If that's

While Gregory Peck in *The Man in the Gray Flannel Suit* chooses family over career, Holden does the reverse, putting his slide rule ahead of June Allyson.

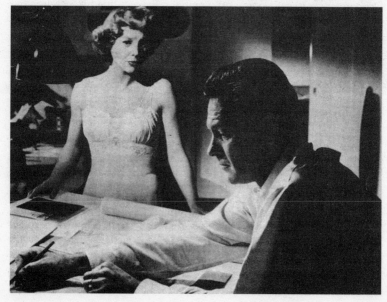

what you really want," she says hoarsely in her June Allyson voice, "that's all that should matter, to either of us." And she gives him a word of encouragement: "Nothing's impossible, remember?" He's right, and she's wrong. Unlike Ann Dadier's judgment in *Blackboard Jungle*, hers here is simply overridden; she is given nothing, no surrogate power in return. She does not become an agent of social control. He, not she, represents culture. He, not she, is the authentic guardian of the dream, which *can* be realized by Tredway; his view that "nothing is impossible" prevails over hers, and she cedes the family's pride of place to business, his business. Again everything works out, but on his terms this time. If, in *The Man in the Gray Flannel Suit*, Rath secures his career by choosing family, in *Executive Suite* Walling secures his family by choosing career.

It is left to Julia Tredway, the superfluous woman, to underline this message at the end, for if Don Walling has to live like Bullard, Mary has to live like her. After Walling has been chosen to head the company, she turns to Mary and says, "You must be very proud of him." "I am, and a little frightened, too," replies Mary. "Because you don't completely understand him?" asks Julia. "We never do," she goes on, answering her own question. "Not men like that. It will make you very lonely at times, when he shuts you out of his life, but then he'll always come back to you, and you'll know how fortunate you are to be his wife." In this film, like *Mildred Pierce*, men's and women's worlds are not only very different, they are mutually exclusive as well, and the one is subordinate to the other.

The reason that Walling's wife has to be put in her place is that conservative films worried that the family might be sapping the moral fiber of the American male. In *Atomic City* (1952), the weak-kneed wife of a top U.S. scientist tries to persuade hubby to give in to Red blackmail in order to save their son, whom the Soviets have kidnapped. Scientist: "The Russians will wreck half the world." Mom: "I only know that Tommy is our world, our whole world." Scientist decides to stand up to the Reds, even if it means his boy ends up in Komsomol. Says an admiring FBI agent, "He wouldn't sell out, not even for the kid." Tom Rath put the problem nicely in *The Man in the Gray Flannel Suit*: "When a man's got a lot of security, money in the bank, other jobs waiting for him, it's a cinch to be fearless and full of integrity, but when he's got a wife and three children to support, and his job's all he's got, what do you think he ought to do about it then?" The family was undermining men's inclination to take risks. Conservative films didn't like that, and tried to do something about it.

In *The Desperate Hours* (1955), Fredric March, a wealthy banker, presided over a typical middle-class family living in a typical suburb somewhere in America. March had been something of a marked man ever since, in *The Best Years of Our Lives*, he had played a liberal banker who got into trouble with his boss for giving loans to vets with no more collateral than their word. March never did learn his lesson, and, in fact, *Best Years* won an Academy Award. But now, when trouble comes in the person of Humphrey Bogart, his Oscar's useless. Family discipline in the March household is lax, and the flab behind the picture window invites a jab or two. In the opening scene, his son, Ralphie, refuses to pick up his bike, which is lying on its side in the middle of the front lawn. As Bogart and the gang cruise the neighborhood, they spot the bike, and it prompts them to seize on March's house. "Why my house?" March asks. "I like people with kids," replies Bogart. "They don't take chances." Sparing the rod has spoiled Ralphie, and threatens to spoil the American dream as well.

March's first response to the invasion of his home is appeasement: give them anything they ask for, he reasons, and they'll go away. For a variety of reasons, they don't, and March is forced to take a stand. When, gun in hand, he finally confronts Bogart, Bogart sneers contemptuously, "You ain't got it in you, Pop." "I got it in me; you put it there," March replies evenly, and drives Bogart out of the house to die in a hail of police bullets. The film doesn't actually make him pull the trigger, but it convinces us that he could. When the film ends, we know that March has earned his plush suburban home, his cushy bank director's job—if anyone was asking. "Lady," he tells his wife, with evident pride, "you don't know what a tough old bird you married," and, in case we haven't gotten the message, *The Desperate Hours* closes with a swipe at permissive child rearing. March finally puts little Ralphie in his place: "I've had about all I'm gonna take from you, young man." From now on, his bike will go in the garage, where it belongs.

The Desperate Hours, like *Executive Suite*, strengthened the man within the context of the family, but better still, conservative films often preferred to separate man and family entirely. Corporate-liberal films like *Strategic Air Command* tried to bring the family to the battlefield. In *Sabre Jet* (1953), the American pilots commuted to their nine-to-five jobs in Korea, bombing Pyongyang and Chosun. After a hard day in the cockpit, they returned to suburban Okinawa, where their wives whisked them away from the airfield in the family station wagon to a dry martini waiting at home. But conservative films tried to cut the umbilical cord. In Joseph H. Lewis's *Retreat, Hell!* (1951), when Marine Capt. Richard Carlson is called up for active duty, he takes his family with him to the base where he's been assigned for training. One day, tough Col. Frank Lovejoy tells the men to say good-bye to their families because the battalion is going twenty miles inland on maneuvers. Carlson breaks out into a cold sweat at the very idea of being separated from the wife and kids, and requests permission to spend the night with them. "Permission denied," snaps Lovejoy, and all the other officers stare at Carlson like he's crazy. "I guess I'm a little confused," he confesses sheepishly. "I'm just a family man." "You're a Marine," bellows Lovejoy, "and don't you forget it." Lovejoy is worried that Carlson won't be able to cut the mustard when he gets to Korea. He's "got a wife and two children; he's going to play it safe, too safe," he says, but of course, by the end of the film, Carlson is shooting gooks like fish in a barrel.

Whereas *Sands of Iwo Jima* interred John Wayne and groomed mild John Agar for civilian life, *Retreat, Hell!* does an about-face and prepares both fathers and sons for war. In addition to family-man Carlson, it also features a callow youth, Russ Tamblyn, whose dad was a gung-ho leatherneck. Russ is anxious to be, like him, the pride of the Marines. The only trouble is, he's so scared of combat he can't move. Eventually, he, too, proves himself, but he's still in trouble, not from the North Koreans, who fall over dead whenever he glances their way, nor from dad, whom he loves dearly, but from doting mom, who has humiliated him by asking Harry Truman to send him home. It seems she has already lost one son at Iwo Jima and another in Korea, and wants the third alive. "I belong here," Russ says despondently, barely audible above the rumble of mortar fire. But just as he's saying a reluctant farewell to his buddies, the enemy launches a surprise attack ("Those soldiers are Chinese!! What are they doing here?"), and Russ gets to stay. The Reds save him from a fate worse than death: mom.

Toward the end of *Retreat, Hell!*, Colonel Lovejoy, taking a moment out from battle, allows as how "it must be wonderful to have a family." "You have," replies Carlson, looking about him at the Marines. "They're all around you." Like *Strategic Air Command*, this film redefined the army as a family, but this time it is a family of men. Conservative films, when they are not toughening up the family, feature men bonding with other men. This is one reason why Wyatt Earp rides off with barely a wave good-bye for poor Clementine, to continue his way west with brother Morg. It was particularly true of war films. In *From Here to Eternity*, Burt Lancaster preferred the company of other men to the considerable charms of Deborah Kerr. "You don't want to marry me," she says shrewdly. "You're already married—to the army," and she's right, he is. Despite the torrid beach scene, he really doesn't need or want a woman. Why should he? As Jap Zeros strafe Wheeler Field, a low-angle shot catches Warden with a machine gun on hip, ecstatically firing away. Kerr finds this a hard act to follow. Similarly, Montgomery Clift leaves Donna Reed for the army. "Please don't go back. We'll go to the States and get married," she pleads. But it's no dice. The army provides a warmer womb. "They'll take care of me," he assures her. "I'll be all right when I get back." In the final scene, it is Kerr and Reed who are going back to the States together, without their men. As Audie Murphy put it in *To Hell and Back*, "I think I'll just let the army do my planning for me." Women in these films threatened to break up that old gang of mine, the male community.

Conservatives' fondness for the army as a community of men often outweighed their mistrust of the army as a bureaucracy. "The military man," observed critic Stanley Cavell, "asserts the myth of community," and he goes on to observe that "the movies' way of asserting community is typically through male comradeship."[28] This won't work as a description of movies in general; as we have seen, men in corporate-liberal films had to integrate the family into the military community, and they were punished if they didn't. But it is an accurate description of conservative films like these, where being soft, womanish, or wearing an apron was a serious business.* In *Flying Leathernecks*, Major Kirby transmits this message to

---

*Even when the attainment of a wife is the goal of the hero's labors, she is often irrelevant. Wolfenstein and Leites, in *Movies: A Psychoanalytical Study*, cite a striking instance of this pattern in *She Wouldn't Say Yes* (1945), where the buddies are the bride's father and his son-in-law. "In a comic reversal of the saying 'It's not your father I'm marrying, it's you,' the hero and the father hold hands and exchange vows in a second marriage rehearsal. In the end, on what was to have been the wedding night, the young man sleeps with the father. His marriage is not yet legal, and the father makes him sleep in the lower berth with him while the daughter occupies the upper."[29]

his tiny son. When his wife says, "Johnny, give your father a kiss," Kirby vetoes it, saying, "He's too big to go around kissing men." In conservative films men, not women, educate the children, and they educate them into toughness. In *Shane*, Alan Ladd got into trouble with mom for teaching Brandon de Wilde how to shoot. But in Anthony Mann's *The Tin Star* (1957), it's okay for an older gunfighter (Henry Fonda) to instruct a wet-behind-the-ears raw youth (Tony Perkins) how to use a gun.

When conservative men came home, they experienced little of the guilt and anxiety that beset pluralist men. Heroism was alive and well, beating strongly in the hearts of men like Audie Murphy, the most decorated soldier in World War II, who came back to be a movie star. If Peck, Clift, Hudson, and Dean were corporate-liberal antiheroes, Murphy joined John Wayne as the ideal conservative hero of the fifties, precisely because he was so ordinary; he was the boy-next-door who could go out and slaughter Germans by the handful one minute and come back with his innocence intact. Not every vet, in other words, returned wounded and/or neurotic. In *The Blue Dahlia* (1946), *Thieves' Highway, Ride the Pink Horse* (1947), and *Bad Day at Black Rock*, vets returned to kick ass, to whip the children—usually boys—into shape, and to take care of business on the home front, which had gone to seed while Johnny was away. If women wanted any part of the action, they had to shape up, like Perkins's girl friend, Millie, in *The Tin Star*, a typical pluralist woman at sea in a conservative film. She won't marry him unless he quits his job. "It's me or that badge," she says, but by the end, she acknowledges that he's been right all along. "A man can't run away from his star," says Perkins. "Neither can a woman," Millie agrees.

Moving right along, leaving the center behind, men become even harder, tougher, and more independent. Whereas conservative films like men in groups, radical-right films like loners, men who do it by themselves.

The Right Man for the Right Job
The Fountainhead and the Triumph of the Will

The Fountainhead (1949), based on Ayn Rand's novel of the same name, was a Wagnerian soap opera for the radical right. Even though the Nietzschean flavor of Rand's melodramatics was somewhat distasteful to home-grown reactionaries, the film is a primer of right-wing attitudes, and in King Vidor's hands, Rand's febrile dialogue (she wrote the script) becomes a tour de force of top-volume ideological filmmaking, Hollywood's *Triumph of the Will*. Strewn with heroic individualists struggling to defend themselves against craven moderates, big men beset by small, Gullivers among the Lilliputians, the film does its best to upset the centrist applecart.

When the planetarium lecturer in *Rebel Without a Cause* announced that "man existing alone seems an episode of little consequence," he sent *angst*-ridden adolescents like Plato scurrying for cover under their seats. In *The Fountainhead*, on the other hand, existential loneliness is Rand's bread and butter, music to her ears. Her heroes would have it no other way. Gary Cooper plays Howard Roark, a young architect expelled from school in the very first scene because his ideas are "too original." Roark is an extremist and proud of it. He has his own ideas about how buildings ought to be built, but he can't get any work because everyone else agrees with Ellsworth Touhy, architecture critic of *The Banner*, who holds that "artistic value is achieved collectively, by each man subordinating himself to the will of the majority." (To Rand, democracy is virtually communism.) Roark's former teacher, likewise a victim of his originality and now a repentant derelict, gives him some sensible centrist advice: "Compromise, before it's too late." An old friend from school says the same: "You can't hope to survive unless you compromise." But Roark is defiant. He rejects the politics of compromise, and with it the personality structure it implies. He is precisely the kind of man pluralist films didn't like. Rather than soft, compliant, and feminized, he is rigid, unyielding, and obsessive. When his friend offers to lend him money, Roark snaps, "I don't give or ask for help."

If John Wayne was the conservative's best man, and Audie Murphy their best boy, Gary Cooper embodied the type of brittle masculinity preferred by the radical right and often the radical left as well, stubborn men of vision and principle like Billy Mitchell, and Will Kane in *High Noon*, for whom compromise, the siren song of the center, meant selling out, acquiescing to the easy virtue of the moderates. In the face of the business-as-usual, pragmatic approach of the center, the characters Cooper played had no choice but to dig in their heels, stiffen their backs, and tough it out. In centrist films, when pluralists tell the heroes to "relax," it's good advice, because they're too uptight; in radical films, when pluralists tell the heroes to "relax," it's an invitation to opportunism, to knuckle under to the bland conformity of society. In *Invasion of the Body Snatchers*, Miles Bennell's pal Jack, now a pod-person, tells him, "Relax. We're here to help you," while in *The Big Heat*, Dave Bannion's boss says, "Dave, you've got to ease up. Take a few days off." The same is true on the left. In *Attack!* Colonel Bartlett, trying to dissuade Lieutenant Woodruff from exposing his crimes, says, "Be flexible, Woodruff, use your horse sense."

Roark shares the drive and ambition of Don Walling in *Executive Suite*, but in him they are carried to extremes; the logic of rugged individualism leads him out of the center into a world of pure will. Roark is a loner. Had he been in Walling's shoes, instead of competing for the executive suite, he probably would have resigned and gone into business for himself. In films like *The Fountainhead*, groups, be they corporations or governments, all men or mixed, are inevitably inimical to personal vision.

One day Roark gets his big break, a chance to design the Security Bank Building. His design, simple, functional—"natural," in fact—is accepted, save for "one small compromise." The bankers are afraid "the public wouldn't like it; it's too original, too different." They clutter Roark's clean lines with a classical façade. "It's the middle of the road," they explain. "Why take chances if you can be in the middle?" When Roark hears the word *compromise*, he sees red; he would rather die than change a comma on his plans; the commission to design the Security Bank Building is an offer he can, and does, refuse. Like the problematic patriarchs in pluralist films, the Tom Dunsons, Cobbs, and Steigers, Roark is a builder, and he'd rather starve than sell out for the security of the bank building. Here, he's not being stubborn, just principled.

Roark is hard as rock, and his principles land him in his element; he's forced to cut stone to make ends meet. Toiling away in the quarry, Roark encounters wealthy Dominique Francon (Patricia Neal), the Valkyrie of the Social Register. When we first meet her, Dominique is asexual, unemotional, repressed. "I'm a woman completely incapable of feeling," she says. "I'll never fall in love." But no sooner does she disburden herself of these sentiments than she confesses to an inordinate passion for Roark, whom she spies far below her, digging away in her father's quarry. As she sits astride her prancing stallion, flicking his flanks with her crop, dyna-mite blasts thunder forth from the sound track, and Dominique and Roark exchange torrid glances, while Roark assaults the rock face with his phallic drill. When we see those glances and hear those explosions, we know that her defenses against emotion, passion, sex are being blown away. Freud meets Wagner. Dominique is being stripped of her civilized restraints. She is becoming more natural, but before this romance of the wills can be consummated, Roark will have to show her who's boss.

In one scene, Roark enters her bedroom at night, while she's in her dressing gown, and knocks her down. She bounces back and slugs him one. They struggle, and—kiss. She begins to weep and passes out. Her will has been broken. She begs him to marry her. "I'll cook, I'll wash clothes, I'll scrub the floor," she cries, a Dostoevskian heroine in an ecstasy of submission. "Yes or no?" "No," replies Roark. He's won. He doesn't need her; she needs him. Dominique has been dominated. When it came right down to it, radical-right heroes had no use for women. There is no woman at all in Billy Mitchell's life, and Bannion's wife is killed in the first scene of *The Big Heat*. When women do appear in these films, they are traditional helpmates; they have to take their cues from men, adopt their values, as they do in conservative films, except now their values are not the center's, but oppositional values.

In films like *Rio Bravo*, women must become less natural, which means more subservient and less sexual. Here they must become more natural, which means more subservient and more sexual. This is their "natural" condition. But ultimately Roark's purposes cannot be deflected by domes-

Roark (Gary Cooper) dominates Dominique (Patricia Neal), establishing the proper power relationship between men and women in *The Fountainhead*.

ticity. While Tom Rath put his family ahead of his job, and Don Walling put his job ahead of his family, here there's no contest, because there's no family, no children, no home, no hearth. Roark has no mother and no father, and neither is even alluded to in the course of the film. The family drops out of right-wing films altogether.

Right-wing heroes had few, if any, ties with others; even other men didn't hold their interest long. For a moment, Roark forms an attachment to Gayle Wynand (Raymond Massey), owner of *The Banner*, also in love with Dominique. Wynand is another of the film's gallery of self-made millionaires (as common on the right as the masses were on the left), another monster of the will. "We have no choice but to submit or rule," he says to Dominique on their first date, enlarging on his philosophy of life. Spurned by Roark, Dominique marries Wynand, but the two men become fast friends anyway. "We're alike, you and I," Wynand tells Roark.

In fact, they like each other more than either likes Dominique. When they're together, she is the odd woman out in their romance of smiles, shared opinions, and mutual admiration. Wynand invites Roark on a cruise. Dominique objects, accusing Wynand of being "obsessed" with Roark. "I believe you're jealous," Wynand observes, and she is. *The Fountainhead* threatens to become a conservative buddy film, until Wynand is taken out of the picture, later on, saving Roark for himself, allowing him to ride off into the sunset alone, playing solitaire. If corporate liberals believed that no man is an island, the radical right acted as if no one else existed.

One day Roark gets another offer, this time to design the Enright House for Roger Enright, another self-made millionaire who began life as a coal miner. But Roark's path is strewn with obstacles. Ellsworth Touhy, *The Banner's* architecture critic, is still on his case and launches a campaign against him in the paper. Touhy is a liberal. He mocks Enright for being a rugged individualist, a capitalist, attacks him for building a luxury apartment building when the poor don't have any place to live at all. When it comes right down to it, however, it turns out that he just can't stand excellence. "I don't like geniuses," he says. "They're dangerous." We've heard all this before. It was one of the right's loudest complaints against the center, and we have also seen that it was largely true. Films as different as *The Gunfighter*, *The Thing*, *In a Lonely Place*, and Hitchcock's *Shadow of a Doubt* all favored Average Joes over geniuses.

The Enright House is a big success, but Touhy manages to destroy Roark's career anyway, and he has to start again from scratch, designing gas stations, humble homes, and family farms. (He's the victim of a liberal blacklist at a time [1949] when the right, in the real world, was blacklisting the left.) But you can't keep a good man down, and pretty soon Roark is on his way up again, twice a self-made man. In a weak moment, he agrees to ghost-design a housing development for the poor, on the condition that his plans be followed to the letter. They aren't, of course. Once again, his brilliant design is messed up by run-of-the-mill, garden-variety, middle-of-the-road architects. Since the buildings have already been built, and since no one is supposed to know that Roark designed them, he is hard pressed to find an appropriate way of expressing his displeasure, but at last he seizes on a simple expedient: he blows them up with dynamite. He takes the law into his own hands, becoming a revenge hero, a vigilante of the right. In pluralist films, Dominique would have been a restraining influence, dissuading Roark from his mad course, but by this time she's had enough of Wynand and allows Roark to persuade her to help him dynamite the development, following him outside society, the way Becky followed Miles Bennell in *Invasion of the Body Snatchers*, helping him dispatch the pods.

Roark is arrested for his prank, but when he gets his day in court, it quickly becomes clear that it is the center that is on trial, not him. The proceedings sound like the Soviet purge trials. When the prosecutor tells the jury that the crucial question of our age is, "Does any man have the right to exist if he refuses to serve society?" we have to remind ourselves that this is supposed to be America, circa 1948, not Moscow, 1938. Roark disdains lawyers and defends himself (an amateur/superman rejecting professional or expert help) in a wordy peroration, the gist of which is that "the great creators stood alone against the men of their time. They lived for themselves, and only by living for themselves did they achieve the glory of mankind." He attacks his enemies for making "robots" out of men of genius, and he defends the "individual against the collective," attacking society's right to exercise social control over its members, to exact sacrifice from its citizens. "The parasite follows the opinion of others," declaims Roark, directing a fusillade at Riesman's peer-pressured, other-directed man. Farther to the right than both *The Big Heat* and *The Court Martial of Billy Mitchell*, *The Fountainhead* rejects the idea of the public interest altogether, or at least relegates it to a distinctly secondary role, way down the line after self-interest. Revenge is transformed into principle.

Rand's was not a populist brand of right-wing thought; she was as contemptuous of the people as the corporate liberals and the left were. In the wake of the dynamiting, Wynand has *The Banner* defend Roark against "the worst storm of public fury" the city has ever seen. Facing disaster when his staff walks out and roving mobs attack his trucks, Wynand finally gives in and, against his principles, editorializes against Roark.

But the mob can't be all bad, because the jury is persuaded by Roark's fulminations and lets him off. As in other right-wing films, Roark manages to bring the community around to his way of thinking. Wynand, on the other hand, his self-respect destroyed, commits suicide, finally allowing Roark to marry Dominique. Roark has won. The rigid, uncompromising, tough-as-nails man has finally come into his own. From the quarry, he has been catapulted heavenward. In the last shot, Dominique rides up to the top of the Wynand Building Roark has designed. "Where's Mr. Roark?" she asks a humble construction worker. "He's way up on top," she's told, and up she goes, in an open elevator, the entire city, a city of ants—the common man—laid out at her feet. We ride up in the elevator with Dominique, which is to say, Roark has pulled both her and the audience up with him. We have learned from him, accepted his values as our own.

The Fountainhead is an American version of the interwar German "mountain films," which, with their passion for heights, glaciers, craggy promontories, and dramatic cloud formations, expressed contempt for the "valley-pigs," as they were called, the Average Joes and Janes who couldn't make the climb. Many of these films were made by, and featured, Leni Riefenstahl, and as we see Dominique rising up to meet her *Führer* in the ethereal realms where mere mortals fear to tread, we finally realize where she's coming from.

The resonance of the last shot of *The Fountainhead* with the romanticized, sublime landscapes of the mountain films reinforces the idea of nature as a counterweight to culture and contrasts with the cautionary, watch-the-skies codas of centrist sci-fi, where space (and transcendence) are regarded with fear and trembling. What was inhospitable nature in those films is grand in this one, the only fit setting for heroic individualism. This is a nature of absolutes—sky, space, and stone—analogous to the clean, elemental simplicity of Roark's designs and antagonistic to the derivative, cluttered, ticky-tacky modifications urged upon him by the small-minded, liberal arbiters of official culture.

Left-wing films also pitted oppositional values against the center, and subordinated women to men, but for the most part they eschewed the singles culture of films like *The Fountainhead* in favor of couples, and traded in uptight monsters of the will like Roark for loose and relaxed heroes like Rock Hudson in *All That Heaven Allows*.

The Man in the Red Flannel Shirt

All That Heaven Allows and the Flight of the Exurbanites

In Douglas Sirk's *All That Heaven Allows* (1955), Jane Wyman plays a widow named Carrie Scott. When her husband dies, she's left well off, still attractive, of course, but on the edge of middle age with two grown children. Carrie is afraid that the best years of her life are over. In the manicured suburb where she lives, daily life is a round of Tupperware parties, country club dances, and charity bazaars. In one shot, she stands deep in the frame, while the foreground is crisscrossed by the lattice of leading that holds the panels of the window through which the scene is filmed. A woman's home is often a prison.

Carrie is prim, proper, reserved, and looking for Mr. Right. The problem is, there may not be any Mr. Right for someone her age. She gazes sadly at a bouquet of dried flowers in a vase. Is this the autumn of her life too? Is there nothing more? Is she dead on the vine at forty-five?

Enter Rock Hudson, as Ron Kirby, the gardener. Ron is young (younger than Carrie), vigorous, and handsome. But he is only a gardener, and therefore not an appropriate match. Appearances, however, are deceiving. Ron may get down on his hands and knees in the dirt, but this is no suburban version of *Lady Chatterley's Lover*, and Ron is no monster from the id threatening to disrupt Carrie's suburban dollhouse. On the contrary, he's soft-spoken, polite, college-educated (agriculture school, naturally), and it turns out that he only tends gardens as something of a hobby. He *owns* a nursery, where he grows trees; we're relieved to discover that he's actually as middle-class as she is. Deep inside his breast there beats the heart of a small businessman.

If Carrie is worried about autumn, Ron appears every spring, and his job is to make her flower like one of his petunias. But next spring, he tells her, he's not coming back. He's getting out of the gardening business to devote himself to raising saplings, and he invites her home to look at his "silver-tipped firs." Ron gives her a tour of the old, broken-down mill near his house—oak beams, stone walls, birds nesting in the rafters, and so on. As she ventures up the wooden stairs to the loft above, a startled bird takes wing and surprises her into Ron's arms. Cut to a shot of a dove, cooing away like a foghorn. Ron, and Ron's world, in case we've been asleep, are nature, as Carrie and her world are culture. One of Carrie's suitors, speaking more truly than he knows, later calls Ron "nature boy," and indeed, he's on a first-name basis with the beasts of the forest. In one shot, a timid fawn nibbles deer food out of his palm. Although intended as one, "nature boy" is no insult in this film, because natural men are noble savages.

Suburban life is suffocating and conventional in *All That Heaven Allows*. Ron (Rock Hudson) teaches Carrie (Jane Wyman) all about the birds and the bees.

In left-wing films, as in right-wing films, men draw women out of culture into nature, often wild, elemental nature. Take *Viva Zapata!* Like Johnny Ringo, Zapata just wants to settle down. He falls in love with Jean Peters (Josefa), daughter of a wealthy bourgeois who doesn't want to end up, she says, squatting in the dirt patting tortillas like an Indian. Zapata wants Josefa to teach him to read, that is, he wants to be civilized, and with the help of a wealthy patron, he gets his foot on the bottom rung of the ladder of success. At the same time, however, he can't help noticing that society is unjust, that the peasants, his brothers, are oppressed. Torn between town and country, he rides off into the mountains to fight. He knows what's good for him, but his heart is with his people.

Zapata is a later incarnation of Brando's Stanley Kowalski, but this time he is unambiguously heroized, like Ron a noble savage silhouetted dramatically against rocks and crags. As long as he stays in the mountains, he is safe. But when he goes to court Josefa in town, he's in danger. Her parents' house becomes his prison. In one scene, uncomfortable in city clothes, he is seated in the parlor trading the traditional conceits of courtship with Josefa's mother. Behind his head is a barred window, and above it swing two birdcages. On another occasion, he is actually arrested as he steps out of the door. For Zapata, to live in society is to die, and so Josefa must live with him in the mountains. In a film like *On the Waterfront*, she would have drawn Zapata out of the mountains into the city, in the same way that Edie Doyle draws Terry out of the jungle into the courtroom. But here he takes her out of culture into nature, and she ends up, just as she feared, patting tortillas like an Indian, although in this film, as she must learn, that is good.

In Joshua Logan's *Picnic* (1956), adapted from William Inge's Broadway hit of the same name, it's Kim Novak's turn to be drawn out of culture (here, parochial small-town life), this time by William Holden, a drifter, another natural man. The schoolteacher who would have been the culturizing heroine of a pluralist film is here found wanting. Played by Rosalind Russell, she is not a woman of principle, like the teachers in *The Gunfighter* and *On the Waterfront*, but a repressed, henpecking harpy who makes a fool of herself over Holden.

Holden, on the other hand, spends a good deal of the movie, like Zapata, stripped to the waist, "naked as an Indian," as someone says, flexing his muscles for the edification of the sex-starved ladies of

Nowheresville. He is a free spirit, a breath of fresh air. After he leaves, one woman says, "He clomped through the house like he was still outdoors. You knew there was a man in the house." Once again, houses—the enclosures that are fortresses in centrist films—are prisons in radical films. Society literally threatens Holden with jail, as it does Zapata, and he has to save Novak from hers—her mother's home, defined by a screen door that separates her from him like the bars of a cage. Running from the cops, he takes refuge behind a waterfall that effectively conceals him, rather than threatening to drown him, as Niagara Falls does to Joseph Cotten in the middle-of-the-road, stick-close-to-the-banks *Niagara*. Nature in *Picnic* is man's best friend, not his enemy.

Picnic was one of a number of films, like *A Streetcar Named Desire* (1951), *Cat on a Hot Tin Roof* (1958), *The Fugitive Kind*, *Splendor in the Grass* (1961), *The Roman Spring of Mrs. Stone* (1961), and *Sweet Bird of Youth*, in which sex-starved women lusted after young studs, usually played by Marlon Brando, Paul Newman, or Warren Beatty. Although these films contained ideological elements that put them on the left side of the political spectrum—the villain of *Picnic*, for example, is the scion of the town's wealthiest family, who vies with lumpen Holden for Novak's favors—their real radicalism lay in their sexual politics. The heroes of these films were easy to distinguish from the rigid men of the right; they were less monsters than martyrs of the id, hounded by society for their threatening sexuality. Roark was a "control freak," to borrow a phrase from *The Deer Hunter* (1978). For him, nature was indeed a jungle, as the Hobbesian centrists maintained, but that was just fine, because man was king of the beasts, and Roark was king of men. In *The Fountainhead*, nature meant domination, but for the heroes of films like *Picnic*, nature wasn't a jungle— good or bad—but a Rousseauistic arcadia. Therefore, being natural meant letting go. Nature was liberation.

Interestingly enough, these films were largely written by homosexuals like Tennessee Williams, or adapted from plays by homosexuals like William Inge. As we have seen, radicals used nature as a stick against culture, because it was a convenient way to attack the center. For homosexuals, this conflict took on a particular significance, because it drew on a tradition of imagery that equated homosexuality with sexual liberation and noble savagery. In their hands, the assault by nature on culture became an attack on the sexual conventions of the center.

When the Kinsey Report landed like a bombshell on the repressive landscape of fifties sexuality, the war between radicals and the sexual center broke out anew, and once again, nature and culture were deployed against each other like two hostile armies. The report attacked conventional attitudes toward sex and argued for more permissive standards of behavior in general, and homosexuality in particular. Sexual centrists rejected the implications of the report and attacked it from the high ground of conventional sexual attitudes, pitting culture against nature.

Lionel Trilling, for example, made great fun of Kinsey's assertion that homosexuality was "natural" because animals, particularly rats, did it too. He didn't like Kinsey's "strong reliance on animal behavior as a norm," nor the way Kinsey used the animal as a category to "establish a dominating principle of judgment, which is the Natural," nor the kind of man who emerged from the report, " 'a picture of an animal who, however civilized or cultured, continues to respond to the constantly present sexual stimuli, albeit with some social and physical restraints.' " Trilling recognized that Kinsey was using nature as a club against culture, and took pains to disarm him. "Surely the problem of the natural in the human was solved four centuries ago by Rabelais," Trilling loftily observed. "Rabelais's solution lay in the simple perception of the *natural* ability and tendency of man to grow in the direction of organization and control."[30] Like the hearts of other pluralists, Trilling's lay with "organization and control," but he wasn't against permissiveness, so long as it didn't go too far. He didn't want to give up nature if he didn't have to, and he didn't have to if he could argue, with Rabelais, that "organization and control" are natural too.

Meanwhile, back in *All That Heaven Allows*, nature and culture are still going at it. Carrie has been introduced to the flora and fauna of Ron's world, but what about the humans? Ron invites her to a party. Inside a rustic split-level house in the woods, his friends are gathered around the fire for some good talk and red wine. As they lay out the red-and-white-checked tablecloths, poke candles into Chianti bottles, and put the lobsters on to boil, Carrie begins to find out who's who in nature's half acre: an assortment of ethnics, eccentrics, and conservationists. First, there's grizzled Grandpa Adams, a beekeeper and artist ("I'm not an abstractionist; strictly primitive"); then "Manuel, the Lobster King"; then a woman from the Audubon Society; and finally Mick Anderson (Charles Drake), who, like Ron, runs a tree nursery. Most of them are fugitives from the rat race. While Ron pulls corks out of bottles with his teeth, Mick's wife, Alida (Virginia Grey), briefs Carrie on the history of this bucolic bohemia. Mick, she says, is a former ad man who chucked Madison Avenue ("the ulcer circuit," as he calls it) and headed for the woods. He once thought that money and an important position would bring him happiness, but he found out that this just wasn't so, so he dropped out.

To Carrie, overdressed and uncomfortable in a suit, these casual, unconventional people represent a whole new world. She picks up a copy of *Walden* that happens to be lying on the coffee table and opens up to the passage where Thoreau writes that "the mass of men live lives of quiet desperation." In *The Lost Weekend*, Ray Milland had described his life this way too, and reached for the bottle to ease the pain, but there he had been wrong, and the film encouraged him to realize his utopian aspirations inside society. In *All That Heaven Allows*, Thoreau is right; Carrie's life *is* one of "quiet desperation," and the utopian alternative represented by the people gathered around her can only be realized outside society. (In 1954, *Walden* was banned from U.S. Information Service libraries overseas because it was "socialistic.")[31] As Carrie reads on about "different drummers," and asks herself, with Thoreau, "Why should we be in such frantic haste to succeed?" Ron plays the piano while Alida confides that although *Walden* is Mick's Bible, Ron's never read it. "He just lives it. I guess all of us are looking for security these days, and when Mick met Ron, who neither had it nor seemed to need it, he was completely baffled."

Ron, it seems, has taught Mick to live like him. He is something of a local guru, which is to say, men, not women, are teachers in this film. Women, not men, are infantilized. His relation to Carrie is precisely one of teacher to student, parent to child. He reminds her to dress warmly when she goes out: "It'll be cold by the time we get back. You'd better take a warm coat." And again, he sees to it that she remembers her boots. As she stoops to put them on, he says, solicitously, "I'll help you. You mustn't catch cold."

Men taught women in conservative films too, but unlike them, where strong men culturized or tamed wild, natural women, Ron deculturizes Carrie, who has been led astray by citified or, more accurately, suburbanized ideas, and helps her to become a naturalized citizen.

Ron is a left-wing version of Roark. "To thine own self be true" is his motto, and like Roark, he's an individualist, an inner-directed man with his own "psychological gyroscope" inside him. As Alida says, "Ron's security comes from inside himself, and no one can take it away from him." The major difference between Ron and Roark is that Ron is a soft, nurturing male, whereas Roark is a hard, domineering male. Although Ron is independent, he's not a loner. He doesn't dispense with the female principle. Not only does he need Carrie, he's more "feminine" than she is. He tutors her in domesticity, not the other way around. Ron is something new under the sun: a feminized, inner-directed male. In other words, whereas masculinized women feminized hard men in films like *Giant*, soft men feminized masculinized women in films like *All That Heaven Allows*. Ron teaches Carrie how to be a woman.

Nature takes its course, and Carrie is surprised to find that Ron has gone ahead and converted the old mill—for them. (Recall that Leslie decorated the Benedict mansion, pitting her taste and values against Bick's in *Giant*; here, Ron has done the decorating, and will shortly pit the new old mill against Carrie's suburban home.) Ron has put in a big picture window, opening up his home to the outdoors. ("You can see for miles," he observes, as we look at the view.) Carrie's house, on the other hand, is often pictured from the outside, and we look through the leaded glass windows at the people trapped inside.

One day Ron pops the question. Carrie, playing the male role, replies, "I hadn't thought about marriage!" "Why do you think I've been seeing you?" asks homebody Ron. But Carrie demurs. "It's impossible," she says, echoing Mary in *Executive Suite*. She's afraid of what her children and the neighbors will say. "It's easy if you're not afraid," Ron reassures her in Rock's husky, honied tones as Sirk cuts to another exterior shot of a deer frisking about in the woods. Like the social-control figures in pluralist films, Ron tells her she must decide for herself. He explains that Mick had to discover for himself that he had to make his own decisions, that he had to learn to be a man. "And you want me to be a man?" she exclaims. "Only in that one way," Ron replies, but the cat is out of the bag. He wants her to become like him, adopt his values, but paradoxically, as we have seen, men's values in films like this are women's.

Carrie gives in; she'll defy convention and marry him. It's eros against civilization. The course of true love, however, rarely runs smoothly, and there is no reason why it should here. Carrie's friends and neighbors are against the marriage. (If this were a sci-fi film, Ron would be an alien, and we know it would be left-wing, because he is benevolent.) Even Carrie's best friend, Sara (Agnes Moorhead), raises her eyebrows. "Your gardener!" she exclaims, warning Carrie that people will talk. But she decides to throw a party for Carrie so that the solid citizens of Stonington can get to know Ron. The party, of course, goes badly. "A gardener—why doesn't he get himself a money-making occupation?" says one man. "Is there any money in trees?" wonders another. *All That Heaven Allows* was *The Graduate* of the fifties.

Stonington, we see, is a bad town, filled with small-minded, back-stabbing people. In this film, pluralists' affection for social control in the guise of peer pressure is derogated as keeping up with the Joneses. Carrie's kids, Kay (Gloria Talbott) and Ned (William Reynolds), momma's girl and poppa's boy, are this film's spokespeople for the center, this film's doc and cop, and they're both wrong. "He won't fit in," objects daughter Kay, confident that Carrie will come around to her point of view. "She's much more conventional than you think she is," she tells priggish brother Ned. "She has an innate desire for group approval." Kay wears glasses, meaning she's a hypercivilized pluralist woman. But here, the Freud she spouts doesn't mean she's on familiar terms with her id, but only with sterile book learning. Kay is repressed herself. From a slightly different angle, she's a younger version of Roz Russell in *Picnic*, the schoolteacher on her way to becoming a spinsterish schoolmarm. (Kay is saved from this fate; she falls in love, doffs her glasses, and becomes feminized, too. In one scene, she puts on mom's nail polish. "Since when have you joined the female ranks?" quips Ned.) Kay doesn't represent Carrie's secret desires, as Veda does Mildred's, but rather, her secret fears. Ned, on the other hand, is a young conservative. "There's a certain sense of tradition," he protests, while the camera traps him behind the other side of those ubiquitous latticed glass partitions, so that he, too, looks like he's behind bars. "Ron's against everything father stood for." Ned tries to fill his dad's shoes by doing things like ostentatiously making cocktails, but here he's just silly.

Carrie increasingly falls under the sway of her children and her neighbors. She bows to peer pressure, and she and Ron fight about it. Once again, competing conceptions of home become symbolic of opposing ideologies. Were we to marry, Ron says angrily, "we would be living just as you always have, probably in your house." "What's wrong with that?" retorts Carrie. "Suppose we did live in my house. It wouldn't change you. You couldn't be changed." "Yes, I could," says Ron. "By who?" "By you." In pluralist films, women had to change men. Here, woman's power to do precisely that is dangerous and has to be guarded against. The wedding is off. Time passes. Mick suggests that Ron call Carrie. "For what? I can't force her. She has to make up her own mind," objects Ron. "She doesn't want to make up her own mind," replies Mick. "No girl does. She wants you to make it up for her." Advised to act like Roark, Ron declines. Nor does he act like a pluralist social-control agent, manipulating her from within. True to his word, he refuses to press her further.

Meanwhile, Carrie is suffering in silence. Her deep-seated need for group approval actually makes her sick, giving her headaches. She tries a doctor. His remedy works, but it's more natural than medical. "Headaches are nature's way of making a protest," the doc patiently explains. Carrie, he implies, has acted "unnaturally" in rejecting Ron. The doc realizes that it is her superego, not her id, that's been giving her trouble. "You're punishing yourself," he says. "Do you expect me to give you a prescription to cure life? Forget for a moment that I'm a doctor and let me give you some advice as a friend: Marry him!"

If Ron won't lift a finger to win Carrie back, fate will. Autumn gives way to winter, and Ron has a bad accident. He slips down a snowbank and gets a concussion, finally allowing Carrie to complete her course in feminization. Notified of the accident by Alida, she rushes to his side. With Ron confined to bed, she can become his nurse, that is, nurse to the owner of a nursery. Ron is out cold, and Carrie has time to take in the changes in the old mill. She's carried away by the interior decoration. "This room," she exclaims, "the beauty that Ron's put into it—and the love." When she realizes how close he's come to death, she understands that she's been wrong and he's been right. "I feel like a coward," she says to herself. "I let others make my decisions." She joins Ron in rejecting pluralism's politics of peer pressure, here depicted as small-minded conformity, and throws in with him, outside the center.

As she stares raptly at his immobile features, the camera looks out the picture window behind him, revealing the deer who have wandered up to the house. Ron wakes up. "Carrie!" he cries, seeing her for the first time. "You've come home." "Yes, darling, I've come home!" In this film, it is the woman who has wandered and must come home, not the man, and once again, home is nature, not culture. The camera tilts up over Ron's head and looks through the glass at the deer on the other side, scampering about in the new spring grass. THE END.

If Ron has been right all the time, what has he been right about? What has Carrie learned? She learns that if civilization is as stultifying as it seems to be in this film, then its discontents have something to tell her; the apparatus of social and psychological repression on which it is based has to be shaken up. Whereas Mildred Pierce was punished for her sexuality, Carrie has to become more "natural," like Dominique Francon in *The Fountainhead*. Early in the film Ned had objected when his asexual mother had worn a revealing, flaming-red evening gown ("I guess it's okay, but isn't it cut kind'a low?"), while Freud-crazy Kay had added, "When we reach a certain age, sex becomes incongruous." Now we know that both were wrong about this too. Harvey (Conrad Nagel), an older man, had proposed to Carrie long before Ron. Pecking lightly at her cheek, he had painted a picture of a sexless future. "I'm sure you feel as I do," he had said soberly. "Companionship and affection are the most important things." But Carrie wanted more, wanted Ron. With his easy rapport with nature, Ron is a male version of *Forbidden Planet*'s Alta. But whereas her garden became a jungle after she and the Skipper kissed, that is, after the serpent sex, the monster from the id, intruded, Ron's garden dies, gives way to winter, when Carrie withholds her kiss, when the gift of sex is withdrawn.

The critique of culture posed by *All That Heaven Allows* is hardly very profound, however. Although the film presents a clash of two sets of values, the conflict between them often boils down to no more than a choice of different life-styles: whiskey against wine, suburbia against exurbia, the garden club against the Sierra Club, Harvey's dinner jacket and gray flannel suits against Ron's Pendleton plaids and corduroy pants. In one scene Carrie and Ron have to choose whether to take his car or hers to the country club party. Carrie's car is a Mercury, Ron's a beat-up woody station wagon. It's supposed to be a subtle and significant difference, but it is really a question of Tweedledum or Tweedledee. Moreover, although the film does sanction a relationship between an older woman and a younger man, does sexualize a neutered mother, it nevertheless fits the two sexes into traditional roles. Ron guides, liberates Carrie, not the reverse.

Yet despite the limited nature of the film's critique, silly and trivial as the options are that it presents, we still find here the seeds of the counterculture back-to-the-land ecological revolt of the sixties and seventies. The attack on the city had begun way back in the late forties with *film noir*. Films like *The Naked City, Edge of the City,* and *Where the Sidewalk Ends* romanticized the city, but they also rejected it as artificial and corrupt. Its mean streets led to the American nightmare: a dead end of failure, suicide, murder, and whatnot. It was a City of Unhappy Endings. As we have seen, many of these films contained utopian interludes in which their heroes and heroines found a few fugitive moments of respite in a park or hideout in the woods. These patches of nature, few and far between in *film noir*, emerged from the shadows of the skyscrapers in fifties *film blanc* to flower in the manicured lawns of suburban communities. The black-and-white *noir* city was left behind when Ike's ambitious interstate highway system encouraged Americans to settle in the sprawling developments that sprang up like mushrooms around the inner cities. Happily ensconced in long cars and ranch-style homes with rectangular picture windows, America's sense of space changed from (city) vertical to (country) horizontal.

The suburbs, where town and country meet, promised the happy endings that *film noir* refused. But *All That Heaven Allows* turned its back on all that. It was the greening of *The Man in the Gray Flannel Suit*. Ron was Tom Rath five years after Rath's film had ended. We had seen Rath reject the rigid, old-style conservative striver for the relaxed pluralist family man. Let the other guy get a coronary at fifty; he was content to do it himself in his own backyard. Years pass. Commuting having become more onerous than ever, Rath quits his middle-level job at United Broadcasting. With the kids out of the house at college, he and the little woman move from Westport to Woodstock, where Rath can become a jolly green giant like Hudson in *All That Heaven Allows*, or even the painter he always wanted to be, like Hudson again in John Frankenheimer's *Seconds* (1966). Before you know it, Rath is marching against the war and voting for Gene McCarthy. Not only has the corporate-liberal attempt to amalgamate nature with culture in the suburbs broken down, but nature has finally emerged as a genuinely oppositional value, has turned definitively against culture. By the time the fifties ended, both men and woman were heading for the woods. As the heroizing of Indians in the sixties would indicate, Geronimo had won after all.

COMING
APART

The vital center was an unstable amalgam of contradictions. As the fifties got ready to become the sixties, the seams started to show. Something wasn't right. Nowhere was the change more evident than in the movies. For one thing, the genres so popular in the fifties had a hard time hanging in. Sci-fi films, with a few exceptions, died out entirely. As the war in Vietnam heated up and became increasingly divisive, war films became fewer and farther between. Westerns started strong, as younger men like John Sturges and Sam Peckinpah picked up the reins from Ford and Mann, but they began to trail off at the end of the decade, when directors such as Penn, Robert Altman, and Peckinpah himself dealt them a succession of blows from which they have still not recovered, in self-critical antigenre films like *Little Big Man* (1970) and *McCabe and Mrs. Miller* (1971).

Flops like Francis Coppola's *Finian's Rainbow* (1968) put an end to musicals, while biblical spectacles, which flourished in the high fifties, also disappeared in the sixties. The superheated rhetoric of films like *Quo Vadis, Samson and Delilah* (1951), and *The Robe* (1953) seemed at the time, in the words of Michael Wood, "just right." "In 1956," writes Wood, "in *The Ten Commandments*, Anne Baxter could say, 'Moses, Moses, you splendid, stubborn, adorable fool,' and get away with it." But not for long. What was just right in the fifties seemed just silly in the decade that followed. And even a film that tried to distance itself from the genre like the 1963 superspectacle *Cleopatra*, filled with self-conscious puns (Richard Burton emerges from a mausoleum to joke about his roommate—"or should I say tombmate?"), fell flat. [1]

Cleopatra's failure nearly bankrupted the studio (Fox) that made it, and signified the end of the studio system, which had suffered throughout the fifties from declining attendance, competition from television, and the rise of independent productions bankrolled by breakaway stars and powerful talent agencies like MCA that were just beginning to flex their muscles. The studio infrastructure, with its army of salaried writers, actors, and directors and its constant stream of films-by-formula, made genre possible; when it disintegrated, genre disappeared.

The other nail in the coffin was the collapse of the shared assumptions on which genre depends and which make its conventions seem natural. In the sixties, under the pressure of Vietnam, the center polarized into right and left. First it turned right. In the late fifties, American complacency sustained three rude shocks. In 1956, Hungary tried to throw off the Soviet yoke, but the same Republicans who had been bellowing "rollback" for a decade contented themselves with kibitzing from the sidelines. Before the smoke had settled over the Hungarian capital, Israel, France, and Britain invaded Egypt. When the Russians bristled and blustered, the United States pressured its allies to give Nasser his canal back, and thereby sustained another defeat in the eyes of the right. *"Over the humiliated forms of our two oldest and closest allies,"* lamented the *National Review* (in italics, yet), *"we clasp the hands of the murderers of the Christian heroes of Hungary,* as we run in shameless—and vain—pursuit of the 'good will' of Asia and Africa's teeming pagan multitudes."[2]

The next year, Americans learned that Hungary was not the only satellite they had to worry about. The Russians launched their eighty-four-pound Sputnik, and the United States plunged into a state of national anxiety, otherwise known as "agonizing reappraisal." When red-faced Americans tried to follow suit with their Vanguard two months later, the rocket blew up on lift-off, and the 3.2-pound satellite it carried (Khrushchev derisively called it an "orange") fell to earth, beeping unhappily. Michigan Governor G. Mennen "Soapy" Williams said it all:

> Oh Little Sputnik, flying high
> With made-in-Moscow beep,
> You tell the world it's a Commie sky,
> And Uncle Sam's asleep.[3]

The feminized man was one of the first victims of the post-Sputnik backlash. The Korean War had shown that American boys were too soft to stand up to enemy brainwashing; Sputnik showed that they were too dumb to compete with Soviet whiz kids. When Charles Van Doren, who had been proving that eggheads were good for something by answering the $64,000 Question on American television, admitted he had been cheating, it was the last straw. Conservatives who had never bought Spock and Dewey in the first place crowed "I told you so," and corporate liberals nodded in agreement.

It was the new president, John F. Kennedy, who best embodied the spirit of the sixties. Jack and Jackie elbowed klutzy Ike and Mamie out of the Oval Office, and brought a fresh glamour, excitement, and class to the presidency. But Jack was tough, too, the author of *Profiles in Courage* and the commander of PT 109; when he faced down Khrushchev over Cuba, he gave old-fashioned male intransigency a good name again. With the Russians growing stronger by the moment, lofting satellites as easily as Americans dunked baskets, placing missiles in Cuba and building walls in Berlin while Uncle Sam was watching "I Love Lucy," Kennedy offered a new virility, a more muscular, conservative version of pluralism, along with a new sense of national purpose.

No film revealed the center's shift to the right better than Alfred Hitchcock's *Psycho*, released in 1960, at the end of one decade and the beginning of another. In the famous opening shot, we find Marion (Janet Leigh) and Sam (John Gavin) in a hotel room in Phoenix, Arizona. Marion is single, a secretary, and she is using her lunch hour to make love to Sam. (Her lunch sits, neglected, on the bedside table.) But Marion wants to get married, and she asks Sam to be her husband. Sam doesn't want to; he doesn't have enough money to get married now. But Marion is insistent. It's marriage or nothing.

No sooner is Marion back at her office than she steals money from her boss, the nest-egg she and Sam need to tie the knot. She hops into her car and begins the journey from Phoenix to Fairvale, where Sam lives. But she never gets there. In a driving rainstorm, she takes a wrong turn, and after making her way through miles of unfamiliar back roads, she comes to a stop before the Bates Motel. There's a sinister-looking mansion high atop a hill behind the motel, but she pays it no heed and rushes inside, where she encounters the proprietor, a shy, awkward, but not unappealing young man named Norman Bates. It's Tony Perkins.

By using Perkins for this role, Hitchcock could not help but make a comment on the kind of masculinity Perkins represented, after playing all those men who wore aprons in the fifties. For Hitchcock, like everyone else, the handwriting was on the wall. Softness in men was a slippery slope. A few tears today might be a flood tomorrow. Suppose men were too sensitive—gay, even? While *Rebel Without a Cause* came out for the feminized man, it was careful, as we have seen, to call a halt, and with Plato we saw where feminization stopped and unhealthy homoeroticism began.

But in real life, as Christine Jorgenson showed, it wasn't so easy to draw the line. The grim deaths of two of the most prominent sensitive male leads, Dean and Clift, dramatized the pitfalls of the new "masculinity." These were the red-blooded American boys who were going to close the missile gap? storm the beaches of the Bay of Pigs? In 1961, "Poppa" Hemingway himself, the big daddy of all the tough guys, shot himself through the head amid rumors of homosexuality. If it could happen to Hemingway, it could happen to anybody.

Had Marion Crane seen *Fear Strikes Out* (or *Touch of Evil*, for that matter), she would have driven right on past the Bates Motel to the Holiday Inn. But it wasn't Marion's fault. Diffident Noman Bates conformed exactly to what Marion had been taught by Spock-symp experts the normal, well-adjusted, sensitive American boy was supposed to be like. While Sam is the traditional reluctant male, offering Marion sex instead of food, Norman gives her food instead of sex, offering her sandwiches and milk when she arrives at the motel after a tiring day on the road. He provides her with a nurturing, supportive environment that allows her to speak relatively freely about herself. He divines her moods and draws her out in conversation. In short, Norman is a feminized man. But there is more to Norman than meets the eye. A few minutes later, in the notorious shower scene, he stabs her to death with a knife while she bathes. In the last shot of this seqence, the water, discolored with blood, is sucked down the drain.

Eventually, Marion's murder is brought to light by Sam and Lila (Vera Miles), Marion's sister, but although they solve the crime, they don't understand it, and it is up to a psychiatrist to explain it. Hitchcock fans have always been embarrassed by this ending because it is so heavy-handed and reductive. But like it or not, it is a psychiatrist who has the last word. "If anybody can get any answers, it'll be the psychiatrist," says the sheriff, the professional deferring to the expert, and he's right. But *Psycho* is a therapeutic film with a difference; pluralism was moving right. "The mother

By 1960, in the wake of post-Sputnik backlash, momma's boys were going crazy.
Here's gentle Tony Perkins getting ready to slice and dice Janet Leigh.

killed the girl," says the psychiatrist. The trouble with Norman is that he
grew up in a matriarchal family. Norman is a momma's boy, dominated
by a bad (overprotective) mom, not a bad dad, as in an orthodox corporate-
liberal film. "A boy's best friend is his mother," he tells Marion. Norman
is like the baby-faced psycho in *While the City Sleeps*. Mom has infantilized him to such an extent that several times he's shown eating candy.
The ultimate revelation of Norman's tenuous grasp on his own gender is,
of course, his appearance in the last shot of the film as a woman (his
mother), wig, dress, and all. Corporate-liberal films like *Giant* had
encouraged boys and girls to exchange roles, and in films like *Some Like
It Hot* (1959), transvestism had become a harmless and humorous metaphor for the feminization of men. But in the atmosphere of post-Sputnik

backlash, such sexual fluidity had to be repudiated, and cross-dressing could only be disturbing, sinister, and pathological, as it was in *Psycho*. By the beginning of the sixties, feminized men were the psychos tough guys were earlier. Feminization was regarded as castration, not humanization.

The corollary to attacking feminized men, of course, is punishing strong women. Marion is altogether too independent and domineering for her own good. But Marion is not murdered to punish her for straying from the straight and narrow. (She is killed *after* she decides to return the money and face the consequences.) Her crime does not lie so much in what she does as in what she is: a woman. She is punished for her sexual attractiveness and the power it exercises over men. Through Norman, *Psycho* retaliates against Marion for what it perceived as the erosion of male power; women who defy men go down the drain, and men who take women for role models go off their rockers.

Psycho, then, has a therapeutic orientation, but it detaches therapy from the attendant constellation of pluralist values and allies it instead with conservative values: the repudiation of the matriarchal family, the domineering mother, the absent father, the sexually promiscuous, pushy young woman who deserves what she gets, and the feminized momma's boy. Moreover, *Psycho* not only colonizes the therapeutic for the right, it goes farther, forging a right-leaning coalition of pluralists, conservatives, and reactionaries. Neither the cops nor the docs can do the job. The cops are too dumb, and although the psychiatrist may understand Norman's crime, he can't act (unlike the gangbusting docs who replaced cops in earlier films), and *Psycho* relies on Sam and Lila, do-it-yourselfers independent of both the cops and the docs, to protect the center.

It would be a mistake to call Sam and Lila vigilantes just because they are private parties outside the law, but this was nevertheless the direction *Psycho*, like other films of the center, was taking. The alliance between the state and right-wing vigilantism characterized the enormously influential James Bond films that followed *Psycho*. Bond was essentially an outsider, a loner, without family or friends, wife or male companions. Nevertheless, he worked directly for the state. He represented a new synthesis of organization man and tough guy, civil servant and vigilante. Each film took pains to situate him firmly within the organization. He had a boss (M), a desultory flirtation with the boss's secretary (Miss Moneypenny), an expense account, and a dazzling array of gadgets fashioned and supplied by the intelligence agency he worked for. Like the private detective, Bond was licensed, but he was licensed to kill. In other words, at the same time that the radical-right loner was taken under the wing of the center, appropriated, as it were, by the state, the state became permeated by the values of the right. Mike Hammer had come home.

In the Bond and male-bonding films of the sixties, pluralist proprieties fell like dominoes. Bond treated women like things, killed often and casually, and exponentially escalated the violence quotient of American movies. The turning point came in the first film, *Dr. No* (1962), where dapper 007 toyed with a poor geologist, allowing him to struggle toward a gun he knew was empty, and then shot him to death cleanly and quietly with his silenced Beretta, showing neither more nor less enthusiasm than it took to flick a fleck of dust off the lapel of his Savile Row suit. For male audiences, the Bond films were filled with a kind of macho exhilaration, allowing them to enjoy sex and empathize with violence without the entanglements, scruples, and guilt required of them by centrist films of the fifties. Sex emerged as a commodity, on a par with Bond's other accouterments of power.

Like *Psycho*, the Bond films shifted the center to the right, but they still drew back from the brink. They evinced a strong sense of the public interest, and the rough-and-ready justice Bond administered was impersonal, even clinical in its stylized brutality. Bond may have been licensed to kill, but he never killed for himself, only for the state. *

Clint Eastwood went considerably further. He buried the code of the cowboy along with the bodies of those who were unlucky enough to come within range of his gun. He showed us that we not only didn't have to be shot at first to shoot back, but that we could shoot in the back if we felt like it. Killing in self-defense was for jerks. Moreover, Clint often killed for personal reasons. His films made revenge respectable, moved it toward what was fast becoming the mainstream, and looked forward to the upscale, white-collar-revenge films of the seventies, like *Death Wish* (1974).

While America was turning right, and therapeutic films like *Psycho* and *Marnie* were holding hands with James Bond, the seeds of the counter-

---

*Hitchcock, incidentally, undoubtedly realized that John Gavin in *Psycho* was not tough enough to put Janet Leigh back in the kitchen where she belonged. In *Marnie* (1964), he stopped fooling around and used Sean Connery himself.

culture, planted in the fifties by pluralism itself, were beginning to germinate. Baby-boomers were rocking to Fats Domino and going to see pictures like *Blackboard Jungle* at the same time that Jack Kerouac went on the road and Norman Mailer, Paul Goodman, and others had formed a small but vocal culture of dissent. By the late fifties, *Playboy*, riding the wave of the new singles culture, had chased the *Saturday Evening Post* off the newsstands. The loose, relaxed, swinging hedonism *Playboy* purveyed cut the umbilical cord that tied consumerism to the family. Much of the energy liberated by the *Playboy* rebellion fed the right (Bond was nothing if not a swinger) but it fed the left as well. It offered a further liberalization of behavior, first for men (*Playboy* preceded *Playgirl* by several decades) and then, courtesy of the pill, for women as well. JFK may have glamorized discipline and a return to basics, but consumerism had discovered the singles culture. Men abandoned lawn mowers for sports cars, while women began postponing babies, not pleasure. Pretty soon, front lawns were overgrown with weeds and dishes were piling up in the sinks of suburbia. Where once there had been marriage, now there were "lifestyles," a bewildering array of relationships, all shored up by the mega-affluence of the sixties, so profligate and wasteful it made the fifties seem chintzy by comparison. Crew cuts gave way to long hair, and as hair grew longer still, adults complained that they couldn't tell if junior was a boy or a girl. Gender was up for grabs, and a new generation gap opened a chasm between parents and their kids.

If movies moved to the right in the early sixties, by mid-decade they were moving to the left as well. The changes in sexual mores, along with the softening of the blacklist, the virtual dismantling of the Production Code, and above all, the fast-growing disenchantment with the Vietnam War, created a climate increasingly conducive to the production of films so critical of American institutions they would have been unimaginable in the fifties. First there was a series of films made by a new, younger crop of directors which implicitly criticized both the arms race and the anticommunist mania that accompanied it. These films did not regard the Bomb as a friendly deterrent, the view adopted by *Strategic Air Command* and *Bombers B-52*, but on the contrary, as itself a danger. In Stanley Kramer's *On the Beach*, (1959), for example, the "post-attack environment" is imagined as a vast Jonestown, with survivors taking government-issued suicide pills from doctors (it's doomsday for the therapeutic) to put them out of their misery. Tony Perkins, Gregory Peck, Fred Astaire, and Ava Gardner don't get to make a new world; instead, they are killed by radiation.

And then, in 1964, there was *Dr. Strangelove*, which mercilessly ridiculed the ideologically tinged conventions of the films that preceded it. From the opening scene—the same lyrical mid-air refueling sequence featured in *Strategic Air Command*—it quickly became clear that instead of hiding behind genre, this film would explode it.

The film begins when Gen. Jack D. Ripper (Sterling Hayden), the deranged commander of SAC's Burpelson Air Force Base, unbeknownst to President Merkin Muffley (Peter Sellers), launches an impromptu, do-it-yourself nuclear attack on the Soviet Union. He reasons that once the attack has begun, the president will have no choice but to follow it up with an all-out first strike, or risk being obliterated by the Russians. Nevertheless, cooler heads prevail. President Muffley calls Premier Kissoff on the hot line, warns him that an attack is immanent, and offers to help him destroy the American bombers by giving away their positions. Then he orders an assault on Burpelson Air Force Base in an attempt to extract from Ripper the "recall code" that will abort the attack. The recall code is obtained, and all the bombers are either summoned home or destroyed by the Russians. Except one.

Had *Strangelove* been a centrist film, Ripper would have been an aberration, a madman acting in defiance of America's well-known record of nuclear restraint. Just as the corrupt waterfront in *On the Waterfront* "ain't like America," so Burpelson Air Force Base wouldn't have been like no other air force base. Here, it is. Ripper is crazy, but so is everybody else. *Strangelove* ridicules all the center's stock characters, and therefore the generic conventions that dictate their responses. Dr. Strangelove himself (also Peter Sellers) is the pluralist as mad scientist, Edward Teller or Herman Kahn. He's the expert in this film, but it's clear that his schemes for preserving the race by sealing selected specimens in mine shafts are pure madness. "Reality" has deserted the corporate liberals. The conservative, on the other hand, gum-chewing Gen. Buck Turgidson (George C. Scott), is only marginally saner than Strangelove. In his heart he knows that Ripper is right.

Ripper is the right-wing vigilante who would have made Billy Mitchell proud. He defies the organization in A-1 style, only here he's not a hero but a psycho. Sixties audiences who saw the film over and over anticipated his famous paranoid speech, chanting, "I can no longer sit back and allow Communist infiltration, Communist indoctrination, Communist subversion, and the International Communist Conspiracy to sap and impurify all of our precious bodily fluids." On the other hand, the by-the-book organization man who won't let Group Captain Mandrake (Sellers again) shoot the lock off a Coke machine—because it's private property—to get a dime to call the president with the recall code is a fool as well. (Remember the wall-eyed GI who won't let Sergeant Warden have the guns to defend Pearl Harbor in *From Here to Eternity?*)

Strangelove forecloses all the options. Both the center's preference for machines over men and the right's preference for men over machines lead to nuclear annihilation. The Soviet Doomsday Device that "rules out human meddling" by automatically detonating when the Russians are attacked destroys the world. Dr. Strangelove, with the metal arm he can't control and his mechanical "Heil Hitlers," is well on his way to becoming a robot of the center. People, on the other hand, are no better. It is Ripper, after all, who starts the trouble. "When you instituted the human reliability tests, you assured me there was no possibility of such a thing occurring," complains the president. "I admit the human element has failed us here," replies Turgidson. Ironically, when the "human element" functions properly, it just makes matters worse. "I'm sorry if they're jamming your radar, but they're trained to do it," Muffley apologizes to Kissoff. "It's initiative." And indeed, it's thanks to pilot Kong's (Slim Pickens) resourceful facility with spit and chewing gum, the saving grace of so many conservative and right-wing heroes, that the faulty bomb-bay doors are repaired, enabling him to deliver the Bomb. When Kong rides it down to its destination, yelling "Yippeee!" and waving his ten-gallon hat (remember Cowboy in *Flying Leathernecks?*), he becomes indeed the Last American Hero.

When *Strangelove* invokes *Strategic Air Command*'s refueling sequence, it does so to turn it inside out. *Strategic Air Command* sought to domesticate war, reconcile civil with martial, public with private, by equating the Air Force with the family, bombers with babies. It tried to convince us that making war and making love were the same. *Strangelove*, on the other hand, severed these metaphorical connections, frustrated the struggle for consensus. To Kubrick, it was strange to love war, a contradiction

The last frontier: "cowboy" Slim Pickens, shortly before he goes down with the ship, taking the conventions of fifties war films with him.

in terms, a perversion. We had to choose babies *or* bombers, and the choice, spelled out several years later on bumper stickers, was obvious: make love, not war. We could no longer have our cake and eat it too.

But although *Strangelove* disentangles love and war, it is to no avail. No utopian possibilities are held out for the salvation of hapless humanity. In the penultimate scenes, drawing on dozens of war movies, *Strangelove* forces us to identify with Major Kong and his crew as they fly breathlessly low over the white expanse of Siberian tundra, eluding Soviet radar and dodging enemy missiles in their crippled B-52. When they finally succeed, they die, and when they die, the film ends, and with it the world. Yet it is precisely the apocalyptic climax of the film, a montage of nuclear explosions, that contains seeds of hope. By getting us to root for the success of the mission, that is, by mobilizing the conventions of the genre and then showing us that success in this case means disaster, *Strangelove* makes us aware of "How [We] Learned to Stop Worrying and Love the Bomb."

The spy films that followed, such as *The Ipcress File* (1965) and *The*

Spy Who Came In from the Cold (1965), in which "our" side was as treacherous as "their" side, presented a duplicitous and grimy picture of finely modulated grays that contrasted sharply with the colorful black-and-white world of James Bond. In the left-wing spy films of the mid-sixties, the hero was less likely to be punched in the jaw by the KGB than shot in the back by his own boss, betrayed by the one person he trusted most. In these films, nothing was the way it seemed, and if the right drafted therapy for its cause, the left used the Cult of Complexity to question cold-war verities.

Strangelove and the left-wing spy films were early birds, harbingers of thing to come. The real shift to the left wasn't evident until several years later, with movies like *Bonnie and Clyde* (1967), *The Graduate* (1967), and *Easy Rider* (1969). Many of these films featured men so feminized they made Tony Perkins look like John Wayne. They endorsed the drop-out counter-cultural life-style of the sixties, and substituted dope, sex, and rock-'n-roll for mom and apple pie. With the exception of the failed cycle of campus-unrest films, the left-wing films of the late sixties were, as opposed to their predecessors of the fifties, major motion pictures. Like the Bond and Eastwood films, they were not peripheral to mainstream movies; they *were* mainstream movies.

In films of the sixties, both right and left, the center's attempts to reconcile contradictions finally broke down. Nature became a value totally oppositional to culture, now experienced as corrupt. Sex, in the hands of both James Bond and Arlo Guthrie, became a weapon against the "system." For the right, individualism became a critique of society, now experienced as thoroughly regimented; patriarchy became an enemy of matriarchy, increasingly experienced as emasculating; vigilante violence became an acceptable alternative to the law, now perceived as ineffectual. For the left, feminism became an attack on patriarchy, now experienced as sexist; leisure became a critique of labor, increasingly experienced as alienated; ethnicity became an alternative to the melting pot, now regarded as racist; and therapy itself came under attack as coercive. The vital center had collapsed: "Things fall apart; the center cannot hold . . ." What Schlesinger had feared a decade and a half earlier when he opened his book with a citation from his dog-eared volume of Yeats had come to pass.

In the sixties, the collapse of the center cleared the way—momentarily, at any rate—for the emergence of oppositional films long relegated to the limbo of extremism by the reigning consensus. These films, on balance, may have been neither better nor worse than the films of the fifties, but they did present a strikingly different picture of American life, one that was at once more passionately utopian (*Woodstock* [1970]) and spectacularly apocalyptic (*Dirty Harry*) than that depicted by their predecessors. Of course, this vision too was ideological. New conventions replaced the old, but despite all that *Dr. Strangelove* showed us about the klunky machinery of genre, we continued to believe what we saw.

Notes

INTRODUCTION. IT'S ONLY A MOVIE

1. Robert Warshow, *The Immediate Experience* (Garden City, N.Y.: Doubleday & Co., Anchor Books, 1964), p. 83.

CHAPTER ONE. WHO'S IN CHARGE HERE?

1. David Riesman and Nathan Glazer, "Intellectuals and Discontented Classes," in Daniel Bell, ed., *The Radical Right* (Garden City, N.Y.: Doubleday & Co., Anchor Books, 1964), p. 121.

2. Arthur Schlesinger, Jr., *The Vital Center*, new ed. (London: André Deutsch, 1970), p. 245.

3. Lionel Trilling, *The Liberal Imagination* (Garden City, N.Y.: Doubleday & Co., Anchor Books, 1953), pp. 208, 289.

4. Daniel Bell, "The Dispossessed," in Bell, ed., *Radical Right*, p. 32.

5. Schlesinger, *Vital Center*, p. 155.

6. Daniel Bell, "Interpretations of American Politics," in Bell, ed., *Radical Right*, p. 70.

7. David Riesman, Nathan Glazer, and Reuel Denney, *The Lonely Crowd* (Garden City, N.Y.: Doubleday & Co., Anchor Books, 1955), p. 211.

8. Quoted in William H. Whyte, Jr., *The Organization Man* (Garden City, N.Y.: Doubleday & Co., 1957), p. 32.

9. Quoted in Christopher Lasch, *Haven in a Heartless World: The Family Besieged* (New York: Basic Books, 1979), p. 97.

10. Thomas S. Szasz, *Ideology and Insanity* (Garden City, N.Y.: Doubleday & Co., Anchor Books, 1970), p. 5.

11. *Variety*, January 16, 1946, p. 18.

12. *New York Times*, March 17, 1946.

13. Michel Ciment, *Kazan on Kazan* (New York: Viking Press, 1974), p. 64.

14. Talcott Parsons, "Social Strains in America," in Bell, ed., *The Radical Right*, p. 223.

15. Quoted in George N. Nash, *The Conservative Intellectual Movement in America* (New York: Basic Books, 1976), p. 208.

16. Quoted in Lasch, *Heartless World*, p. 99.

17. Riesman and Glazer, "Intellectuals and Discontented Classes," in Bell, ed., *Radical Right*, pp. 118, 125, 135.

18. Schlesinger, *Vital Center*, pp. xxiii, 165.

19. Whyte, *Organization Man*, p. 235.

20. William F. Buckley, *Up from Liberalism* (New York: McDowell, Obolensky, 1959), p. 194.

21. Nash, *Conservative Intellectual Movement*, pp. 128, 129.

22. Quoted in Joseph McBride and Michael Wilmington, *John Ford* (New York: Da Capo Press, 1975), p. 108.

CHAPTER TWO. THE ORGANIZATION MAN GOES TO WAR

1. Daniel Bell, ed. *The Radical Right* (Garden City, N.Y.: Doubleday & Co., Anchor Books, 1964), p. 19.

2. Arthur Schlesinger, Jr., *The Vital Center*, new ed. (London: André Deutsch, 1970), p. xii.

3. William H. Whyte, Jr., *The Organization Man* (Garden City, N.Y.: Doubleday & Co., Anchor Books, 1957), pp. 7–8.

4. Quoted in Douglas T. Miller and Marion Nowak, *The Fifties* (Garden City, N.Y.: Doubleday & Co., 1977), p. 237.

5. David Riesman, Nathan Glazer, and Reuel Denney, *The Lonely Crowd* (Garden City, N.Y.: Doubleday & Co., Anchor Books, 1955), p. 105.

6. Robert Warshow, *The Immediate Experience* (Garden City, N.Y.: Doubleday & Co., Anchor Books, 1964), p. 104.

7. I. F. Stone, *The Haunted Fifties* (New York: Random House, 1963), p. 105.

8. Quoted in Barbara Ehrenreich and Deirdre English, *For Her Own Good: 150 Years of the Experts' Advice to Women* (Garden City, N.Y.: Doubleday & Co., Anchor Books, 1978), p. 192.

9. Schlesinger, *Vital Center*, p. 41.

10. Julian Smith, *Looking Away: Hollywood and Vietnam* (New York: Charles Scribner's Sons, 1975), p. 43.

11. Ibid., p. 50.

12. Barbara Deming, *Running Away from Myself: A Dream Portrait of America Drawn from the Films of the 40's* (New York: Grossman Publishers, 1969), p. 9.

13. Miller and Nowak, *The Fifties*, p. 129.

14. Lionel Trilling, *The Liberal Imagination* (Garden City, N.Y.: Doubleday & Co., Anchor Books, 1953), p. 242.

15. Whyte, *Organization Man*, p. 269.

16. Smith, *Looking Away*, pp. 18, 221.

17. William F. Buckley, *Up from Liberalism* (New York: McDowell, Obolensky, 1959), pp. 95, 97, 99.

CHAPTER THREE. PODS AND BLOBS

1. Daniel Bell, ed., *The Radical Right* (Garden City, N.Y.: Doubleday & Co., Anchor Books, 1964), p. 32.

2. Quoted in George N. Nash, *The Conservative Intellectual Movement in America* (New York: Basic Books, 1976), p. 39.

3. Talcott Parsons, "Social Strains in America," in Bell, ed., *Radical Right*, p. 209.

4. Quoted in Douglas T. Miller and Marion Nowak, *The Fifties* (Garden City, N.Y.: Doubleday & Co., 1977), p. 96.

5. David Riesman, Nathan Glazer, and Reuel Denney, *The Lonely Crowd* (Garden City, N.Y.: Doubleday & Co., Anchor Books, 1955), p. 152.

6. Daniel Bell, "Interpretations of American Politics," in Bell, ed., *Radical Right*, p. 47.

7. Daniel Bell, "The Dispossessed," in Bell, ed., *Radical Right*, p. 43.

8. Quoted in Nora Sayre, *Running Time: Films of the Cold War* (New York: Dial Press, 1982), p. 13.

9. Quoted in Victor Navasky, *Naming Names* (New York: Viking Press, 1980), p. 24.

10. William H. Whyte, Jr., *The Organization Man* (Garden City, N.Y.: Doubleday & Co., Anchor Books, 1957), p. 129.

11. William F. Buckley, *Up from Liberalism* (New York: McDowell, Obolensky, 1959), p. 195.

12. Lionel Trilling, *The Liberal Imagination* (Garden City, N.Y.: Doubleday & Co., Anchor Books, 1953), p. 95.

13. I. F. Stone, *The Truman Era* (New York: Random House, Vintage Books, 1973), p. xxvii.

14. Bell, "The Dispossessed," pp. 19, 45.

15. Alan F. Westin, "The John Birch Society," in Bell, ed., *Radical Right*, p. 268.

16. Bell, "The Dispossessed," p. 3.

17. Westin, "The John Birch Society," pp. 266–67.

18. Parsons, "Social Strains in America," p. 224.

19. Arthur Schlesinger, Jr., *The Vital Center*, new ed. (London: André Deutsch, 1970), pp. 254, 161, 162.

20. Quoted in Miller and Nowak, *The Fifties*, p. 222.

21. Ibid., p. 85.

22. This follows the discussion of *Adventure* in Barbara Deming, *Running Away from Myself: A Dream Portrait of America Drawn from the Films of the 40's* (New York: Grossman Publishers, 1969), chap. 3.

23. Quoted in Bell, "The Dispossessed," p. 9.

24. Susan Sontag, *Against Interpretation* (New York: Dell Publishing Co., Delta Books, 1967), p. 222.

25. Quoted in Nash, *Conservative Intellectual Movement*, p. 49.

26. Quoted in ibid., p. 258.

27. Raymond Durgnat, *Films and Feelings* (Cambridge, Mass.: MIT Press, 1971), p. 262.

28. Schlesinger, *Vital Center*, p. 250.

29. Quoted in Nash, *Conservative Intellectual Movement*, p. 150.

30. Quoted in David Pirie, ed., *Anatomy of the Movies* (New York: Macmillan Co., 1981), p. 276.

31. Ibid., pp. 277, 280.

CHAPTER FOUR. THE ENEMY WITHIN

1. Daniel Bell, "Interpretations of American Politics," in Daniel Bell, ed., *The Radical Right* (Garden City, N.Y.: Doubleday & Co., Anchor Books, 1964), p. 55.

2. David Riesman, Nathan Glazer, and Reuel Denney, *The Lonely Crowd* (Garden City, N.Y.: Doubleday & Co., Anchor Books, 1955), p. 255.

3. Ibid., p. 187.

4. William H. Whyte, Jr., *The Organization Man* (Garden City, N.Y.: Doubleday & Co., Anchor Books, 1957), p. 440.

5. Eric F. Goldman, *The Crucial Decade—and After: America, 1945–1960* (New York: Random House, Vintage Books, 1960), pp. 192, 196.

6. Sidney Hook, *Heresy, Yes—Conspiracy, No* (New York: John Day & Co., 1953).

7. Arthur Miller, *The Crucible* (New York: Bantam Books, 1971), p. 137.

8. Victor Navasky, *Naming Names* (New York: Viking Press, 1980), p. xi.

9. Penelope Houston, "On the Waterfront," *Sight and Sound* 24 (October–December 1954): 85.

10. Daniel Bell, *The End of Ideology* (New York: Collier Books, 1961), p. 176.

11. Christopher Lasch, *Haven in a Heartless World: The Family Besieged* (New York: Basic Books, 1979), p. 13.

12. Peter Biskind, "Review of *Kazan on Kazan*," *Quarterly Review of Film Studies* 1 (May 1976): 170–73.

13. Navasky, *Naming Names*, p. 210.

14. Carlos Clarens, *Crime Movies* (New York: W. W. Norton & Co. 1980), p. 257.

15. Jack Lait and Lee Mortimer, *U.S.A. Confidential* (New York: Crown Publishers, 1952), pp. 13, 15, 28, 29.

16. Quoted in Clarens, *Crime Movies*, p. 257.

17. John Howard Lawson, *Film in the Battle of Ideas* (New York: Masses & Mainstream, 1953), p. 23.

18. Douglas T. Miller and Marion Nowak, *The Fifties* (Garden City, N.Y.: Doubleday & Co., 1977), p. 280.

19. Quoted in Eugene Rosow, *Born to Lose: The Gangster Film in America* (New York: Oxford University Press, 1978), p. 281.

20. Quoted in Lasch, *Heartless World*, p. 100.

21. Ibid., pp. 15–16.

22. Whyte, *Organization Man*, p. 425.

23. William F. Buckley, *Up from Liberalism* (New York: McDowell, Obolensky, 1959), p. 52.

24. Mark Thomas McGee and R. J. Robertson, *The J.D. Films* (Jefferson, N.C.: McFarland & Co., 1982), p. 30.

25. Andrew Dowdy, *The Films of the Fifties: The American State of Mind* (New York: William Morrow & Co., 1975), p. 142.

26. McGee and Robertson, *J.D. Films*, p. 47.

27. Buckley, *Up from Liberalism*, p. 88.

28. McGee and Robertson, *J.D. Films*, pp. 91–92.

29. Mortimer and Lait, *U.S.A. Confidential*, p. 37.

30. McGee and Robertson, *J.D. Films*, p. 24.

31. Arthur Schlesinger, Jr., *The Vital Center*, new ed. (London: André Deutsch, 1970), p. 191.

32. Michael Wood, *America in the Movies* (New York: Basic Books, 1975), pp. 133–34.

33. Penelope Houston, "Mr. Deeds and Willie Stark," *Sight and Sound* 19 (November 1950): 278ff.

34. Buckley, *Up from Liberalism*, p. 88.

35. Quoted in George N. Nash, *The Conservative Intellectual Movement in America* (New York: Basic Books, 1976), p. 200.

36. Richard Combs, ed., *Robert Aldrich* (London: British Film Institute, 1978), p. 53.

CHAPTER FIVE. ALL IN THE FAMILY

1. Quoted in Douglas T. Miller and Marion Nowak, *The Fifties* (Garden City, N.Y.: Doubleday & Co., 1977), p. 147.

2. David Riesman, Nathan Glazer, and Reuel Denney, *The Lonely Crowd* (Garden City, N.Y.: Doubleday & Co., Anchor Books, 1955), pp. 23, 31.

3. Barbara Deming, *Running Away from Myself: A Dream Portrait of America Drawn from the Films of the 40's* (New York: Grossman Publishers, 1969), p. 141.

4. Daniel Bell, *The End of Ideology* (New York: Collier Books, 1961), pp. 308, 301.

5. Riesman, Glazer, and Denney, *Lonely Crowd*, p. 23.

6. Miller and Nowak, *The Fifties*, p. 97.

7. Pauline Kael, *I Lost It at the Movies* (New York: Bantam Books, 1966), p. 50.

8. Betty Friedan, *The Feminine Mystique* (New York: W. W. Norton & Co., 1963), p. 36.

9. Quoted in ibid., p. 132.

10. Ibid., p. 216.

11. Ibid., pp. 42, 60.

12. Robert Warshow, *The Immediate Experience* (Garden City, N.Y.: Doubleday & Co., Anchor Books, 1964), p. 91.

13. Friedan, *Feminine Mystique*, p. 204.

14. Molly Haskell, *From Reverence to Rape* (Baltimore: Penguin Books, 1974), pp. 253, 268.

15. Ibid., p. 262.

16. Lee Mortimer and Jack Lait, *U.S.A. Confidential* (New York: Crown Publishers, 1952), pp. 2, 46–53.

17. William F. Buckley, *Up from Liberalism* (New York: McDowell, Obolensky, 1959), p. 86.

18. Robert Sklar, " 'Red River'—Empire to the West," *Cineaste* 9 (Fall 1978): 14–19.

19. Riesman, Glazer, and Denney, *Lonely Crowd*, p. 102.

20. William H. Whyte, Jr., *The Organization Man* (Garden City, N.Y.: Doubleday & Co., Anchor Books, 1957), p. 78.

21. Mary P. Ryan, *Womanhood in America* (New York: Franklin Watts, New Viewpoints, 1975), p. 346.

22. Quoted in Barbara Ehrenreich and Deirdre English, *For Her Own Good: 150 Years of the Experts' Advice to Women* (Garden City, N.Y.: Doubleday & Co., Anchor Books), p. 196.

23. Philip Wylie, *Generation of Vipers* (New York: Rinehart & Co., 1946), p. 185.

24. Quoted in George N. Nash, *The Conservative Intellectual Movement in America* (New York: Basic Books, 1976), p. 66.

25. Leo Braudy, *The World in a Frame* (Garden City, N.Y.: Doubleday & Co., Anchor Books, 1976), p. 131.

26. Raymond Durgnat, *Films and Feelings* (Cambridge, Mass.: MIT Press, 1972), p. 189.

27. Whyte, *Organization Man*, p. 279.

28. Stanley Cavell, *The World Viewed: Reflections on the Ontology of Film* (New York: Viking Press, Compass Books, 1971), pp. 47–48.

29. Martha Wolfenstein and Nathan Leites, *Movies: A Psychological Study* (Glencoe, Ill.: Free Press, 1950), p. 114.

30. Lionel Trilling, *The Liberal Imagination* (Garden City, N.Y.: Doubleday & Co., Anchor Books, 1953), pp. 226, 227, 229.

31. Miller and Nowak, *The Fifties*, p. 407.

CONCLUSION. COMING APART

1. Michael Wood, *America in the Movies* (New York: Basic Books, 1975), pp. 16, 15, 14.

2. Quoted in George N. Nash, *The Conservative Intellectual Movement in America* (New York: Basic Books, 1976), p. 263.

3. Paul Dickson, "How a Little Beep-Beep-Beep Scared America Half to Death," *The Washingtonian*, September 1982, pp. 117–28.

Photo Credits

page 9   *12 Angry Men:* Copyright © 1957. Orion-Nova. All rights reserved. Released through United Artists Corporation.

page 13   *12 Angry Men:* Copyright © 1957. Orion-Nova. All rights reserved. Released through United Artists Corporation.

page 27   *Panic in the Streets:* Copyright 1950 Twentieth Century-Fox Film Corporation. All rights reserved.

page 35   *My Darling Clementine:* Copyright 1946 Twentieth Century-Fox Film Corporation. All rights reserved.

page 46   *High Noon:* Stanley Kramer, Courtesy of the Academy of Motion Picture Arts and Sciences.

page 51   *Strategic Air Command:* Paramount.

page 65   *Strategic Air Command:* Paramount, Courtesy of the Museum of Modern Art.

page 73   *Flying Leathernecks:* RKO, Courtesy of RKO General Pictures.

page 76   *Twelve O'Clock High:* Copyright 1949 Twentieth Century-Fox Film Corporation. All rights reserved.

page 80   *From Here to Eternity:* Columbia, Courtesy of the Academy of Motion Picture Arts and Sciences.

page 90   *The Court Martial of Billy Mitchell:* Warner Brothers, Courtesy of the Academy of Motion Picture Arts and Sciences.

page 96   *Attack!:* Copyright © 1956. The Associates & Aldrich Co., Inc. All rights reserved. Released through United Artists Corporation.

page 101   *It Came from Outer Space:* (1953) Universal, Courtesy of Universal Pictures.

page 114   *Forbidden Planet:* Copyright © 1956 Loew's Inc. From the MGM release.

page 125   *Them!:* Warner Brothers, Courtesy of the Museum of Modern Art.

page 128   *The Thing:* RKO, Courtesy of RKO General Pictures.

page 141   *Invasion of the Body Snatchers:* Allied Artists/Walter Wanger, Courtesy of the Museum of Modern Art.

page 148   *It Came from Outer Space:* (1953) Universal, Courtesy of Universal Pictures.

page 151   *The Day the Earth Stood Still:* Copyright 1951 Twentieth Century-Fox Film Corporation. All rights reserved.

page 161   *Blackboard Jungle:* Copyright © 1955 Loew's Inc. Copyright renewed 1983 by MGM/UA Entertainment Co. From the MGM release.

page 175   *On The Waterfront:* Columbia, Courtesy of the Museum of Modern Art.

page 184   *Underworld USA:* Columbia.

page 192   *The Big Heat:* Columbia, Courtesy of the Museum of Modern Art.

page 195   *Force of Evil:* MGM/Enterprise, Courtesy of Phototeque.

page 211   *Rebel Without a Cause:* Warner Brothers.

Index

Adams, Julia, 121, 302
African Queen, The (1951), 267
Agar, John, 256–57, 313
Aherne, Brian, 23
Albert, Eddie, 92
Aldrich, Robert, 55, 92, 244
All About Eve (1950), 264
All My Sons (1948), 253
All Quiet on the Western Front (1930), 92
All That Heaven Allows (1956), 258, 323–33
  critique of culture in, 332–33
  nature vs. culture in, 324–30
  peer pressure in, 330–31
All the King's Men (1949), 164
Allyson, June, 64, 307
Altman, Robert, 60, 336
Andrews, Dana, 25, 273, 297
Andrews, Edward, 199
Angry Red Planet (1960), 154–55
Animal Farm (1954), 112
Apache (1954), 244–5
Apache Woman (1955), 240
Apaloosa, The (1966), 261
Arden, Eve, 304
Arness, James, 124
Arnold, Jack, 105, 121, 147, 159, 221, 224
Arrowhead (1953), 243
Arthur, Jean, 252
Astaire, Fred, 344
Astor, Mary, 252
Atomic City (1952), 311

Attack! (1956), 83n, 92–97, 317
  class distinctions in, 93, 95
  group vs. individual in, 94–95

Baby Doll (1956), 272
Bad Day at Black Rock (1954), 228–29, 315
Bad Seed, The (1956), 218
Baker, Carroll, 272
Balsam, Martin, 171
Barefoot Contessa, The (1954), 253n, 263
Barker, Lex, 240
Basehart, Richard, 89
Battle Circus (1953), 60
Battle Cry (1955), 60, 84–85
Battleground (1949), 61
Battles of Chief Pontiac (1953), 240
Baxter, Anne, 264, 336
Beatty, Warren, 257, 326
Beginning of the End, The (1957), 107, 126
Begley, Ed, 11–12, 17–19
Bel Geddes, Barbara, 268
Bell, Bernard Iddings, 29
Bell, Daniel, 15, 17–19, 52, 104, 106, 111–12, 164, 171–72, 255
Bellamy, Ralph, 88
Bendix, William, 57
Bend of the River (1952), 252
Bennett, Bruce, 296

Bergman, Ingrid, 23, 24, 267
Best Years of Our Lives, The (1946), 251,
    273, 312
biblical spectacles, 115n, 258
Bickford, Charles, 86
Big Heat, The (1953), 56, 189–94, 317–
    18
    corruption in, 190–91
    professionalism attacked by, 193
    public interest in, 191–94
    revenge as motive in, 192–93
    use of force endorsed by, 193
Big Knife, The (1955), 253n, 270, 283,
    295
Big Sleep, The (1946), 56
Bissell, Whit, 218
Blackboard Jungle, The (1955), 107,
    162–63, 202–7, 212–17, 228, 266,
    274, 282, 308
    conservatives vs. liberals in, 204–6
    criticism of, 216
    culture vs. nature in, 203–5
    delinquency as anomaly in, 203
    divide-and-conquer strategy in, 205–
    7, 214–16
    fairy tale in, 212–14
    peer group portrayed in, 205–6
Black Scorpion, The (1957), 107
Blob, The (1958), 117, 224
Blue Dahlia, The (1946), 315
Blyth, Ann, 276, 300
Boetticher, Bud, 56
Bogart, Humphrey, 37, 60, 198, 252,
    267, 312
Bombers B-52 (1957), 58, 69, 93n, 105
Bond, James, 341–42
Bond, Ward, 40
Bonnie and Clyde (1967), 194, 347
Boorstin, Daniel, 115
Borgnine, Ernest, 81, 258
Boys' Town (1938), 198
Bradbury, Ray, 147
Brando, Jocelyn, 190
Brando, Marlon, 171, 177, 224, 257,
    260–61, 326
Braudy, Leo, 302
Brave New World (Huxley), 112

Brennan, Walter, 278
Bridge on the River Kwai, The (1957), 92
Bridges, Lloyd, 45
Bright Leaf, The (1950), 252–53
Bringing Up Baby (1938), 22
Broken Arrow (1950), 37, 163, 166,
    230–40, 257–58
    enemy in, 232–33, 238
    Geronimo in, 236–37
    hierarchical view of society in, 235
    humanism in, 238–39
    Indians as sympathetic characters in,
    230–31
    nature vs. culture in, 233–36
    shaving scene in, 235
    social control in, 239–40
Broken Lance (1954), 240
Brooks, Richard, 107, 203
Brothers Rico, The (1957), 190
Brown v. Board of Education (1954), 243
Buckley, William, 91, 109, 214n, 218,
    243, 276
Burton, Richard, 336
Bus Stop (1956), 267, 271–72

Cagney, James, 218–19, 252, 273, 297
Caine Mutiny, The, 252
Calhern, Louis, 204
Carefree (1938), 22
Carey, Macdonald, 37
Carlson, Richard, 147, 313
Carroll, Leo G., 105
Cat on a Hot Tin Roof (1958), 326
Cat People, The (1942), 22, 108
Caught (1949), 253, 268
Cavell, Stanley, 314
centrism and centrist films, 20, 147
    class divisions in, 93n
    God and, 115–16
    internal vs. external conflicts in, 162
    plurality of meanings in, 135
    polarization of, 337–48
    sexuality in, 133
    utopianism attacked by, 112–13

values reinforced by, 163
Chambers, Whittaker, 38
Chandler, Jeff, 233, 240
Chase, Borden, 281
Chase, The (1946), 251, 260–61
children, 270, 315
  deaths of, 298–99
  parents taught by, 282, 290–91
Chisholm, C. B., 29–30
Clarens, Carlos, 190
Cleopatra (1963), 336
Clift, Montgomery, 60, 79, 257, 258,
  267, 271, 279, 314
Cobb, Lee J., 12–13, 16–19, 24, 170–
  71, 254–55, 283
Cobweb, The (1955), 268
Command Decision (1949), 60
Communism, 48, 111–12, 132–35,
  140–41, 169
Conquest of Space, The (1955), 116, 254
conservatism and conservative films, 19,
  35–36, 40, 42–43, 134–36, 218–23
  army as family in, 313–14
  career women in, 296–303
  children in, 314–15
  corporate liberals caricatured by, 128n
  culture and patriarchy in, 275, 301–2
  doubling structure in, 222
  family in, 311–13
  feminized men and, 274
  geniuses derided by, 37
  heroism in, 315
  individual vs. group in, 139
  matriarchy and, 274
  peer groups in, 222–23
  "the people" and, 38–39
  professionals in, 182
  public vs. private in, 186–89
  sex roles in, 274–76, 302–4
  social control in, 182–89, 217–23
  technology and, 109–10
  theology in, 116–17
  therapeutic and, 110, 341
  tolerance rejected in, 241
  use of power in, 36, 185–86, 223,
  242
Considine, Tim, 310

Conte, Richard, 24, 193, 264
Cook, Elisha, Jr., 256
Cooper, Gary, 44, 86, 88, 252–53, 273
Coppola, Francis Ford, 177n, 336
cops:
  doctors vs., 23–24, 27–28, 34–36
  as individualists, 56–57
  as sadists and psychopaths, 24–25
Corman, Roger, 105
Cornthwaite, Robert, 127
corporate liberalism and corporate liberal
  films, 15–20, 35–36, 42–43, 172–
  73, 176–77
  career vs. family in, 309–10
  conservative caricatures of, 128n
  culturization in, 275
  dissidents and, 163
  doctors and, 21–22, 25
  doubles in, 206, 210
  family in, 308–9, 312–13
  force rejected in, 175–76
  globalism and, 29–30
  individual vs. groups in, 139
  "the people" in, 130
  power in, 164
  therapeutic strategy and, 25, 110
  utopia and, 177
Cotten, Joseph, 36–37, 56
Count Three and Pray (1955), 185–86
Court Martial of Billy Mitchell, The
  (1955), 86–91
  army in, 87–88
  group vs. individual in, 86–91, 144n
  hierarchical view of society overturned
  in, 89–90
  press in, 90
  public in, 90–91
Crain, Jeanne, 163
Crawford, Broderick, 25n,
Crawford, Joan, 296, 302
Creature from the Black Lagoon, The
  (1954), 107–8, 115
Creature Walks Among Us, The (1956),
  121
crime films, 56, 168–96
  corporate-liberal, 172–73, 176–77
  left-wing, 194–96

crime films, *(cont.)*
  mob in, 183–84, 255
  right-wing, 189–94
Criss Cross (1949), 252
Crowther, Bosley, 23
Crucible, The (Miller), 170
"Cry" (Ray), 258
Cukor, George, 263
Cult of the Cobra, The (1955), 108
Cultural and Scientific Conference for
  World Peace, 153
Curtis, Tony, 262
Curtiz, Michael, 296

Dassin, Jules, 194
Daves, Delmer, 163, 230
Davis, Bette, 264
Day, Doris, 271, 273, 290
Day the Earth Stood Still, The (1951),
  145–47, 150–59
  Christian symbolism in, 152
  Earth as dystopian in, 157–58
  East/West congress in, 153–54
  Einsteinian figure in, 153–54
  individual vs. center in, 152
  "the people" in, 154–55, 157
  utopia in, 157–58
Deadly Mantis, The (1957), 104, 107
Dean, James, 163, 200, 257, 258, 261–
  62, 285
Death Wish (1974), 342
Deer Hunter, The (1978), 326
Defense Department, U.S., 83n
de Havilland, Olivia, 24, 264–65, 267–
  68
delinquency films, 197–227
  cause represented in, 199
  conservative, 218–23
  extremists in, 206–7, 209–10
  gangs in, 199, 255
  good vs. bad delinquents in, 207
  left-wing, 224–27
  right-wing, 223–24
  therapeutic and, 200, 202

DeMille, Cecil B., 223, 263
Deming, Barbara, 59–60, 116n
Democratic Party, 15, 111
Derek, John, 198, 218
Desperate Hours, The (1955), 312
Destination Moon (1950), 102–3
Detective Story (1951), 24, 56–57, 186,
  192, 256, 258
Dichter, Ernst, 266
Dickinson, Angie, 187, 302
Dietrich, Marlene, 176
Dirty Harry (1971), 48, 348
doctors, 21–28, 34–36, 60–61
Donen, Stanley, 268
Don't Bother to Knock (1952), 272
Douglas, Gordon, 58, 123
Douglas, Kirk, 24, 97
Douglas, Paul, 26, 306
Dracula (1931), 102
Dragnet (1954), 56
Drake, Charles, 147, 327–28
Dr. Cyclops (1940), 104
Dr. No (1962), 342
Dr. Strangelove (1964), 68, 344–46
Dru, Joanne, 282
Duel in the Sun (1947), 272
Durgnat, Raymond, 134, 303
Dwan, Alan, 71

Earth vs. the Flying Saucers (1956),
  124n, 225
East of Eden (1955), 254, 261
East Side, West Side (1949), 272–73
Eastwood, Clint, 105, 342
Easy Rider (1969), 347
Einstein, Albert, 103, 153
Eisenhower, Dwight D., 15, 43, 57, 91–
  92, 115–16
Enforcer, The (1951), 183–84
Erickson, Leif, 170–71
ethnics, 31, 177, 228–44
Ewell, Tom, 262, 269–70, 272
Executive Suite (1954), 305–11
  business vs. family in, 308–11

experts, 28, 34–36, 40–42, 60–61
extremists, 18–19, 34, 39–40, 91

Face in the Crowd, A (1957), 164
family, 250–52, 267, 311–13, 319
Fear Strikes Out (1957), 23, 259–60,
    294
Feminine Mystique, The (Friedan), 263
Ferrer, Jose, 24
Fine, Benjamin, 197
Finian's Rainbow (1968), 336
Five (1951), 120
Fixed Bayonets (1951), 71–72, 89
Flame Within, The (1935), 22
Flaming Star (1960), 240
Flight to Mars (1951), 114
Fly, The (1958), 116
Flying Leathernecks (1951), 71–77, 202,
    306, 314–15
    group vs. individuals in, 71–73, 77,
        81
    Marine Corps in, 74
    therapeutic repudiated in, 77
Fonda, Henry, 10–19, 34, 40, 254–55,
    315
Forbidden Planet (1956), 105–6, 108–
    15, 133, 157, 222, 275
    technology in, 105–6, 108–11
    utopia in, 113
Force of Evil (1948), 194–96, 253
Ford, Glenn, 25n, 56, 190, 202
Ford, John, 40, 42–43, 170, 237, 241–
    42, 302
Foreman, Carl, 48
For Her Own Good (Ehrenreich and
    English), 197
Fort Apache (1948), 40–42, 128n, 242n
    conservative ideology in, 40–42
    experts vs. professionals in, 40–42
    loyal opposition in, 41–42
    populism in, 40–41
Fountainhead, The (1949), 316–22, 326
    center on trial in, 321
    existential loneliness in, 316

nature vs. culture in, 322
    revenge as principle in, 320–21
Foxfire (1955), 293–95, 298n
Francis, Anne, 108, 199, 216
Frankenheimer, John, 333
Frankenstein (1931), 102
Friedan, Betty, 263, 266, 270, 271, 277
Friendly Persuasion (1956), 273
From Hell It Came (1957), 107–8, 115
From Here to Eternity (1953), 59, 79–
    84, 93n, 128n, 222, 298n
    army in, 82–84
    court martial in, 80–81
    group vs. individual in, 79–84
    promotions in, 82–83
Fromm, Erich, 29, 110, 250
Fugitive Kind, The (1959), 272, 326
Fuller, Sam, 62, 71–72, 83n, 89, 142n,
    183, 187–88, 197, 237

Gable, Clark, 60, 116n, 252–53, 267,
    283, 302
gangster films, *see* crime films
Gardner, Ava, 252, 263, 272–73, 302,
    344
Garfield, John, 194, 198, 251
Garland, Judy, 263, 270
Garment Jungle (1957), 107, 254, 283
Gates, Larry, 183
Gavin, John, 338
Generation of Vipers, A (Wylie), 297
Genn, Leo, 267–68
Gentlemen Prefer Blondes (1953), 262
Gesell, Arnold, 291
Giant (1956), 256, 285–93, 329, 340
    decay of patriarchy in, 290–93
    sex roles in, 287–93
Giant Claw, The (1957), 103
Girl Can't Help It, The (1956), 272
Glass Key, The (1942), 252
Glazer, Nathan, 14–15, 31
Godfather, The (1972), 177
Going My Way (1944), 22
Gomez, Thomas, 194

Graduate, The (1967), 347
Grahame, Gloria, 37
Greatest Show on Earth, The (1952), 263
Great Sioux Uprising, The (1953), 240
Grey, Virginia, 328
Group, The (McCarthy), 58
Gunfighter, The (1950), 250, 255, 268, 283, 320
Gwenn, Edmund, 124

Haley, Bill, 202
Halls of Montezuma (1950), 60–61
Harris, Julie, 258
Has Anybody Seen My Gal? (1952), 253, 309
Haskell, Molly, 271
Hathaway, Henry, 272
Hauser, Virginia, 168
Hawks, Howard, 47, 126, 186, 302
Hayden, Sterling, 303, 344
Hayes, Helen, 165–66
Hayes, Margaret, 204
Heflin, Van, 60, 84–85, 240, 252
Heinlein, Robert, 103
Hell and High Water (1955), 142n, 187–88
Hellman, Lillian, 59, 153
Henreid, Paul, 23, 199
Hepburn, Audrey, 271
Hepburn, Katharine, 267
Heston, Charlton, 132, 243
High and the Mighty, The (1954), 41
High Noon (1952), 37, 44–48, 253
   anti-populism of, 47–48
   centrist models attacked in, 46–47
   teacher in, 47
High School Confidential (1958), 198, 221
Hitchcock, Alfred, 23, 36, 54, 252, 297, 320, 338
Holden, William, 24, 263, 306, 325
home, portrayal of, 250–51, 264–67
Home of the Brave (1949), 23, 60, 228, 251

Hook, Sidney, 15, 169
Hopper, Dennis, 291
Hopper, Hedda, 216
House Un-American Activities Committee (HUAC), 169
Houston, Penelope, 171, 229
How to Marry a Millionaire (1953), 262
Hudson, Rock, 61, 253, 256–59, 285, 290, 302, 323
Hunter, Jeffrey, 241
Hunters, The (1958), 59
Hutton, Betty, 263

I Accuse My Parents (1944), 199
I Married a Monster from Outer Space (1958), 117
In a Lonely Place (1950), 37, 252, 320
individualism, 48–57, 251–52
   decline of, 52
   in left-wing films, 96–97
   private eyes and, 55–56
   radical right and, 48
Inferno (1953), 193
Informer, The (1935), 170
Inge, William, 325
Invaders from Mars (1953), 201n, 225, 254
Invasion of the Body Snatchers (1956), 137–44, 150, 317, 321
   as activist film, 143–44
   common sense vs. expertise in, 138–39
   individual vs. group in, 144
   "take-over" symbolism in, 139–41
   women and children in, 138
Invasion of the Brain Eaters (1958), 134
Invisible Boy (1957), 118
Ipcress File, The (1965), 346
I Remember Mama (1948), 31
It Came from Beneath the Sea (1955), 104
It Came from Outer Space (1953), 147–51, 156–59
   aliens in, 149–51

Earth as dystopian in, 157
hysteria suppressed by, 156
individual vs. center in, 150, 156–57
"the people" in, 156
It Conquered the World (1956), 105
I Was a Teenage Werewolf (1957), 108,
217–23, 272, 275
failure of nature in, 219–21
failure of social control in, 219–22
popularity of, 223
school in, 221
therapist in, 219–21

Jaffe, Sam, 153
Jagger, Dean, 306
J. D. Films, The, 219
Johnny Angel (1945), 275
Johnny Belinda (1948), 22
Johnny Guitar (1953), 115n, 286, 302–3
Johnson, Nunnally, 294, 308
Jones, Jennifer, 263, 272
Joy Ride (1958), 224
juvenile delinquency, 197–227
gangs and, 199
as sickness, 199
social factors behind, 197–98
see also delinquency films

Kael, Pauline, 261
Karson, Phil, 190
Kay, Beatrice, 187
Kazan, Elia, 20, 26–27, 31, 162, 164,
169–72, 179n, 254, 260
Keel, Howard, 268–69
Kefauver, Estes, 168, 191, 197
Kelly, Grace, 44, 271, 302
Kelly, Nancy, 218
Kennedy, Arthur, 176
Kennedy, John F., 338
Kerr, Deborah, 82, 314
Kiley, Richard, 204

Killer Is Loose, A (1956), 56
Killers, The (1946), 252
King, Henry, 70, 250, 263
King Dinosaur (1955), 108
King Kong (1933), 118–19
Kinsey Report, 327
Kiss Me Deadly (1955), 55–56, 107
Kiss Me Kate (1953), 275
Knock on Any Door (1949), 198
Korean War, 59
Kramer, Stanley, 47–48, 224, 343
Kronos (1957), 118
Kubrick, Stanley, 68, 92, 97, 345–46

Ladd, Alan, 315
Ladies Home Journal, 267
Lait, Jack, 191, 274
Lancaster, Burt, 79, 244, 252, 258,
270–71
Landon, Michael, 217, 223
Lang, Fritz, 56, 115n, 143, 176, 190,
275, 297
Lasch, Christopher, 177, 202
Lawless Breed, The (1952), 302
Lawson, John Howard, 59, 196, 254
Lederer, Charles, 130
Left-Handed Gun, The (1958), 25n,
176, 275
left-wing films, 96–97, 194–96, 224–
27, 244–45
aliens in, 120–21, 149–50
class distinctions in, 93, 95, 97–98
couples in, 277
gangsters in, 194
individual vs. community in, 96–97,
150–52, 156–57
intellectuals in, 154
metaphorical parricide in, 227
nature vs. culture in, 325–30, 333
panic avoided in, 154
peer groups in, 224–25
science and technology in, 119, 157–
58
tolerance in, 224–45

left-wing films, *(cont.)*
  utopias and, 120, 150
  women in, 276–77
Lehigh, Janet, 338
LeRoy, Mervyn, 272
Lewis, Joseph H., 313
liberalism, *see* corporate liberalism and
  corporate liberal films
Lindner, Robert, 54
Lion Is in the Streets, A (1953), 164, 273
Little Big Man (1970), 336
"Little White Cloud That Cried, The"
  (Ray), 258
Litvak, Anatole, 264
Locket, The (1946), 23
Logan, Joshua, 267, 325
Lonely Crowd, The (Riesman, et al.), 18,
  54
Lost Continent (1951), 104
Lost Weekend, The (1945), 267, 328
Love is a Many Splendored Thing (1955),
  263
Lovejoy, Frank, 37, 62, 66, 313
Luce, Clare Booth, 216
Lumet, Sidney, 10
Lupino, Ida, 267, 270

McCabe and Mrs. Miller (1971), 336
McCambridge, Mercedes, 286, 303
McCarthy, Kevin, 137
McCarthy, Mary, 58
McCary, Leo, 162
McCormack, Patty, 218
McCrea, Joel, 283
McIntire, John, 245
McLaglen, Victor, 40, 170
Macready, George, 57, 97
Magnani, Anna, 270–71
Magnificent Obsession (1954), 259, 298
Malden, Karl, 58, 61, 69, 105, 171, 259
Malloy, Terry, 165
Maltese Falcon, The (1941), 252
Maltz, Albert, 59
Man from Planet X, The (1951), 121

Man in the Gray Flannel Suit, The
  (1956), 107, 267, 270, 308–9
Mankiewicz, Joseph, 264
Mann, Anthony, 252, 254, 315
Mann, Delbert, 255
Man of the West (1958), 254, 255
Mansfield, Jayne, 271–72
Man Who Shot Liberty Valance, The
  (1962), 42–43, 257
  conservatives betrayed in, 43
  grass-roots democracy in, 43
  teacher in, 47
March, Fredric, 306, 308, 312
Marlowe, Hugh, 154
Marlowe, Philip, 55
Marnie (1964), 342
Marshall, E. G., 12, 14, 16–19
Martin, Dean, 186
Martin, Strother, 92
Marty (1955), 255
Marvin, Lee, 93, 193
M*A*S*H (1970), 60
Mason, James, 89n, 263, 268, 272–73
Massey, Raymond, 95, 254, 319
Maté, Rudolph, 237
Mature, Victor, 34
Mellen, Joan, 261
men, 250–62
  as bad dads, 254–55
  children and, 270
  emotional flexibility and, 256–62
  feminization of, 257–62, 274–76,
    281–84, 337–41
  as group members, 255
  as heroes, 255–56
  home and, 250–51
  as individualists, 251–52
  infantilization of, 270–72, 292–93
  macho, 260–61
  as misogynists, 251–52
  as neurotics and psychotics, 252–53
  in radical films, 316–17
  as revenge characters, 255
  self-made, 253–54
  tough guys, 251–52
Men, The (1950), 60, 251, 261
Merrill, Gary, 70

Mildred Pierce (1945), 296–304
  children in, 304
  crime in, 300–301
  male alternatives in, 301
  pluralism in, 304
Miles, Vera, 339
Milestone, Lewis, 61, 92
Milland, Ray, 267, 328
Millican, James, 64
Mills, C. Wright, 164
Mineo, Sal, 200, 257
Misfits, The (1961), 252–53, 267, 271
Mitchell, Millard, 70–71
Mitchum, Robert, 25n, 59–61, 276
Moby Dick (1956), 253
Mogambo (1953), 302
Monolith Monsters, The (1957), 108
Monroe, Marilyn, 262, 267–68, 269–
  73
Monster That Challenged the World, The
  (1957), 107–8
Montalban, Ricardo, 229
Moorhead, Agnes, 330
Morrow, Vic, 206
Mortimer, Lee, 191, 274
Mostel, Zero, 31
Movies: A Psychoanalytical Study (Wol-
  fenstein and Leites), 314n
Murphy, Audie, 82–83, 314–15
Murray, Don, 267, 271–72
Murray, Henry A., 22
My Darling Clementine (1946), 34–40,
  235, 242, 274
  conservative values in, 36–39, 188
  cops vs. doctors in, 34–36, 39
  historical context of, 35–36
  normalcy stressed in, 36–37
  "the people" in, 37–39
  teacher in, 36, 47
  two-front war in, 34, 39–40
My Son John (1952), 162, 165–166, 297

Nagel, Conrad, 332
Naked and the Dead, The (1958), 92,
  95, 119n

Naked City, The (1948), 194, 333
Naked Jungle, The (1954), 132
Naked Spur, The (1953), 252
Naming Names (Navasky), 170
Nash, George, 38
National Review, 118, 141, 243, 337
Navasky, Victor, 170, 179n
Neal, Patricia, 59, 152, 318
Neanderthal Man, The (1953), 219n
Neemeyer, Gerhart, 132
Neumann, Kurt, 116
New Deal, 15, 48, 53
Newman, Paul, 25n, 257, 326
New Science of Politics, The (Voegelin),
  119
Niagara (1953), 272–73, 326
Nielsen, Leslie, 108
Night the World Exploded, The (1957),
  117
1984 (1956), 112
Niven, David, 264, 267
North, Edmund, 152
Not of This Earth (1957), 114
Novak, Kim, 325

O'Connell, Arthur, 267–68
Oh Men! Oh Women! (1957), 294
On Dangerous Ground (1951), 267
One-Eyed Jacks (1961), 260–61
1,000,000 Delinquents (Fine), 197
One Minute to Zero (1952), 60–61, 276
On the Beach (1959), 343–44
On the Waterfront (1954), 162–63, 165,
  169–82, 199, 260–61, 267, 274,
  283
  Christian iconography in, 178–79
  Father Barry in, 174–76, 178–79
  frame of reference for, 173
  good guys vs. bad guys in, 170–71
  informing as emphasis in, 169, 179–
    82
  the mob in, 177–78, 184–85
  natural imagery in, 178–79, 181n
  problem defined in, 171–72
  public vs. private in, 178–82

On the Waterfront, (cont.)
  revenge rejected in, 176
  utopian aspirations in, 176, 180–81
Operation Pacific (1951), 59
Organization Man, The (Whyte), 53,
  77–78
Other Love, The (1947), 263–64, 267,
  298

Paget, Debra, 233
Pal, George, 117
Palance, Jack, 31, 92, 243, 256
Panic in the Streets (1950), 20–33, 163,
  268, 270
  complexity of reality in, 28
  cops vs. doctors in, 27–28
  local vs. national needs in, 28–30
  as national emergency film, 26
  "the people" in, 30–32
  public vs. private in, 180–81
  reporter in, 30–31
Parson and the Outlaw, The (1957),
  185–86
Parsons, Talcott, 29, 105, 112, 263
Partisan Review, 115
Paths of Glory (1957), 92, 97–98
Peacemaker, The (1956), 185–86
Peale, Norman Vincent, 105, 259
Peck, Gregory, 24, 70, 75, 228, 250,
  253, 267, 308, 344
Peckinpah, Sam, 336
Perkins, Tony, 257, 259–60, 315, 338,
  344
Persuader, The (1957), 185–86
Peters, Jean, 272, 325
Pevney, Joseph, 293, 298n
Pickens, Slim, 345
Picnic (1956), 325–26
Pidgeon, Walter, 108, 306
Pillow Talk (1959), 290
Pinky (1949), 163, 228
Playboy, 343
pluralism and pluralist films, 16–20
  army and, 66

  career women in, 296
  conservatives in, 40
  dissident Third Force and, 164–65,
    173
  doctors and, 22
  family and, 250–51
  groups vs. individuals and, 54–55,
    128n, 178–82, 205
  leadership and, 165
  as other-directed, 256
  persuasion vs. coercion and, 163–64,
    166
  poor despised in, 31–32
  relativism in, 181–82
  tolerance and, 228, 239
Podhoretz, Norman, 54
Poitier, Sidney, 205
police, *see* cops
Polonsky, Abraham, 194
Powell, Jane, 268, 273
Preminger, Otto, 25, 86
Price, Vincent, 23, 275
Pride of the Marines (1945), 251
private eyes, 55–56
Protestant Ethic, 53, 61, 77, 107, 251,
  282, 309n
psychiatrists, 22–23, 166, 339–41
Psycho (1960), 338–41

Quo Vadis? (1951), 258, 336

radical films, 45–48, 117–21
  aliens in, 120–21, 149–50
  compromise in, 317–18
  defined, 45n
  houses in, 325–26
  ideology confused in, 48
  individual vs. group in, 139
  leaders' betrayal of followers in, 95
  living outside town in, 149
  technology in, 117–19

utopias in, 119–20
values subverted by, 163
see also left-wing films; right-wing
films
Rancho Notorious (1952), 115*n*, 176
Rand, Ayn, 38, 316
Randall, Tony, 271–72, 294
Rankin, John, 153
Ray, Johnny, 258
Ray, Nicholas, 25, 37, 71, 115*n*, 162,
198, 218, 286
Reagan, Ronald, 216
Rebel Without a Cause (1955), 162–63,
200–202, 207–12, 261–62, 272,
282–84, 339
divide-and-conquer strategy in, 207–
10
expert in, 201–2
family in, 210–12
society in, 201
values defined in, 211–12
Red Planet Mars (1952), 120, 132
Red River (1948), 278–84
Reed, Donna, 81, 314
Rennie, Michael, 145, 151
reporters, 30–31, 129–30
Republican Party, 15, 19, 111
Retreat, Hell! (1951), 62, 313–14
Reynolds, Debbie, 264, 268, 269, 270,
271, 273
Reynolds, William, 330
Rhapsody in Blue (1945), 253, 271,
309*n*
Ride the Pink Horse (1947), 315
Riefenstahl, Leni, 322
Riesman, David, 14–15, 18, 31, 54,
106, 165, 166, 181, 187, 251, 256,
282
right-wing films, 48, 189–94, 223–24,
243
aliens in, 120, 151
centrist views in, 142
couples in, 277
family in, 319
individual vs. group in, 139, 317,
321–22
men in, 316–17

nature vs. culture in, 142
paranoia in, 143–44, 191
"the people" in, 193
public interest in, 191–94
revenge in, 192–93
technology in, 117–19
utopias in, 119–20
women in, 142*n*, 276–77, 318*n*
Rio Bravo (1959), 47, 186, 193, 275,
302, 318
Robe, The (1953), 336
Robertson, Cliff, 95, 183
Robinson, Edward G., 253
"Rock Around the Clock" (Haley), 202
Rocketship XM (1950), 102, 120
Rogers, Ginger, 294
Roman Spring of Mrs. Stone (1961), 326
Romero, Cesar, 104
Roosevelt, Eleanor, 218
Rose, Reginald, 14
Ruby Gentry (1952), 272
Run for Cover (1955), 218
Running Away from Myself (Deming),
59–60
Rush, Barbara, 147
Rusher, William, 141
Russell, Jane, 271, 293
Russell, Rosalind, 325
Ryan, Joseph P., 169
Ryan, Mary, 291
Ryan, Robert, 25, 71, 193, 253, 267

Saboteur (1942), 54
Sabre Jet (1953), 312–13
Saint, Eva Marie, 171, 267
Samson and Delilah (1951), 336
Sanders, George, 322
Sands of Iwo Jima (1949), 71, 256–57
Saturday Evening Post, 197
Saxon, John, 199
Scarface Mob (1962), 194
Schlesinger, Arthur, Jr., 15–16, 18, 32,
53, 112–13, 136, 228, 347
Schulberg, Budd, 170

science fiction movies, 102–59
  aliens and monsters in, 104, 120–21,
    149–51
  anti-utopianism in, 112–15, 141
  bureaucracies in, 131–32
  center coalition in, 103–6
  conservative, 104–5, 110, 116
  corporate-liberal, 103–4, 110, 116,
    126
  culture vs. nature in, 106–8, 118,
    132–35
  dissent in, 158–59
  emergencies in, 102
  federal government in, 103, 117,
    123–24, 143
  interchangeable actors in, 102–3
  nuclear weapons in, 104, 107
  Other in, 107–12, 117
  power as used in, 164
  radical, 117–21
  restrained style of, 102–3
  soldiers vs. scientists in, 103–5, 117,
    124–29
  technology in, 105–6, 117–19
  theology in, 116–17, 152
  women in, 133–35, 138, 166
Scott, George C., 344
Scott, Zachary, 253n, 298
Scourby, Alexander, 190
Screen Guide for Americans (Rand), 38
Search, The (1948), 60
Searchers, The (1956), 241–43, 252
Seconds (1966), 333
Sellers, Peter, 344
Senate, U.S., 168, 197
Seven Brides for Seven Brothers (1954),
  268–69, 273–75
Seven Year Itch, The (1955), 262, 269–
  70
Shadow of a Doubt (1943), 36–37, 320
Shane (1953), 164, 176, 252, 255–56,
  315
Sherman, Vincent, 107, 254
Sherwood, John, 121
Shock (1946), 23
Siegel, Don, 137
Sign of the Ram (1948), 22
Simmons, Jean, 271, 273

Sinatra, Frank, 81, 264, 269, 270
Singin' in the Rain (1952), 273
Sirk, Douglas, 253, 258–59, 275, 323
Sklar, Robert, 281
Sleep My Love (1948), 23
Smith, Julian, 59
Smithers, William, 93
Snake Pit, The (1948), 23, 264–65,
  267–68
social control, 163–244
  anti-authority alliances in, 206–7
  child-rearing as, 290–92
  in conservative films, 182–89, 217–
    23
  factionalization as means of, 164–65,
    173
  force rejected for, 163–64
  internalization of, 174–75, 216–17,
    239
  leadership and, 165
  male doctors and, 267–68
  minorities and, 229–44
  in peacetime, 167
  by professionals, 182
  tolerance in, 228, 239
  utopian aspirations and, 176, 180
  of women, 265–66
Social Ethic, 53–55, 61, 77, 115n, 195
Somebody Up There Likes Me (1956),
  267
Some Like It Hot (1959), 262, 340
Somewhere in the Night (1946), 251
Sontag, Susan, 102, 107, 118, 158, 271,
  277
Southern Tradition, The (Weaver), 104
Soviet Union, 58, 111, 120, 132–35,
  159, 337
So Young, So Bad (1950), 23, 199
Space Children, The (1958), 224–26
Spellbound (1945), 23, 24, 267
Spillane, Mickey, 55
Splendor in the Grass (1961), 326
Spock, Benjamin, 291
Sputnik, 337
spy films, 346–47
Spy Who Came In from the Cold, The
  (1965), 346–7
Stack, Robert, 41, 275

Stanwyck, Barbara, 263–64, 267, 272–73, 307
Star Is Born, A (1954), 263
Stark, Jim, 283
Stars in My Crown (1950), 185–86
Steel Helmet (1951), 71–72, 83n, 187
Steiger, Rod, 89, 171, 253n, 283, 295
Stevens, Craig, 104
Stevens, George, 31, 164, 285
Stevens, Mark, 264–65
Stevenson, Adlai, 106, 267
Stewart, Jimmy, 42, 64, 230, 237, 242, 252, 257–58
Stewart, Paul, 75
Stone, I. F., 57, 111
Strangers on a Train (1951), 297
Strategic Air Command (1955), 64–69, 105, 275, 294, 308, 312, 345
  Air Force in, 67–68
  equivalence between babies and bombers in, 67–68
  expert and organization man wedded in, 74
  sexual metaphors in, 68
Streetcar Named Desire (1951), 260, 326
Strode, Woody, 237
studio system, 336–37
Sturges, John, 336
Success Story (Lawson), 254
Sullivan, Harry Stack, 22, 201n
Susan Slept Here (1954), 268
Szasz, Thomas, 22

Talbott, Gloria, 330
Tall Men, The (1955), 253, 283
Tamblyn, Russ, 313
Tarantula (1955), 105, 107, 108
Taylor, Elizabeth, 285
Taylor, Robert, 24, 253n, 258
Taylor, Rod, 285–86
technology, portrayal of, 105–6, 108–11
Teeters, Negely, 197
Ten Commandments, The (1956), 336
Tender Trap, The (1955), 264, 269, 270

Them! (1954), 123–36, 139, 163, 167, 282
  federal government in, 123–24
  "the people" in, 129–30
  scientists in, 124–27
  women in, 133
therapeutic philosophy, 21–28, 200, 202
  as authority, 28
  conservatives and, 110, 341
  corporate liberals and, 110
  delinquency and, 200, 202
  political issues neutralized by, 25
  in war films, 71, 75–77
Thieves' Highway (1949), 193, 275, 315
Thing, The (1951), 115, 126–36, 320
  bureaucracy in, 131–32
  nature vs. civilization in, 133–35
  populism in, 130–31
  reporter in, 130
  science vs. military in, 127–29
This Day and Age (1933), 223
This Island Earth (1955), 114, 155, 157
Thompson, Dorothy, 267
Thrill of it All, The (1963), 273
Time, 216
Time Limit (1957), 92
Tin Star, The (1957), 315
Tobey, Kenneth, 127
To Hell and Back (1955), 82, 314
Tomahawk (1951), 240
Toomey, Regis, 224
Tracy, Spencer, 198
Tree Grows in Brooklyn, A (1945), 31
Trilling, Lionel, 17, 74, 110, 327
Truman, Harry S, 58, 228
Trumbo, Dalton, 59
12 Angry Men (1957), 10–20, 163, 199, 254–55, 282
  as centrist film, 20
  characters as symbols in, 10–11, 14, 16
  complexity of reality in, 16–17
  consensus dramatized in, 10, 16, 18–20
  group pressure in, 52, 54
  individual rights guaranteed in, 54
  new political alignments represented in, 14–16

12 Angry Men, (cont.)
    pluralism in, 16–20
    system legitimized in, 10
    verdict in, 19–20
Twelve O'Clock High (1949), 70–77,
    167, 253, 256, 258, 306
    Air Force in, 74
    doctor in, 74–76
    group vs. individuals in, 70–77
Two Mrs. Carrolls, The (1947), 252
Twonky, The (1953), 119
Two Rode Together (1961), 237, 242

Underworld USA (1960), 183–89, 197,
    275
    Big Business in, 195
    crime as widespread in, 185
    individualism respected in, 186–87
    informing in, 185–87
    professionalism attacked by, 193n
    public vs. private in, 186–89
    syndicate in, 183–84
    use of force in, 185–86
Unforgiven, The (1960), 240
Unguarded Moment, The (1956), 199
Unknown World (1950), 105
utopias, portrayal of, 112–16, 141–42,
    157, 176–77, 180

Van Cleef, Lee, 105
Variety, 23
Vengeance Valley (1951), 255
Vertigo (1958), 252
Vidor, King, 316
Viereck, Peter, 297
Village of the Damned (1960), 222
Viva Zapata! (1952), 164, 325
Voegelin, Eric, 119

Walden (Thoreau), 328
Walker, Robert, 297
Walsh, Raoul, 84, 95, 164, 196, 253,
    302
War Arrow (1954), 240
Warden, Jack, 11–12, 16–19
war films, 57–98
    army in, 61–63, 66, 74, 82, 87–88
    cast of characters in, 60
    cold war and, 57–58, 167
    command changes in, 71
    conservative, 60–62, 79, 82, 84–86
    corporate-liberal, 61, 69, 71, 86
    courts martial in, 80–81, 91, 94, 97–
        98
    doctors in, 60–61
    group vs. individual in, 57, 59, 61–
        62, 64–98
    ideological pressures on, 83n
    insubordination vs. mutiny in, 96–98
    left-wing, 62, 92, 96–98, 119n
    officers as heroes in, 60
    pluralist, 60
    right-wing, 62, 86, 91
    sexual and familial metaphors in, 68–
        69
    therapeutic themes in, 71, 75–77
War of the Worlds (1953), 102, 117
Warshow, Robert, 38, 47, 57, 270
Wasp Woman, The (1959), 108
Wayne, David, 262
Wayne, John, 40, 42, 59, 71, 89n, 186,
    241, 252, 256–57, 275, 278, 313
Weaver, Richard, 104
Welcome Stranger (1947), 22
Weldon, Joan, 124
We're Not Married (1952), 262
westerns, 229–44
    anxiety of power in, 176
    as commentary on race relations, 229,
        240
    good vs. bad Indians in, 236–38, 240,
        242–43
    Indianization in, 238
    left-wing, 244
    outlaw communities in, 115n
    "the people" in, 37–38